Celebrating African-American Achievements

WHO'S WHO
in BLACK Chicago®

THE SECOND EDITION

Scenes from the 2006
Who's Who In Black Chicago® Unveiling Reception

Celebrating African-American Achievements

WHO'S WHO
IN BLACK
Chicago®

THE SECOND EDITION

Who's Who In Black Chicago®
is a registered trademark of
Briscoe Media Group, LLC

Purchase additional copies online @
www.whoswhopublishing.com

Corporate Headquarters
Who's Who Publishing Co., LLC
1650 Lake Shore Drive, Suite 250
Columbus, Ohio 43204

All Credit Cards Accepted

*Inquiries for bulk purchases for youth
groups, schools, churches, civic or
professional organizations, please call
our office for volume discounts.*

Corporate Headquarters
(614) 481-7300

**Copyright © 2007 by C. Sunny Martin,
Briscoe Media Group, LLC**

ISSN Number: 1938-8438

Photo Credits
C. Sunny Martin, Johnson Publishing Company
& Powell Photography

**ISBN # 1-933879-35-1 Hardback
$50.00 each-U.S. Hardback
Commemorative Edition**

**ISBN # 1-933879-34-3 Paperback
$34.95 each-U.S. Paperback**

"It took us longer to play the course
than it did to get to Bermuda."

Eight world-class golf courses. Over 70 fantastic tennis courts. And dozens of delightful spas. There's no place like Bermuda when it comes to indulging all your passions. And at just under two hours from the East Coast, there's no island paradise that's easier to reach. So come relax, hit the ball, and feel the love in Bermuda.

For full details, and to book tickets and reservations, call **1-800-BERMUDA**, or visit **www.bermudatourism.com**

BERMUDA
feel the love.

Table of CONTENTS

MEET THE TEAM

WHO'S who
PUBLISHING CO., LLC

C. Sunny Martin
Founder & CEO

Ernie Sullivan
Senior Partner

Paula Gray
VP Customer Care

Carter Womack
Regional VP

Melanie Diggs
Executive Editor

Beverly A. Coley
Chicago Associate Publisher
(312) 942-1995

Nathan Wylder
Senior Editor

Tamara Allen
Production Manager

Sarah Waite
Webmaster

Yulanda Thomas
Sr. Account Manager

Angela Coley
Sr. Account Manager

Christina Llewellyn
Production Assistant
Graphic Designer

Diane Winters
Graphic Designer

Monica Sherchan
Graphic Designer

Cammie Bridges
Sr. Account Manager

Mallori Fair
Sr. Account Manager

Monica Lehman
Business Manager

Adam DeDent
Copy Editor

Rachel Bobak
Copy Editor

Sarah Longacre
Receptionist

Alisha Martin
Executive Assistant

CORPORATE OFFICE
1650 Lake Shore Drive, Suite 250 • Columbus, Ohio 43204 • (614) 481-7300
Visit Our Web Site - www.whoswhopublishing.com

THIS BOOK WAS MADE POSSIBLE BY THE GENEROUS SUPPORT OF OUR

SPONSORS

PLATINUM SPONSOR

Allianz

OFFICIAL AIRLINE

▲ DELTA

DIAMOND SPONSORS

RR DONNELLEY

EMERALD SPONSORS

 **BERMUDA** *feel the love.*

UNVEILING RECEPTION SPONSORS

MEDIA PARTNERS

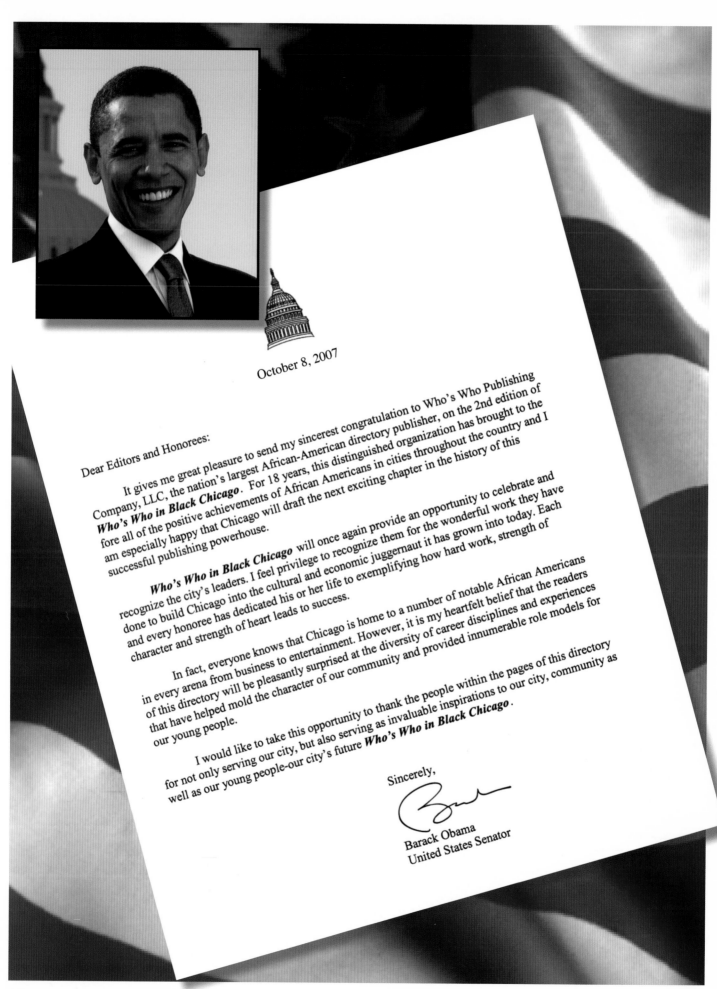

October 8, 2007

Dear Editors and Honorees:

It gives me great pleasure to send my sincerest congratulation to Who's Who Publishing Company, LLC, the nation's largest African-American directory publisher, on the 2nd edition of *Who's Who in Black Chicago*. For 18 years, this distinguished organization has brought to the fore all of the positive achievements of African Americans in cities throughout the country and I am especially happy that Chicago will draft the next exciting chapter in the history of this successful publishing powerhouse.

Who's Who in Black Chicago will once again provide an opportunity to celebrate and recognize the city's leaders. I feel privilege to recognize them for the wonderful work they have done to build Chicago into the cultural and economic juggernaut it has grown into today. Each and every honoree has dedicated his or her life to exemplifying how hard work, strength of character and strength of heart leads to success.

In fact, everyone knows that Chicago is home to a number of notable African Americans in every arena from business to entertainment. However, it is my heartfelt belief that the readers of this directory will be pleasantly surprised at the diversity of career disciplines and experiences that have helped mold the character of our community and provided innumerable role models for our young people.

I would like to take this opportunity to thank the people within the pages of this directory for not only serving our city, but also serving as invaluable inspirations to our city, community as well as our young people-our city's future *Who's Who in Black Chicago*.

Sincerely,

Barack Obama
United States Senator

OFFICE OF THE GOVERNOR
JRTC, 100 W. Randolph, Suite 16
Chicago, Illinois, 60601

ROD R. BLAGOJEVICH
GOVERNOR

GREETINGS

As Governor of the State of Illinois, I am pleased to congratulate the Who's Who Publishing Company on the release of Who's Who in Black Chicago.

Who's Who in Black Chicago celebrates and recognizes outstanding leaders whose contributions have made a significant impact in numerous communities. With that in mind, I extend my fondest congratulations and appreciation to each honoree in this publication. Your hard work has certainly made a lasting impact on the State of Illinois, and will undoubtedly continue to do so in the years to come. I am very proud to be a part of this wonderful book.

On behalf of the citizens of Illinois, I offer my best wishes for continued health, happiness and success in the years to come.

Sincerely,

Rod R. Blagojevich
Governor

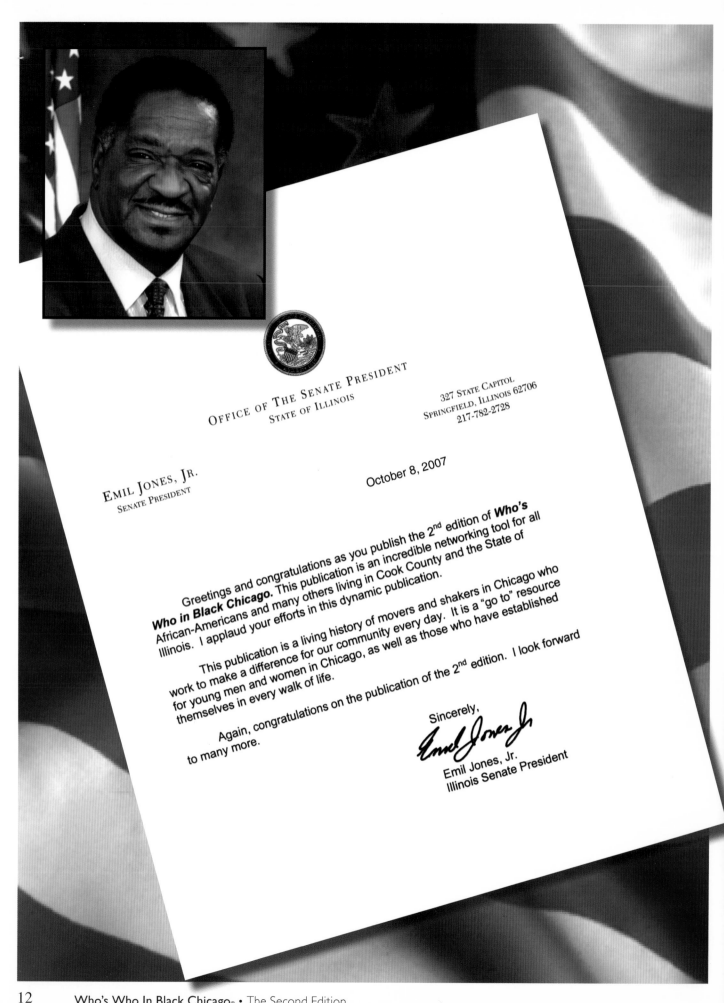

OFFICE OF THE SENATE PRESIDENT
STATE OF ILLINOIS

327 STATE CAPITOL
SPRINGFIELD, ILLINOIS 62706
217-782-2728

EMIL JONES, JR.
SENATE PRESIDENT

October 8, 2007

Greetings and congratulations as you publish the 2nd edition of **Who's in Black Chicago.** This publication is an incredible networking tool for all African-Americans and many others living in Cook County and the State of Illinois. I applaud your efforts in this dynamic publication.

This publication is a living history of movers and shakers in Chicago who work to make a difference for our community every day. It is a "go to" resource for young men and women in Chicago, as well as those who have established themselves in every walk of life.

Again, congratulations on the publication of the 2nd edition. I look forward to many more.

Sincerely,

Emil Jones, Jr.
Illinois Senate President

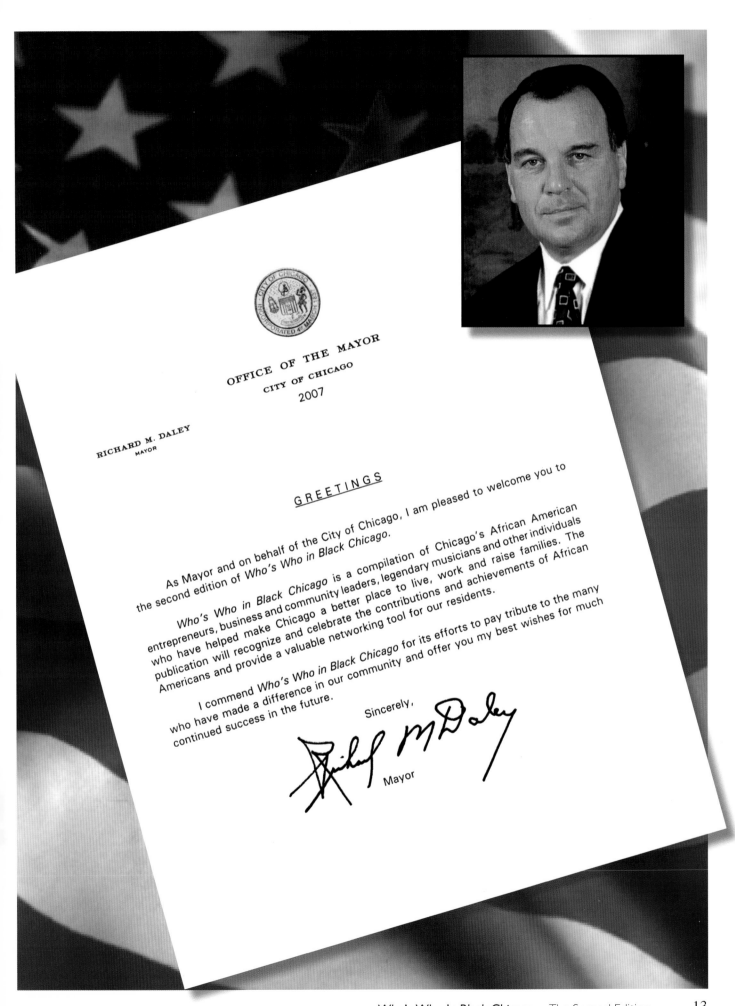

OFFICE OF THE MAYOR
CITY OF CHICAGO
2007

RICHARD M. DALEY
MAYOR

GREETINGS

As Mayor and on behalf of the City of Chicago, I am pleased to welcome you to the second edition of *Who's Who in Black Chicago.*

Who's Who in Black Chicago is a compilation of Chicago's African American entrepreneurs, business and community leaders, legendary musicians and other individuals who have helped make Chicago a better place to live, work and raise families. The publication will recognize and celebrate the contributions and achievements of African Americans and provide a valuable networking tool for our residents.

I commend *Who's Who in Black Chicago* for its efforts to pay tribute to the many who have made a difference in our community and offer you my best wishes for much continued success in the future.

Sincerely,

Richard M Daley

Mayor

JESSE L. JACKSON, JR.
2ND DISTRICT, ILLINOIS

Congress of the United States
House of Representatives
Washington, DC 20515—1302

Dear Who's Who:

It is with great pleasure that I congratulate your company for producing the second annual edition of *Who's Who in Black Chicago*. I know that this was a labor of love and will be a phenomenal success.

From late heroes like Emmett Till and Lorraine Hansberry to living legends such as Koko Taylor and Bernie Mac, African-American Chicagoans have a legacy of which everyone should be proud. In fact, one cannot talk about Black history without mentioning Chicagoans and one cannot talk about Chicago without mentioning Black Americans. I salute you for documenting the lives of a significant population in this magnificent city.

Once again, thanks for this publication! *Who's Who* will be an important resource for all people, in Chicago and throughout the nation.

Sincerely,

Jesse L. Jackson, Jr.
Member of Congress

2419 RAYBURN HOUSE OFFICE BUILDING
WASHINGTON, DC 20515-1302
(202) 225-0773

2120 EAST 71ST STREET
CHICAGO, IL 60649
(773) 241-6500

17926 SOUTH HALSTED
HOMEWOOD, IL 60430
(708) 798-6000

THIS MAILING WAS PREPARED, PUBLISHED, AND MAILED AT TAXPAYER EXPENSE

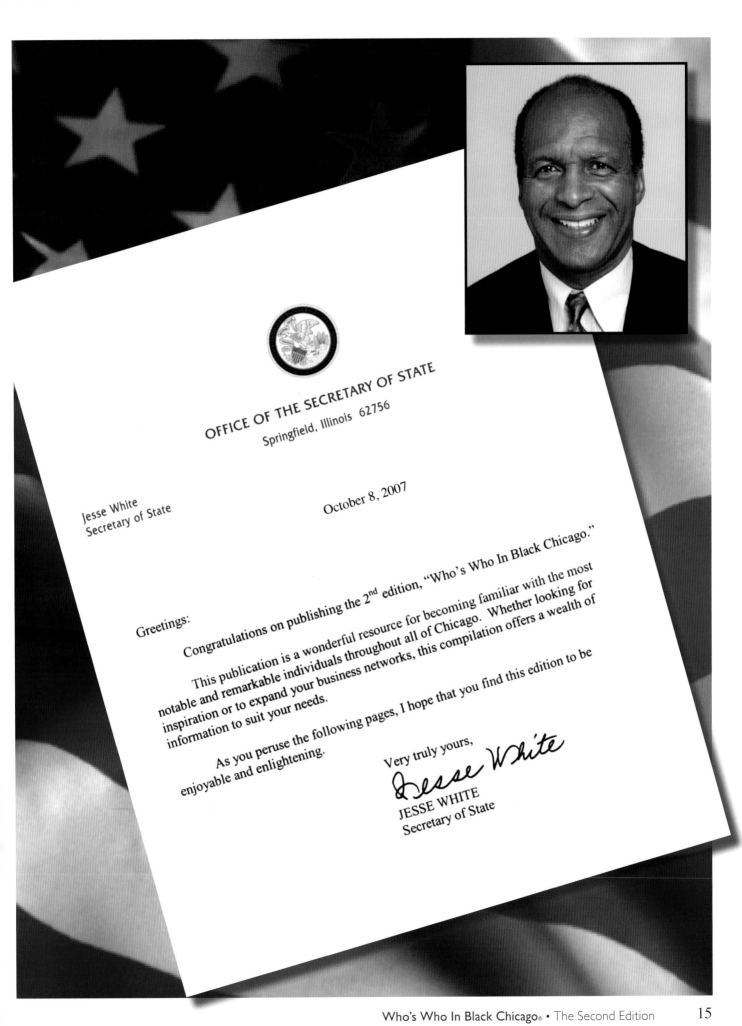

OFFICE OF THE SECRETARY OF STATE
Springfield, Illinois 62756

Jesse White
Secretary of State

October 8, 2007

Greetings:

Congratulations on publishing the 2nd edition, "Who's Who In Black Chicago."

This publication is a wonderful resource for becoming familiar with the most notable and remarkable individuals throughout all of Chicago. Whether looking for inspiration or to expand your business networks, this compilation offers a wealth of information to suit your needs.

As you peruse the following pages, I hope that you find this edition to be enjoyable and enlightening.

Very truly yours,

Jesse White

JESSE WHITE
Secretary of State

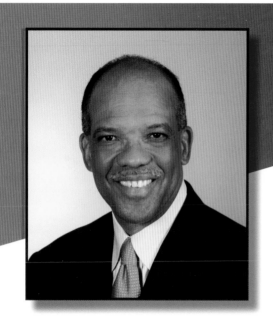

Premier of Bermuda

Greetings,

It is with great pleasure and pride that I welcome you to the 2nd edition of Who's Who in Black Chicago.

Who's Who in Black Chicago is a community experience that creates a feeling of strength and triumph among all of us. These pages are a sweeping display of the African American community's most outstanding members – their great achievements and notable accomplishments. From civic leaders to elected officials to business executives, every person profiled in this book has positively impacted our society and set the standard for future generations to come.

Furthermore, these truly inspirational success stories remind us all – young and old alike – that the work of our community is not yet completed. We must press on.

I am honored to be a part of the Who's Who Publishing Company's remarkable legacy. I trust this book will be a resource for opening lines of communications and building networks so that the community may continue to grow and prosper, may continue to strive for the kind of excellence exhibited in these pages.

Sincerely,

Premier Dr. the Hon. Ewart F. Brown, J.P., M.P.

Diversity
empowers us.

ComEd is committed to developing
leaders and building a workforce that
reflect the diverse communities we serve.

ComEd

EVERY GREAT LEADER HAD A BEGINNING.

Who knows where the next great dream will find its voice. Where future leaders

might find their inspiration. We're proud to inspire the great African-American

minds of today so that they can become the great visionaries of tomorrow.

BOEING

Chicago, with its rich culture and prominent black history, is a place I am proud to call home. As a Chicago native and CEO of the world's largest African-American-owned publishing company, I have witnessed firsthand the growth and international acclaim of a city brewing with limitless possibilities.

By Linda Johnson Rice

It is exhilarating to experience all that Chicago has to offer and all that African Americans give to Chicago. From Jean Baptiste Pointe DuSable, the founder of our city, to Harold Washington, our first black mayor, and now Barack Obama, our black U.S. Senator, Chicago has an inspiring story that continues to unfold. These stories are skillfully documented in this second edition of *Who's Who In Black Chicago*®.

Historical Perspective

Thanks to the efforts of early pioneers of journalism, such as Ida B. Wells and Claude A. Barnett, as well as the achievements of my father, the late John H. Johnson, founder of Johnson Publishing Company, Chicago has become one of the greatest black media capitals in the world. I can remember as a young child when my father would reflect on how he brought *Ebony* and *Jet* magazines to the forefront of America. Despite the racism and prejudices, my father always said, "Failure is a word I don't accept." His tenacity, along with the perseverance of institutions like the *Chicago Defender* and the *Chicago Bee* newspapers, has kept Chicago's black roots strong and vibrant. As a result, we are everywhere, increasing our presence in a city that has thrived because of our talents and drive. We are media, we are business, we are politics, we are leaders. We are Chicago.

For many, Chicago became "The Promised Land" as black southerners moved here during the Great Migration. Many settled and fostered the growth and development of successful black businesses. Anthony Overton, whose empire included the *Chicago Bee* newspaper, a bank, insurance company and cosmetic corporation; Andrew "Rube" Foster, founder of the Negro National Baseball League; Jesse Binga, founder of Binga Bank; and Bessie Coleman, the first African-American female pilot are among Chicago's first black Who's Who.

Vision for the Future

In this edition, we celebrate the achievements of African Americans in Chicago while reflecting on the past. Historic pioneers, my father among them, have inspired me to drive forward with unfailing passion. I see the same commitment to excellence in our present leaders. As you will see in these pages, the growth of Black Chicago is phenomenal, and with budding leaders on the rise—standing on the shoulders of those who have come before us—the best is yet to come!!!

A Message From The Founder & CEO

Founder & CEO

C. Sunny Martin

You are what you aspire to be, and not what you now are; you are what you do with your mind, and you are what you do with your youth.

— Maltbie D. Babcock

Greetings Chicagoans!

I am honored and excited to welcome you to the second edition of **Who's Who In Black Chicago®**. Since its founding by Haitian fur trader Jean Baptiste Pointe DuSable, this city is comprised of foundation upon foundation of legendary and history-making African Americans. I am amazed at the depth of talent, resources, energy and wisdom that exists within your communities.

To that end, this edition is filled with stories and biographies of people in your city, who, facing incredible odds, continue to make strategic strides. Many lessons can be learned with a simple turn of each page. For starters, the Living Legends we feature this year have made their mark in a variety of fields, not just locally, but nationally and internationally. Additionally, the Interesting Personalities are just the tip of the iceberg in the massive amount of talent that exists within the Chicago metropolitan area. The youth of your city are blessed to have world-renowned contemporaries among them, and it is my hope that you will reach back and give back by ensuring this historical volume is made available to them. You have a great deal to be proud of, and I encourage our readers to share this edition with both the young and the old.

I would like to thank our Chicago associate publisher, Beverly Coley, for her efforts in making this another great networking guide. Likewise, without the support of our sponsors and advertisers, we would not be able to create such a comprehensive and quality publication. I also want to thank the corporate headquarters staff for their tireless efforts and my senior partner, Ernie Sullivan, for his committed and persistent efforts in assisting with this edition.

Live life to the fullest,

C. Sunny Martin
Founder/CEO
sunny@whoswhopublishing.com

Criteria for Inclusion

Who's Who In Black Chicago® is an opportunity for us to afford a measure of recognition to the men and women who have made their mark in their specific occupations, professions, or in service to others in the Chicago community.

A sincere effort was made to include those whose positions or accomplishments in their chosen fields are significant and whose contributions to community affairs, whether citywide or on the neighborhood level, have improved the quality of life for all of us.

The names of those brief biographies included in this edition were compiled from customary sources of information. Lists of a wide variety were consulted and every effort was made to reach all whose stature or civic activities merited their inclusion.

In today's mobile society, no such publication could ever claim to be complete; some who should be included could not be reached or chose not to respond, and for that we offer our apologies. Constraints of time, space and awareness are thus responsible for other omissions, and not a lack of good intentions on the part of the publisher. Our goal was to document the accomplishments of many people from various occupational disciplines.

An invitation to participate in the publication was extended at the discretion of the publisher. Biographies were invited to contribute personal and professional data, with only the information freely submitted to be included. The editors have made a sincere effort to present an accurate distillation of the data, and to catch errors whenever possible. However, the publisher cannot assume any responsibility for the accuracy of the information submitted.

There was no charge for inclusion in this publication and inclusion was not guaranteed; an annual update is planned. Comments and other concerns should be addressed to:

C. Sunny Martin, CEO
Who's Who Publishing Co., LLC
1650 Lake Shore Drive, Suite 250
Columbus, Ohio 43204
Phone: (614) 481-7300

E-Mail: sunny@whoswhopublishing.com
www.whoswhopublishing.com

A MESSAGE FROM THE

Chicago

ASSOCIATE PUBLISHER
Beverly A. Coley

"The glory is not in never failing…but rising every time we fall."

The story continues as we embark upon our second edition of ***Who's Who In Black Chicago***®. It is the story of a city and a race of people who have made this city strong and vibrant.

Success ultimately comes after making many mistakes and sacrifices along the way. None of us who grace these pages or who are reading this second edition have been immune to disappointments, struggles, losses or temporary defeats. It is with these life experiences that we realize we must continue to get up and keep going. We are all but links in a chain of humanity. The billions who have passed away before us are watching us and understanding our struggles and cheering us on in silent support. Can you feel their presence?

We are honored to have Linda Johnson Rice, president and CEO of Johnson Publishing Company Inc., pen the foreword to our second edition. The Johnson Publishing Company and its founder, John H. Johnson, is an institution in our community and in the world of publishing. Her outstanding leadership sets an exemplary example for the next generation of family- and black- owned businesses.

It gives me great pleasure to include a Living Legends section in this edition. They are only eight of the thousands of African Americans in this city who have made significant contributions to our community…and yes they got up every time they stumbled, fell or were knocked down by the forces that attempted to silence them for their stance on civil rights and injustices.

The renowned Timuel D. Black has once again graced our pages with a continuation of Chicago's Emerging History, bringing the historical perspective to the present. It was an enormous treat to spend time with Mr. Black, who will be 89 years young in December. His incredible memory, energy and spirit are a wonderful force in action!

Again my thanks and gratitude goes to the Who's Who staff and founder and CEO C. Sunny Martin for the opportunity to highlight many of the historical and contemporaneous experiences shared by African Americans in the city of Chicago. Special, special thanks goes out to Almae Publisher's Representatives team, my sister and business partner, Angela L. Coley, the entire Coley family and especially my mother, Lillie M. Coley for her unwavering love and support and my late father, Allen B. Coley.

The story has to continue for those who come behind us, especially our youth. We hope that when they read this book, they will understand that their dreams are not limited and feel a sense of pride when looking at accomplished people who look like them. As a community of people we must show kindness in another's struggles and continue the courage in our own.

All my best,

beverly

LEADING THROUGH INSPIRATION

By leading through inspiration, we can affect education, economic development and community empowerment. From one dynamic organization to another, we congratulate your accomplishments and support your future.

U.S. Cellular
We connect with you.

www.uscellular.com

You've Made All The RIGHT MOVES

Make your next one at Hewitt. We take great pride in turning strong individuals into even stronger professionals. Through diversity, teamwork, and a positive working environment, we can help you become the kind of leader you strive to be. At work. At home. And in your community. Making the world a better place to work. For everyone.

A Global HR Outsourcing and Consulting Firm

www.hewitt.com/rightmove

©2005 Hewitt Associates LLC

OPPORT**UNITY.**

Harris is committed to helping build vibrant communities and is driven by corporate values that foster a diverse workforce and an equitable, supportive workplace in which all employees are given the opportunity to meet their professional goals.

At the very heart of our promise is the drive to create a culture that encourages diversity and inclusion, recognizes the importance of being a strong corporate citizen and rewards those who deliver exceptional service to our customers.

It's called leading by example.

Chicago's
EMERGING
BLACK HISTORY

By Timuel D. Black Jr.

In the inaugural edition of **Who's Who In Black Chicago**®, I attempted to give the reader a broad understanding of the physical layout and social and cultural climate that existed in Chicago with the first Great Migration, without writing much content about individual personalities. In this volume, I will address some of Chicago's leadership and the legislation that changed the dynamics of populations with the African-American community.

First and Second Great Migrations

During the period roughly between 1915 and 1950, the first Great Migration of blacks from the South to Chicago took place. Upon arrival, they were racially segregated on the south, west, and near north sides of Chicago by an agreement between landlords and landowners wherein they would not rent or sell certain areas of those neighborhoods to persons of color. These types of agreements were known as restrictive covenants and remained in effect until the 1940 U.S. Supreme Court *Hansberry vs. Lee* ruling. However, this Supreme Court decision only applied to a small section of the Chicago neighborhood of Woodlawn. Subsequently, in a 1948 U.S. Supreme Court decision, *Shelley vs. Kramer*, restrictive covenants were ruled unenforceable nationwide. This caused a quick exodus from the densely overcrowded "Black Belt" (now known as Bronzeville) to nearby predominately white and fleeing white neighborhoods such as Hyde Park-Kenwood, Park Manor, Chatham, Englewood, South Shore and Beverly on the South Side, and Austin, Garfield and Douglas Park on the West Side.

Alley in Bronzeville, circa 1947
Migrants from the South did not find "heaven" in Chicago. Much of the housing in historic Bronzeville was built before World War I. The back stairs of buildings often led to rubble-strewn alleys, with poor drainage and unsanitary conditions. The migrants had to make their own pathways upward. Photo by Wayne Miller.

Vivian G. Harsh Research Collection of Afro-American History and Literature, Chicago Public Library

The former Black Belt residents took their urban experiences in politics and education, as well as their work, recreational, entertainment and social skills with them to their new neighborhoods. As a result, the social, cultural, academic, professional and entrepreneurial diversification of the black community was shattered and left barren. What remained was a community of impoverished people from the rural agricultural South who possessed few academic, social, cultural, professional and/or entrepreneurial skills.

Boycotts and Beyond

Later, in the 1950s and through the 1960s with the assassination of Emmett Till and the rise of the Montgomery Bus Boycott in 1955, Rosa Parks and Dr. Martin Luther King Jr. were launched to the forefront. The civil rights movement was accelerated. It is important to remember the unanimous 1954 U.S. Supreme Court decision, *Brown vs. Board of Education*, in which deliberately segregated schools were deemed unconstitutional. This decision had immediate impact on Chicago, which was experiencing overcrowded housing, as well as overcrowded double-shift schools in the black communities.

Organizations such as the local NAACP and the Chicago Urban League began to lobby for integration of these concerns. Their lobbying was actively supported by national labor alliances founded by A. Phillip Randolph such as the Negro American Labor Council, formed in 1960, and the Brotherhood of Sleeping Car Porters, formed in 1925. On a local level, I served as president of the Chicago chapter of the Negro American Labor Council. I was also active through the newly revived CORE (Council Of Racial Equality) and the Chicago area friends of SNCC (Student Nonviolent Coordinating Committee). Made up of scores of young people, these organizations picketed and boycotted places and organizations guilty of segregation.

Pre-school and kindergarten students at Parkway Community House, 1945
Parkway Community House, which opened at 51st and South Parkway in 1940, was an innovative settlement house. Horace Cayton, co-author of *Black Metropolis*, served as its director. This pre-school program offered an educational advantage to young children, many of them born to recently arrived migrants. The pre-school program, run by Frances Reese, was a precursor to Head Start.

Vivian G. Harsh Research Collection of Afro-American History and Literature, Chicago Public Library

July 22, 1963, Chicago C.O.R.E. members at a sit-in in the lobby of the Chicago Board of Education.
Vivian G. Harsh Research Collection of Afro-American History and Literature, Chicago Public Library

Asa Philip Randolph and Timuel Black during the 1961 National Alliance of Labor Council Convention, Chicago.

Vivian G. Harsh Research Collection of Afro-American History and Literature, Chicago Public Library

Dr. King and the SCLC were inspirations and guided much of the independent leadership in Chicago — mainly blacks. Chicagoans marched with him in Birmingham, Alabama, in 1963; Selma, Alabama, in 1965; and of course on August 28, 1963 in the historic March on Washington. There were more than 3,000 Chicagoans present in D.C. when he delivered his great "I Have a Dream" speech. Later, through the Coalition of Community Organization, Dr. King was convinced to come to Chicago in 1966 to attempt to break the continued segregated housing barrier.

It was while planning that action that we enlisted one of Dr. King's former young supporters from South Carolina, Jessie Louis Jackson, who was attending the divinity school at The University of Chicago, to take on Chicago leadership of the store merchant boycott efforts called Operation Breadbasket. It has now expanded its activities under Rev. Jackson's leadership and is renamed Operation PUSH (People United to Serve Humanity). Rev. Jackson was unsuccessful in running for president of the United States twice, in 1984 and 1988. It is very possible these two unsuccessful but very exciting attempts helped convince Illinois Senator Barack Obama that his campaign for United States president could be successful despite the color of his skin.

Timuel Black with students attending the March on Washington, August of 1963

Vivian G. Harsh Research Collection of Afro-American History and Literature, Chicago Public Library

Martin Luther King Jr., Timuel Black and others, 1962
Vivian G. Harsh Research Collection of Afro-American History and Literature, Chicago Public Library

From 1960 to the present, because of the physical separation of blacks by class and income levels in Chicago, there developed not only a physical separation, but also an emotional and psychological separation as well. This was evidenced by the building of huge amounts of public housing in old neighborhoods, poverty-stricken single-parent households and seemingly powerless and hopeless people. Joblessness, isolation and poor education within impoverished communities may have laid the groundwork for some street gangs, drug use and trafficking, and may have helped stimulate violence in once thriving, safe and optimistic areas.

Harold Washington, Timuel Black and others during Washington's campaign for mayor.
Vivian G. Harsh Research Collection of Afro-American History and Literature, Chicago Public Library

Current Political Leaders

During the late Mayor Harold Washington's elections in 1983 and 1987, and in between, there was an enthusiasm and unity in black Chicago that had not been evident since the late 1960s. Both Dr. King's assassination in Memphis, Tennessee, and Mayor Harold Washington's sudden death in November of 1987, re-demoralized an already divided and skeptical community. However, there have been numerous political successes since this period. This includes the first black U.S. female senator, Carol Moseley-Braun; U.S. Congressmen Bobby Rush, Danny K. Davis and Jesse Jackson Jr.; U.S. presidential candidate Barack Obama; Illinois State Senate President Emil Jones Jr.; former Illinois State Comptroller and State Attorney General Roland Burris; Illinois Secretary of State Jesse White; former president of the Cook County Board of Commissioners, John H. Stroger Sr. and his son, Todd; Cook County Circuit Court Chief Judge Timothy Evans; and former mayoral successor to Harold Washington, Eugene Sawyer.

Currently, the physical character of the Black Belt/Bronzeville area is swiftly changing because of the relatively ideal location, which is downtown near Lake Michigan, with good public transportation routes and an almost complete tear-down of affordable public housing. The old Black Belt is gentrifying. The old yet beautiful architectural housing is being restored and modernized, and new expensive housing is being built on the abundance of vacant land. Additionally, the 2016 Olympics are proposed to take place in historic Washington and Jackson Parks, because there is little possible organized community resistance.

In Chicago, we have more college presidents and professors, and an increased number of wealthy African-American men and women. Unfortunately, the economic poor class is also greater than before and growing. With an increase in poverty, the social distance between the haves and have-nots has increased. The cohesiveness that existed during the first Great Migration did not transfer to most of those who moved to Chicago in the second Great Migration. The beneficiaries of the first Great Migration have a responsibility to help our less fortunate brothers and sisters. Those in power, the upwardly mobile professional, entrepreneurial and wealthier classes must reach back to the ever-growing population of the poor and disenfranchised. This is a challenge that is extended to those represented in this and future generations of *Who's Who In Black Chicago*®.

Timuel D. Black Jr.

A lifetime Chicago resident, Timuel D. Black Jr. is a retired social sciences professor emeritus, political activist, historian and philosopher. Born in Birmingham, Alabama, at the age of eight months, his family moved to Chicago in August of 1919. He is the author of a series of oral histories, *Bridges of Memory: Chicago's First Wave of Great Migration* (Northwestern University Press), which chronicles interviews of three generations of southerners who came to Chicago with the first wave of migrants.

Black has taught at several high schools in Chicago and Gary, Indiana, City Colleges of Chicago and Roosevelt University. He earned a master's degree in social sciences from The University of Chicago and a bachelor's degree in sociology from Roosevelt University.

In addition to serving as the local chapter president of the Negro American Labor Council, he has served on several boards, including the ACLU and Americans for Democratic Action. His awards and honors are too numerous to mention. A U.S. Army veteran, Black served in combat in World War II and experienced four major battles. Almost 89 years old, he is still writing history that keeps Chicago's African-American heritage alive.

CONFIDENT DRIVEN QUALITY DISTINCTIVE VALUABLE EXPERTISE RESOURCEFUL UNIQUE TALENTED INNOVATIVE KNOWLEDGEABLE SHREWD ATTENTIVE PROFICIENT KIND TEAMWORK FRIENDLY INCISIVE INSIGHTFUL DYNAMIC QUALIFIED ANALYTICAL DETERMINED BRIGHT PROFESSIONAL ORIGINAL EXPERT GENEROUS PRUDENT VERSATILE UNDERSTANDING TIRELESS CLEVER STRONG OBSERVANT IMAGINATIVE DRIVEN PERCEPTIVE KEEN CONSISTENT TACTFUL EAGER BRILLIANT RATIONAL CAPABLE BUSINESSLIKE INFORMED CREATIVE IMPACTFUL PERCEPTIVE SMART ORGANIZED INTEGRITY PRIDE DISCERNING LEADERSHIP ASTUTE THOUGHTFUL CONFIDENT DRIVEN QUALITY DISTINCTIVE VALUABLE EXPERTISE RESOURCEFUL UNIQUE TALENTED INNOVATIVE KNOWLEDGEABLE SHREWD ATTENTIVE PROFICIENT KIND TEAMWORK FRIENDLY INCISIVE INSIGHTFUL DYNAMIC QUALIFIED ANALYTICAL DETERMINED BRIGHT PROFESSIONAL ORIGINAL EXPERT GENEROUS PRUDENT VERSATILE UNDERSTANDING TIRELESS CLEVER STRONG OBSERVANT IMAGINATIVE DRIVEN PERCEPTIVE KEEN CONSISTENT TACTFUL EAGER BRILLIANT RATIONAL CAPABLE BUSINESSLIKE INFORMED CREATIVE IMPACTFUL PERCEPTIVE SMART ORGANIZED INTEGRITY CONFIDENT DRIVEN QUALITY DISTINCTIVE VALUABLE EXPERTISE RESOURCEFUL UNIQUE TALENTED INNOVATIVE KNOWLEDGEABLE SHREWD ATTENTIVE PROFICIENT KIND TEAMWORK FRIENDLY INCISIVE INSIGHTFUL DYNAMIC QUALIFIED ANALYTICAL DETERMINED BRIGHT PROFESSIONAL ORIGINAL EXPERT GENEROUS PRUDENT VERSATILE UNDERSTANDING TIRELESS CLEVER STRONG OBSERVANT IMAGINATIVE DRIVEN PERCEPTIVE KEEN CONSISTENT TACTFUL EAGER BRILLIANT RATIONAL CAPABLE BUSINESSLIKE INFORMED CREATIVE IMPACTFUL PERCEPTIVE SMART ORGANIZED INTEGRITY PRIDE DISCERNING LEADERSHIP ASTUTE THOUGHTFUL CONFIDENT DRIVEN QUALITY DISTINCTIVE VALUABLE EXPERTISE RESOURCEFUL UNIQUE TALENTED INNOVATIVE KNOWLEDGEABLE SHREWD ATTENTIVE PROFICIENT KIND TEAMWORK FRIENDLY INCISIVE INSIGHTFUL DYNAMIC QUALIFIED ANALYTICAL DETERMINED BRIGHT PROFESSIONAL ORIGINAL EXPERT GENEROUS PRUDENT VERSATILE UNDERSTANDING TIRELESS CLEVER STRONG OBSERVANT IMAGINATIVE DRIVEN PERCEPTIVE KEEN CONSISTENT TACTFUL EAGER BRILLIANT RATIONAL CAPABLE BUSINESSLIKE INFORMED CREATIVE IMPACTFUL PERCEPTIVE SMART ORGANIZED INTEGRITY CONFIDENT DRIVEN QUALITY **DISCERNING DRIVEN EXPERTS ENERGETIC SHREWD IMAGINATIVE SAVVY** INNOVATIVE KNOWLEDGEABLE SHREWD ATTENTIVE PROFICIENT KIND TEAMWORK FRIENDLY INCISIVE INSIGHTFUL DYNAMIC QUALIFIED ANALYTICAL DETERMINED BRIGHT PROFESSIONAL ORIGINAL EXPERT GENEROUS PRUDENT VERSATILE UNDERSTANDING TIRELESS CLEVER STRONG OBSERVANT IMAGINATIVE DRIVEN PERCEPTIVE KEEN CONSISTENT TACTFUL EAGER BRILLIANT RATIONAL CAPABLE BUSINESSLIKE INFORMED CREATIVE IMPACTFUL PERCEPTIVE SMART ORGANIZED INTEGRITY PRIDE DISCERNING LEADERSHIP ASTUTE THOUGHTFUL CONFIDENT DRIVEN QUALITY DISTINCTIVE VALUABLE EXPERTISE RESOURCEFUL UNIQUE TALENTED INNOVATIVE KNOWLEDGEABLE SHREWD ATTENTIVE PROFICIENT KIND TEAMWORK FRIENDLY INCISIVE INSIGHTFUL DYNAMIC QUALIFIED ANALYTICAL DETERMINED BRIGHT PROFESSIONAL ORIGINAL EXPERT GENEROUS PRUDENT VERSATILE UNDERSTANDING TIRELESS CLEVER STRONG OBSERVANT IMAGINATIVE DRIVEN PERCEPTIVE KEEN CONSISTENT TACTFUL EAGER BRILLIANT RATIONAL CAPABLE BUSINESSLIKE INFORMED CREATIVE IMPACTFUL PERCEPTIVE SMART ORGANIZED INTEGRITY CONFIDENT DRIVEN QUALITY DISTINCTIVE VALUABLE EXPERTISE RESOURCEFUL UNIQUE TALENTED INNOVATIVE KNOWLEDGEABLE SHREWD ATTENTIVE PROFICIENT KIND TEAMWORK FRIENDLY INCISIVE INSIGHTFUL DYNAMIC QUALIFIED ANALYTICAL DETERMINED BRIGHT PROFESSIONAL ORIGINAL EXPERT GENEROUS PRUDENT VERSATILE UNDERSTANDING TIRELESS CLEVER STRONG OBSERVANT IMAGINATIVE DRIVEN PERCEPTIVE KEEN CONSISTENT TACTFUL EAGER BRILLIANT RATIONAL CAPABLE BUSINESSLIKE INFORMED CREATIVE IMPACTFUL PERCEPTIVE SMART ORGANIZED INTEGRITY PRIDE DISCERNING LEADERSHIP ASTUTE THOUGHTFUL CONFIDENT DRIVEN QUALITY DISTINCTIVE VALUABLE EXPERTISE RESOURCEFUL UNIQUE TALENTED INNOVATIVE KNOWLEDGEABLE SHREWD ATTENTIVE PROFICIENT KIND TEAMWORK FRIENDLY INCISIVE INSIGHTFUL DYNAMIC QUALIFIED ANALYTICAL DETERMINED BRIGHT PROFESSIONAL ORIGINAL EXPERT GENEROUS PRUDENT VERSATILE UNDERSTANDING TIRELESS CLEVER STRONG OBSERVANT IMAGINATIVE DRIVEN PERCEPTIVE KEEN CONSISTENT TACTFUL EAGER BRILLIANT RATIONAL CAPABLE BUSINESSLIKE INFORMED CREATIVE IMPACTFUL PERCEPTIVE SMART ORGANIZED INTEGRITY PRIDE DISCERNING LEADERSHIP ASTUTE THOUGHTFUL CONFIDENT DRIVEN QUALITY

IT'S HOW WE DELIVER DESTINCTIVE CLIENT VALUE.

www.aon.com

FOCUS

True visionaries never lose sight of their goals.

We proudly salute Who's Who in Black Chicago
and all of those who are making a difference in the community.

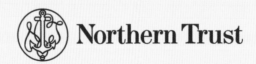

Private Banking | Asset Management | Financial Planning | Trust Services | Estate Planning Services | Business Banking

interest

limelight

CORPORATE SPOTLIGHT

attention

prominence

highlight

celebrate

headline

focus

recognition

Allianz ⑪

From Awareness to Action:
One Company's Mission to Embrace Diversity

By Walter Lancaster, Director of Multicultural Markets
Allianz Life Insurance Company of North America

You might be asking yourself "Who is Allianz?" We're a provider of life and long term care insurance and annuities in the United States. And while we may not be a household name, our parent company – Munich-based Allianz SE – is one of the world's leading integrated financial services organizations: It's the second-largest insurance company in the world based on revenue[1] and the third-largest money manager.[2] You probably know our U.S.-based sister companies, which include Fireman's Fund® and PIMCO.

That established, when we made the business decision at Allianz to make multicultural markets a priority, we took all the right steps. We identified key market segments. We hired top talent. We translated collateral into multiple languages. We created a dedicated Web site. We networked with associations and organizations. We sponsored awards and events.

What became apparent early on was that we needed to establish the inherent and critical link between multicultural markets and diversity. While diversity was an integral part of our external marketing effort, it wasn't necessarily embraced internally in our company. We knew we had to move from talking about the concept of diversity to making diversity a core element of our business philosophy and our culture. We had to take diversity from "awareness" to "action."

When discussing the topic of "diversity," there's always a danger of misinterpretation. Our first order of business was getting a definition of "diversity" that made sense. Allianz defines diversity as a concept that is far broader than race and gender. In the context of our workplace, diversity means creating a work environment that respects and includes differences, recognizing the unique contributions that individuals with different abilities and life experiences can make toward new and innovative ideas – and toward building a work environment that maximizes the potential of all employees.

With "diversity" clearly defined, we set about implementing a five-point strategic plan to make sure our company began to reflect the diverse communities we serve:

1. Recruitment

We held the various lines of business at Allianz accountable for diversity competency and for increasing their efforts to recruit top talent through minority-specific associations, organizations for people with disabilities, and GLBT networks.

2. Diversity training

We implemented a number of in-house educational opportunities for employees to become personally engaged and view themselves as true diversity "champions" including monthly diversity learning workshops with topics ranging from inter-racial communications, to understanding accents, to generation and gender gaps.

3. Workplace inclusion and retention

To ensure that all types of people could "fit in" and be successful, Allianz formed a Diversity Advisory Group whose role is to serve as an advocate, so that everyone has a "voice" in the organization.

4. Supplier diversity

We began to identify, include, and help develop diverse businesses that can provide Allianz with competitive products and services. We joined the National Minority Supplier Development Council. Today, we source and include at least one minority supplier in all formal bids where there's a minority supplier available for that product or service.

5. External recognition

To provide objective feedback and to benchmark our

Allianz ⓘ

diversity efforts in the industry and communities we serve, Allianz now utilizes multiple external diversity and social responsibility rankings.

With an internal diversity-friendly culture firmly in place, we're now positioned with true cultural competency to focus on our customers – the financial professionals who sell Allianz products. This is where our Multicultural Markets team comes in.

Allianz Multicultural Markets Advisory Services goes out into the field and works directly with multicultural financial professionals and agencies, providing support through multiple programs and resources including:

•In-language collateral and support services via our responsive telephone support team.

•An Allianz Multicultural Web site, which provides timely access to information, marketing materials, and sales support for Asian, African-American, and Hispanic markets.

•Our Allianz Multicultural Advisory Board, which provides a valuable feedback mechanism to ensure that we're on track with our marketing focus, support efforts, and product offerings

•A dedicated Multicultural Consulting Team, which serves the African-American, Asian, and Hispanic markets.

•The 2007 Allianz Multicultural University, which embraces all financial professionals who want to be involved with and support multicultural efforts. Allianz is conducting what's projected to be the nation's largest multicultural conference in Las Vegas in September. We also created a dedicated Web site–www.allianzmu. com – so that more people can have access to information

about the event, programs, and featured guest speakers.

Throughout our journey from supporting multicultural markets to embracing diversity, we've learned an important lesson at Allianz: You can't have one without the other. Unless an organization fully adopts an internal diversity policy, it cannot credibly communicate externally to cultural markets.

[1] Forbes 2000, www.forbes.com, March 29, 2007.
[2] P&I Wyatt World 500: The world's largest managers, as of 12/31/2005, Pensions & Investments, September 4, 2006.

Vera Banks, CMFC

Financial Advisor
Perennial Wealth Solutions

Gwendolyn V. Kirkland, CFP

Managing Principal
Turnbo & Associates

Vera Banks is an independent broker who services primarily baby boomers and the senior market. She understands that retirement and savings must be handled with the utmost care, and has devoted much of her career to educating others about these topics. Prior to becoming an independent broker, she spent six years as a life insurance agent for Prudential.

Vera earned a Bachelor of Arts degree in business management from National-Louis University in Evanston, Illinois. She currently hosts a radio talk show and co-hosts the Chicagoland *Community Calendar* on cable as a financial advisor. A frequent guest speaker on financial topics for churches and community organizations, she was recently a guest speaker at the Midwest Leadership Conference in Tinley Park, Illinois.

Currently, Vera is working on several community-building and community relations projects. She and her husband, Elijah, have been married for 15 years. They have two daughters and a grandson.

Gwendolyn V. Kirkland is a managing principal of Turnbo & Associates, an independently owned office of Sterne Agee Financial Services. She enjoys working with a diverse client base that includes athletes, business owners and high-net-worth individuals, as well as approximately 1,200 other clients who are striving to increase their net worth.

Gwendolyn earned a Bachelor of Science degree from Bradley University in Peoria, Illinois, and a Master of Education degree from DePaul University. She has been working in the securities industry since 1983, and holds National Association of Securities Dealers Series 7 and insurance licenses.

In her spare time, Gwendolyn is a sought-after speaker and author, and is active in a number of professional organizations, including the Chicago Urban League, the National Female Executives and the Certified Financial Planners Board of Standards. She is also currently enrolled at Chicago Theological Seminary in the Master of Divinity Program.

Nathan A. Majors Jr.

Independent Advisor
Major Financial Planning

Matthew Sapaula

President
MatthewSapaula, Inc.

Nathan A. Majors Jr. has been an independent advisor with his own firm, Major Financial Planning, since 2004. He has a passion for helping his clients work toward achieving a successful retirement without outliving their financial resources. He also helps business owners establish retirement savings programs and business continuation plans.

Nathan has a degree in accounting and has been working in financial services since 1999. He holds National Association of Securities Dealers Series 7 and 65 licenses.

In his spare time, Nathan volunteers for various organizations, including the Black Star Project, the Ultimate Goal Ministries, and as a tutor with the Delta Literacy Project. He and his wife, Dana, live in the southern suburbs of Chicago. They have four children, of whom three will be in college this fall.

Matthew Sapaula is president of Matthew Sapaula, Inc., a Chicago-area financial planning firm that specializes in retirement planning and real estate equity management. For more than eight years, his customized approach has designed progressive financial strategies to help his clients uncover hidden assets and increase their wealth.

Personally trained by Douglas R. Andrew, author of *Missed Fortune 101*, Matthew offers complimentary seminars on traditional and nontraditional wealth-building strategies. He also credits his ten years of military service for instilling in him the values and discipline that he now applies to his business. He served in Somalia and the Persian Gulf as a U.S. Marine, and was meritoriously promoted to staff sergeant.

In his spare time, Matthew enjoys spending time with his three children, who are active in sporting and ministry activities. He is also a member of The Executives' Club of Chicago, the National Association of Insurance and Financial Advisors, and the Chicago Real Estate Investment Club.

Tony Wiley & Cathy Augustine

Founders
Genesis Wealth Management

Tony Wiley and Cathy Augustine are founders of Genesis Wealth Management, a financial services firm that helps clients with wealth accumulation, saving for education, estate and retirement planning, and more. Genesis Wealth Management has also been retained by the Chicago Board of Education to provide financial education and service to 403(b) participants through a partnership with ING Securities.

Tony and Cathy are both chartered senior financial planners and registered investment advisor representatives. They have more than 35 years of combined experience in the financial services industry, and are both fully licensed in all aspects of financial planning.

In addition to offering financial wellness workshops, Tony and Cathy also host a bi-quarterly cable show, the *Genesis Report*, and frequently make guest appearances on radio and television shows.

Ed passed away three years ago.

But thanks to you, he helped pay his granddaughter's tuition bill.

With your know-how and our insurance products, Ed found a way to help his granddaughter get her college degree – even though he couldn't be there on graduation day.

You change people's lives. We just give you the tools. And the reason you rely on us is *because they're counting on you.*SM

Allianz (ll)

Introducing Multicultural Markets Advisory Services

The strong business backgrounds of our Advisory Services team demonstrate that we are a forward-thinking leader in expanding various markets for a new business generation.

Baron Carr
Vice president of Multicultural Markets, Allianz Life Insurance Company of North America

Baron Carr is the head of Multicultural Markets Advisory Services, with responsibility for building a multicultural distribution channel and creating a brand within the African-American, Asian, and Hispanic markets. Prior to joining the company, Baron held key positions in the multicultural markets at JPMorgan Chase. He was head of emerging markets group in the Auto Finance division, and led the Corporate Marketing and Communications' multicultural marketing efforts. Baron holds a B.A. in Media Arts and an M.B.A. in Accounting from Long Island University.   **763.765.5685**

Lily Fong
Director of Asian Markets

Lily brings 10 years of multicultural marketing/diverse recruiting, and women in marketing experience from New England Financial/MetLife, General Motors Acceptance Corporation, and Prudential. She graduated Summa Cum Laude with an M.B.A. in international marketing.   **763.765.5462**

Rafael Gutierrez
Director of Hispanic Markets

Rafael comes to us with 17 years in the insurance business, and has experience with Western & Southern Life and AIG in Chile and Peru in the areas of product development, recruiting, and training. He has a B.S. in computer science and an M.B.A. in marketing and management.   **763.765.7874**

Walter Lancaster
Director of African-American Markets

Walter comes to us with over 35 years of experience in multicultural marketing and diversity initiatives with Fortune 500 companies like Loew's Inc., the Gannett Group, Metromedia Inc. and most recently JPMorgan Chase. He holds a B.A. from CCNY and is a recipient of the coveted Black Achievers in Industry Award.   **763.765.5671**

Mission statement:

Multicultural Markets Advisory Services

Our mission is to become a world-class consulting team and secure long-term, profitable growth for our FMOs, AFMOs, broker/dealers, and producers through projects that range from existing business improvements to full-scale transformational change. Our work extends beyond the strategic dimension through our commitment to helping our clients build organizational capabilities that ensure long-term economic advantages within the multicultural markets.

www.allianzlife.com

Allianz Life Insurance
Company of North America
5701 Golden Hills Drive
Minneapolis, MN 55416-1297
800.950.7372

Allianz Life Insurance
Company of New York
One Chase Manhattan Plaza, 38th Floor
New York, NY 10005-1422
877.796.6880

For financial professional use only – not for use with the public.

Chicago's
LIVING
LEGENDS

Photo by Powell Photography, Inc.

- CHICAGO'S LIVING LEGEND -
THE REVEREND WILLIE BARROW
Her Sacred Commission

By Ingrid E. Bridges

The Reverend Willie Barrow will be forever remembered in history books as a spiritual and social activist, and as the woman who walked alongside the late Dr. Martin Luther King Jr. during the height of the civil rights movement. During that time she organized marches, transportation and meetings for eight long years, but has since grown by leaps and bounds.

"I managed Dr. King's schedule as he marched around the nation," she recalls. Barrow traveled monthly to Atlanta, Georgia, to work by his side in a time when blacks were described as Negroes and colored, labeled as inhuman, and ordered to sit at the back of the bus because of the color of their skin.

Subsequently, Barrow's empowering touch continued to connect people's lives. This was apparent when she became one of the founding members of Operation Breadbasket, an organization which provided a sense of direction and empowerment to the downtrodden and mistreated in communities across Chicagoland.

After decades of defining lawful methods to crack the code of inequalities against people of color, earning the title "little warrior," she admits it has been a tough, long road. "I think I paid the price," said Barrow, from her busy office at RainbowPUSH (formerly known as Operation Breadbasket) headquarters on Chicago's South Side, where she currently serves as chairperson emeritus.

Despite losing her only son in the prime of his life, a husband of merely six decades, and her only sister (a twin) this year, today she remains just as diligent as in her former years in the movement. At 80-plus years young, serving people and their needs remains her sacred commission. People compel Rev. Barrow get up in the morning and lay down with peace late at night—the needs of people drive her.

"It's not easy when you have a commitment toward people," said Barrow. "If you really want a sense of great relationship, great power—connect with other people. We must connect with people of all races and backgrounds today in order to make it," she advised.

Barrow manages to stay afloat not only perfectly, but profoundly so, adapting to society's rapid changes stemming from the onslaught of the computer age, cell phones and text messaging technology, with ease and comfort. "It's a different world. Today you can't make a difference by yourself."

No longer managing marches nor overseeing schedules of mighty men who change the world, her undying wit is sought out by dozens who admire her, who need her advice to move forward in their businesses, organizations, and yes, their lives, whether they are a politician or media personality. Rev. Barrow fulfills humanity's needs even more as an associate pastor of the Vernon Park Church of God in the Windy City. Serving on countless boards, speaking at podiums from the school house to the White House, she remains committed to the movement of perfecting and connecting the lives of God's people everywhere she goes. "We are not as much divided as we are disconnected," she shares.

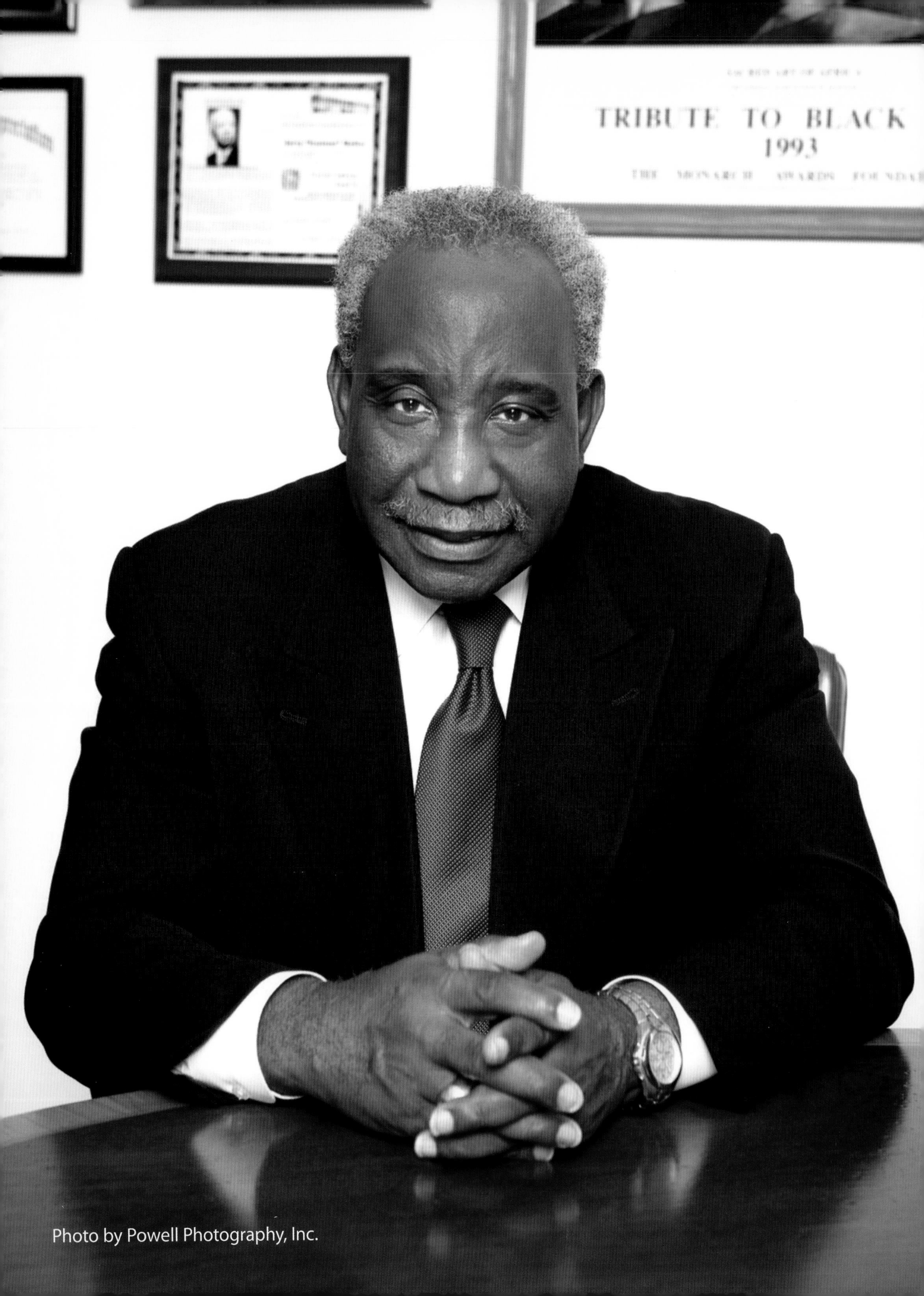

Photo by Powell Photography, Inc.

- CHICAGO'S LIVING LEGEND -
JERRY BUTLER
A Lasting Impression

By Barbara Kensey

Chicagoans have a certain affection for Cook County Commissioner Jerry Butler that is usually not accorded to politicians. But that's because Chicagoans knew Jerry before he was Commissioner Butler. Or at least they knew his music. Many of them grew up listening to songs like "For Your Precious Love" and "Only the Strong Survive." So when he made the transition from full-time musician to a full-time political career with weekend performances, Chicagoans elected him with the highest vote total of any county commissioner in Chicago history.

Jerry "Iceman" Butler is currently serving his sixth four-year term as Cook County Commissioner where, along with 17 other duly elected commissioners, he is responsible for making laws, establishing rules and setting policy for the second-largest county in the United States with an annual budget in excess of $3 billion.

Butler began his life wanting to be a chef, influenced by his uncle John Bennett who "had more money than anybody in the family," owned his own restaurant and had his own automobile. "He was a hard-working guy and he'd always give me a job, and out of having the job I'd wind up having some money," he said. "I was going to go around the world cooking and eating good food."

Fortuitously, two brothers, Arthur and Samuel Brooks, moved into the neighborhood and his life took a turn. "They thought they could sing and make records," Butler recalls. "Some friend told them about me and they asked if I could help. I joined the group and I talked Curtis Mayfield into coming into the group. We changed the name to The Impressions because Curtis said we should make a lasting impression."

And a lasting impression was made from the onset, starting with a poem the 18-year-old Butler had written called "For Your Precious Love." It became a major hit record and a career was launched. "I was always working to better myself, to get out of poverty," Butler recalls. "I was motivated by a whole bunch of desires and needs and wanting to be."

An award-winning performer, producer and composer, Butler has been nominated for three Grammys and is the recipient of many awards, including several from ASCAP for his songwriting and publishing work. He has had numerous million-selling recordings both with The Impressions and in his solo career. They include *For Your Precious Love* (Vee-Jay, 1958); *He Will Break Your Heart* (Vee-Jay, 1960); "Never Gonna Give You Up" (Mercury, 1976); and "Ain't Understanding Mellow" (Mercury, 1973). In 1991 Butler was inducted into the Rock & Roll Hall of Fame.

These days he splits his time between his two mistresses—politics and music—and Annette, his wife of 48 years. As the elder statesman on the Cook County Board, he is gliding along as only an "Iceman" can, wracking up honors such as being elected grand master of the Prince Hall Masons in the state of Illinois. It is an achievement he stacks alongside of a Board of Governors degree and a master's degree in criminal justice studies from Governors State University and, of course, his gold records.

JEAN BAPTISTE POINTE DuSABLE
The Father of Chicago

- CHICAGO'S LIVING LEGEND -
DR. MARGARET BURROUGHS
Artistic Icon

By Ingrid E. Bridges

Dr. Margaret Burroughs is an icon of artistic flare and African culture known not only throughout Chicago, but throughout the world as founder of the DuSable Museum of African American history and for her untiring dedication to the arts.

Burroughs' devout love for black art, and its rich history, drove her and husband Charles Burroughs to start the Ebony Museum of Negro History in their home on the city's South Side, back in 1961. People came by to view their unique collection, which sat on pedestals, tables and bookshelves back then. The couple's growing collection of some of the world's richest African art soon caught the eye of elementary and high schools around the city, and soon the buzz was on.

In 1968 the museum was renamed after Jean Baptist Pointe DuSable, a Haitian fur trader who was the first permanent resident of Chicago. After years of growing by leaps and bounds, in 1971 the Chicago Park District granted the museum use of a former park administration building in Washington Park. In 1993 after much negotiation and favor, Burroughs managed to have a new wing bearing the name of the late Mayor Harold Washington added to the building, consisting of two floors and a theater. Today the museum remains at that same location as the DuSable Museum.

Burroughs' powerful presence is just as rich as the items on display throughout the various corridors of the DuSable Museum. Her ageless wit is exemplified in her many personal works, for she too is an artist. Many art collectors and artists will attest that her amazing litho cuts and pen and ink prints are an intricate part of their private collections. Her ink creations of the late singer Mahalia Jackson, activist Malcolm X, and a special piece entitled "In School Together," are just spectacular.

Traveling the world speaking on the rewards of art collecting, Burroughs remains humble as one of the most sought-out women of her time. And, despite the grace of years, she maintains a wonderful sense of humor about her amazing life and her deep creations which are also displayed in museums around the world, as well as in art galleries, corporations and schools alike.

The recipient of 60 honors and six honorary degrees, this poet, author, educator and civic leader still finds time in her busy schedule to serve humanity by teaching and lecturing in countless institutions of art, culture and education.

Today, Dr. Burroughs says of her life, "It's a simple one." However, because her name is synonymous with DuSable Museum and the arts, statesmen call on her and honor her. President Jimmy Carter honored her as one of the ten outstanding black artists in America.

Thanks to her devotion, the museum remains in the black community as a much sought-out institution, serving the needs of those interested in the rich culture and history of black art.

- CHICAGO'S LIVING LEGEND -

CIRILO A. MCSWEEN

Hard Work, Passion and Commitment

By Melody M. McDowell

The journey that took Cirilo A. McSween from the depths of poverty to the heights of success began in his native Panama. There he gained prominence as a member of the Panama Track and Field team by shattering the country's individual records in several international competitions, including the Olympics.

Cirilo matriculated to the University of Illinois and continued his record-setting athletic feats while earning a degree in economics. He set his sights on a career in insurance and boldly hitched a ride to New York to meet with executives at New York Life. Undaunted that the insurance industry had never had an African-American agent, he nonetheless applied for a job. After being paced through exercises that would have disheartened most, Cirilo was eventually hired by New York Life and launched what would be a milestone-studded career.

He turned the industry on its heels by becoming the first African-American ever to sell as much as $1 million in a year and $2 million in a month. These feats earned him a lifetime membership in the prestigious Million Dollar Roundtable.

Conflicted over the plight of those being denied human rights, in the '60s, he put his career on hold to risk his life in the civil rights movement. He developed a bond with Dr. Martin Luther King Jr. and became a board member and national treasurer of the Southern Christian Leadership Conference.

When King was felled by an assassin's bullet, Cirilo was one of the pallbearers. After his death, McSween joined forces with the Reverend Jesse Jackson, becoming a board member and vice chairman of RainbowPUSH and a vanguard in the movement. He also distinguished himself as the campaign treasurer when Harold Washington made his successful—and historic—run for mayor of Chicago.

In the '80s, McSween blazed new trails by becoming an owner/operator of a McDonald's restaurant. McSween's McDonald's was the first business to open on the State Street Mall and the first to report $3 million in annual sales. This sales triumph earned him the prestigious Ronald McDonald Award and The Golden Arch Award twice. He now owns and operates 11 stores including six at O'Hare Airport.

In what is hailed as a "climactic high point" of his career, his civil rights and business life were chronicled in an exhibit mounted at Chicago's famed DuSable Museum of African American History in 2004. Titled McSween Meets King: A Civil Rights Story, the retrospective graphically captured his struggles for equality in 20th century America and journalized his pioneering business role.

In 2005 New York Life instituted the Cirilo A. McSween – New York Life Rainbow/PUSH Excel Scholarship Award in recognition of his historic place with the company and the industry. The stipends are presented yearly to full-time college students whose commitment to scholarship and their communities mirrors McSween's.

McSween remains devoted to Panama and helped ratify the Panama Canal Treaty. His loyalty and advocacy have earned him Panama's highest honors. A close confidante to the current president, he played a role in his successful election.

Ultimately, Cirilo A. McSween is a living legend who is the embodiment of what hard work, passion and commitment can achieve.

- CHICAGO'S LIVING LEGEND -

THE REVEREND ADDIE WYATT

"I would come the same way."

By Ingrid E. Bridges

The Reverend Addie Wyatt could easily be pegged as a modern-day Harriet Tubman for her determination toward changing the face of the labor movement during the height of the civil rights movement.

Changing how women were regarded in the workplace was her divine mission, a vocation that began shortly after being employed at a meat packing house in 1941. It was then and there she became a union activist. She served as an activist and international representative in the Union Food and Commercial Workers International Union, and was director of women's affairs.

Her mission for equality and fairness was depended upon by hundreds wanting equal rights where they worked in a time when blacks in America were regarded as colored people with no hope or future in society's professional arena. Despite constant opposition from every side, Wyatt galvanized people who would believe in her plight, no matter how difficult the times. Still, people came from far and wide to examine her moves, politicians and community folk, alike.

For years she fought, rallied and served as a campaign worker. Eventually she prevailed in getting justice within the industry, and in 1953 was elected vice president of her branch, Local 56. She was the first black woman to hold a senior office in an American labor union. The mother of two children

regrets not one decision she made back then, "If I had my life to live over again, I would come the same way, learning to work with men and women; learning how to fight against wicked injustice and inequality. It has been a marvelous experience for me," said Wyatt.

Her success would not be possible without concerned friends and powerful allies who saw her through the tough times. She admits that no man is an island. "The late Congressman Charles Hayes was my partner, my supporter, giving constant support where he could. I learned to respect and appreciate the brothers. I learned to honor them and they will honor you. When you honor one another, you're protective, you don't want to let harm come to one another," Wyatt shared.

In 1974 she helped form the Coalition of Labor Union Women, and in 1976 became the international president of the United Food and Commercial Workers, making her the first African-American woman to lead an international union. She held this post until she retired to become a full-time pastor at the Vernon Park Church of God along with her husband, Claude Sr.

"The Bible tells us we have a responsibility of being a true partner, male or female, young or old, black or white," said Rev. Wyatt. "Being faithful unto God is being faithful to his purpose for us living here as women."

- CHICAGO'S LIVING LEGEND -

R. EUGENE PINCHAM

"I know I've been blessed."

By Barbara Kensey

Retired Appellate Court Judge R. Eugene Pincham lives in a sprawling home surrounded by a white picket fence and containers of red geraniums in a quiet residential community on the South Side of Chicago. The walls and all the surfaces of his home office are filled with awards and honors. He is well known and highly respected both professionally and personally. Not bad for a man who grew up thinking everyone went to bed hungry. "I came up the rough side of the mountain," he affirms. "I know I've been blessed."

Born in Chicago, June 28, 1925, Pincham moved with his family to Athens, Limestone County, Alabama, as an infant. There, he attended Trinity, an American Missionary Association school run by dedicated white Christian missionaries, mainly from New England. His grandmother and mother also attended Trinity which was both an elementary and a high school. The school was burned down three times by hostile whites who resented blacks being educated and each time the missionaries rebuilt it – better than the last time. The lessons he learned from that experience were about injustice and commitment which laid the foundation for his life. That and indoctrination by the missionaries that not doing your very best was a sin.

The superior education he received at Trinity prepared him to graduate with honors in 1947 from Tennessee State University. After marrying his college sweetheart Alzata Cudalia Henry—a marriage that lasted 57 years until her death in 2005—he returned to Chicago where he attended law school at Northwestern University, the only black in a class of 80 students. Alzata worked as a substitute teacher in order to help him through school. "She trusted and believed in me," he shares.

Pincham built a successful law practice litigating many high profile criminal and civic cases before being elected a judge in 1976. Then in 1990, after 14 years on the bench, he resigned in protest when the Cook County Illinois Democratic Party refused to slate the black chairman of the Finance Committee for president of the Cook County Board of Commissioners despite the fact that that trajectory was a time-honored tradition.

Taking the injustice personally, Pincham ran for president of the Cook County Board himself and although he lost that election, he won the right to be a candidate in the general election.

Now retired, this social activist continues to take on select cases that impact the community socially, economically or politically. In 1992, for example, he successfully litigated the Chicago ward reapportionment case which resulted in a more accurate reflection of Chicago's racial composition.

At this point in his life, he still sees work to be done. Asserts Pincham, "I'm tremendously disturbed by the immunity with which police officers can treat black people and get away with it." He is also troubled by the fact that black people are not fulfilling their responsibilities by voting.

If there is anything that can be done about either situation, Pincham is the person to do it. The missionaries taught him well and he fully understands that "the sole purpose of life is to use your life to help somebody else."

Photo by Powell Photography, Inc.

- CHICAGO'S LIVING LEGENDS -
WESLEY SOUTH & PERVIS SPANN
Still Talking Today

By Barbara Kensey

Wesley South and Pervis Spann, co-owners of Chicago's WVON Radio are like night and day, Spann is a gregarious, outgoing personality who delights in a joke while South is more laid-back with a memory so sharp it belies his 93 years on the planet. They first met in the 60s when both were on-air personalities at WVON Radio – "back in the day" when VON stood for the "Voice of the Negro."

When it comes to black talk radio, South is the pioneer. Nearly 20 years Spann's senior, South was already at WVON hosting a popular one-hour talk show called *Hotline* five nights a week from 11 p.m. to midnight when Spann arrived.

Leading political figures of the day—Dr. Martin Luther King Jr., Malcolm X, the Honorable Elijah Muhammad, Medgar Evers, Dick Gregory and others—made it a point to stop by WVON and South's *Hotline*. At one point the show was so hot that during that one-hour time slot Illinois Bell Telephone Company logged so many calls coming in simultaneously, the lines serving the area were completely jammed.

"The Chess brothers got the money, but we got the praise," South says, referring to the owners at that time. "We got very little money."

South was a known commodity with an established reputation as a journalist. He had worked at the *Chicago Defender*, *Ebony* and *Jet* magazines. He also had a column in the *Chicago American* called "South Side Lites," reporting on the goings on in the black community. And for a brief stint, he owned his own publication, *Now*.

Spann was "the man" for live shows in Chicago, promoting headliners such as Redd Foxx, Al Green, Sam Cooke and Aretha Franklin. He also owned one of the city's most popular night clubs, The Burning Spear, where he discovered and showcased emerging talent including Chaka Khan, The Jackson 5, and the Five Stair Steps.

A self-proclaimed workaholic, he also owned radio stations in Tennessee, Georgia and Florida. Going by the moniker "The Blues Man," Spann followed South at midnight and would hold his devoted blues lovers until 4 or 5 in the morning.

Spann has traveled quite a distance from Itta Bina, Mississippi, where he raised and picked cotton. He was never afraid of hard work. "I've been a workaholic all my days," he says. At one point, he attended Moody Bible Institute where he considered the idea of becoming a minister.

South, a native of Muskogee, Oklahoma, came from a solidly middle-class family. His grandfather, father and older brother were all physicians. Yet he says his greatest motivation was a "desire to get out of poverty." South attended Northwestern University where it took him nine years working full-time to earn a degree.

Despite dissimilar beginnings and different routes, they arrived at the same place at the same time. By 1980, these giants of the "Midway," the name of their company, had moved from on-air personalities to the owners of WVON Radio. Six years later, the station went all-talk and it is still talking today. The "Voice of the Nation," beams black talk worldwide 24 hours a day.

- CHICAGO'S LIVING LEGEND -
LERONE BENNETT JR.

"I fell in love with history."

By David Smallwood

Lerone Bennett Jr.'s passion for the written word, beginning at age 6, led him to become one of the pre-eminent historians, journalists and scholars of our time. He is all three rolled into one.

Named editor emeritus of *Ebony* magazine upon his retirement in 2005 after working at Johnson Publishing Company for 52 years, Bennett is the celebrated author of ten books, including the historic *Before The Mayflower* and the controversial *Forced Into Glory: Abraham Lincoln's White Dream.*

Mayflower, a history of the black experience in America starting with its origins in western Africa, has been named one of the 100 most significant black books of the 20th century, one of the top ten most influential black books ever by *American Legacy*, and has been referenced by more than 100 other books.

Forced Into Glory caused a raging national debate by making the case that Abraham Lincoln was hardly a friend of the American Negro. This October, *Glory* will appear in paperback for the first time, and *Mayflower* will be re-issued in its eighth revised edition.

Bennett also wrote *What Manner of Man?*, the biography of his Morehouse College classmate, Dr. Martin Luther King Jr., and he assisted legendary publisher John H. Johnson in preparing his classic autobiography, *Succeeding Against The Odds.*

Bennett is the beneficiary of numerous honors and awards, including honorary degrees from almost 20 colleges or universities. He was recently inducted into the International Civil Rights Walk of Fame, the Chicago Journalism Hall of Fame and the National Association of Black Journalists Hall of Fame.

Earlier this year, Bennett received a commendation from the Mississippi State Legislature and told the assembled group, "I want to thank the great black teachers of Mississippi, who literally saved my life. Almost everything I could see in the old Mississippi told me I was nothing, that I was dirt. The teachers told me that I was somebody and there was no limit to what I could dream and do."

He was born in Clarksdale, Mississippi, on October 17, 1928. Early on, Bennett says, "I fell in love with history, with the black press and with the written word. I believed foolishly that if I could learn how to read, if I could understand why Mississippi was what it was, if I could tell that story, then the whole thing would change."

He wrote his first article at age 14 for a black paper in Jackson, joined the *Atlanta Daily World* the day after he graduated Morehouse in 1949, and was recruited by John Johnson to *Ebony* in 1953, becoming executive editor in 1987. Bennett has never had any boss other than the black press.

His historical articles were an *Ebony* hallmark, and in striving for a more accurate and inclusive interpretation of black and American history, Bennett was what he calls a "witness-participant."

"You can't find truth just by reading and watching; you have to get involved," he says. "So, I've not only written about the struggle for equality and racial issues, but I've marched, boycotted and organized from Mississippi to Selma to Gage Park here in Chicago."

Bennett and his wife, Gloria, have four children: Joy, Constance, Courtney and Lerone III.

Slow and steady brings out the stars

Ariel Fund

*Overall Morningstar Rating™
as of 5/31/07
(out of 383 domestic
mid-cap blend funds)*

The Overall Morningstar Rating for a fund is derived from a weighted average of the performance figures associated with its three-, five- and ten-year (if applicable) Morningstar Ratings.

Ariel Fund was rated two stars among 383, three stars among 310 and five stars among 132 domestic mid-cap blend funds for the three-, five- and ten-year periods ended 5/31/07, respectively. For each fund with at least a three-year history, Morningstar calculates a Morningstar Rating™ based on a Morningstar Risk-Adjusted Return measure that accounts for variation in a fund's monthly performance (including the effects of sales charges, loads and redemption fees), placing more emphasis on downward variations and rewarding consistent performance. These ratings change monthly. The top 10% of funds in an investment category receive five stars, the next 22.5% receive four stars, the next 35% receive three stars, the next 22.5% receive two stars, and the bottom 10% receive one star. Morningstar does not guarantee the accuracy of this information.

Patience has so many rewards

At Ariel Mutual Funds, our disciplined approach to value investing has helped investors like you achieve long-term goals since 1983. In fact, we chose the tortoise as our symbol because it illustrates our faith in the moral of Aesop's fable—*slow and steady wins the race.* Call an Ariel Investment Specialist today and bring the value of patient investing to your portfolio with the no-load Ariel Mutual Funds.

ARIEL MUTUAL FUNDS

arielmutualfunds.com 800-292-7435

Past performance does not guarantee future results. Investing in small and mid-cap stocks is more risky and more volatile than investing in large cap stocks. *For a current prospectus, which includes the investment objectives, risks, management fees, charges and expenses as well as other information, call 800-292-7435. Please read the prospectus carefully before investing. ©2007, Ariel Distributors, LLC.*

©2007 Morningstar, Inc. All Rights Reserved. The information contained herein: (1) is proprietary to Morningstar and/or its content providers; (2) may not be copied or distributed; and (3) is not warranted to be accurate, complete, or timely. Neither Morningstar nor its content providers are responsible for any damages or losses arising from any use of this information.

Our policy is people.

When we create our line of products, we have one thing in mind, you: who you are, how you live, and what matters to you most. That's why American Family Insurance offers you an array of products that cater to your unique needs and lifestyles, and for less than you'd expect. Whether it's home, auto, life, health, or commercial insurance, our knowledgeable and responsive agents will give you complete information so that you can make the right decisions for you, your family or your business.

American Family Mutual Insurance Company and its Subsidiaries
Home Office - Madison, WI 53783
www.amfam.com

©2006   003731287 - 04/06

All your protection under one roof ®

Proud to Support
WHO'S WHO IN BLACK CHICAGO

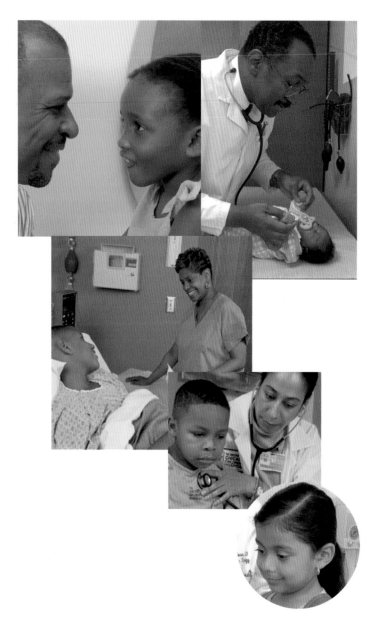

Like *Who's Who*, the University of Chicago Medical Center (UCMC) is committed to supporting the diverse business community.

Our business diversity initiative assures the inclusion of minority- and woman-owned businesses in all aspects of our supply chain. Last year alone we spent over $10 million dollars with supply and professional services firms.

Our initiative has been honored, in particular, for the participation of diverse contractors in the construction of the University of Chicago Comer Children's Hospital opened in 2005. Nearly 40 percent of the new hospital's construction contracts went to minority- and women-owned businesses.

Groups that have honored our business diversity initiative include Black Contractors United, Chicago Urban League and the Chicago Minority Business Development Council, Inc.

As we expand into the future, a diverse supplier pool will help us remain at the Forefront of Medicine.

THE UNIVERSITY OF
CHICAGO
MEDICAL CENTER

AT THE FOREFRONT OF MEDICINE®

profound

captivating

INTERESTING PERSONALITIES

distinct

impassioned

original

inspiring

remarkable

individual

prodigious

Photo By: POWELL PHOTOGRAPHY, INC.

ZERRIE CAMPBELL

Empowerment through Education

By David Smallwood

As president of Malcolm X College (MXC) for the past 15 years, Zerrie Campbell has led that institution longer than any of the college's six other presidents, and has been in office longer than her three predecessors combined.

Not a bad track record for someone who originally thought she would go "five years and out." Campbell, MXC's first female head, is also the longest-tenured president at any of the seven City Colleges of Chicago (of which MXC is one).

Half of her 30-year educational career has been spent as Malcolm X's president, and she was the college's vice president for several years prior. "So this place is really home for me," Campbell says.

She calls her proudest achievement "helping to create a top-of-the-mind presence of Malcolm X as a quality institution with a premiere health science program, a great comprehensive general education curriculum and a wonderful commitment to the community."

Campbell strongly credits her staff for that accomplishment. "I could leave here today and things would be on a fine, firm footing," she says. "This institution is not Zerrie Campbell."

Calling the school "a cultural hub of the city, not just the City Colleges," Campbell notes that Malcolm X hosts more than 1,000 meetings and community activities that bring upwards of 150,000 people to the college every year.

A premiere event is the college's full-blown, seven-day celebration of Kwanzaa. MXC's celebration, one of the largest in the nation, has for the past 14 years been held in conjunction with Shule Ya Watoto (School For Children), which has elevated Campbell to "Queen Mother" status.

Under Campbell's leadership, Malcolm X has been awarded more than $12 million in federal grants, and has won three coveted awards for excellence from the Illinois Community College Board in the areas of teaching and learning, institutional effectiveness and strategic planning, and workforce preparation.

A big source of Campbell's pride is the school's health programs. "There's not a hospital in the area that most likely does not have a graduate from Malcolm X College," she boasts. "We have one of only six physician assistant programs in the country, and a radiology program that for two years now has won statewide competition among 18 other radiology programs."

That is personal to Campbell, who, when she fell ill several years ago and was hospitalized, was serviced by several students who were MXC graduates. Good thing that she was a good president to them? "Nope," she responds, "better thing that they were trained well!"

Campbell, one of a trio of City Colleges presidents who actually managed the entire system for 15 months in the early 1990s, says she is "humbled and grateful by the way this West Side community has embraced the college and me personally."

She thinks part of that acceptance comes from the college trying to live up to the mission of the man for whom the college is named.

"People comment that we have such a beautiful facility," she notes, "but what better tribute to a man than for an institution to be stately and truly represent his philosophy of empowerment through education? You can change the quality of your life through an education."

CEDRIC THURMAN

"There are more ways to serve."

By Barbara Kensey

He has been a bank president, an entrepreneur who founded his own general management consulting services firm and, at one point, he considered becoming a priest. Now he is the chief diversity officer for a real estate money management company. And he is only 42 years old.

Cedric Thurman was appointed chief diversity officer for Jones Lang LaSalle's North America region in April of 2007. In this position he is responsible for nurturing and cultivating a culture of diversity and inclusion, and for designing and implementing programs to increase the diversity of individuals who are developed and promoted within the firm. It is an important position that he is well suited for.

Born and raised a Catholic, church and religion were always important in his life. "I think that helped to shape who I am," he says. His parents were a huge influence. "My father always said you're not better than anybody else and nobody else is better than you. You always treat everybody the same."

He attended Catholic grammar school, was an altar boy and went to seminary for high school. In his senior year, Thurman was selected to assist the teacher with the religion class. He wound up teaching a freshman religion class and was so good at it his teacher asked him to continue to teach. As a result, he received an award for being the religion assistant of the year.

"My parents raised me with traditional Southern values," he says. "My father had rules you had to follow. Education was not an option. You were going to college even if you went to be a musician. You were going to go to school." His father was an excellent role model, himself having gone to school on the GI Bill, picking cotton to help pay his expenses.

When the time came to make a decision about college, his father asked him if he wanted to be a priest. When he indicated he did, his father proposed a deal. Thurman's brother was already at the University of Illinois so he suggested that Thurman also consider U of I. If it didn't work out, he said, then he could attend seminary. Thurman went on to earn a degree in finance from the University of Illinois and an MBA in management strategy and marketing from Northwestern University's Kellogg School of Management.

Thurman has a strong sense of responsibility to the community. He believes it is important to help those who can't help themselves and to have a positive impact on society. He also believes it is important that he be a role model for his 10-year-old son. "I want to make sure I give my son a road map," he declares.

Always an active participant in life, he currently serves on the boards of Junior Achievement Chicago Division, INROADS, the President's Council for the Museum of Science and Industry and the University of Illinois' College of Business Alumni. He is also active with the African American Employee Resource Group. Thurman affirms, "I learned that there are more ways to serve than being a priest."

BOBBIE STEELE

A Heart for People

By Ingrid E. Bridges

The first-ever female to serve as Cook County government president, Bobbie L. Steele, made headlines across Chicago in 2006. Her short-lived interim post of only four months will forever say a lot about the powerful woman she really was within the political arena across the Windy City.

Known as a pioneer of many movements, Steele made her debut in politics, not by chance, but by appointment of the people, through standing for the betterment of humanity. This former Chicago Public Schools elementary teacher of 20-plus years and mother of seven changed careers after being encouraged by the late Mayor Harold Washington, who was impressed with her involvement in countless progressive organizations.

Standing behind her all the way was Mayor Washington and numerous powerful black leaders. Steele was overwhelming elected to the Cook County Board of Presidents with more than 500 votes. Her political savvy gained momentum throughout the years as she sat on the board. For example, in 1987 she introduced an amendment to the board's purchasing ordinance which established a goal of 25 percent participation for minorities and 10 percent participation for women on all county purchases.

Since her inauguration, Steele has led the charge to re-open Provident Hospital and sponsored the Class 9 tax incentive for all multi-unit buildings in the county. While serving as a commissioner, she served the longest term as chair of the Finance Committee of the Forest Preserve District.

Steele admits she learned early on from her mother how to balance a checkbook as a teenager, which spilled over into her early marriage and later into her profession, where she oversaw billion-dollar budgets as chair of the Alpha Kappa Sorority, Inc. and later as president of the County Board.

Her dedication toward the people of Cook County was as simple as a mother's desire for her child, a better life for all concerned. This includes providing quality and accessible health care for indigents, which pushed her to lead the charge in naming the new Cook County Hospital after John H. Stroger Jr., former Cook County Board president. Her concern for the downtrodden and mistreated led her to do even more than those who came before her.

In 2004 President Steele introduced the Cook County Re-Entry Employment Project Ordinance, which seeks to reinforce the evidence that formerly incarcerated individuals can succeed if they are employed. The ordinance provides 100 jobs for adults who are first-time nonviolent offenders through Cook County government or through vendors who provide service to county government.

Between wanting to establish an on-site daycare center for county employees to leading the charge for a new state-of-the-art Domestic Violence Court building to keep families closer, Steele has touched the people like any mother figure would, through the heart. "I have a heart for the people every day; people are my heart," she said.

GEORGE A. WILLIAMS

A Pioneering Penchant for Excellence

By Jeff Burdick

The "first-mover advantage" refers to how the first company into a new market can often become the dominant long-term player. Think of what Starbucks is to premium coffee and Amazon.com to online retailing.

The same applies to individuals with the courage to be pioneers within their professions, as the career of ComEd's George A. Williams demonstrates. In 1992, Williams became the first African American at Philadelphia-based PECO Energy to earn a senior reactor operator license to operate a nuclear power plant, and in 1994 was named that company's youngest-ever manager of a fossil generating plant.

Building on this early career momentum, in 2003 Williams became the first African-American site vice president of a nuclear power plant for New Orleans-based Entergy Corporation. In 2005 and 2006, Williams was named one of the 50 and 100 most important blacks in technology by *U.S. Black Engineer & Information Technology*. Then last year, he became the first African American in ComEd history to be named senior vice president of operations. In this role, he oversees one of the nation's largest electrical distribution systems, serving eight million residents within ComEd's 11,300-square-mile Northern Illinois service territory.

"Often minorities will look for someone else to be the trailblazer before they're willing to venture into a new field. If I had taken that approach, I wouldn't have pursued engineering and made the energy field my lifelong passion," said the 23-year electric and nuclear industry veteran.

After 15 years in Philadelphia, he continued his corporate ascent with moves to Carolina Power & Light; PPL Susquehanna in Allentown, Pennsylvania; and Entergy, which culminated with three years as operations vice president of the Grand Gulf Nuclear Station in Port Gibson, Mississippi.

"I'll admit being a pioneer can sometimes be awkward. You aren't always well received. Some may think you only got your chance or a promotion because of your race," he said. "But I never used those misperceptions as an excuse and always let my actions, results and leadership be the final arbiter."

It helped that being out front came naturally to Williams.

"I was always one to venture out on my own. I was captain of my football team, first in my family to go to college, and first to earn a master's degree. Also growing up in a neighborhood rife with drugs and gangs, I understood early on the need to strive to be the very best."

It's a drive for excellence that doesn't end once you've established yourself – a trait he brought with him to ComEd.

"You must continually find new ways to differentiate yourself from competitors. This applies to companies and people alike. How can you provide a more reliable product? What innovations are you bringing to the table? What leadership skill are you missing?" Williams said.

In other words, once a pioneer, always a pioneer.

CHERYL BURTON

A Unique Perspective

By David Smallwood

Multiple Emmy Award-winner Cheryl Burton, who co-anchors the 5 p.m. news at ABC 7, is a Chicago native who feels fortunate to have achieved her major success right here at home.

"It's an amazing comfort because my family is here," says Burton, who has been with Channel 7 for 16 years. "They're only a phone call or drive away, so I don't have to get on a plane or boat to visit my 77-year-old mom and my sisters."

Broadcasting is a field that has brought her fame and fortune, but not one she intended to get into. The Lindblom grad, who never missed a day of high school and was the first alumnus inducted into the school's Hall of Fame back in April, originally intended to be a doctor.

She graduated from the University of Illinois at Champaign/Urbana with a degree in biology and psychology, but found the cost of medical school prohibitive. Health care's loss was TV's gain as the natural showperson in Burton took over. She had done several commercials around town, and in college was a member of the Marching Illini band that performed in the Rose Bowl and Liberty Bowl.

She was also a contestant on the old *Star Search* talent show and won several times in the spokesmodel category. "As spokesmodel, you were basically [host] Ed McMahon's assistant, kind of like the emcee for the whole hour besides him," Cheryl says. "But you had to talk about issues, and that helped prepare me for this career. That's also when I fell in love with this business."

Her broadcasting career took off in earnest when she co-anchored WGN's weekly syndicated series, *The Minority Business Report*, in 1989. The next year, she was a general assignment reporter in Peoria, and then moved to Wichita, Kansas, as a weeknight anchor for two years before coming home to join ABC 7 News in 1992.

"I know the city, I was born and raised here," Burton says. "I know the politics, the history, and I can relate issues of today to what was happening here when I was a young kid growing up, so I have a unique perspective that few others have."

As the top black journalist at the top-rated news station in the city, Burton feels that one of her primary responsibilities is affecting the kind of news coverage the station gives the black community.

"When I see stories that are covered improperly or don't project the image they should, I have to speak up," she says. "Children are watching and we need to show them a brighter future. Not all African Americans walk in handcuffs or are shot in drive-bys. I have the responsibility to make sure people see the good side of the African-American experience."

One of Burton's most memorable moments was interviewing Archbishop Desmond Tutu. "He said, 'Cheryl, I would rather you be in jail and speak your mind than be free and silent.' I've never forgotten that," she says.

Burton was born on Christmas Day, but instead of accepting gifts, she holds an annual toy drive to benefit victims living in domestic violence shelters.

ERIC WHITAKER, M.D., STEPHEN A. MARTIN JR., PH.D., AND TERRY MASON, M.D.

Changing Lives for the Better

By David Smallwood

Surprisingly, little public mention has been made of the fact that since the beginning of 2006, the health of the residents of the City of Chicago, the County of Cook, and the State of Illinois—a combined population of 12.4 million—has been in the hands of three African-American doctors.

That is unprecedented, a first.

The three health czars—all black men, at that—are Eric Whitaker, director of the Illinois Department of Public Health since 2003; Stephen Martin, chief operating officer of the Cook County Department of Public Health since 2003; and Terry Mason, Chicago health commissioner since January of 2006.

As the head medical doctors of their respective municipalities, these men do far more than say, "stick out your tongue and say aaahhh," or, "turn your head and cough."

Together, they take care of the health of the people of Illinois and visitors flowing through, from infrastructure to health promotion to disease prevention.

Whitaker's Illinois Department of Public Health has 1,100 employees, a budget of $400 million, 250 programs that touch virtually every age, aspect, and life cycle, and it coordinates with 95 local health departments throughout the state.

Martin's operation is part of the third-largest health care network in the country, the Cook County Bureau of Health Services. The bureau provides more than 150,000 annual health service visits to residents of suburban Cook County.

In the city of Chicago, Mason directs 1,200 employees, a $200 million budget, seven multiservice community health clinics that provide more than half a million visits a year, and 12 mental health centers that serve 12,000 patients.

The doctors arrived at their positions through various paths. Whitaker attended St. Rita High School and remains an assistant professor at Rush Medical College. He had created a 30-year "to do" plan and running the state's health department "*was* on my list for about ten years from now," he says.

Martin received his doctorate in epidemiology and says he "thought down the road, I would eventually have an opportunity to run a health department."

Mason, a Hyde Park High School grad who hosts WVON's *Doctor In The House* Saturday talk show, is a nationally renowned urologist who says he accepted the city position because "I had a feeling that God had something more for me to do than what I was doing; it was a divine calling."

Explaining their work in public health policy Whitaker says, "Many African Americans are concerned about the poor state of health in our community, which often motivates us to get into medicine in the first place. You deal with cases one-on-one, but when you feel the need to make a bigger impact, you get involved in public health."

Mason continues, "In these seats, we have the opportunity to affect *systems*, and systems affect thousands and millions of people. The three of us can change those systems, the way things get distributed, where funding goes, how decisions are made. You don't do that if you're not sitting at the table."

Martin concludes, "The three of us openly share resources and information and we have the opportunity to really change peoples' lives for the better."

DOROTHY BROWN

Achieving Against the Odds

By Barbara Kensey

Dorothy Brown is a woman of faith. Reared in the segregated south of Minden, Louisiana, she grew up feeling inferior because of her complexion and because her mother was a devout member of the Church of God in Christ in a town where everyone else was Baptist. "To be able to break out of the [inferiority] complex to hold a countywide office in the largest county in the state, has a lot to do with grace," she says.

Indeed, she is serving her second term as the first African American to hold the position of clerk of the Circuit Court of Cook County. It is a powerful position where she manages an annual budget of more than $100 million and a workforce that exceeds 2,300. But Dorothy Brown has been achieving heights for a long time. As a high school student, she distinguished herself as captain of the girl's varsity basketball team, graduated in the top ten percent of her class and went on to graduate magna cum laude from Southern University in Baton Rouge.

She has a law degree, is a certified public accountant, holds an MBA in business administration and has distinguished herself in every arena she has ever entered. She even made a credible run for mayor of the City of Chicago. What makes Dorothy run?

Raised in a household where religion, morality and discipline were enforced, Brown grew up knowing three things about herself: that she loved the Lord, that she wanted to be successful and that she was willing to work for it. The same dedication and fervor that she brought to her spiritual growth — as a seventh grade student she read the Bible every night — she brought to every aspect of her life. "God was really teaching me at that time and giving me a good foundation," she says.

Brown was surrounded by role models. This included her parents who demanded high academic standards, her oldest sister who set the bar, her uncle and aunt who were active in the civil rights movement, and her grandfather, who she says was "a brilliant man who talked to us like we were adults."

She also had tough teachers who recognized something in her and held her to a higher standard.

Brown has done an amazing job of building on that foundation despite the inevitable obstacles. She has experienced racism and sexism firsthand on more than one occasion. For example, despite graduating number one as a CPA, not a single accounting firm offered her a position.

Since taking over the clerk's office, she has brought a new level of professionalism to the department. Her slogan is "Professionalism over Politics." And she is committed to developing well-trained and motivated staff who, in turn, will deliver friendly, professional service to the public.

Dorothy Brown remains highly motivated to achieve against the odds. She is nowhere near done yet. The competitiveness and discipline she acquired on the basketball court and the faith she leans heavily on are assurances that Dorothy Brown will run on to see what the end will be.

CALVIN G. BUTLER JR.

A Will to Succeed

By Ingrid Bridges

Sage advice goes a long way for those with a plan to rise above the norm. Just ask Calvin G. Butler Jr., senior vice president of external affairs of RR Donnelley Corporation. Butler serves as the primary point of contact for elected officials, community organizations and small businesses across the country. Did I also mention he is responsible for leading two strategic sales initiatives in the organization?

Only a few short years ago, as senior director of government affairs at RR Donnelley, Butler began turning his colleagues' heads when he first began lobbying day-to-day on issues impacting the organization in its various locales. Butler's expertise, and his ability to build relationships with key stakeholders in local and state governments, led him to be promoted twice within five years of joining the corporation. It was a significant milestone for a lawyer, with limited manufacturing experience, to become a leader running plant operations in a manufacturing company.

As a graduate of Bradley University and Washington University School of Law, the dynamics of this 38-year-old negotiator, who never officially practiced in a law firm, have changed things at the top from where he stands. His will to succeed in diverse areas is the spice that drives Butler in an industry where African-American men are few. His willingness to see opportunities and leverage relationships to help grow the bottom line has been a key to his success.

Butler's thoughts of unifying businesses in a greater capacity and understanding the role that business should play in the community serves him well as president of the RR Donnelley Foundation.

"I look for partnerships in each city and/or county that RR Donnelley has a facility. It is important for me to service our operations scattered across the nation. All of our employees should feel a connection with the company and partnering with them in their charitable pursuits is a great way to demonstrate we care," shared Butler.

Butler believes in making a difference in all arenas, not just as a black man; but as a man. "I am very confident in who I am and what I bring to the table. My goal is to continue to perform for RR Donnelley, while continuing to grow as a person and serve as a role model for young people in both my professional and personal life."

Thanks to the plan he began perfecting as a young man—to never quit—his ultimate dream to someday become president of a major conglomerate remains possible, and today he is loving it all the way to the top. Additionally, he maintains a position of gratitude that he openly shares with his wife of 13 years, Sharon, and two children, son Blake Calvin, 12, and daughter Raini Alexis, 9, by his side.

Photo By: POWELL PHOTOGRAPHY, INC.

JOYCE E. TUCKER & YASMINE T. BATES

"Good enough is not good enough for you."

By Barbara Kensey

Joyce Tucker relates the story of cutting grass as an 11-year-old when the lawn mower suddenly stopped. She went to tell her uncle, who said, "When you find out what happened, let me know." Investigating, she discovered it had run out of gas and again went to tell him. He inquired, "What are you going to do about that?" She read the directions, found out about oil and gas and went to the gas station. Problem solved.

"This man was teaching me how to think," she says. "I'm never going to bring a problem without adding what I think should be done."

Problem-solving and successful outcomes appear to run in this trailblazing family. Joyce, vice president of global diversity and employee rights for The Boeing Company, is the older sister of Yasmine T. Bates. Yasmine is executive vice president for community affairs and economic development at Harris Bank, where she is responsible for overseeing the company's community investment and development activities in the Chicagoland area.

Yasmine was the first African-American female executive vice president of a major bank in Illinois and the first at Harris Bank.

An attorney, Joyce is a nationally recognized expert with more than 28 years of experience in equal employment opportunity (EEO) and affirmative action in both the public and private sectors. Among her many successes, former President George H. W. Bush appointed Tucker as commissioner of the U.S. Equal Employment Opportunity Commission (EEOC), where she served from 1990 to 1996. Prior to her appointment as an EEOC commissioner,

she served for ten years in the Illinois Governor's cabinet as the first director of the State of Illinois Department of Human Rights.

Not bad for two sisters whose humble story begins on Maypole Street on the West Side of Chicago.

Raised in a working class family where expectations were high, not attending college was never an option. Says Yasmine, "We understood the need to go to college and we were really motivated to make something of ourselves." Both are graduates of the University of Illinois.

Their uncle, who was also their guardian, was a dominant role model. A medical doctor who strove for success, Yasmine says of him, "He believed in us and our ability to achieve. He taught independence. 'Oh, you can do it.'" Their grandmother provided the spiritual base and a solid foundation of core values. "We had a great, encouraging grandmother who was there for emotional support," says Joyce. "She said, 'Good enough is not good enough for you.'"

A strong work ethic, a desire for independence and excellence are hallmarks of success, but what makes their story really special is the relationship they share as sisters. No sibling rivalry here. The mutual love, adoration and closeness they developed as children, continues today. They not only look up to each other, they motivate and inspire one another. And all their lives they've looked out for one another.

"I saw my baby sister as a gift to me," Joyce says. "I felt it was my responsibility to look out for her, to protect her, to make sure that she was okay."

HAKI MADHUBUTI

"I believe in us."

By Barbara Kensey

Without a word, Haki Madhubuti's office at Third World Press speaks volumes about who he is. The space is bright and comfortable, conducive to serious contemplation. Everywhere there are books and the walls are alive with the dynamism of African-American art, a colorful Southern quilt and framed black and white posters of the jazz musicians he admires. "Literature, music, art saved my life," he declares.

Ask him a question and the story just pours out. After all, he is a storyteller of the highest degree. He speaks of growing up in a family of hustlers and of his introduction to literature through Richard Wright's *Black Boy*; how reading it opened up a whole new world for him. Of joining the service at 16 where he learned two valuable lessons that he carries with him to this day: one, that he would never bend to anyone again; and two, the power of ideas. The latter was driven home when the sergeant ripped apart his copy of Paul Robeson's *Here I Stand*, the book he was reading on his way to Ft. Leonardwood, Missouri, in the United States Army.

Haki Madhubuti is a powerful voice for black pride and self-sufficiency. An internationally renowned poet, publisher, editor, educator, activist and scholar, he consciously searched early on for what he could do that would make a difference in the world. With his wife, Dr. Safisha, they decided on education and communication.

In 1972 he founded Third World Press with $400 and a used mimeograph machine. Today, it is the second-oldest, continuously operating independent black publishing house in the country. Along with his wife, he is also the co-founder of four schools – New Concept Preschool; Betty Shabazz International Charter School, the flagship school; Barbara A. Sizemore Academy Middle School; and DuSable Leadership Academy, a college preparatory high school.

Leading by example, he accepts no salary for his work with the press or the schools. "This is a service for me," he says. "I believe in us," referring to black people.

Besides institution building, Haki is the distinguished university professor at Chicago State University where he directs the only MFA program in creative writing in the world that is centered around African-American literature.

A prolific writer, he has published more than 28 books, including *Black Men Obsolete, Single, Dangerous?: The Afrikan American Family in Transition* which sold more than one million copies, and *YellowBlack: The First Twenty-One Years of a Poet's Life, A Memoir*. He has also edited numerous books on the African-American experience by such distinguished authors as Gwendolyn Brooks, Chancellor Williams, John Henrik Clarke, Amiri Baraka and Sonia Sanchez.

A highly disciplined man, he has never smoked, drank or partied. He has been a vegetarian since 1970 and a vegan since 1979. An avid cycler, at 65 years of age, he clocks close to 100 miles a week.

As to his legacy he says he will be happy if "All my [biological] children and my cultural children say, 'He did a good job. He was a good man. He was a half-way decent poet.'" It is likely he will get his wish.

TAYLOR MOORE

Wisdom beyond Her Years

By Barbara Kensey

Taylor Moore has been praying since she began talking at 2 years old. At 3, she accepted Christ as her personal savior and her minister agreed to do what few ministers would have done at that age. He baptized her. At 9, a custodian at the public school she attended asked her mother if Taylor could participate in a Back to School Rally at her church. Her mom agreed. Taylor attended the rally and delivered a powerful message on the importance of her peers turning off the video games and television and getting focused so that they could be the people God wants them to be. At that point, a career was born.

You don't have to be in her presence long to know that Taylor Moore is anointed. She is an old soul, wise beyond her years. Not only is she a motivational speaker, traveling all over the country delivering messages of abstinence, nonviolence and excellence, but she is also a percussionist, the leader of a band called Just Friends, an actress, a singer, rapper and television host of not one, but two cable television shows. And she just turned 18!

"I'm trying to make my mark," she says. "When people say 'Taylor Moore,' I want them to think excellence, hard worker, an advocate for positive and healthy choices, one who is always aiming for more, striving for more ... because there's more to be done."

A resident of Chicago's South Shore community where she lives with her mother, Taylor recently graduated from Kenwood Academy, ninth in a class of 379 with a 4.0 grade point average. In fall of 2007, she will enter the University of Illinois in Champaign, Urbana, where she will major in music education and minor in communications.

Taylor feels it is her responsibility to be a role model for other young people, something she is accustomed to being. "There was never a moment when there wasn't somebody watching me. And when someone is always watching you, you always have to be on point. That's when you really have to be focused and know who you are," she declares.

She also says she doesn't mind people watching her because she practices what she preaches. And she practices it *before* she preaches it.

As the teen spokesperson for an organization called Project Reality, Taylor recently released her first professional compact disc titled *Wait for Me* with a message that encourages abstinence. One particular tune is "I'm Worth Waiting For." She sings and raps on the CD which was produced by a producer who has worked with the likes of Shirley Caesar and India.Arie. It is marketed through the schools to promote abstinence.

Additionally, Taylor is producer, director and host for the cable show *Words to Live By*. Her mom, Trudy, who left her job as a public school teacher to become her manager, produces and Taylor hosts a second show titled *Making It*.

"I want to let children in the inner cities and public schools know that if you just stay focused, you can have whatever it is that your heart desires," she says.

SANMAR
FINANCIAL NETWORK

Photo By: POWELL PHOTOGRAPHY, INC.

ROGER F. SALTER

Creating Wealth Legacies

By David Smallwood

If you've got a couple of bucks you want to make grow, you could do worse than hand them over to Roger F. Salter, who is acknowledged as one of the top 1,000 financial planners in the entire world.

For 33 years, Salter has headed Sanmar Financial Planning, a network of professionals with more than 150 years of combined experience in insurance, taxes, stocks/bonds, accounting, mutual funds, pensions, legal services, real estate and financial planning. Together, they help individuals and businesses achieve financial independence and create wealth legacies.

An insurance and financial professional since 1962, Salter just three years later became only the third African American to earn a spot on the Million Dollar Roundtable. That international body represents less than two-tenths of one percent of 350,000 life insurance producers worldwide, those who have sold more than $1 million of life insurance in one year.

Salter co-founded America's first black life insurance general agency in 1969, and was American General Financial Group's General Agent of the Year in 1997. He is the recipient of more than 100 awards, including Man of the Year honors from different groups, spanning 40 years from 1965 and 2005.

Sanmar, founded in 1974, routinely puts more than $100 million in life insurance policies in force for its customers annually and invests millions in mutual funds on their behalf. Such superior service has garnered the company upwards of 1,000 clients, including Ernie Banks, Diann Burns, Robin Robinson, Merri Dee, Barbara Bates, Tim Hardaway, Roland Burris, attorney Jim Montgomery, the Leak and Rayner funeral homes, entertainers Steve Harvey, Ronald and Ernest Isley, Anthony Anderson, Teddy Riley, Howard Hewitt, Richard T. Jones, and several Illinois lottery winners, among others.

Salter attended Chicago State University, was a member of DuSable High School's 1958 class, and has been married to wife Jacqueline for almost 50 years. Their son, Roger J. Salter, is Sanmar's senior vice president, and also a certified financial planner.

Salter, who started out selling door-to-door insurance in black neighborhoods, says his fascination with money came as a child. "When I found out that if I shined shoes, I could have my own money and wouldn't have to ask my parents for it, I took to it like a duck to water," says Salter.

He also sold magazines, newspapers, watermelons and coal as a kid, "but what I really have is a knack for selling ideas," Salter explains. "Selling is really just providing someone with something they want to have, so I introduce a concept, ask people what they want to do, and see if I have a solution to fit the individual.

"If you give me a million today and I get ten percent interest on it, in seven years you'll have two million," Salter continues. "I know where to get you ten percent; that's what I study."

He also studied at American College to become a chartered life underwriter and at the College of Financial Planning to become a certified financial planner, both four-year schools that supply two of the highest educational designations in the financial field.

And if that isn't enough, Salter has one extra skill to help protect your money—he is a third-degree brown belt in karate!

Photo By: POWELL PHOTOGRAPHY, INC.

AVA YOUNGBLOOD

Providing High-Impact Leadership Talent

By David Smallwood

YES, Ava Youngblood knows leadership when she sees it!

The president of Youngblood Executive Search Inc. founded YES in 2002 as a retained recruiting firm to provide high-impact leadership talent for a group of very select clients.

"Our clients range from the largest and most respected multinational corporations to the most innovative startups," says Youngblood. "And, for those clients, we identify, evaluate and recruit board members, presidents, executive directors, senior vice presidents, vice presidents, general managers, division heads, functional directors and C-level executives."

Youngblood, who has more than 25 years of high-level corporate and recruiting experience, says YES focuses on identifying and attracting highly qualified leadership talent who cannot only enhance a company's immediate performance, but also innovate existing organizations and build new ones.

"We go beyond finding people who match position specifications," Youngblood says. "It is our belief that strong leadership at all levels is a company's key competitive advantage."

Therefore, she says, YES recruits leaders with "integrity, accountability, and intellectual curiosity who have demonstrated the ability to provide vision, embrace and drive change, act decisively, drive team results, and develop diverse leadership talent."

Her company identifies appropriate prospects on a nationwide basis through assessment interviews, leadership profiles, and thorough reference checks, and that's just for starters. YES then assists clients with the difficult task of job offers and negotiation with finalist candidates, and also assists those candidates with the sensitive issue of leaving current employers where they are highly regarded. Youngblood believes so strongly in the quality of her firm's work that she offers her clients a one-year candidate replacement guarantee should the hired chosen prospect not remain on the job.

She is a Lindblom High School graduate who earned a bachelor's degree in chemical engineering at Northwestern University. As a member of INROADS, Youngblood had 11 job offers upon graduating, and chose to go with her INROADS sponsor, Amoco. She stayed there for 19 years in a string of increasingly responsible positions, including research and development, operations planning, logistics, quality management, sales and marketing, executive development and strategic planning. Her forte at Amoco eventually became leadership assessment, competitive strategy development, strategic marketing, organizational change and information technology utilization.

In her early years with the global petrochemical energy company, she also went to school at night to earn an MBA in marketing strategy and economics from The University of Chicago's Graduate School of Business. All the while, she was married and raising a family.

At a certain point in her Amoco career, Youngblood was the object of recruitment by the Deborah Snow Walsh Inc. executive search firm, which ended up hiring Youngblood itself. She was senior vice president of that firm, responsible for business development and maintaining client relationships, before founding YES.

This obviously brilliant woman serves on the board of trustees of Northwestern University and the board of directors of its School of Engineering's advisory council. She is also past director of INROADS/Chicago, past chairman of the Conference Board's Competitive Analysis Council, sits on the National INROADS Executive Alumni Roundtable, and is a member of The University of Chicago's Women's Business Group, among many other impressive affiliations.

Photo By: POWELL PHOTOGRAPHY, INC.

MARGARET GARNER

More than Bricks and Mortar

By Ingrid E. Bridges

Across America women in construction trades are far and few in between, but in Chicago, Margaret Garner, the CEO of Broadway Consolidated Construction Companies (BCCC), begs to differ. Beyond captivating her peers and clients with her glamorous style and amazing wit, Garner has taken the construction business to another level in the Windy City, making what seemed difficult in years past for a black contractor, seem simple.

In only five years of existence, BCCC has grossed more than $30 million, with current projects exceeding the annual goal of $10 to $15 million. Living up to her philosophy of "more than bricks and mortar" could not be timelier, as she succeeds with her latest venture of building a Wal-Mart store in Chicago and as the first black female contractor to do the work.

Garner's participation made national headlines in everything from the local paper to *Time* magazine, where her credibility and integrity was placed under a microscope. Once again, she persevered successfully executing the project with diligence, making her someone to watch and learn from in the construction trades.

This graduate of the University of Pittsburgh earned degrees in business and economics with flying marks. Her humble beginnings in construction management landed her an important position with the local U.S. Department of Housing and Urban Development Housing Authority in Pittsburgh, Pennsylvania. It was there Garner began to better understand what her journey was leading to. She soon discovered her career was bigger than her silent dreams; it was for building people's lives and their communities.

Recruited early on by the assistant secretary of HUD for its internship program in Washington, D.C., Garner heavily worked on the "Re-invention of HUD" project, where she successfully designed methods to move residents from welfare to work within their communities. Serving as an intricate part of the HUD team, she soon tackled the nation's third-largest housing authority in the country, the Chicago Housing Authority (CHA), as the director of modernization.

Managing people has always been one of her strong attributes. Under the CHA umbrella, Garner managed the architects and engineering division, environmental division, capital funding and the construction division, comprised of 300 tradesmen. She succeeded at every challenge that knocked at her door. Her modernization team in conjunction with a leading construction company was able to fast-track the renovations of a high rise for temporary relocation of residents and rehabilitate 234 new townhouse units in a record-setting time of 120 days.

Today, Garner's career has taken astounding turns, leaping further and wider than most of her peers in the construction business. Due to her undying efforts to achieve excellence, in 2004 she became president of the Federation of Women Contractors, making her someone that those in the construction world should know.

Despite how her firm becomes more and more in demand, family life remains a major priority for Garner. She makes it her business each day to spend quality time with her only daughter, Margarite, who also aspires to succeed in the construction business.

Photo By: POWELL PHOTOGRAPHY, INC.

KENNY WILLIAMS

A Climb to the Top

By David Smallwood

For six months, from March until September of 2003, Chicago was the epicenter for African Americans in leadership positions in professional sports.

Bill Cartwright was the Bulls coach. The Bears signed Kordell Stewart as quarterback. Dusty Baker was close to managing the Cubs to a World Series. The White Sox had a black manager in Jerry Manuel, and a black general manager, Ken Williams.

Of the five, only Williams is still on the job, and he succeeded gloriously in 2005 when his White Sox captured the World Series, their first championship since 1917.

Williams was appointed to his position in 2000 and his .537 winning percentage after six years is the best in club history for a general manager. He is the first black GM in Chicago sports, and the third in baseball, following Bill Lucas at Atlanta, and Bob Watson, who led the Yankees to a World Series title.

A Berkeley, California, native, Williams played football and baseball at Stanford University, was drafted by the Sox in 1982, and played outfield for the Sox, Detroit, Toronto and Montreal from 1986-1991.

After his playing days, Williams served the Sox as a scout, director of minor league operations, television studio analyst, special assistant to chairman Jerry Reinsdorf, and vice president of player development, before becoming GM.

He says that early on, he experienced more problems than you'd want to imagine for being an African American in his position. "Stalkers, things written on the side of the house and garage, a couple of people had to be locked up," he cited as examples. "But that's just ignorance."

Williams has a long history with racial issues. His father and another man were the first two black firefighters in San Jose, California, and they had to go to court to get those jobs. His father also ran track with John Carlos (his godfather) and Tommie Smith, the track athletes who gave the Black Power salute during the 1968 Olympic Games in Mexico, and sprinter Lee Evans. "With all the things associated with that, the political discussions in my house started very early on," Williams said.

"The gift they gave me with all the discrimination they faced—and John was blackballed for a long time—was that they never once said anything about treating a white man any different than a black man. They said you treat a man in front of you as he treats you. If he gives you respect and he's truthful and honest with you, you return that; if he doesn't, you still try to give him that in hopes he will reciprocate."

A low-keyed man who doesn't seek the limelight, Williams and his wife, Jessica, have five children.

Assessing his own position of being the only black GM in the game, he says, "When it's not referred to as a black hire or black fire, and the numbers aren't counted—there's one black general manager and six black NFL coaches—when you don't have to count any more, that's when we'll know there's been a little progress. I understand how far we've come, which is great, but we have a long way to go, too."

Photo By: POWELL PHOTOGRAPHY, INC.

NORMA JEAN WHITE

"She got her break and everybody else benefited."

By Barbara Kensey

Norma Jean White tells the story of her mother working at the Schulze Bakery on 55th and State back in the day when the bakery was segregated. White females were allowed to take a break, but black women were not. One day her mother just walked away from the conveyor belt while the Dolly Madison cakes were running, creating havoc, and went home. The manager called her mother and asked her to come back. She agreed, but only if she got a break. "She got her break and everybody else benefited," says Norma. "She's my 'shero.'"

Coming from a root like that, it is no surprise that Norma Jean White would become the first black female business representative for the Chicago Teachers Union in 1975. But it was not an easy journey. At a very young age she found herself in a marriage that did not encourage her independence. She wanted to be educated but her abusive husband resisted, so she found the courage and strength to leave him, to enroll in school and to graduate with a teaching degree from Chicago Teacher's College.

She began her career in the Chicago Public Schools system in January of 1970. She says she learned how to be a teacher by the teachers she had as a student. "African-American teachers were firm, but they wouldn't embarrass you. I learned from the positive and the negative." Among her major influences she names Dr. Margaret Burroughs, her art teacher, and Nell Matilda Woodard, her music teacher, both at DuSable High School.

While teaching she became interested in what was going on in the teacher's union. "I was interested in how they were representing us. So I just voluntarily went to meetings and kept my eyes on what was going on." This was during the tenure of Chicago Teachers' Union President Robert Healy and Vice President Jacqueline Vaughn. "The person who represented the school I was at would rarely attend meetings and then when she went, she wouldn't tell us anything. So they elected me."

White's job was to visit schools in the inner city and communicate with the faculty and career service employees regarding policies, programs or changes that might affect them. "I wasn't prepared," she says. "I just learned as I went along." When Vaughn ascended to union president, she tapped White to become the union's financial secretary. Later she would become vice president of the Illinois Federation of Teachers and the American Federation of Teachers, and a business rep for Teamsters Local 743 where she groomed others to become leaders in their worksites.

"I did bring a lot of people along with me with both unions. I looked for people who could take my place. They all say that I got them started." Like her mother before her, what Norma Jean did also benefited others. Now retired, she says she wants to be remembered as a person who lived a life that was dedicated to bringing others along with her. "I didn't just want to be a shining star," she declares. "I wanted to be a part of the constellation."

etA
CREATIVE ARTS
FOUNDATION INC
Photo By: POWELL PHOTOGRAPHY, INC.

ABENA JOAN BROWN

"Culture tells us who we are..."

By Barbara Kensey

Abena Joan Brown is clear about what she wants her legacy to be: "A cultural institution that helps us to define ourselves in the true genesis of what culture is," she says. Raised to believe that she could do anything that she wanted to do, not only for herself, but for the family and the race, Brown has built a major cultural institution whose mission is to "preserve, perpetuate and promulgate" the African-American aesthetic. Now she is working on expanding it.

Brown is the co-founder, president and producer of eta Creative Arts Foundation, a performing and cultural arts organization now in its 36th year. Founded in 1971 to provide professional training and opportunities in the arts, eta—which means 'head' in the Ewe language of West Africa—has grown into a full-fledged cultural institution that serves a large and diverse population in the performing, visual and literary arts and in arts education.

Now, fueled by an outstanding board of directors chaired by educator Nancy C. McKeever, Brown is on a mission to expand on that vision and build the first African-inspired, state-of-the-art cultural center in the city of Chicago. The sprawling compound-like structure will house a second theater, a cabaret, galleries, a visitors' center and an outdoor pavilion. It will be connected to the current space by an overhead bridge fittingly named Sankofa, the Ghanaian word that signifies the need to go back to the past in order to move forward.

Always keenly aware of history and responsibility, Brown believes that "We stand on the shoulders of those who went before us. And we *must* be the ones that the next generation stands on."

Involved in the arts all her life, Brown began dancing at the age of 3. She has been an actress, company manager, stage manager, director and producer and is an internationally acclaimed arts administrator and fund raiser.

Reared on the South Side of Chicago in a "race" family, Brown was educated at Roosevelt University and earned a master's degree in community organization and management from The University of Chicago. Before assuming the helm of eta full-time, she was responsible for the overall operations of the YMCA of Metropolitan Chicago.

A product of the civil rights movement, the black arts movement and the black consciousness movement, she bristles when queried about her responsibility to the community. "I don't feel a responsibility to the community," she says. *"I am the community. You do things for the race."*

A great inspiration and mentor to many, Brown's own influences have been numerous. Some of them will be honored by having their names attached to various spaces in the new facility. Among them are Dr. Margaret Burroughs, Gwendolyn Brooks, Hoyt W. Fuller, Etta Moten Barnett, W.E.B. DuBois and eta's first board chairman, Milton Davis, ShoreBank chairman emeritus.

Culture, commitment and consciousness are extremely important to Abena Joan Brown. She doesn't espouse an African world view for nothing. "Culture tells us who we are, where we've been and where we need to go," she declares. "If we ever get that straight, we'll be fine."

JESUS CHRIST IS LORD

Photo By: POWELL PHOTOGRAPHY, INC.

BISHOP ARTHUR M. BRAZIER

"Churches have to help people, not just preach."

By David Smallwood

Bishop Arthur M. Brazier, head of the 20,000-member Apostolic Church of God that sits on 12 acres of land on the city's South Side, is one of Chicago's most prominent religious personalities.

The still-spry octogenarian, who just turned 86 on July 22, has also been one of the foremost builders of the black community in this city.

Bishop Brazier was a founder and early president of The Woodlawn Organization (TWO), one of the most successful community organizations in the country, which was prominent in the civil rights movement of the 1960s.

TWO successfully blocked the southern expansion of The University of Chicago in 1963 during the urban renewal era. The next year, Brazier, along with the Chicago Urban League's Bill Berry, formed the Coordinating Council of Community Organizations to fight segregation in Chicago schools. He was also active in Dr. Martin Luther King's visit to Chicago in 1966.

Under TWO, Brazier's vision for Woodlawn has been to turn it into an affordable, viable mixed-income community. To accomplish that goal, which is well under way, Brazier founded The Woodlawn Preservation and Investment Corporation, as well as The Fund for Community Redevelopment and Revitalization, to rebuild one of the poorest areas in Chicago.

To date, along with The University of Chicago, which became a partner 20 years ago instead of an adversary, Brazier's various organizations have built dozens of single-family homes and town-houses as part of an eight-block development along 63rd Street that will eventually have 233 homes in all, with a fifth of them affordable for working families.

Brazier's interest in this economic development came from seeing the deep needs of people during his 57 years of serving as a pastor.

Soon after he felt God's calling in the late 40s and before he had a church, Brazier was a street preacher. "I was preaching on 31st and Indiana one day and a man told me, 'Reverend, I hear what you're talking about, but I'm hungry.' So I took him across the street and bought him a meal, and afterward he said, 'Now, Rev., I can understand you a bit better!'" Brazier recalled. "It taught me that churches have to help people, not just preach."

Brazier started Apostolic Church of God in 1960 with just 100 members. As it grew, he felt that he couldn't just stand at his pulpit and preach against social ills, but had to go out and do something about them.

"That's why I got involved in community organizations," Brazier says. "One of the greatest sins of this country at the time—still is—was racial discrimination and segregation because it destroyed a lot of people before they could get started in life, and they were blocked simply because of the color of their skin. I saw this evil and tried to do something about it."

Bishop Brazier has been married for 59 years to his wife, Isabelle, whom he met at a church picnic, ironically during a period when Brazier himself had stopped attending church. They have four children: Lola, Byron, Janice and Rosalyn.

PEOPLE TO PEOPLE

Photo By: POWELL PHOTOGRAPHY, INC.

GLORIA BROWN

Longevity and Glorious Success

By David Smallwood

"Glorious" Gloria Brown, as her many friends—and there are many—call her, has been with Channel 9 since it was... Channel 8!

No, not really, but Brown is a trailblazer who broke the color barrier at WGN-TV in 1964 when she was hired as the station's first black professional employee.

That was the year the Beatles first visited America and appeared on *The Ed Sullivan Show*. Ed and the Beatles are long gone, but the vibrant, always smiling Gloria still looks today like a teeny-bopper from that era.

She literally worked her way up in the television business, from a typist, purchasing department assistant, and news room secretary, to her current positions as business manager for WGN-TV News and Emmy Award-winning producer of *People To People*. Her primary responsibilities are assisting the director in day-to-day news department operations, scheduling staff, preparing and overseeing budgets, and handling all business-related matters pertaining to news.

For her longevity and success, Brown was inducted into the Silver Circle of the National Association of Television Arts and Sciences in May of 2006.

The show she produces, *People To People*, hosted by Allison Payne, is a weekly news and public affairs talkfest that has featured everyone from President Bill Clinton, to Rev. Jesse Jackson, to Michael Jordan's mom, Deloris. Brown's work on that show has been awarded by the Associated Press, the National Association of Black Journalists (NABJ), and with the Illinois Broadcasters' prestigious Silver Dome Award.

Brown, a Hattiesburg, Mississippi, native whose family moved to Chicago in the 1950s, graduated from DuSable High School and earned her degree in business from Chicago State University.

As far as being a trailblazer, she claims she was not a product of the civil rights movement. "This was in 1964 and the movement was just kicking in," she says. Instead of integrating or trying to make a statement, Brown says she was just looking for a job.

"I could write well," she says, "type over a hundred words a minute, take shorthand, knew all the business machines — and could fix them! As far as being a mold-breaker, my attitude was, why can't I do it? I had all these business skills, why *not* give me a job?"

Still, it didn't work that way. Gloria's maiden name is Leggett, which does not sound black, and she said she didn't "sound" black on the phone. So, she could call and make appointments, but "when I got there and they saw I *was* black, the job had just gotten filled," she recalls.

That went on until she got a summer job at Encyclopedia Britannica, which was next door to the *Tribune*. She asked about jobs there, was hired and quickly made her way to *Tribune*-owned WGN-TV.

After 40 years, it is home for her and she is widely acknowledged as the mother hen for black and white employees alike, the glue that keeps the WGN family together.

Gloria serves on the boards of Habilitative Systems Inc. and the NABJ-Chicago Chapter. More importantly, she says, she is the "mother of a wonderful daughter, Jeneene Brown-Moseley, the proud grandmother of Lance Joseph Moseley, and married to the remarkable Joe Brown."

MELODY M. MCDOWELL

Results and Repeat Business

By Ingrid E. Bridges

For more than 25 years, entrepreneur Melody M. McDowell, founder of MELODY'service, a communications boutique, continues to put prominent faces on the world map. Highly regarded as a prominent Chicago firm, McDowell believes MELODY'service works because of her diverse ability to combine her skills as a public relations specialist, editor, writer and marketer with her devotion to efficiency, competence and professionalism.

Humbled that her first client, McDonald's restaurateur, Cirilo McSween, remains with MELODY'service. Her major clients consist of individuals, nonprofits, corporations and global operations. The list includes Real Men Cook; Dr. Mae C. Jemison, the first black woman astronaut to be launched into space; Ben & Jerry's Ice Cream; Kraft Foods; the Chicago Symphony Orchestra; and many more.

McDowell has survived and thrived in a tough industry because she adheres to the six Rs: She is Reliable, Resourceful and Responsible. These qualities yield Results, Repeat business and Rewards!

Some prospects tend to be reluctant to work with the firm because hers is a one-woman operation. However, she challenges them with her record. "We do the work faster, call the client back faster, write the press releases, speeches and presentations with more clarity and make decisions faster than the mega-firms. We also maintain a 100 percent on-time performance and believe in being nice to everybody. So, it's not about being bigger, it's about the quality of the work and the results." And once they are exposed to the MELODY'service brand of customer service, they join the client fold.

While proud of her professional triumphs, McDowell has scored success in other arenas. Unafraid to venture outside of her comfort zone, in 2005 she joined a local Toastmasters Club. Within six months, she was elected president. By drawing from her marketing skills, she increased membership fivefold elevating it to an award-winning club from one on the verge of extinction. Most significantly, she shocked the organization by winning first place in the Area Toastmasters Evaluation contest, one of the organization's most demanding competitions. It was the first time McDowell competed and, in winning, she beat out several veterans. She has also climbed Paradise Pic in St. Maarten, citing it as an example of her adventurous spirit.

McDowell earned a master's degree in library science from Chicago State University and a Bachelor of Science degree in English from Spelman College. While in her '20s, she wrote a play that enjoyed a successful eight-week run at the Experimental Black Actors Guild. She has also acted in community theater and hopes to return to her playwriting and acting one day.

This recipient of two Kizzy Awards also received the Media Cornerstone Award from the U.S. Department of Commerce Minority Business Development Agency on the local level, and for the ten-state Midwest region. Currently, McDowell is chair of Alpha Kappa Alpha's Centennial Communications Committee and its first chief information officer—testimony to the respect she commands.

PARIS DELANE

Songs of His Own

By David Smallwood

He's got a seven-octave vocal range and can sing in Hebrew. He has mastered martial arts, yet performs healing massage therapy he learned in Japan. He was taught by South Dakota Indians how to catch fish with his hands, the same ones he uses to play drums, guitar and piano.

He grew up on the South Side deep in gang territory, but became friends with one of the richest families in the world. He has been a bodyguard and bouncer, but performs innumerable concerts to raise funds for children with a host of problems.

This mountain of a man breaks bricks with his hands, but wouldn't hurt a flea. Gentle giant Paris Delane is not a walking contradiction, just a guy who takes a big bite out of life.

Delane is best known as a founding member of the acclaimed rock-soul-gospel band Sonia Dada. From its formation in 1990 to its breakup in 2003, Sonia Dada developed a worldwide fan base and its six albums sold hundreds of thousands of copies.

Delane now tours with his own group, Tye Dye Skye, and has a CD, *The Learning Tree*, set for release soon.

Paris, whose brother is actor Michael Clarke Duncan, got his splendid voice from his father, "Big Hank," a 6'9" gambler and construction company owner, and mother Lillian, a gospel singer who was friends with Mahalia Jackson and Ella Fitzgerald. Lillian bought Paris bongos and a guitar and taught him to sing and scat as a child.

After a beloved girlfriend died, one winter evening Paris began singing in the Chicago subway to soothe his soul. "People were digging it, so I went back the next day and it was just as good, so I kept doing it," he says.

Delane convinced two friends, Sam Hogan and Michael Scott to join him, and they became an underground sensation performing as the trio Rough, Smooth and Silk (Paris was Rough).

"One day this little Jewish man came up to us and said, 'that was amazing, I'd like to make some music with you guys,'" Delane says. "He wrote songs and played guitar and we liked his music. He turned out to be Danny Pritzker of *the* Pritzker family, Jay's son, but we didn't know it at the time."

They all ended up putting Sonia Dada together with Paris as lead singer, and he says, "Being around the Pritzkers, I saw things in three months that some people never see in their lives!"

The group performed with the likes of Bob Dylan, the Rolling Stones, Santana, the Neville Brothers, and the Alman Brothers, toured the world, and once appeared before a crowd of 850,000 in Holland. Delane was befriended by ultra-A list celebrities—Keith Richards showed up at Paris' birthday party—but he remains humble and kind.

On her deathbed in 2002, his mother Lillian told Paris it was good working with all those folks but that he had songs of his own, and made him promise he would start performing his own work.

"She said, 'God's got your back and I'll be your biggest agent in heaven,'" Paris recalls. "That night I went home and wrote a song called 'The Learning Tree,' which is the name of the new album."

Photo By: POWELL PHOTOGRAPHY, INC.

JINNIE ENGLISH

Helping Others Overcome

By Barbara Kensey

Jinnie English has spent her entire life trying to overcome. Now her mission is helping others overcome as the CEO of a niche executive mental health maintenance firm for high achievers like herself.

Born to a Korean mother and an African-American father, English grew up in Chicago's impoverished Englewood community where being biracial just didn't fit in. "I grew up across the street from a park with no swings and lots of broken glass. I remember the first time I saw someone with a gun, saw a man hit a woman." Getting out of that environment was her greatest motivator.

Education was important in her household. Her father graduated high school and although her mother only went to the sixth grade, she ran a very successful business. Her mother also planted the seed for Jinnie's career because she was always helping people.

English is a licensed clinical social worker (LCSW) and president of English Consulting which she founded in 1999 as a private sector mental health services agency. A graduate of the University of Chicago's School of Social Service Administration, she is a Ph.D. candidate at the Institute for Clinical Social Work.

A psychotherapist and management consultant for 17 years, English developed and continues to refine the concept of business therapy. She specializes in workplace issues, management assessments and supervision, corporate trainings and ethical practice. She also works with individuals on minority issues, anxiety, depression, stress, power and control, interpersonal skills, personality disorders and survivors of abuse and trauma, something she knows about personally.

"Growing up, people were always having problems in their relationships," she recalls. "I remember asking questions and thinking a lot about that. I learned to listen and people felt comfortable because I listened. When I decided to practice therapy, it seemed like an accident, but looking back it was natural."

According to her Web site, English Consulting is "known for moving professionals from good to great by developing their capacity to become visionary leaders while bridging their personal and professional lives." The eight-year-old company has seven locations with the main office in suburban Calumet Park. There are also three downtown Chicago locations and offices in Highland Park and Hinsdale.

Recently, English founded Chicago's High Achievers, the only think tank and sustaining environment for ambitious and bright individuals in Chicago.

"I think I have a huge responsibility to people—not just my community—people who have potential, who have ambition. It doesn't matter what they look like or where they come from. My obligation is to help because somebody helped me."

English has experienced lots of trauma in her life, and while she is helping others she is still working on herself. "My greatest challenge was looking at me. It's always been for me about fitting in. It was painful and it's still painful," she says. "I have to accept the fact that I will never fit in."

EARL JONES

Committed to Reaching Out

By David Smallwood

He is one of the more recent additions to town, but his influence is felt across the entire metropolitan area. Meet Earl Jones, who heads one of the largest radio conglomerates in the third-largest market in the country as president and market manager of Clear Channel Radio Chicago.

Jones arrived in 2005 as regional vice president for Clear Channel stations in Chicago, as well as Milwaukee, Madison, and Eau Claire, Wisconsin. Last year, he was elevated to president and allowed to focus exclusively on the Chicago cluster of stations, which consists of WGCI, V103, WNUA, WLIT, WKSC and WGRB. Jones is the first African American to hold both those positions in the Chicago area for Clear Channel.

His success is all the more remarkable because he has only been in radio nine years, since joining Clear Channel Atlanta in 1998 as director of sports marketing. He previously worked in television sales from 1985-1997, at FOX, the WB, and Paramount/Viacom stations in Atlanta and Washington, D.C.

The Tuscaloosa, Alabama, native earned a chemistry degree from Norfolk State University in 1980, but also played defensive back on the football team and was so good that the Atlanta Falcons drafted him (in the third round) when he graduated. He actually had a decent five-year career until he suffered a knee injury and retired to pursue other options.

His wife, Dolores, to whom he's been married for 21 years, with three children, was a national radio sales manager who showed him how much he could make in that profession. While Jones got a foothold in the industry, she was the family's breadwinner.

The jovial, down-to-earth Jones brought the team-oriented approach he learned in sports with him to the business world and it has proven successful. "I've had great teams wherever I've been," he says, "and I have a great team here—people really out in the trenches day-to-day, which makes us all winners."

The team concept, he says, "has worked well for Clear Channel Chicago Radio from a financial standpoint; exceptionally well from a cultural standpoint; in terms of outreach and the different charities we're involved with; and with our advisory board, which has been extremely helpful and contains people from all walks of life."

Jones, who has been elected to the boards of the Chicago Urban League and Chicagoland Chamber of Commerce, says he is committed to reaching out to people at all levels to ask, "What do we need to do as the stations you listen to, to get more involved in the community?"

He says his right-hand, Angela Ingram, Clear Channel Radio Chicago's vice president of communications, "has put a lot on my plate, and in choosing and picking from that, what I understand is that winning here means being close to it out there—going to the different events, talking to all the people, just being a part of the community."

"I've grown tremendously in getting an idea of what it means to be a Chicagoan and to live here," he says. "That's been very helpful to me."

Photo By: POWELL PHOTOGRAPHY, INC.

ELEANOR CHATMAN

A Love of Adventure and the Exotic

By David Smallwood

Sometimes you just have to do the thing yourself!

That's what Eleanor Chatman figured out when the travel bug hit her in the early 1970s, but travel agents couldn't arrange itineraries for the exotic locales she wanted to visit.

"I got tired of going to travel agents asking for destinations they knew nothing about," Chatman says. "The first time I wanted to go to Ghana, the travel agent's eyes bucked and I had to explain that it was in West Africa."

Another travel problem she ran into were "agents, white and black, who once they saw you were black, would book you into lesser accommodations—sometimes because they didn't think you had the money, but mostly because they assumed you'd settle for less," she says.

Fed up, Chatman started Mahogany Travel Service. "I had ended up planning my own trips anyway, since the agents didn't know, so I decided I could do this myself," she says.

Mahogany blossomed into a worldwide agency that offered domestic and international travel; bus, Amtrak and plane tours, including a Black Big Band tour; Disney/Bahamas cruises; and gambling excursions on riverboats and to Las Vegas and Atlantic City.

The agency gave special attention to convention packages for churches, sororities, fraternities, and other such organizations, and it became so successful that Chatman sold Mahogany to Johnson Publishing Company in 1991. But she turned right around and founded African Travel Advisors, which specializes in group tours to Africa and other countries of the Diaspora.

Since the early days, Chatman has visited 65 countries, 32 states, and her beloved Ghana eight times now. She says her love of travel grew out of having a double major of history and physical education in college.

"I was adventurous, curious about the people I had studied in history. I wanted to go to some of the exotic locations they were from—Africa, South America and Asia," says Chatman. "The travel was almost a by-product of my desire to know about people, and as a phys ed major, I was healthy enough to get out there and see what was going on."

The Chicago native graduated from East Washington State University in Spokane, Washington, because her husband was in the Air Force and they and their three children moved extensively. Chatman started Mahogany when she was back in Chicago teaching history and physical education at Harlan High School. To this day, her former students and their children, sometimes three generations, still travel with her.

Chatman quickly ticks off her favorite travel destinations: "Swaziland, between South Africa and Mozambique, is the most beautiful country you'd ever want to see. It has a 37-year-old king who has 17 wives now!

"Brazil is fun and I like the Orient. I went to Vietnam for the first time in April; blew my mind! The best food truly is in Italy. And I love shopping in Rome in September after the new season's shows when they put last year's clothes on sale!"

African Travel Advisors' group tours in 2008 are to Venezuela in January, Senegal and South Africa in March, Kenya and Zanzibar in July, and Vietnam and Hong Kong in September.

Diversity is a Requirement For Our Success

At Abbott, every day is filled with new discoveries and leading-edge innovation. Our professionals are passionate about life, health care and the contributions they can make. With over 60,000 employees worldwide and $22 billion in sales in more than 130 countries, we're not just poised to enhance the health of the world – we're positioned to make it happen.

An EOE, Abbott is committed to employee diversity.

"Our diversity – of people and products – makes our company strong. We count on having a variety of perspectives to foster the innovation we need to bring our science, and our company, to a higher level."

– Miles White, CEO

www.abbott.com

Abbott
A Promise for Life

Exceptional products are an outgrowth of an **inclusive workplace** where ideas are free to thrive. The development of breakthrough products is an example of the way our employees anticipate and meet the needs of customers in a **global marketplace**. It all begins with a **diverse workforce** committed to developing exciting, innovative products.

Experience Motorola: Workplace, Marketplace, and Workforce

www.motorola.com

DIVERSITY IS NOT JUST A HEADLINE.
IT'S THE FULL STORY.

elevision viewing habits vary from person to person,
ousehold to household and city to city. As the TV
atings company, we work hard to accurately
measure the differences in television viewership.
That's why, at Nielsen, having a workforce reflective
f these differences is a priority.

nielsen
· · · · · · · · ·
Every view counts.

learn more, go to www.nielsenmedia.com   © 2007 The Nielsen Company   All Rights Reserved.

influence
You have the power to beat the flu.®

Over the past

Unfortunately, some people think you can get influenza (flu) from the injectable vaccine. **NOT SO.**

Injectable influenza vaccine is made from killed virus, so you cannot get the flu from the vaccine. Some people may experience a sore arm or a fever that usually goes away within 24 hours, but these side effects are not symptoms of the flu. You can easily catch influenza from an infected person—so vaccination is your best defense against the flu.

While most people get immunized in October or November, vaccination is beneficial throughout influenza season because most people get infected from December through March.

years, hundreds of millions

of influenza (flu) shots have been administered

Immunization offers **SAFE** and **SIMPLE** protection against influenza. So join the crowd and get IMMUNIZED.

where **PROMISE** of discovery becomes **POWER** to

SAVE LIVES

Ikenna Madueke '07, Presidential Scholar, Pre-Med

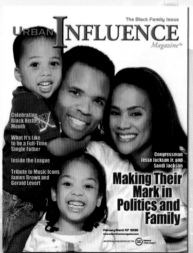

Supplier Diversity
A Natural Resource

In today's naturally evolving business climate, developing opportunities for diverse suppliers is not just our corporate responsibility, it's good for business and ultimately makes us a stronger, more productive, and increasingly successful company.

To learn more about Nicor's Supplier Diversity Program, please contact Dave Thomas at 630 388-2870 or dthoma1@nicor.com

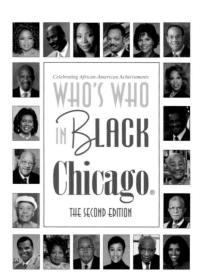

WHERE BUSINESSES ARE BORN

The Joseph Business School was established in 1997 as part of Dr. Bill Winston's vision to help entrepreneurs start and grow successful businesses by providing Bible-based business instruction, consultation, financial services, and state-of-the-art business offices. The goal of The Joseph Business School is to provide a "one stop" shop for business development, entrepreneurship and career and workforce development training. It is the only faith-based Small Business Development Center (SBDC) in the country sponsored by the Small Business Administration (SBA).

To learn more about the many services available through The Joseph Business School please call 1-866-791-4JBS (4527).

JOSEPH BUSINESS SCHOOL

www.josephbusinessschool.com

RUSH UNIVERSITY MEDICAL CENTER PROUDLY SALUTES *WHO'S WHO IN BLACK CHICAGO.*

To build sustainable diversity, you need a strong foundation of inclusion. For more than three decades, health care professionals and students at Rush University Medical Center have volunteered their time and skills to address the needs of Chicago's underserved communities. Community service is a vital part of Rush education and employment.

Shaping the health care leaders of tomorrow. Recognizing diversity as the cornerstone of scientific discovery. Putting patients first in everything we do.

Quite simply, it's how medicine should be.

For more information about Rush and its programs, visit www.rush.edu or call (888) 352-RUSH.

RUSH UNIVERSITY MEDICAL CENTER

M4009 7/07

powerful

effective

Influential

MOST INFLUENTIAL

guiding

prominent

momentous

significant

authoritative

leading

meaningful

Carol L. Adams, Ph.D.

Secretary of Human Services
State of Illinois

Dr. Carol L. Adams is secretary of the Illinois Department of Human Services. Appointed by Governor Rod Blagojevich in February of 2003, Adams directs the state's human services programs with a staff complement of more than 13,000 people and a $4 billion budget. The agency offers services at more than 300 locations statewide. Its major components are alcoholism and substance abuse, community health and prevention, developmental disabilities, human capital development, mental health and rehabilitation services.

Adams has made substantial contributions to human services, community development, sociological research and African-American education and culture for more than 30 years. She has been a consultant in social development throughout the United States, as well as in Africa and the Caribbean.

A sociologist, Adams attended Fisk University, Boston University, The University of Chicago and Union Graduate School, as well as special programs at Yale and Harvard universities. She is a member of Alpha Kappa Alpha Sorority, Inc., and holds the prestigious Phi Beta Kappa Key.

Adams is a native of Louisville, Kentucky, and is the mother of one daughter, Nia.

Tracey Alston

President & Chief Executive Officer
Danielle Ashley Communications

Tracey Alston is the founder of Danielle Ashley Communications, a full-service integrated marketing, advertising and public relations agency established in 1994. As chief executive officer, Alston has an extraordinary talent for developing advertising and marketing programs that positively impact her clients' bottom line. Her services are especially sought after for political campaigns. For two consecutive years, Danielle Ashley Communications has been recognized as one of the fastest-growing urban businesses in the nation by *Inc.* magazine's Inner City 100.

Alston is a passionate believer in community involvement and grassroots outreach. She is a board member of Jack and Jill of America, Inc., South Suburban Chicago chapter, and a dedicated member of the League of Women Voters. By combining her two loves, business and people, Alston has created a company that puts her in touch with both.

She received a Bachelor of Arts degree in communications from Columbia College of Chicago. With 14 years of radio management experience, Alston became the youngest female radio station owner (WBEE-AM Chicago) in the United States. She is the loving mother of three girls.

nthony "Tony" Anderson is the vice chair and Midwest managing partner of Ernst & Young. Since taking the role in July of 2006, Tony oversees a practice of 3,400 audit, tax and transaction professionals serving clients in Illinois, Indiana, Iowa, Minnesota, Missouri, Nebraska, western Michigan and Wisconsin. Tony is also a member of Ernst & Young's governing body, the Americas Executive Board.

Prior to his current position, Tony worked in Los Angeles where he served as the Ernst & Young managing partner for the Pacific Southwest area since July of 2000. He was admitted to the partnership in 1989 and relocated to Los Angeles in 1996 to oversee the Pacific Southwest area's financial services and insurance practice.

An active civic leader, Tony serves on the boards of the Chicago 2016 Bid Committee, the Chicago Urban League, The Field Museum, and Lyric Opera of Chicago. He is also on Chicago State University's Foundation board and the president's advisory board of the National Association of Black Accountants, Inc. – Chicago Chapter.

Tony received his bachelor's degree in accounting from Chicago State University.

Anthony "Tony" K. Anderson

Vice Chair &
Midwest Managing Partner
Ernst & Young LLP

he Honorable Carrie M. Austin is a four-term alderman of Chicago's 34th Ward. She works effectively to run city government and accommodate city services for her constituents and the greater metropolis. Appointed by Mayor Daley on May 23, 2007, to chair the Committee on the Budget and Governmental Operations, she spearheads the second most powerful and prestigious chairmanship. She co-chairs the Committee on Committees, Rules and Ethics, and sits on the Energy, Environmental Protection and Public Utilities; Finance; Health; Housing and Real Estate; Police and Fire; and Zoning committees.

Austin has been a staunch member of the 34th Ward Democratic Organization since 1972. Her commitment to public service includes working under former 34th Ward Aldermen Wilson Frost and her late husband, Lemuel, as well as State Representative Nelson Rice Sr.

Austin is active at her church, Logos Baptist Assembly, which includes membership in the Pastors Aide Club. A trendsetting advocate of quality in public education, she enjoys strong support from ward principals.

She is the mother of seven children and the grandmother of 25.

The Honorable Carrie M. Austin

Alderman, 34th Ward
City of Chicago

Shawn D. Baldwin

Chairman
Capital Management Group

Shawn D. Baldwin is chairman of Capital Management Group (CMG), a Chicago-based investment bank. CMG provides sales/trading and investment banking services to pension funds and corporations. CMG has participated in 75 capital markets transactions for more than $68 billion.

CMG has a network of fiduciaries and academics via its economic conferences. The event draws the world's largest plan sponsors and institutional investors to discuss market trends. CMG's conference attendees represent $400 billion in plan sponsors and $2 trillion in investment managers. Baldwin is the second African-American member of the Chicago Stock Exchange and has Series 7, 24 and 63 licenses. He is a member of the CFA Institute and the National Association of Securities Dealers.

Baldwin was featured in *The Economist, Business Week, Forbes, Fortune, Money, Investment Dealers' Digest* Top 40 Investment Bankers Under 40, *Black Enterprise*'s Top 75 Blacks on Wall Street, and *Black Enterprise*'s Top 40 Under 40. He is a speaker on Bloomberg, CNN, CNNfn, CNBC and CBS Radio. He is an invitee to the Money Summit, Milken Global Institute, *Fortune*'s CEO Strategies Summit and *Forbes* CEO Forum.

William Bates Jr.

Executive Vice President
& General Counsel
Seaway National Bank

William Bates Jr. is executive vice president and general counsel for Seaway National Bank. He is responsible for the oversight of legal and compliance matters and several bank departments including trust, internal audit, loan collections, administrative services and security. He has been a board member of the bank and its holding company, Seaway Bancshares, Inc., since 1990. Prior to joining Seaway in 1982, Bates worked for six years as a senior auditor for Arthur Andersen and Company.

Bates serves on the boards of United Way of Metropolitan Chicago, South-Southwest Suburban United Way, The John Marshall Law School Alumni Association, and the Seaway Community Development Corporation, a nonprofit affiliate of the bank that renovates homes for sale to low- and moderate-income families. He is also a member of Omega Psi Phi Fraternity, Inc.

Bates earned a Bachelor of Arts degree from the University of Illinois at Urbana-Champaign and a Master of Business Administration degree from The University of Chicago. He also received a juris doctorate from The John Marshall Law School.

D r. Traci P. Beck, a native of Minneapolis, Minnesota, is a graduate of Stanford University, where she received a Bachelor of Science degree. Beck obtained her medical degree from The University of Pittsburgh and completed a urology residency at The University of Chicago. Upon completion of her urology residency, she furthered her urologic training by completing a fellowship in female urology, voiding dysfunction and genitourinary reconstruction at Cedar-Sinai Hospital in Los Angeles, California.

Currently, Beck serves as the co-director of the Women's Center for Continence and Pelvic Medicine at the Illinois Masonic Medical Center in Chicago. She is the only board-certified African-American female practicing urology in the city of Chicago.

Beck is the recipient of the Dr. Chester E. Harris Award for Community Leadership and Service to Humanity, The Pfizer Scholars in Urology Award and *Today's Chicago Woman*'s 100 Women Making a Difference Award. She is a member of the National Medical Association, the American Urological Association, the Society for Urodynamics and Female Urology, and Alpha Kappa Alpha Sorority, Inc.

Traci P. Beck, M.D.

Co-Director, Women's Center for
Continence and Pelvic Medicine
Illinois Masonic Medical Center

D r. Carl C. Bell is president and chief executive officer of Community Mental Health Council & Foundation, Inc., a comprehensive community mental health center in Chicago. He is the principle investigator of a NIMH R-01 grant for using CHAMP to prevent youth HIV risk in a South African Township. He is also an international fellow with the Centre for Ethnicity & Health & Institute for Philosophy, Diversity & Mental Health, faculty of health, University of Central Lancashire, Preston, United Kingdom.

Bell is the director of public and community psychiatry, and co-director of the Interdisciplinary Violence Prevention Research Center at the University of Illinois – Chicago (UIC), where he is also a clinical professor of psychiatry and public health.

He has published more than 350 articles and books on mental health, including *The Sanity of Survival: Reflections on Community Mental Health and Wellness*, and has also produced *Eight Pieces of Brocade*, a chi kung exercise DVD.

A graduate of UIC, Bell earned his doctorate degree from Meharry Medical College. He completed his psychiatric residency in 1974 at the Illinois State Psychiatric Institute in Chicago.

Carl C. Bell, M.D.

President &
Chief Executive Officer
Community Mental Health
Council & Foundation, Inc.

James A. Bell

Executive Vice President &
Chief Financial Officer
The Boeing Company

J ames Bell is executive vice president and chief financial officer of The Boeing Company. From March through June of 2005, he also served as Boeing president and chief executive officer on an interim basis.

A 34-year company veteran, James oversees business performance and strategic growth initiatives at the world's largest aerospace company. He is responsible for overall financial management of the company, its financial reporting, treasury, investor relations and customer-financing activities. Under his leadership, Boeing is further strengthening internal financial controls, enabling improved business decision-making and achieving superior financial performance that matches the quality of Boeing technology and people. Before becoming chief financial officer, James was corporate controller and held leadership positions in auditing, program management, contracts and pricing, among other functions.

He is a member of the board of directors of Dow Chemical Company, the Joffrey Ballet, the Chicago Urban League and The Economic Club of Chicago, among others.

A Los Angeles native, James is a graduate of California State University at Los Angeles.

Robert D. Blackwell Sr.

Chair
Blackwell Consulting Services

R obert "Bob" D. Blackwell Sr. is chair of Blackwell Consulting Services. A well-known leader in management and information technology, Bob's computer industry expertise spans more than 35 years. He is known in the industry as a visionary and dynamic leader.

After working for more than 25 years with IBM, Bob founded Blackwell Consulting Services in 1992. Today, the company is a national full-service, full life-cycle management and information technology consulting firm, serving the Global 1,000 and middle market enterprises. With more than 200 consultants and revenues of $43 million in 2005, Blackwell has grown to become one of the largest minority-owned management and IT firms in the U.S.

Holding a bachelor's degree from Wichita State University, Bob is a member of The Executives' Club of Chicago, The Economic Club of Chicago and The Metropolitan Club of Chicago. Bob sits on the board for the Illinois Institute of Technology, and is a trustee of Lakeside Bank and the Museum of Science and Industry.

Bob passionately supports the Arts and Business Council, the Neighborhood Writing Alliance and the eta Creative Arts Foundation.

William "Bill" Bonaparte Jr. is owner, president and chief executive officer of Bonaparte Corporation, the largest full-service, African-American-owned electrical contractor in Chicago. Under Bill's leadership, the company has grown to an average annual revenue base of $20 million, providing middle class jobs to more than 100 full-time employees.

He began his career in telecommunications as the first African-American PBX installer with Illinois Bell. Bill later retired from corporate America, and formed Bonaparte Connection, supplying communication connectivity services.

He is the proud recipient of many awards, honors and recognitions, a few of which include his induction into the University of Illinois at Chicago Business Hall of Fame in 2002 and becoming archived by *The HistoryMakers* in 2003.

Bill earned a Bachelor of Science degree from the Milwaukee School of Engineering and a certificate from the Massachusetts Institute of Technology.

He has two sons, William III and Jason, whom he hopes will succeed him in operating the company. Bill lives in metropolitan Chicago, has a special interest in sport fishing and history, and loves his mother's cooking.

William Bonaparte Jr.

President &
Chief Executive Officer
Bonaparte Corporation

Barbara Bowles, CFA, is vice chair of Profit Investment Management, an investment advisory firm with more than $1.2 billion in assets. In 1989 she founded The Kenwood Group, Inc., an equity investment advisory firm that merged into Profit in 2006.

Barbara holds a Master of Business Administration degree in finance from The University of Chicago Graduate School of Business and a bachelor's degree from Fisk University. She received the chartered financial analyst designation in 1977.

She serves as a director for Black & Decker Corporation, Wisconsin Energy Corporation, Children's Memorial Hospital, the Chicago Urban League, the Museum of Science and Industry and Hyde Park Bank. Barbara is a member of the CFA Society of Chicago and the National Association of Securities Professionals. She is a trustee of Fisk University, and serves on The University of Chicago School of Business advisory council.

Barbara has been recognized by *The HistoryMakers* of Chicago, the YWCA of Metropolitan Chicago and the African-American MBA Association of The University of Chicago. She and her husband, Earl, are residents of the Hyde Park-Kenwood community.

Barbara Bowles

Vice Chair
Profit Investment Management

CHICAGO'S MOST INFLUENTIAL

Charles E. Box

Chair
Illinois Commerce Commission

Charles E. Box was appointed chair of the Illinois Commerce Commission in January of 2006 by Governor Rod Blagojevich. He is the first African American to head the agency. The ICC is responsible for regulatory oversight of investor-owned utilities, including telecommunications, electricity, water and gas companies, as well as transportation issues related to trucking insurance certification, household goods moving and railroad safety.

A native of Rockford, Charles served as the city's mayor from 1989 to 2001. Prior to that, he held the positions of city administrator and legal director. He has served on several boards and commissions since 1977, including the Illinois Growth Enterprises, Rockford College board of trustees and the Illinois Children's Healthcare Foundation.

Charles has been recognized with a number of awards, including the 1991 Dr. Nathan Davis Award for Outstanding Service and Leadership, the 2001 Rockford Area Arts Council's Mayor's Art Award and the 2002 Edward Potter Lathrop Medal.

Charles graduated, magna cum laude, from Dartmouth College with a Bachelor of Arts degree in history in 1973 and a juris doctorate from the University of Michigan Law School in 1976.

Jeanna Bridges

Regional President
Homewood-Flossmoor
Harris N.A.

Jeanna Bridges is a regional president for Harris N.A., an integrated financial service organization providing more than one million personal, business and corporate clients with banking, lending, investing and wealth management solutions.

Bridges joined Harris in 1979 as a retail banking representative and held a succession of increasingly more senior positions in sales, sales management and operations. Her broad range of experience and leadership excellence led to her promotion to president of Harris Wilmette in March of 2002. She was appointed to her current role in 2006.

Bridges attended DePaul University and Hunter College. She is the chair-elect for the National Able Network, which provides full-service counseling, training and placement programs that empower individuals and businesses. Bridges is a board member for South Suburban College Foundation, and an advisory board member for the Habitat Humanity of Chicago South Suburbs. She is also a past president of the Chicago Chapter of Urban Financial Coalition Services, and a former Family Reserve board member. Additionally, Bridges is a recipient of the YMCA of Metropolitan Chicago Black & Hispanic Achiever Award.

In 1989 Dr. Irene Hale Brodie was elected mayor of the Village of Robbins, a suburb of Chicago. The first woman mayor of Robbins, she was responsible for getting a $2.5 million HUD debt forgiven from Washington, D.C., attracting quality new home builders to Robbins, and building a $403 million industrial park, which has become Robbins Community Power.

Some of Mayor Brodie's accomplishments include serving on one of President Clinton's environmental think tanks in 1996 and 1997; guest lecturing in 1993 and 1994 to the Graduate School of Business at Harvard University; serving as vice president of the Illinois Municipal League; and a 2002 U.S. Region V benefactor to Moraine Valley Community College. She was also appointed to three transition teams for the current governor of Illinois. Currently, Brodie is the assistant secretary of the board of the National Conference of Black Mayors.

Dedicated to assisting grade school and college-bound students with scholarships, Brodie has scholarship commitments of $80,000 per year to be received from businesses beginning in 2008. She personally contributes $2,000 each year to eighth grade graduates.

The Honorable
Dr. Irene H. Brodie

Mayor
Village of Robbins

The Honorable Howard B. Brookins Jr. was elected alderman of the 21st Ward in April of 2003, and is currently in his second term. Brookins continues a tradition of public service in the footsteps of his father, former State Senator Howard B. Brookins Sr. He has had a distinguished career in the public sector, serving as an assistant public defender, assistant state's attorney and special assistant attorney general. He is currently a partner in the Brookins & Wilson law firm.

Brookins is a graduate of Mendel Catholic High School, Southern Illinois University in Carbondale and Northern Illinois University Law School. He participates in a number of committees and organizations, including Trinity United Church of Christ, Prince Hall Mason Eureka Lodge #64 and Alpha Phi Alpha Fraternity, Inc.

Brookins is a longtime resident of Chicago, and is committed to improving the quality of life for the area he serves. He is a devoted husband to Ebonie Taylor-Brookins and proud father of Howard B. Brookins III and Harihson Bilal Brookins.

The Honorable
Howard B. Brookins Jr.

Alderman, 21st Ward
City of Chicago

Marc Brooks

Chair & Chief Executive Officer
MKMB Corporation

Marc Brooks is chair and chief executive officer of MKMB Corporation, an investment firm that has placed capital in a wide range of industries. Some notable investments include an ownership stake in the nation's tenth-largest cable television company, WOW Internet and Cable, and a national distribution partnership with U.S. Cellular through a sister company, Urban Media Group.

In addition to his responsibilities with MKMB, Brooks serves as vice chair of Brooks Food Group, a food manufacturer with 300 employees and $100 million in revenue. Some of Brooks' other ventures include multiple partnerships with famed restaurateur Jerry Kleiner, including an upscale banquet facility and two restaurants in Chicago.

Some of Brooks' notable achievements include Retail Firm of the Year recipient by the Minority Enterprise Development Council in 2003, recognition as one of Chicago's 100 Most Influential African-Americans by *N'DIGO* magazine in 2004 and 2005, and recipient of U.S. Cellular's Top Agent Award in 2006.

Brooks currently serves on the boards of WOW Internet and Cable, Brooks Food Group, Providence-St. Mel School and De La Salle Institute.

Carole Brown

Managing Director &
Head of Central Region
Lehman Brothers

As a managing director, Carole Brown heads Lehman Brothers' Chicago-based Midwest Municipal Finance Office and has primary responsibility for managing the firm's municipal business within the United States central region. She serves as the senior investment banker for local municipal clients and maintains primary responsibility for the firm's client relationships in several major national markets.

In September of 2003 Mayor Richard M. Daley appointed Carole as chair of the Chicago Transit Authority board, where she oversees policy for the nation's second-largest transportation agency.

A native of Baltimore and a graduate of Harvard College, she received a master's degree in management from Northwestern University's Kellogg Graduate School of Management.

Carole serves on several boards, including the Chicago Children's Museum, Mercy Foundation and the Illinois Council Against Handgun Violence. She is a member of The Economic Club of Chicago and The Executives' Club of Chicago. She also serves on the advisory boards for the Chicago Public Schools' School Partner Program and Uhlich Children's Home. Carole is a 2002 fellow of Leadership Greater Chicago, and was named their 2007 Distinguished Fellow.

Edwin A. Burnette was appointed chief executive and chief attorney of the Law Office of the Cook County Public Defender in March of 2003. His responsibilities include establishing policies and procedures for representing clients and designating liaisons to all county and court agencies involved in the administration and funding of the law office.

Burnette earned the rank of major over the course of 15 years of service in the U.S. Marine Corps. He served in Camp Lejeune, North Carolina; Quantico, Virginia; Washington, D.C.; and Okinawa, Japan, among other places. Burnette held several positions, including operational law specialist, senior defense counsel, company commander, chief prosecution attorney, trial defense counsel for the Office of the Staff Judge Advocate, and appellate defense counsel for the Department of the Navy.

Burnette speaks and teaches at DePaul University College of Law, The University of Chicago Law School, the National Legal Aid and Defender Association, and many others institutions and organizations. He currently serves on numerous boards.

He is a graduate of the United States Naval Academy and DePaul University College of Law.

Edwin A. Burnette

Chief Executive &
Chief Attorney
Law Office of the Cook County
Public Defender

Karen Caldwell-Fleming, CPA, is co-head of risk and portfolio management at LaSalle. She has 20 years' experience in the capital markets, and is highly regarded by Wall Street firms' sales, banking, structuring and trading divisions.

She has responsibility for the interest rate hedging of the $120 billion balance sheet of LaSalle. This includes generating income by implementing relative value decisions in duration, curve and volatility for the total return-based $30 billion-plus fixed income portfolio, which consists of $17 billion in mortgages, $7 billion in municipals, $8 billion in securitized products and a $5 billion wholesale residential loan portfolio. Caldwell-Fleming founded the bank's securitized credit portfolio, which included developing and implementing underwriting procedures and relative value matrices.

She earned a bachelor's degree in accounting from Florida A&M University and a Master of Management degree in finance from Northwestern University.

Previously, Caldwell-Fleming traded foreign currency as manager of overnight trading. In that role, she developed the operations for the prime brokerage, where hedge funds trade on a leveraged basis. Earlier she was responsible for restructuring problem corporate debt.

Karen Caldwell-Fleming

Senior Vice President
ABN-AMRO
LaSalle Bank

Warrick L. Carter, Ph.D.

President
Columbia College Chicago

D r. Warrick L. Carter is president of Columbia College Chicago. He joined Columbia in 2000, following four years as director of entertainment arts for Walt Disney Entertainment.

Carter spent 12 years in academic leadership at Berklee College of Music in Boston. His previous academic appointments were at Governors State University and the University of Maryland, Eastern Shore. He received a Bachelor of Science degree from Tennessee State University and a Doctor of Philosophy degree in music education from Michigan State University.

Carter has consulted on music education for organizations throughout the United States and internationally, including the National Endowment for the Arts and the Ministry of Culture in Paris. He has published and lectured on education, jazz and African-American music history and culture worldwide.

As a performer and a composer of commissioned works, Carter has an international reputation. He is a two-time recipient of the National Black Music Caucus Achievement Award and a member of the International Jazz Educators Hall of Fame.

Carter has served on many boards, currently including the International House of Blues Foundation and the Federation of Independent Colleges.

The Honorable
N. Keith Chambers

Executive Director
Illinois Human Rights Commission

T he Honorable N. Keith Chambers is the executive director of the Illinois Human Rights Commission. In this position, he has oversight responsibility for processing adjudications of violations to the Illinois Human Rights Act. He is also a three-term trustee of the Village of South Holland, where he chairs the Public Safety Committee and serves as co-chair on the Finance Committee.

A 20-year veteran of government, Keith has served in leadership roles for three Illinois governors and a Cook County Board president. He is a graduate of the University of Illinois in Springfield, where he received a bachelor's degree and is currently completing his master's degree in public administration.

He is proud to have received the Outstanding Community Service Award from the Springfield Urban League and the Springfield Chapter of the NAACP, the Community Leadership Award from the Village of South Holland and the Outstanding Service to the Business Community Award from the Illinois Black Chamber of Commerce.

A native of Springfield, Keith and his wife, Tina, are the proud parents of two sons, Ryan Nicholas and Nicholas Keith II.

In October of 2006, James Compton retired from the Chicago Urban League and the Chicago Urban League Development Corporation. He became executive director in 1972, and was elected president and chief executive officer in 1978.

Compton serves as a life trustee of the Field Museum of Natural History, and is a trustee of DePaul University. He is a member of The Chicago Club, The Economic Club of Chicago, The Executives' Club of Chicago and The Commercial Club of Chicago. Compton's board affiliations include Ariel Mutual Funds, Commonwealth Edison Company, Seaway National Bank and the eta Creative Arts Foundation.

He received an honorary doctorate from Aurora University; the 2002 National Urban League's Whitney M. Young Jr. Leadership Award for Advancing Racial Equality; the City Club of Chicago's 2002 John A. McDermott Award for Civic Leadership; and the 2000 Illinois Action for Children Service Award.

A Morehouse College graduate, Compton received the Merrill Scholarship to study French literature at the University of Grenoble in France. He was awarded the Doctor of Humane Letters honorary degree from Columbia College Chicago.

James W. Compton

Retired President &
Chief Executive Officer
Chicago Urban League

Lester Coney joined Mesirow Financial in 2006 as executive vice president, Office of the Chairman. He is responsible for originating and nurturing new business opportunities as well as expanding and maintaining client relationships across all lines of business. Les keeps the company connected to ethnic, minority and community organizations by providing corporate support for key initiatives and events.

Les is chair of the Goodman Theatre, founding chair of the Congo Square Theatre and vice president of the DuSable Museum of African American History board of trustees. He also serves on the board of directors for the School of the Art Institute of Chicago, Roosevelt University and Lincoln University. Additional honors include the 2007 Executive Leader Award from AFP Chicago and the 2007 King Legacy Award from the Boys and Girls Club of Chicago.

Les resides in Chicago's West Loop, and he is the father of two children, Chanel and Javon.

Lester Coney

Executive Vice President
Office of the Chairman
Mesirow Financial

Bob Dale

President &
Chief Executive Officer
RJDale

Bob Dale is president and chief executive officer of the RJDale marketing communications network, which includes RJDale Advertising & Public Relations, RJDale Interactive and Impacto Dale.

Originally established 27 years ago as an African-American-focused agency, RJDale's practice areas have expanded to include general market advertising, digital communications and new media, and the full range of multicultural in-language communications capabilities.

In addition to winning numerous awards for communications excellence and innovation in both advertising and public relations, RJDale ranked among the leading black-owned marketing firms in the U.S. by *Black Enterprise* and among the top 100 minority-owned companies by DiversityBusiness.com.

Dale, a native Chicagoan, is a strong advocate for education. He is board president of the Institute of Positive Education and co-founder of Betty Shabazz International Charter School. He is also a member of the Association of Business Leaders and Entrepreneurs.

Dale earned his master of business administration from Stanford University. He has four sons and resides in Chicago's Bronzeville community with his wife, Cathy.

Elnora D. Daniel, Ed.D.

President
Chicago State University

Dr. Elnora D. Daniel was appointed president of Chicago State University (CSU) on August 1, 1998. She assumed this presidential post after more than three decades of administrative, consultative and grantsmanship experience in higher education throughout the United States and abroad.

Daniel has facilitated institutional transformation. Under her administration, the university has enjoyed consecutive years of balanced budgets, increased federal funding from $17 million in 1998 to $23 million in 2001, and the securing of funds for five new buildings and major building renovation. The university has also seen a significant increase in contributions to the Foundation, more than doubling the size of the CSU endowment.

She sits on a myriad of local and national boards, and advisory panels addressing diverse constituencies. These appointments include the National Association for Equal Opportunity in Higher Education, Junior Achievement, Chicago United, The Economic Club of Chicago, the University Club of Chicago and the Commercial Club of Chicago.

Daniel earned master's and doctorate degrees in education from Teachers College, Columbia University, and holds the rank of colonel [retired] in the United States Army Reserve.

D r. Blondean Davis has been superintendent of Matteson School District 162 since 2002. Reversing a downward trend in test scores as minority enrollment increased, she has led the district's schools to extraordinarily high levels of performance. One of her schools was recognized by the U.S. Department of Education and the Illinois State Board of Education as one of the ten best elementary schools in the state.

Previously, Davis was in charge of daily management of the 601 Chicago public schools from 1995 until August of 2001. She also served Chicago Public Schools as deputy chief education officer, district superintendent, principal, assistant principal, counselor and teacher.

A graduate of the Chicago Public Schools, Davis holds a master's degree and a doctoral degree from Loyola University. She has served as associate professorial lecturer at St. Xavier University and as a senior consultant to the Illinois State Board of Education. Davis was the first woman president of a Phi Delta Kappa chapter. A recipient of many awards and honors, she is also active on the boards of many local and national organizations.

Dr. Blondean Y. Davis

Superintendent of Schools
Matteson School District 162

T he Honorable Danny K. Davis (D-IL07) was chosen by the people of the Seventh Congressional District of Illinois as their representative in Congress in 1996. He has been re-elected by large majorities to succeeding Congresses.

Davis serves on the Government Reform, Small Business, and Education and Labor committees. He is chair of the House Postal Caucus, and is a member of numerous other caucuses, including the Black Caucus and the Progressive Caucus.

Davis has distinguished himself as an articulate voice for his constituents and an effective legislator who is able to move major bills to passage. He practices a unique style of communication and interaction with his constituents through advisory task forces, town hall meetings, weekly television and radio shows featuring audience call-in, periodic written public reports and regular attendance at other community events.

Prior to his election to Congress, he served on the Cook County Board of Commissioners and the Chicago City Council. Before seeking public office, Davis had productive careers as an educator, community organizer, health planner and administrator, and civil rights advocate.

The Honorable Danny K. Davis

Representative, Seventh
District of Illinois
U.S. House of Representatives

The Honorable
Monique D. Davis

Representative, District 27
Illinois House of Representatives

The Honorable Monique D. Davis was born and raised on the South Side of Chicago. Her legislative district covers part of the city's South Side, where she maintains her constituent service office.

As representative, Davis serves as chair of the General Services Appropriations Committee, as well as vice chair of the Elementary and Secondary Education Committee. Additionally, she is a member of the Higher Education Appropriations, Financial Institutions, State Government Administration, Public Utilities, Gaming, and Juvenile Justice Reform committees.

Davis has a bachelor's degree in elementary education and a master's degree in guidance and supervision from Chicago State University. She has also earned 42 graduate hours in administration supervision and special education, as well as credit toward her doctorate degree from Roosevelt University.

Prior to being elected state representative, Davis taught in the Chicago Public Schools system, served as coordinator for the Chicago Board of Education, and was a training specialist with City Colleges of Chicago. She is a member of Trinity United Church, and has served on the Board of Christian Education.

Shani Davis

Olympic Champion
Ice Speed Skating

Speed skater Shani Davis won two Olympic medals at the 2006 Winter Games in Turin, Italy, a gold medal in the 1,000-meter event, and a silver medal in the 1,500-meter event. He is a two-time world all-round champion (2005, 2006), and is the current world record holder for fastest time in both the 1,000- and 1,500-meter events.

Born in Chicago, Davis was raised by his mother on the South Side. He started roller-skating at local rinks at age 2 but was quickly bored with it. At 6, Davis switched to ice, and joined the Evanston Speedskating Club, where he began competing locally after two months. At 8, Davis was winning regional competitions in his age group.

He won five National Age Group Championships (1995, 1997, 1999, 2000, 2003) and a North American Championship (1999). Davis made history at 17 when he became the first U.S. skater to earn spots on the short and long track junior world teams three years in a row (2000-2002). His first international medals came at the 2002 Junior Country Match and 2002 Junior World Championships.

Jacoby Dickens is chair of Seaway National Bank of Chicago. Elected to the board of directors in 1979, Dickens served as vice chair until 1983 when he was elected to his current position. During his tenure, Seaway National Bank has risen to become the largest black-owned bank in the Midwest.

After spending 14 years as an engineer with the Chicago Board of Education, he embarked on his entrepreneurial career by investing in real estate, and later acquired part ownership in a bowling recreation center. At one time, his total bowling facilities ranked him as the country's No. 1 black proprietor.

Dickens serves on the boards of the Chicago Urban League and the Chicago State University Foundation, and is a principal of Chicago United. He is a member of The Economic Club of Chicago, a trustee at Chicago State University and a former trustee at DePaul University and the Museum of Science and Industry.

His honors include induction into the Chicago Business Hall of Fame in 1996.

Dickens is married to Veranda Jolliff Dickens.

Jacoby Dickens

Chair, Board of Directors
Seaway National Bank

Donna Dunnings is the first African American and female chief financial officer of Cook County. As chief financial officer, Donna is responsible for the strategic direction and management of the six departments that compromise the Bureau of Finance: Budget and Management Services, Comptroller, Contract Compliance, Purchasing, Revenue and Risk Management.

The Bureau of Finance is responsible for the financial oversight of the Cook County government. The bureau coordinates and supervises all the financial activities of the county, and monitors the expenditures of each budgetary unit while striving to ensure that the county taxpayers' dollars are expended in an economical and fiscally responsible manner.

Donna graduated, summa cum laude, from the University of Arkansas Pine Bluff with a degree in accounting. She received a Master of Management degree from the Kellogg Graduate School of Management at Northwestern University.

A native of Helena, Arkansas, Donna is now a resident of the South Side of Chicago. She is a member of the Apostolic Church of God, and is a proud mother of two daughters, Martia and Meygan.

Donna Dunnings

Chief Financial Officer
Cook County Government

CHICAGO'S MOST INFLUENTIAL

R. Martin Earles, M.D.

Dermatologist & President
Dr. Earles, PC

D r. R. Martin Earles is a practicing dermatologist in Chicago and a pioneer in hair transplants among African Americans. He was the first to publish a paper on hair transplants in black women, "Hair Transplants in Black Women," in the *Journal of Dermatologic Surgery and Oncology* (1986).

Earles developed an acne treatment line and treatment products for razor bumps. He also developed dandruff treatment products, for one of which he holds a U.S. patent. His son, Robert, is chief executive officer of Dr. Earles, LLC, and directs placement of products in the general marketplace. Andrea Earles, his daughter, is marketing director, and the children's mother, Eve Earles, is the media consultant.

He holds bachelor's and master's degrees from Howard University, and completed his residency in dermatology at Rush Medical Center in Chicago.

Earles has appeared in many popular magazines, including *Ebony*, *Jet*, *Essence* and *Vogue*. He is a member of the National Medical Association, Sigma Pi Phi Fraternity, Inc., and Kappa Alpha Psi Fraternity, Inc.

Earles' hobbies include golfing and writing poetry.

The Honorable Timothy C. Evans

Chief Judge
Circuit Court of Cook County

T he Honorable Timothy C. Evans serves as chief judge of the Circuit Court of Cook County, the largest of the 22 judicial circuits in Illinois. Evans oversees the circuit's approximately 400 judges whom he assigns throughout the court's eight divisions and six geographic districts. He also oversees an annual budget of $166.4 million, and more than 2,700 employees who work in 14 non-judicial offices.

Evans was first elected chief judge in 2001, and was re-elected to a second three-year term in 2004. Only the fourth person to serve as chief judge of the Circuit Court of Cook County, he is the first African-American to serve in this position.

Evans has expanded opportunities for women and minorities, appointing the first Hispanic American as presiding judge of the Fourth Municipal District and the first woman as presiding judge of the Chancery Division. His efforts also led to the creation of a new, state-of-the art court facility for domestic violence cases in Chicago.

A 1965 graduate of the University of Illinois, Evans received a juris doctorate from The John Marshall Law School in 1969.

Born Louis Eugene Walcott in 1933, Minister Louis Farrakhan was reared by his mother in a highly disciplined, spiritual household in Roxbury, Massachusetts. Known as "The Charmer," he achieved fame in Boston as a vocalist, calypso singer, dancer and violinist. He joined the Nation of Islam in 1955 and decided to dedicate his life to the teachings of the Honorable Elijah Muhammad.

Farrakhan became the leader of the Nation of Islam in 1977. In 1979 he founded *The Final Call*, an internationally circulated newspaper, and penned *A Torchlight for America* in 1991. He led 2,000 blacks from America to Accra, Ghana, for the Nation of Islam's first International Saviours' Day in October of 1994.

In 1995 Farrakhan led the Million Man March on the Mall in Washington, D.C., which drew nearly two million men. He returned to the Mall in 2000 with the Million Family March.

Additionally, Farrakhan launched a prostate cancer foundation in his name in 2003. First diagnosed with prostate cancer in 1991, he survived a public bout with the disease, and currently maintains a rigorous work schedule.

The Honorable Minister Louis Farrakhan

Leader
Nation of Islam

Lula M. Ford presently serves as a commissioner for the Illinois Commerce Commission. She is the first African-American woman to be appointed as a commissioner in the agency's 90-year history. Before her appointment, Ford was the assistant director of Central Management Services for the State of Illinois. For nearly 35 years, she served as an elementary school teacher, principal, assistant superintendent, instruction officer and school leadership development officer for Chicago Public Schools.

Ford has received numerous awards for her dedicated work as an educator, child advocate and public servant. She has won accolades from former President Bill Clinton and Chicago Mayor Richard M. Daley for her excellent performance and contribution to Chicago's inner-city schools.

Ford is an active member of many civic organizations including Delta Sigma Theta Sorority, Inc., The Links, Inc., Crusade of Mercy, the Chicago Urban League and the United Negro College Fund. She received a bachelor's degree from the University of Arkansas-Pine Bluff, and was awarded master's degrees from Northeastern University and the University of Illinois-Champaign/Urbana.

Ford is also the proud mother of one adult daughter, Charisse.

Lula M. Ford

Commissioner
Illinois Commerce Commission

Paul Freeman

Music Director
Chicago Sinfonietta

Maestro Paul Freeman was proclaimed in *Fanfare* magazine as "one of the finest conductors which our nation has produced." Born in Richmond, Virginia, in 1987, he became the founding music director of the Chicago Sinfonietta. In January of 1996 he was appointed music director of the Czech National Symphony Orchestra in Prague, a position which he holds simultaneously with his Chicago Sinfonietta music directorship.

Freeman is in constant demand as a guest conductor all over the world, having conducted more than 100 orchestras in upwards of 30 countries. As one of America's most successful recording conductors, he has more than 200 releases to his credit. Moreover, his nine-LP series tracing the history of black symphonic composers from 1750 to the present garnered a great deal of attention in the mid 1970s, and was recently updated on CDs with the Chicago Sinfonietta's *African Heritage Symphonic Series*.

Robert Marsh wrote of Maestro Freeman in the *Chicago Sun-Times*: "Freeman conducts performances which are remarkable for their beauty and communicative force. He brings the sound of the Chicago Sinfonietta to the heights of angels."

Helen Davis Gardner, M.D.

Staff Psychiatrist
DuPage County

Dr. Helen Davis Gardner is a physician specializing in medicine and psychiatry. She is a board-certified diplomat in psychiatry.

Gardner was valedictorian of Aquinas Dominican High School and magna cum laude graduate of Fisk University. She completed an internship at Nashville's Meharry Medical College. Her residencies were completed at Meharry Medical and Chicago Medical, where she was chief resident and faculty executive council member. Gardner practices in the Chicago area and lectures throughout the country.

Gardner is a staff psychiatrist for DuPage County and attending staff psychiatrist for the Illinois Masonic. She is a noted contributor to *Ebony* magazine, and has been heard on numerous radio stations. Gardner was also a physician contributor on WMAQ-TV NBC5 television in Chicago. Additionally, she served as acting medical administrative director of DuPage County, and completed the Rush University Medical Center Bipolar Fellowship.

Gardner is a member of Beta Kappa Chi Scientific Honor Society, the National Medical Association, the American Medical Association, the Massachusetts General Psychiatry Academy and the Chicago Medical Society.

Gardner is the proud mother of Fisk University student Kossie Gardner III.

Walter E. Grady is a career banker with 40 years of experience. Born in Memphis, Tennessee, he moved to Chicago in 1965 after serving in the U.S. Air Force, and began his career with Continental National Bank in 1967. He joined Seaway National Bank in 1972 and steadily moved up the ranks in management to attain his current position as president and chief executive officer of Seaway in 1980. Under Grady's leadership, Seaway has grown to become the largest black-owned bank in the Midwest.

For years Grady taught as an adjunct professor in business and finance for Chicago State University and the American Institute of Banking. He is active on several boards, including the Illinois Bankers Association and the Illinois Commission on Volunteerism and Community Service, and has received numerous citations for his civic work. He is also a member of Alpha Phi Alpha Fraternity, Inc. and United Methodist Church.

An avid coin collector and outdoors enthusiast, Grady resides in the South Suburbs with his wife, Janyth.

Walter E. Grady

President & Chief
Executive Officer
Seaway National Bank

The Honorable Deborah L. Graham, state representative of Illinois' 78th District, was born and raised on the west side of Chicago, and has devoted her life to community service. Deborah's commitment to community affairs dates back to her youth, where she volunteered with her grandmother through her church to help feed the homeless and coordinate services and activities for seniors. As a legislator, she has worked with senior groups to pass long-term care reforms and passed measures to protect seniors from exploitation. She has worked to protect the interest of Illinois' youth by holding the State Board of Education accountable for educational standards, and by requiring hospitals to report injuries or deaths of children caused by being backed over by large vehicles.

Deborah has supported a measure to close the loophole of ex-convicts failing to register as sex offenders, and she has championed legislation that requires stricter gun control laws.

Deborah holds a bachelor's degree in business administration from Robert Morris College. She is a member of Truth and Deliverance Christian Church under the leadership of Pastor John T. Abercrombie.

The Honorable
Deborah L. Graham

Representative, 78th District
Illinois House of Representatives

Stedman Graham

Chair & Chief Executive Officer
S. Graham and Associates

S tedman Graham is chair and chief executive officer of S. Graham and Associates (SGA), a management and marketing consulting firm based in Chicago. SGA designs and implements programs that help individuals, businesses and organizations excel and achieve success.

SGA offers professional speaking, workshops and seminars based on the 9-Step Success Process™, which was first introduced in Graham's *New York Times* bestsellers, *You Can Make It Happen* and *Teens Can Make It Happen*. He is the author of ten books, including his latest release *Diversity: Leaders Not Labels*, through which he helps people understand how to increase and improve their talent and performance, deliver their full potential and recognize that success is truly based on results and excellence.

Graham is a former adjunct professor at Northwestern University, and is currently a visiting professor at several universities across the nation. Active in philanthropy and community work, he is on the international board of Junior Achievement, a founder of Athletes Against Drugs and a member of The Economic Club of Chicago.

**The Honorable
Leslie Hairston**

Alderman, 5th Ward
City of Chicago

T he Honorable Leslie Hairston, a Chicago native, has built a professional career dedicated to public service. In 2007 she was sworn in to her third term as alderman of Chicago's 5th Ward, having won 75 percent of the vote. The ward encompasses The University of Chicago, Museum of Science and Industry, two stellar public parks and historic venues on Lake Michigan. She sits on seven committees, including finance, energy, environmental protection and public utilities, and rules and ethics.

Leslie served as assistant attorney general for the State of Illinois and staff attorney and special prosecutor for the State's Attorney's Appellate Prosecutor's Office, where she argued before the Illinois State Supreme Court. An active member of the Illinois State Bar Association, she was appointed to the assembly in June of 2007 and to the Real Estate Law Section Council.

In addition to her professional and social service activities, Leslie is a founder of B.R.I.D.G.E. and a longtime member of the South Shore Cultural Center Advisory Council, the Hyde Park-Kenwood Community Council, Alpha Kappa Alpha Sorority Inc. and the board of Kaleidoscope, Inc.

As president and chief executive officer of the Chicago-based Hartman Publishing, Inc., Hermene Hartman is one of the most significant and influential black women in American publishing.

Her flagship publication, *N'DIGO*, was founded in 1989 and has since achieved the largest African-American newspaper circulation in the nation and the largest alternative newspaper circulation in Chicago. The weekly publication has an audited circulation of 150,000, and a readership of 600,000.

In 1995 *N'DIGO PROFILES* was established as a special annual publication, with a targeted insert in the *Chicago Tribune* and *Crain's Chicago Business* magazine and a circulation of 325,000.

Hartman is founder and president of the N'DIGO Foundation, a 501(c)(3) nonprofit organization which began in 1995. It sponsors an annual black tie gala to raise funds for educational purposes. In 2004 Hartman became the president of the Alliance of Business Leaders and Entrepreneurs, a business group dedicated to entrepreneurial pursuits, with 70 members and nearly $1 billion in collective annual revenues.

She has received more than 200 awards for outstanding achievement in media, business, community services, education and communication.

Hermene Hartman

President &
Chief Executive Officer
Hartman Publishing, Inc.

Ron Hawkins is vice president and national ombudsman for McDonald's Corporation. He is the first African American to ever hold this position at McDonald's. In this role, Hawkins acts as the conscience to the McDonald's system and evaluates the application of policies, practices and procedures to reach equitable solutions with the U.S. franchisees and corporate staff.

Hawkins joined McDonald's in 1971 as a crew person. In 1973 he moved up to restaurant management in the Washington, D.C., area. He has worked in every level of restaurant management, mid-management and various regional operations department positions. In 1993 Hawkins advanced to director of operations in Philadelphia, director of diversity operations in 1995 and senior director of franchise relations in 1997. He was promoted to AVP in 1999 and into his current position in January of 2003.

Hawkins received a business degree from Prince George's Community College in Largo, Maryland. He resides in Bolingbrook, Illinois, with his wife of 29 years, Santá, and two daughters, Tanisha and Sharday. He is active in his church and community, serving on several boards.

Ron Hawkins

Vice President &
National Ombudsman
McDonald's Corporation

CHICAGO'S MOST INFLUENTIAL

Gregory T. Hinton

Senior Director
Talent Strategies & Diversity
U.S. Cellular®

Greg Hinton joined U.S. Cellular in 2002, where he is currently the senior director of strategic sourcing talent and diversity. He is responsible for sourcing talent, staffing strategies, equal employment opportunity compliance and diversity program development. His human resources career began in 1978, and he worked for major corporations such as RR Donnelley, Amtrak, Pepsi-Cola and Abbott Laboratories before joining U.S. Cellular.

Greg sits on various boards including the League of Black Women, Hispanic Alliance for Career Enhancement, Chicago Minority Business Development Council, Employment Management Association, Staffing.org, Black Data Processing Association and the Recruiting Roundtable. In addition to his professional achievements, he founded a local human resources organization, the Chicago Association of Minority Recruiters, designed to meet the development needs of minority human resources professionals.

Greg earned a Bachelor of Science degree from the University of Illinois and a Master of Science degree from Loyola University Chicago. He has three children, and when they are not keeping him busy, he enjoys cooking, reading and sporting activities. He is currently finishing a cookbook entitled *Tales of Two Cooks*.

Mellody Hobson

President
Ariel Capital Management, LLC

Mellody Hobson is president of Ariel Capital Management, LLC, an investment management firm and mutual fund company with nearly $16 billion in assets under management. She is responsible for firmwide management and strategic planning, overseeing all operations of Ariel's business outside of research and portfolio management. She is also chair of the Ariel Mutual Funds board of trustees.

Mellody has become a nationally recognized voice on financial literacy and investor education. She is a regular financial contributor on ABC's *Good Morning America*, a columnist for *Black Enterprise* and a spokesperson for the annual Ariel/Schwab Black Investor Survey, which examines the investing habits of black and white Americans.

Beyond her work at Ariel, Mellody is actively involved in various professional and civic organizations. She serves on the board of directors of DreamWorks, Estée Lauder and Starbucks. She is also on the board of governors of the Investment Company Institute. Mellody is a former trustee of Princeton University, where she received a Bachelor of Arts degree from Princeton's Woodrow Wilson School of International Relations and Public Policy.

Louis Holland is the managing partner and chief investment officer of Holland Capital Management, L.P., where he oversees the management of the firm's equity and fixed-income investment strategies. Prior to founding Holland Capital, he formed the investment advisory firm of Hahn Holland & Grossman, where he was responsible for security and industry research and portfolio management.

Holland's investment experience was augmented by 15 years at A.G. Becker Paribas Inc. There, he was vice president specializing in asset and portfolio management for corporations, endowments, foundations, public funds, Taft-Hartley, and high-net-worth individuals. He has been a special guest and a 20-year veteran panelist on *Wall $treet Week With Louis Rukeyser*, and *Louis Rukeyser's Wall Street*. Holland has also appeared on *The MacNeil/Lehrer NewsHour*, CNN's *Moneyline*, CNBC, and is a frequent guest on the *Chicago Tonight Show*. The National Association of Securities Professionals honored him with the 2004 Maynard Jackson Entrepreneur of the Year Award.

Holland received a Bachelor of Science degree in economics from the University of Wisconsin and attended the Loyola University Chicago's Graduate School of Business.

Louis A. Holland

Managing Partner & Chief
Investment Officer
Holland Capital Management, L.P.

Robert Howard is president and chief executive officer of Boys & Girls Clubs of Chicago, where he oversees a budget of $16 million. The Clubs serve a diverse population of 18,000 youth, ages 5 to 19, providing structured after-school and summer programming at 28 clubs and ten child care centers.

Howard was a "Club kid" while growing up on Chicago's South Side. He credits the Clubs for the positive values and guidance he received from caring adult professionals, which contributed to his success in corporate America (senior vice president at Payless Shoes). He holds an MBA from Harvard and a master's degree from Roosevelt University.

Howard is an active member of several civic institutions including the capital improvement advisory committee of the City of Chicago. He was featured in *Crain's Chicago Business*; inducted into the University of Illinois at Chicago's Alumni Leadership Academy and Phi Alpha Theta's historical honors society at Roosevelt University; and recognized for outstanding community service by the Association of Collegiate Business Schools and Programs. Additionally, Howard has appeared on numerous television programs stressing mentorship and community involvement.

Robert Howard

President &
Chief Executive Officer
Boys & Girls Clubs of Chicago

The Honorable Mattie Hunter

Senator, Third District
Illinois Senate

The Honorable Mattie Hunter, a native Chicagoan, has represented the Third Legislative District in the Illinois Senate since 2003. She presently serves as chair of the Appropriations III Committee.

Hunter worked for the Human Resources Development Institute, Inc., where she developed and managed a shelter for battered women and children, and was managing director for the Center for Health and Human Services in Johannesburg, South Africa. She participated, coordinated and presented lectures at joint health and human services conferences in Zimbabwe, Nigeria and Zambia.

Hunter received a bachelor's degree from Monmouth College and a master's degree from Jackson State University. In 2004 she attended the John F. Kennedy School of Government at Harvard, and received a certificate in Leadership for the 21st Century: Chaos, Conflict, and Courage. She also attended a Salzburg Seminar on multicultural health care in Salzburg, Austria.

Some legislation passed by Hunter includes SJR31, a Slave Trade Commission to study the slave trade and its consequences on the black community, and SB1, "Ticket for the Cure," a scratch-off lottery ticket with all proceeds going to breast cancer awareness and treatment.

Perri L. Irmer

Chief Executive Officer
Illinois Sports Facilities Authority

Perri L. Irmer is the chief executive officer of the Illinois Sports Facilities Authority, the public agency that built, owns and operates U.S. Cellular Field, home of the Chicago White Sox. She is responsible for all facets of the construction and renovation of the ballpark and surrounding property.

An architect and a lawyer, Irmer has 30 years of experience in all aspects of the real estate and construction industries, having worked for Skidmore, Owings & Merrill, Holabird & Root, Merchandise Mart Properties and Mesirow Financial.

Irmer's public service record includes positions as deputy commissioner of the Chicago Department of Buildings, director of construction services for the Chicago Public Building Commission and assistant general counsel for the Chicago Board of Education. She has overseen nearly $6.5 billion in public works projects in the Chicagoland area.

Irmer serves on the boards of several nonprofits and is a member of The Economic Club of Chicago. She earned a Bachelor of Architecture from the Illinois Institute of Technology in 1981 and a juris doctorate from The University of Chicago Law School in 1991.

Dr. Brooke Jackson was raised in Washington, D.C. After graduating from Wellesley College and Georgetown University Medical School, she completed an internship at the University of Chicago and her dermatology residency at Henry Ford Hospital. As a board-certified dermatologist and dermatologic surgeon, she became the first African American to be awarded fellowship training in laser surgery at Harvard University, where her interests and research helped to pioneer the uses of lasers in ethnic skin.

After completing a second fellowship in skin cancer surgery (mohs micrographic surgery), Jackson joined the staff of the prestigious M.D. Anderson Cancer Center, where she founded the Mohs Surgery Unit. She is currently the medical director of the Skin Wellness Center of Chicago, SC and Skin Spa.

In addition to publishing numerous articles and book chapters, Jackson lectures nationally on the use of lasers and cosmetic procedures in ethnic skin. She is an ambassador and frequent speaker for the American Cancer Society.

An avid runner, Jackson has completed six marathons and seven triathlons. She is married to James Lackland and has twin daughters, Avery and Reese.

Brooke A. Jackson, M.D.

Medical Director
Skin Wellness
Center of Chicago, SC

In October of 2006, Cheryle Robinson Jackson was appointed president and chief executive officer of the Chicago Urban League. She is the first woman to hold either position in the 90-year history of the venerable social and civil justice organization. The league focuses on the city's African-American workforce and business community to empower and inspire individuals to reach and exceed their economic potential.

Prior to her history-making appointment at the league, Cheryle served in the administration of Illinois Governor Rod R. Blagojevich, most recently as deputy chief of staff of communications.

Cheryle serves as a director on the boards of the Metropolitan Planning Council, the Field Museum, the Chicago Manufacturing Renaissance Council and the Chicagoland Chamber of Commerce. She also serves on the Northwestern University board of trustees, the 2016 Chicago Olympics Committee and the Daniel Burnham Anniversary Planning Committee.

Cheryle is a native of Chicago, and graduated from Northwestern University in 1988. She and her husband, Charles, reside on Chicago's South Side.

Cheryle Robinson Jackson

President &
Chief Executive Officer
Chicago Urban League

Rev. Jesse Louis Jackson Sr.

Founder & President
RainbowPUSH Coalition, Inc.

B orn in Greenville, South Carolina, Jesse Jackson Sr. graduated from North Carolina A&T State University in 1964 and earned a Master of Divinity degree in 2000.

In 1965 he became a full-time organizer for the Southern Christian Leadership Conference (SCLC). Shortly thereafter, Dr. Martin Luther King Jr. appointed him to direct SCLC's Operation Breadbasket program. Jackson went on to found Operation PUSH (People United to Serve Humanity) and the National Rainbow Coalition, which eventually merged in 1996 to become the RainbowPUSH Coalition.

Jackson's 1984 presidential campaign registered more than one million new voters and won 3.5 million votes. His 1988 campaign registered two million-plus new voters and won seven million votes.

A renowned orator and activist, Jackson has received the prestigious NAACP Spingarn Award, more than 40 honorary doctorate degrees, and the Presidential Medal of Freedom. Additionally, he has written two books, *Keep Hope Alive* and *Straight from the Heart.*

Jackson married his college sweetheart, Jacqueline Lavinia Brown, in 1963. They have five children, Santita Jackson, Congressman Jesse L. Jackson Jr., Jonathan Luther Jackson, Yusef DuBois Jackson, Esq., and Jacqueline Lavinia Jackson Jr.

The Honorable Sandi Jackson

Alderman, 7th Ward
City of Chicago

T he Honorable Sandi Jackson has been actively involved in Democratic Party politics for close to two decades. Since her inauguration on May 21, 2007, she has served Chicago's 7th Ward as alderman.

Prior to her election, Sandi served as the deputy director of training for the Democratic National Committee. In that role, she traveled the country educating state parties, constituent groups and progressive organizations on methods of outreach and campaign strategy.

A veteran of five presidential campaigns for the White House, Sandi has directed scheduling operations for the Reverend Jesse L. Jackson. She also served as a presidential appointee in the Clinton administration as vice president of congressional and external affairs for the Export-Import Bank of the United States.

She earned a bachelor's degree from Bowling Green State University in 1985 and a juris doctorate from the University of Illinois School of Law in 1992.

Sandi has resided in the 7th Ward for 13 years with her husband, Congressman Jesse L. Jackson Jr., and is the proud mother of Jessica and Jesse L. Jackson III.

Valerie B. Jarrett is the president and chief executive officer of The Habitat Company. As one of the nation's premier developers and managers of residential apartments, the company has developed more than 25,000 housing units and currently manages more than 30,000 units.

Before joining The Habitat Company in 1995, Jarrett served for eight years in the City of Chicago government as deputy corporation counsel for finance and development, and deputy chief of staff for Mayor Richard M. Daley. She also served as commissioner of the Department of Planning and Development for the City of Chicago. Prior to her government services, Jarrett practiced law with two private law firms specializing in areas of commercials real estate.

From 1995-2003, Jarrett served as chair of the Chicago Transit Authority, and she is currently chair of The University of Chicago Medical Center. Additionally, she serves as director of several corporate and nonprofit boards, including USG Corporation, Inc., Navigant Consulting, Inc., RREEF America II and The University of Chicago.

Valerie B. Jarrett

President &
Chief Executive Officer
The Habitat Company

The Honorable Lionel Jean-Baptiste has served as alderman of Evanston's second ward since 2001. He is a husband, father of three and grandfather of one. After coming from Haiti at the age of 14, Lionel earned a degree in political science from Princeton University in 1974.

In Brooklyn, New York, he taught on the elementary and collegiate levels, served as director of special housing for the New York City Housing Preservation and Development Department, and organized for jobs and worker's rights and against police brutality.

Lionel earned a law degree from Chicago-Kent College of Law. He went into private practice working in the areas of immigration, personal injury, real estate and probate. Likewise, he worked on political cases such as the reparations case that is being litigated against several U.S. corporations.

He was a member of the African Liberation Support Committee and the Durban 400. Lionel is co-founder of the Haitian Relief Fund of Illinois and the Haitian Congress to Fortify Haiti. A member of the Governor's Task Force on Racial Profiling, he is listed in *Who's Who Among American Lawyers*.

**The Honorable
Lionel Jean-Baptiste**

Alderman, Ward 2
City of Evanston

William A. Johnson, M.D.

President, Executive Director &
Medical Director
Luck Care Center

William A. Johnson, M.D. is president, executive director and medical director of the Luck Care Center, a private not-for-profit HIV/AIDS clinic. The Luck Care Center is the only HIV/AIDS clinic independently operated by African Americans in the state of Illinois.

Johnson dedicates time to HIV/AIDS organizations and to the relief efforts of organizations such as the Foundation for Hospices in Sub-Saharan Africa. In recognition of his and his wife's contributions to the cause, the AIDS Legal Council in Chicago named them Provider Advocates of the Year in 2002. He is the immediate past president of the Cook County Physicians Association and an active member of the National Medical Association, serving as chair of the Committee on International Affairs.

Board-certified in internal medicine and hospice and palliative medicine, Johnson completed a medical degree at The University of Chicago Pritzker School Of Medicine, where he attained honor status. He was the recipient of the Monarch Award in Medicine in 2001 and Trailblazer in Healthcare by the RainbowPUSH Coalition in 2005.

**The Honorable
Emil Jones Jr.**

President
Illinois Senate

The Honorable Emil Jones Jr. has been a member of the Illinois General Assembly since 1973. He is an independent-minded and progressive legislator with a solid reputation of fairness and advocacy. He is a strong proponent of social justice and fair and adequate funding of public education in Illinois. Jones has served as Senate president since 2003, receiving the unanimous support of his caucus in 2003 and 2005.

A 1953 graduate of Chicago's Tilden Technical High School, Jones graduated from Loop Junior College. He also attended Roosevelt University, which awarded him a Doctorate of Humane Letters degree, honoris causa, in 2004. Additionally, he received an honorary Doctor of Humane Letters degree at Chicago State University. In 2004 he was named to the board of directors of the Forum of Senate Presidents, and he was inducted into the Phi Theta Kappa International Honor Society of Harold Washington College. Moreover, he serves on the board of directors of the State Legislative Leaders Foundation.

Jones has four children and is married to Dr. Lorrie Jones.

Born in Brooklyn, New York, in 1963, Michael Jordan grew up in Wilmington, North Carolina. He attended Emsley A. Laney High School where he participated in football, baseball and basketball, and was named to the McDonald's All-American Team as a senior. After earning a scholarship to the University of North Carolina at Chapel Hill, he led the team to a national championship in 1982.

His 13 seasons with the Chicago Bulls were monumental: six NBA championships; ten league scoring titles; five-time league Most Valuable Player; NBA Finals MVP six times; and All-Star Game MVP three times. Following his second retirement, he returned to basketball for two seasons with the Washington Wizards. Jordan is the NBA's all-time leader in most points per game (30.1) and is third on the NBA's list of all-time scorers (32,292 points). He also won two Olympic gold medals.

In addition to his triumphs on the court, Jordan is one of the most marketed athletes in history. He has served as a spokesperson for numerous brands, and is a successful restaurateur and businessman. He has three children.

Michael Jordan
Basketball Legend

Robin L. Kelly was appointed chief of staff to Illinois State Treasurer Alexi Giannoulias in January of 2007. Prior to joining the treasurer's office, she was elected to serve a third term as Illinois state representative of the 38th District located in South Cook County.

In recognition of her work in the General Assembly, Kelly received awards from numerous organizations, including SEIU Local 880, Independent Voters of Illinois-Independent Precinct Organization and the Illinois Environmental Council. In addition, Kelly is a fellow of the Flemming Leadership Institute, a program for emerging leaders across the country, and a member of the Cook County Human Rights Commission and Place Matters, a national task force on health care disparities. She also serves on the boards of Rich Township Food Pantry and the Illinois Theatre Center.

A native of New York City, Kelly moved to Illinois to attend Bradley University, where she received a Bachelor of Arts degree and a Master of Arts degree and now serves on the board of trustees. She received a Doctorate of Philosophy degree from Northern Illinois University.

Robin L. Kelly
Chief of Staff
Illinois State Treasurer

Avis LaVelle

President
A. LaVelle Consulting Services, LLC

Avis LaVelle is president and founder of A. LaVelle Consulting Services, LLC, a strategic communications consulting company founded in 2003. A. LaVelle Consulting Services seeks to provide government and corporate clients with guidance on public affairs, public relations, government relations and crisis communications.

LaVelle formerly served as an assistant secretary of the U.S. Department of Health and Human Services during the Clinton administration. Likewise, she was press secretary to Chicago Mayor Richard M. Daley. In the private sector, LaVelle was the vice president of communications and government relations for The University of Chicago Hospitals, and was vice president of community relations and communications for Waste Management, Inc.

LaVelle is a graduate of the University of Illinois at Urbana-Champaign and Keller Graduate School of Management. With a commitment to public education, she served six years as vice president of the Chicago School Reform Board. She is a member of Apostolic Church of God and Delta Sigma Theta Sorority, Inc.

LaVelle and husband Osekre D. Hoes are the parents of one son, Robert.

**The Honorable
Casandra Lewis**

Judge
Circuit Court of Cook County

Judge Casandra Lewis serves as a circuit court judge in Chicago, Illinois. She primarily hears personal injury cases and contract disputes. The *Chicago Daily Law Bulletin* wrote of Lewis, "she is proficient and has a demeanor about her that keeps control in her courtroom while making very intelligent decisions."

Prior to being elected to the bench in 2002, Lewis was a successful trial lawyer. While in practice, she was recruited to teach at the National Institute of Trial Attorneys, an intensive training program designed to help lawyers hone their trial skills. She is an alumna of Roosevelt University and The John Marshall Law School, respectively.

Lewis is an active member of the Cook County Bar Association and the National Bar Association. She is an executive officer of the Illinois Judicial Council (IJC) and chairs its Law Day Program, which provides inner-city high school students with the opportunity to shadow judges for a day. In 2005 Lewis received the IJC Chair Person's Award for her outstanding work with the Law Day Program.

Michael W. Lewis began his career with Harris in 1976. He currently serves as executive vice president and central district executive. His responsibilities include strategically integrating the management of business segments across the network of Harris bank branches in the city of Chicago. He has specific accountability for growing the bank's commercial business, community development and consumer loans and services sectors throughout the region.

Mike is an active member of the Chicago business community and serves on several boards. He is chair of the board of Chicago United and a member of the executive committee for the Local Initiatives Support Corporation. He serves on the dean's advisory council at Western Michigan University and various other local community-based organizations. In addition, he acts as executive sponsor for the Asian-American Coalition of Employees at Harris and actively participates in the Harris Diversity Council.

Mike received an undergraduate degree in business from Western Michigan University, and was awarded a Master of Business Administration degree from Indiana University. Mike and his wife, Jacqueline, have two children.

Michael W. Lewis

Executive Vice President &
Central District Executive
Harris N.A.

State Senator Kimberly A. Lightford was re-elected to her third four-year term in the Illinois State Senate on November 7, 2006 by an overwhelming majority. First elected in 1998, she merits the distinction of being the youngest woman and African American elected to the State Senate. Lightford has served as chair of the Illinois Senate Black Caucus since she was a freshman legislator, another first.

Lightford has received numerous awards, including the Western Illinois University Alumni of the Year, the Proviso/Leyden NAACP Good Government Civic Award, and the Chicago Teachers Union Certificate of Commendation for Support of Public Education.

She holds a Bachelor of Arts degree in public communication from Western Illinois University and a Master of Public Administration degree from the University of Illinois at Springfield. She is also a member of Delta Sigma Theta Sorority, Inc.

Lightford is the devoted mother of son Isaiah. When the senator is not busy fighting for domestic policies for her communities, she enjoys spending time with her family in Maywood.

**The Honorable
Kimberly A. Lightford**

Senator, District 4
Illinois Senate

Connie L. Lindsey

Executive Vice President
Group Head, Public Entities
& Institutions
Northern Trust

Connie L. Lindsey is an executive vice president at Northern Trust. She is group head of the Public Entities and Institutions segment in Corporate and Institutional Services. Prior to this appointment, she served as director of enterprise relationship management within Worldwide Operations and Technology, where she also served as deputy business unit head. Her responsibilities there included the oversight of finance, strategic planning and business recovery functions.

Previously, Connie served as a senior vice president in Northern Trust's Personal Financial Services, responsible for community, personal and business banking for Illinois. She received a Bachelor of Arts degree in finance from the University of Wisconsin.

Connie is a board member of the Joffrey Ballet, Women Employed and a national board member of the Girl Scouts of the USA. Likewise, she is board of governors member for The Metropolitan Club of Chicago. A 2001 class fellow of Leadership Greater Chicago, she is also a member of the Chicago Finance Exchange, The Economic Club of Chicago and the School of Education advisory council at DePaul University.

Lyle Logan

Executive Vice President
Managing Director, Institutional
Sales & Client Servicing
Northern Trust

Lyle Logan is an executive vice president at Northern Trust. He is managing director of institutional sales and client servicing for Northern Trust Global Investments. Previously, he was senior vice president and head of Chicago Private Banking within Personal Financial Services (PFS). Lyle joined the company in April of 2000 as a senior vice president in PFS-Midwest. As part of the management team, he oversaw the business unit's growth strategies, and focused on the development and marketing of Northern Trust's array of services to current and prospective clients.

Prior to Northern Trust, Lyle worked at Bank of America in Chicago since 1981, where he held several leadership positions as a senior vice president in the Private Bank and Domestic Portfolio Management Group.

Lyle holds a Bachelor of Arts degree in accounting and economics from Florida A&M University and a Master of Business Administration degree in finance from The University of Chicago. His community involvement activities include serving on the boards of Chicago Public Radio, Children's Memorial Hospital, National Public Radio, The Spencer Foundation, The Field Foundation of Illinois and Scholarship Chicago.

I rwin Loud oversees the development of Muller & Monroe's private equity investment programs and serves on the investment committee. A private equity innovator, Irwin was named one of 25 to Watch over the next 25 years by *Pensions & Investments* in 1999.

Previously, he was senior portfolio manager and private equity investor for the Florida State Board of Administration (FSBA), which manages the state's $110 billion pension fund. While at FSBA, Irwin played a prominent role in launching the industry's first partnership focused exclusively on private equity co-investments. He was also the architect of the formal structuring and growth of the portfolio to $3.2 billion in commitments.

Irwin began his career at Chase Manhattan Bank, N.A., New York, where he served as a loan officer in the international and investment banking divisions.

Irwin received a Bachelor of Science, summa cum laude, and a Master of Business Administration degree from Florida A&M University, School of Business & Industry.

Irwin C. Loud III

Chief Investment Officer
Muller & Monroe Asset
Management, LLC

N ationally recognized workforce and supplier diversity expert James H. Lowry is a senior advisor for The Boston Consulting Group (BCG).

Previously a senior vice president and global diversity director, Lowry led the firm's workforce diversity, ethnic marketing and minority business development consulting practice. Prior to joining BCG, he had his own firm, James H. Lowry & Associates (JHLA), which was established in 1975. In 1978 JHLA prepared the first major study on minority business enterprise development for the Department of Commerce, entitled "New Strategy for Minority Business." In 2005 Lowry authored a new study, "Realizing the New Agenda for Minority Business Development," sponsored by the Kauffman Foundation, in conjunction with the Billion Dollar Roundtable.

Lowry received an undergraduate degree in political science from Grinnell College and a master's degree in public international affairs from the University of Pittsburgh. He attended the Program for Management Development at Harvard Business School and was elected president of his class. Lowry was honored in the inaugural class of the Minority Business Hall of Fame.

James H. Lowry

Senior Advisor
The Boston Consulting Group

**The Honorable
Blanche M. Manning**

U.S. District Court for the
Northern District of Illinois

The Honorable Blanche M. Manning was appointed in 1979 as an associate judge for the Circuit Court of Cook County. In 1984 she was selected to be the supervising judge of the largest division in the Cook County court system. In 1986 she was elevated to the Illinois Appellate Court, where she served until 1994, when she was appointed as a federal district judge. Prior to ascending to the bench, Manning was a distinguished trial lawyer and a Chicago public school teacher.

Manning earned a bachelor's degree in education from the Chicago Teachers College (now Chicago State University), a juris doctor degree from the John Marshall Law School, a Master of Arts degree from Roosevelt University and a Master of Laws degree from the University of Virginia Law School. She also received honorary degrees from Chicago State University, Roosevelt University and Lake Forest College.

In addition to belonging to numerous legal and community-based organizations and committees, Manning is a talented musician and composer and is often found playing her saxophone or clarinet with a wide variety of orchestras and jazz groups.

Michael Mayo

Partner
Deloitte & Touche LLP

Michael Mayo is a partner serving the public sector and higher education practice for Deloitte & Touche's Chicago office. He has also served as the firm's Midwest regional director for public sector services. Throughout his 30-year career, Mike has provided accounting, auditing and consulting services for some of the firm's largest government clients. He is also one of the firm's leading partners in the areas of counseling and mentoring, practice development, training and community outreach. He is active in the firm's diversity initiatives and currently serves as the advisory partner for the Chicago office's Black Employee Network.

Mike has received recognition and numerous awards, including *Crain's Chicago Business*' Forty Under Forty award, Illinois State University's Outstanding Young Alumni award and Harold Washington College's Business Professional of the Year award. He has served on the transition teams of various state and local elected officials, and has served on boards of directors and trustees for numerous organizations.

Mike received a Bachelor of Science degree in accounting and business administration from Illinois State University, and attended Loyola University's health care law program.

Pamela McElvane is chief executive officer of P&L Group, Ltd., a Chicago-based business of specialty companies offering an innovative approach to diversity recruiting business solutions. Additionally, she is currently on the boards of directors for Legacy Bancorp, the American Cancer Society and the Gamaliel Foundation. Pam was featured in the 2006 inaugural edition of *Who's Who In Black Chicago®*, and she received 2005 Women of the Year honors from the American Society Institute.

Pam is founder of *Diversity MBA Magazine*, a publication designed to reach an inclusive and global business audience. She also owns IT Professional Online publications, which include Diversity IT, Black IT and Hispanic IT online magazines. Moreover, DRI Staffing is an online community that provides professional development resources, and DRI Consulting provides leadership development and training.

Pam received a bachelor's degree in English, sociology and social welfare; an MBA in finance and international marketing; and a master's degree in public policy from the University at California, Berkeley.

Josh, 7, and Cameron, 5, are her two boys. She attends Triedstone Full Gospel Baptist Church, where she leads their strategy team.

Pamela A. McElvane, MBA

Chief Executive Officer
P&L Group, Ltd.

Lester McKeever, an attorney and certified public accountant, is head of the Chicago CPA and consulting firm of Washington, Pittman & McKeever, one of the oldest African-American-owned accounting firms.

McKeever received a Bachelor of Science degree in accountancy from the University of Illinois at Champaign-Urbana and a juris doctorate from the IIT-Chicago-Kent College of Law. His professional accomplishments include a three-year term as chair of the Federal Reserve Bank of Chicago, currently serving as chair of United Way of Metropolitan Chicago and past chair of the Chicago Urban League.

Through the years, McKeever has committed his time and financial resources to numerous civic causes. He is a member of the Civic Committee of the Commercial Club of Chicago and treasurer of the University of Illinois board of trustees, currently serving his 13th year. Recently, DePaul University conferred upon him an honorary doctorate degree.

He and his wife, Nancy, have two adult children, who are also attorneys, and five grandchildren.

Lester H. McKeever Jr.

Managing Principal
Washington, Pittman &
McKeever, LLC

CHICAGO'S MOST INFLUENTIAL

Cheryl Mayberry McKissack

Founder, President &
Chief Executive Officer
Nia Enterprises, LLC

Cheryl Mayberry McKissack is the founder, president and chief executive officer of Nia Enterprises, LLC, a Chicago-based research, systems integration and marketing services firm founded in January of 2000. Nia Enterprises, LLC provides opt-in, permission-based marketing data solutions for the growing and specialized market of African-American women and their families.

Prior to founding Nia Enterprises, McKissack enjoyed a successful 23-year corporate career in technology. In 2005 she was named an associate adjunct professor of entrepreneurship at the Kellogg School of Business, Northwestern University. McKissack recently co-edited *The Nia Guide* series of books for black women focusing on career, work-life balance, and health and wellness.

McKissack, a native of Seattle, Washington, received a Bachelor of Science degree from Seattle University, and in two-and-a-half years earned a Master of Business Administration degree from Northwestern's J.L. Kellogg School of Management.

She serves on the board of directors of The PrivateBanCorp (NASDAQ: PVTB), and as a director of the Deluxe Corporation (NYSE: DLX).

Deryl McKissack

President & Chief Executive Officer
McKissack & McKissack

Deryl McKissack is president and chief executive officer of McKissack & McKissack, an architectural, engineering and program management firm. The firm was established in 1990 with $1,000 and no clients or employees. Today, McKissack & McKissack has 150 employees with four office locations. In 2002 McKissack expanded to Chicago, Illinois, building on the successes she had established. She recently opened offices in Miami, Florida, and Baltimore, Maryland. The firm was recently recognized in *Engineering News-Record* as the 54th largest construction management firm.

McKissack & McKissack provides quality service to health care, environmental, government, education, residential, sports and recreational, commercial, and transportation-related construction projects. Notable projects include the National Institutes of Health, the restoration of the Thomas Jefferson and Lincoln Memorials, the renovation of the main Treasury Building, the Chicago and D.C. Public Schools, the Chicago Housing Authority, the New Washington Convention Center, RFK Stadium, O'Hare International Airport Modernization Program, and Chicago's McCormick Place expansion.

McKissack holds a bachelor's degree in civil engineering from Howard University.

The Honorable Reverend James T. Meeks is the senior pastor of Salem Baptist Church of Chicago. Under his leadership, the church has served the Roseland Community since 1985 and has more than 22,000 members. Serving in the Illinois Senate since 2003, Meeks has supported legislation to improve the lives of underserved people in Illinois, particularly in his fight for education-funding reform.

In 1998 Meeks led the rally to "dry up" Roseland by collecting votes to close 26 area liquor stores in oversaturated areas. He also established the House of Hope, a $50 million, 10,000-seat worship and community activity center.

In addition to serving the 15th Illinois Senatorial District, he chairs the Illinois Legislative Black Caucus, and serves as the executive vice president of the National RainbowPUSH Coalition.

A native of Chicago, Meeks is a graduate of Bishop College in Dallas. He and Jamell, his wife of more than 26 years, have four children.

**The Honorable
Rev. James T. Meeks**

Senator, District 15
Illinois Senate

Marquis D. Miller is executive director of the Chicago State University Foundation. He is responsible for all institutional advancement activities, including fundraising and resource development, public and media relations, and alumni programs for the university.

A member of Omega Psi Phi Fraternity, Inc., Miller is a proud graduate of The Ohio State University. Currently, he is a member of the board of directors of the Association of Fundraising Professionals (AFP) Chicago chapter, and co-chair of the diversity and fellows committee. He is also a member of the board of directors of the Trinity Higher Education Corporation and chair of the program development committee.

Miller is a member of the Leadership Council of Chicago United, Inc., and serves as a member of the Audience Diversity and Development Committee of the Museum of Contemporary Art. Additionally, he has served as a member of the Mid-Ohio Regional Planning Commission and on the boards of Lakefront Supportive Housing, The Harvard School of Chicago, Prevent Blindness America and Prevent Blindness Ohio, and the Columbus Speech & Hearing Center.

Marquis D. Miller

Executive Director
Chicago State University Foundation

Ralph G. Moore

Founder
Ralph G. Moore & Associates

Ralph G. Moore, a certified public accountant, is the founder of Ralph G. Moore & Associates (RGMA), a leading consultant in the area of supplier diversity and minority business development, worldwide.

Before founding RGMA in 1979, Moore was a staff accountant at Arthur Andersen & Co., vice president for Chicago Community Ventures, Inc. and a controller for Parker House Sausage Company.

A graduate of Southern Illinois University, he has contributed to the *Harvard Business Review* and *MBE Magazine*, and has lectured internationally, including multiple engagements in Canada, South Africa and the United Kingdom.

Moore's various civic activities include the director/chair of Habilitative Systems, Inc., the co-founder and past president of the Alliance of Business Leaders and Entrepreneurs, and the director of Junior Achievement of Chicago and the Chicago Minority Business Development Council. He is also on the board of trustees for The University of Chicago Medical Center and City Colleges of Chicago. Additionally, he has been named Entrepreneur of the Year by *Inc.* magazine and Ernst & Young, and has received the Minority Business Advocate Award, to name a few.

Minister Ishmael R. Muhammad

Assistant Minister to
The Honorable Louis Farrakhan
Nation of Islam

In 1964 Minister Ishmael R. Muhammad was born in Albuquerque, New Mexico, to the leader of the Nation of Islam, the Most Honorable Elijah Muhammad, and to the multitalented Tynnetta Muhammad. He enjoys the distinct honor of serving as the assistant minister to the Honorable Minister Louis Farrakhan at the Nation of Islam's headquarters in Chicago.

Ishmael served as one of the principal coordinators of the historic Million Man March that drew more than one million black men to Washington, D.C. He has planned and organized events and conferences throughout the U.S., and has been featured in local, national, and international print and broadcast media.

His travels have taken him to Egypt, Saudi Arabia, Jerusalem, Pakistan, West Africa, Europe, New Zealand and South America. Ishmael studied in Cuernavaca, Mexico, for 17 years, and is bilingual, speaking fluent Spanish and English.

A loving husband and father of seven, Ishmael is an outstanding spokesman for the upliftment of blacks throughout the world in the new millennium. His greatest desire is to help resurrect, redeem and restore black people in America and throughout the world.

D r. Anthony E. Munroe is president of Munroe Management Group, LLC and Advocate Trinity Hospital. He was named one of the Top 25 Minority Healthcare Executives in the United States by *Modern Healthcare* magazine, and was honored with the Robert S. Hudgens National Award as Healthcare Executive of the Year in 2003 by the American College of Healthcare Executives. He is internationally recognized for expertise in strategy, cultural competency, health systems leadership and as a health care futurist.

Munroe completed a Doctor of Education degree in health education at Columbia University. He holds a Master of Business Administration degree from Northwestern University and a Master of Public Health degree from Columbia University.

A life member of Alpha Phi Alpha Fraternity, Inc., Munroe was one of the first ten Kellogg Foundation and Congressional Black Caucus Foundation's national public health fellows. The mayor of Miami-Dade, Florida, recognized him for service and expertise with a proclamation designating an Anthony E. Munroe Day. The recipient of a prestigious congressional certificate for his work in health care, Munroe has presented at the International AIDS Conference.

Anthony Earle Munroe, Ed.D., FACHE

President
Munroe Management Group, LLC
Advocate Trinity Hospital

T he Honorable Stephanie D. Neely, a native Chicagoan from the Southside, brings to the Office of Treasurer of the City of Chicago more than 20 years of financial services experience with leading investment banking institutions. As treasurer, she is responsible for investing public dollars to insure the best return for taxpayers.

A former vice president at Northern Trust Global Investments, Neely was responsible for working with public and corporate pension funds. As treasurer, her duties also include serving on five public pension boards. As an African-American woman, Neely created opportunities for minority- and women-owned financial services firms by fostering relationships with Northern Trust, and thereby helped them establish a foothold in the industry.

Neely holds a degree in economics from Smith College and a Master of Business Administration in finance from The University of Chicago. She has served on the board of several civic and business organizations.

Neely was appointed city treasurer by Mayor Richard M. Daley in December of 2006, and won a citywide municipal election in February of 2007.

The Honorable Stephanie D. Neely

Treasurer
City of Chicago

Martin Nesbitt

President &
Chief Executive Officer
The Parking Spot

Martin Nesbitt is president and chief executive officer of The Parking Spot. He founded and conceptualized the company in 1997 in partnership with Chicago's Pritzker family, and is responsible for running all strategic and operating aspects of the business, which generates $80 million in revenue and has 19 locations and 900 employees. The company has been featured in *The New York Times*, *USA Today*, *Fortune Small Business* and *Entrepreneur* magazine for its innovative approach to an old-line business.

Prior to creating The Parking Spot, Nesbitt was an equity partner at Jones Lang LaSalle, one of the nation's leading corporate real estate firms. Before that, he was employed by General Motors Acceptance Corporation in the area of financial planning, where he became a GM fellow.

Nesbitt is currently a trustee of Chicago's Museum of Contemporary Art, chairman of the board of commissioners of the Chicago Housing Authority, and a board member of The University of Chicago Laboratory Schools.

Nesbitt received a Master of Business Administration degree from The University of Chicago and a bachelor's degree in economics and management from Albion College.

The Honorable Barack Obama

Senator, Illinois
U.S. Senate

The Honorable Barack Obama has dedicated his life to public service as a community organizer, civil rights attorney and leader in the Illinois State Senate. He continues his fight for working families in Illinois and throughout the country.

Senator Obama serves on the Health, Education, Labor and Pensions Committee, the Senate Committee on Homeland Security and Government Affairs, the Veterans' Affairs Committee, and is a member of the Foreign Relations Committee. He focuses on the challenges of a globalized world with fresh thinking and bold ideas. Recognizing the threat posed by weapons of mass destruction and America's addiction to oil, he guides nonproliferation efforts and promotes responsible energy use. He has championed congressional ethics reform and continues to lead on the issues that will define America in the 21st century.

Obama graduated from Columbia University and Harvard Law School, where he was the first African-American president of the *Harvard Law Review*.

Obama is especially proud of being a husband and a father of two daughters. He and his wife, Michelle, live on Chicago's South Side, where they attend Trinity United Church of Christ.

Dr. Nuru-Deen Olowopopo is the president of Irok Obstetrics and Gynecological Services Ltd., a corporation that takes care of women's health issues. He is also a member of Chicago's Commission on Human Relations, and chairs the Mayor's Advisory Committee on African Affairs.

In 2002 President George Bush appointed Olowopopo to the United States Selective Service Board for the state of Illinois. Additionally, he is on the board of directors of Advocate Health Partners of Illinois, The Provident Foundation, African International House, the Trinity Hospital Governing Council and the Association of Nigerian Physicians in the Americas. He is also the president of Advocate Trinity Health Partners.

Olowopopo received a bachelor's degree from the University of Illinois in Chicago (UIC) and a Doctor of Medicine degree from the Abraham Lincoln School of Medicine at UIC. He completed his internship in internal medicine and his residency in obstetrics and gynecology at Cook County Hospital.

Olowopopo was born in Lagos, Nigeria. He is married to Cilla Esiri-Olowopopo, and the couple has two daughters, Fausat and Sherifat, and two grandsons, Raheem and Qudus.

Nuru-Deen Olowopopo, M.D.
President & Chief Executive Officer
Irok Obstetrics and
Gynecological Services Ltd.

In 1989 Hoyett Owens founded I Like It Communications, Inc., a minority-owned and operated advertising/public relations agency specializing in consumer promotions. The firm's clients include TV One, Darden Restaurants, Quaker Oats and Wm. Wrigley Jr. Owens' leadership is represented by his successful signature programs and creative, results-driven strategies.

He began his professional career with one of the nation's Fortune 500 jewelers. After tripling the region's annual sales, which exceeded $25 million, he was promoted to vice president of operations.

In 1983 Owens was recruited by WVON, a Chicago radio station. His entrepreneurial skills quickly led to his promotion to general manager, and he changed the format to talk radio. In 1996 Owens purchased All Printing & Graphics, Inc., a full-service, commercial sheet-fed printing company that is now the largest African-American-owned printing company in the country.

Owens graduated from Jackson State University with a bachelor's degree in speech communications. He is on the board of directors of PII and is treasurer for ABLE. He also serves on panels and provides presentations to help other businesses pursue economic development and partnerships.

Hoyett W. Owens Jr.
President &
Chief Executive Officer
I Like It Communications, Inc.

Mary K. Palmore, M.D.

Chair, Section of
Obstetrics & Gynecology
Advocate Trinity Hospital

Chicago native Mary K. Palmore, M.D., is a graduate of Kenwood High School. She earned a Bachelor of Arts degree in biology premed from Hampton University and a Doctor of Medicine degree from Rush University, where she was the only African-American woman in her class. Palmore is board-certified in obstetrics and gynecology, and is the current chair of the section of obstetrics and gynecology at Advocate Trinity Hospital.

She has been honored with many awards, including The Distinctive Imprint Award and the Trailblazer Award from the North Dallas Business and Professional Women's Organization for being the first African-American female OB-GYN in Dallas. She is also a 2006 graduate of Leadership America.

Palmore enjoys lecturing and presenting seminars for the church, civic organizations and her sorority, Alpha Kappa Alpha Sorority, Inc. She currently serves on the International Conference Planning Committee for Alpha Kappa Alpha. As a member of Trinity United Church of Christ, she sings in the women's chorus and is a member of the praise and worship teams.

Palmore is in private practice and is currently developing Rophe Med-Spa.

Roderick A. Palmore

Executive Vice President,
General Counsel & Secretary
Sara Lee Corporation

Roderick A. Palmore is executive vice president, general counsel and secretary of Sara Lee Corporation. He is a member of the company's senior management team, and he chairs Sara Lee's Global Business Practices Committee. He is also responsible for the company's internal audit, special investigations, risk management, environment and safety functions.

Rick is a director of Nuveen Investments, Inc. and a member of the board of directors of the Chicago Board Options Exchange. He has served on the board of directors of the Association of Corporate Counsel, Chicago Bar Foundation, the Legal Assistance Foundation of Chicago, the Public Interest Law Initiative and United Way of Metropolitan Chicago. He has also served on the Chicago Bar Association's board of managers. In addition, Rick is a member of the board of trustees of the Chicago Symphony Orchestra.

Rick received a Bachelor of Arts degree in economics from Yale University, where he received such honors as National Achievement Scholar, Kenneth MacLeish Scholar and Yale Alumni Association of Pittsburgh Scholar. He received a juris doctorate degree from The University of Chicago Law School.

The Honorable Dr. Sallie D. Penman is the first African-American woman to hold an elected office in South Holland. She was appointed in 2003 and elected in 2004.

In addition to serving the Village of South Holland, Penman is the director of the Illinois Administrators' Academy in Chicago, providing leadership development for 1,800 administrators of Chicago Public Schools. She has received Phi Delta Kappa Educator of the Year twice and the Distinguished Leadership Award, and was featured in *South Holland Today* as a resident you should know.

Penman holds a bachelor's degree in education and a master's degree in administration and supervision from Chicago State University, and a doctorate in educational leadership from Nova Southeastern University.

From politics to education, Penman has provided an African-American voice in key policy decision-making by serving on boards, such as the South Holland Planning and Development Commission and the Illinois State Action Education Leadership Project. She is also president of the Illinois Staff Development Council and chair of the Continuous Improvement Partnership, an advisory board to the state superintendent of education.

The Honorable Dr. Sallie D. Penman

Clerk
Village of South Holland

Aurie Pennick is the executive director and treasurer for the Field Foundation of Illinois, where she oversees approximately $65 million in foundation assets. Pennick is an attorney with many years of experience in the civic and philanthropic sector. She is the recipient of numerous awards and appointments, which include the U.S. delegation for the 1996 Global Conference on Cities in Istanbul, Turkey; the Aspen Institute Fellowship in 2002; the 2003 Human Relations Award from the Chicago Commission on Human Relations; and the 2006 Handy Lindsey Award for Inclusiveness and Diversity in Philanthropy. She recently co-authored an article on affordable housing published in the book *The New Chicago*.

Pennick has a bachelor's and a master's degree from the University of Illinois-Chicago and a law degree from John Marshall Law School. She serves on the boards of the Field Museum, the Rosalind Franklin University of Medicine and Science and the Chicago Network.

Pennick has two very talented daughters.

Aurie A. Pennick

Executive Director & Treasurer
Field Foundation of Illinois

**The Honorable
Toni Preckwinkle**

Alderman, Ward 4
City of Chicago

The Honorable Toni Preckwinkle has served as alderman of the Fourth Ward in Chicago since 1991 and represents approximately 60,000 residents. She serves on several city council committees, including the Finance, Rules and Ethics, Energy, Environmental Protection and Public Utilities, Parks and Recreation, and Landmarks committees. She also consults with developers and other business entities on the building of new housing in the ward.

In 2003 Toni formed Quad Communities Development Corporation with a diverse group of neighborhood leaders. She has received more than 25 awards from government, civil rights, religious, business and community organizations for her innovative ideas and service.

A past president of Disabled Adult Residential Enterprises (1985-1987), Toni serves on the board of directors of the Illinois Council Against Hand Gun Violence. Additionally, she is political director of the South Side chapter of the Independent Voters of Illinois, and executive director and coordinator for economic development for the Chicago Jobs Council.

Toni holds a bachelor's and a master's degree from The University of Chicago. Her husband of 38 years is Zeus Preckwinkle, a schoolteacher, and they have two children.

Quintin E. Primo III

Chairman & Chief Executive Officer
Capri Capital Advisors

Quintin Primo is chairman and chief executive officer of Capri Capital Advisors, a real estate investment management firm headquartered in Chicago. The firm has more than $2.7 billion in real estate assets currently under management, representing pension funds, governmental agencies and other institutional investors. He co-founded the firm in 1992. He is also chairman of Capri Select Income, a real estate mezzanine investment fund.

Primo received a Master of Business Administration degree from Harvard University Graduate School of Business Administration and a Bachelor of Science degree in finance from Indiana University. He is a voting member of the Pension Real Estate Association and Urban Land Institute and a board member of the Real Estate Roundtable.

Quintin is a member of the Federal Reserve Bank of Chicago Seventh District Advisory Council and The Economic Club of Chicago. He also serves as a board trustee of The Chicago Community Trust, (Episcopal) Church Pension Group and The University of Chicago Hospitals. Additionally, he is chairman of the Primo Center for Women and Children, and founder and chairman of the Real Estate Executive Council.

The Honorable Kwame Raoul was appointed to fill the vacancy of U.S. Senator Barack Obama on November 6, 2004. He hit the ground running in the Illinois legislature by successfully advancing legislation promoting civil justice, early childhood education, domestic violence prevention and political reform. Raoul was assigned the leadership role of chair of the of the Senate's Pensions and Investment Committee, where he has championed the effort to expand opportunities for minority- and women-owned financial services firms. In his short time in the General Assembly, he has been elected chair of the Senate's Black Caucus.

Raoul is a graduate of DePaul University and Chicago-Kent College of Law. He is a former county prosecutor and higher education attorney, and has served on the board of directors of the Cook County Bar Association, International Child Care and Kappa Alpha Psi Fraternity, Inc.

Raoul was born on September 30, 1964, to Haitian immigrants, Janin Raoul, M.D., and Marie Therese Raoul. He is a lifelong resident of the Hyde Park and Kenwood community, where he lives with his wife, Kali, and his children, Che and Mizan.

The Honorable Kwame Raoul

Senator, District 13
Illinois Senate

James Reynolds Jr. is founder, chairman and chief executive officer of Loop Capital Markets, LLC (LCM), one of the largest minority-owned investment banking and brokerage firms in the country. A native Chicagoan, he is responsible for all investment banking, trading and institutional sales activity. LCM has more than 75 professionals in its Chicago headquarters and ten offices around the country.

In forming LCM in September of 1997, the client was Reynolds' primary focus, which allowed the firm to work for some of the top corporate, money management and municipal institutions in the United States. Previously, he was a top municipal salesman and manager at Smith Barney, PaineWebber and Merrill Lynch.

Reynolds is actively involved on many nonprofit boards, including the Chicago Historical Society, the Chicago Urban League, Chicago State University, the Levy Institute/Kellogg School of Management, Lincoln Academy of Illinois, the Lyric Opera of Chicago, The University of Chicago Hospitals and Viterbo University.

Reynolds holds a Master of Management degree in finance from Northwestern University's Kellogg School of Management and a bachelor's degree in political science from the University of Wisconsin-La Crosse.

James Reynolds Jr.

Founder, Chairman &
Chief Executive Officer
Loop Capital Markets, LLC

CHICAGO'S MOST INFLUENTIAL

Linda Johnson Rice

President & Chief Executive Officer
Johnson Publishing Company, Inc.

Linda Johnson Rice is president and chief executive officer of Johnson Publishing Company, Inc., publishers of *Ebony* and *Jet* magazines and the No. 1 African-American publishing company in the world. Rice oversees the corporation's domestic and international business operations, which include Fashion Fair Cosmetics, Ebony Fashion Fair, Ebony/Jet Entertainment Group, JPC Consumer Products and the JPC Book Division.

Rice is the recipient of the Robie Award for Achievement in Industry, the Tower of Power Award of The Trumpet Awards from Turner Broadcasting, and the Alumni of the Year Award from the Northwestern University Kellogg Graduate School of Management's Black Management Association.

Rice serves on the board of directors of Bausch & Lomb, Inc., Kimberly-Clark Corporation, Omnicom, MoneyGram International, Inc., The Art Institute of Chicago, the United Negro College Fund and several others. She also sits on the Smithsonian Institution National Museum of African-American History and Culture advisory council, and is a member of the Magazine Publishers Association.

Rice holds a bachelor's degree in journalism from the University of Southern California and a Master of Business Administration degree from Northwestern University.

Julieanna L. Richardson

Founder & Executive Director
The HistoryMakers

Julieanna L. Richardson is a public historian, and the founder and executive director of *The HistoryMakers*. She has a unique and diverse background in theatre, television production and the cable television industry.

Richardson is a magna cum laude graduate of Brandeis University, where she double-majored in theatre arts and American studies. After conducting oral histories on the Harlem Renaissance and Langston Hughes, she attended Harvard Law School. Following graduation, she worked as a corporate lawyer, prior to serving in the early 1980s as the cable administrator for the City of Chicago Office of Cable Communications. While there, Richardson established the Chicago Cable Commission, the city's regulatory body. She went on to found Shop Chicago, a regionally based home shopping channel.

Richardson was driven to start *The HistoryMakers* out of a strong desire to make a difference and to leave a living legacy. Last year, the University of Illinois at Chicago's Great Cities Institute named her its Vernon D. Jarrett Fellow.

The Honorable Al Riley represents the 38th District of Illinois. He also serves as the Rich Township supervisor. Prior to these positions, he served as a township trustee in Rich Township and three terms as a trustee in the Village of Olympia Fields.

Riley is on the board of numerous organizations, including the executive board of the Calumet Council, Boy Scouts of America; and the Illinois Philharmonic Orchestra. He is also the former vice president of the Unity Coalition of the South Suburbs.

A certified urban planner and statistician by profession, Riley has held executive posts in the public and private sectors. He also has numerous publications in education, economic analysis, cancer research and health planning.

He holds a bachelor's degree in geography from Chicago State University, master's degrees in urban planning and statistics, and he completed a doctoral study in public policy analysis at the University of Illinois at Chicago. Additionally, Riley has taught at three universities, most recently at Governors State University, where he has worked for ten years as an adjunct professor, specializing in statistics and policy courses.

The Honorable Al Riley

Representative, District 38
Illinois House of Representatives

Theresa Robinson joined MetLife in San Francisco, California, and after numerous financial positions, was promoted to vice president and chief financial officer. She is currently senior financial advisor to the Agency Distribution Group's executive vice president and responsible for the departments that support the MetLife Career Agency sales force and the New England Financial sales operations.

Her responsibilities include strategic planning, financial management and analysis, with the goal of managing field agency profitability to improve the Agency Distribution Group's profit and loss, and contribution to individual business earnings. She manages a $1.5 billion expense portfolio to drive top-line performance through profitable growth.

Theresa is passionate about helping associates and partners understand how each piece of the financial puzzle contributes to MetLife's success. She is happy when partners and associates reach career milestones and discover new ways to achieve business success.

Theresa has a bachelor's degree in finance and managerial accounting from California State University, and is a member of the National Association of Black Accountants. She lives in Aurora with her husband, Glenn, and is the proud mother of three children.

Theresa Robinson

Vice President &
Chief Financial Officer
MetLife

CHICAGO'S MOST INFLUENTIAL

Desirée Rogers

President
Peoples Gas and North Shore Gas

D esirée Rogers is recognized as an innovative leader with a proven track record of developing creative solutions to transition organizations in challenging circumstances. She is also known as an exceptional communicator and a community advocate.

Rogers has headed up two major organizations, the Illinois Lottery and Peoples Gas. While at the Illinois Lottery, her team's promotion of instant tickets helped to establish a new paradigm in the industry. As the president of Peoples Gas, she has helped transform a traditional utility into a responsive, customer-centric, gas delivery company.

Consistently acknowledged for her business leadership, Rogers was named one of the Top 25 Women to Watch by *Crain's Chicago Business* (2007), as well as one of the Top 50 Most Powerful African American Business Women (2006), and Top 75 Most Powerful Blacks in Corporate America (2005) by *Black Enterprise*. She serves on the board of directors of Equity Residential and Blue Cross Blue Shield of Illinois.

Rogers earned a Master of Business Administration degree from Harvard University and a Bachelor of Arts degree from Wellesley College.

John W. Rogers Jr.

Chair, Chief Executive Officer &
Chief Investment Officer
Ariel Capital Management, LLC

J ohn W. Rogers Jr. founded Ariel Capital Management, LLC in 1983 on the idea that wealth can be created over time. By adhering to a consistent investment philosophy based on patience and independent thinking, John has transformed Ariel into a widely recognized mutual fund company and money management firm with nearly $16 billion in assets under management. He is the lead portfolio manager of Ariel Fund, which celebrated its 20-year anniversary in 2006; Ariel Appreciation Fund; and the firm's small and mid-cap institutional portfolios.

John serves on the boards of many professional and civic organizations, including Aon, Exelon and McDonald's. He is a director of the Chicago Urban League, and the John S. and James L. Knight Foundation, and a trustee of The University of Chicago. Additionally, his investment expertise has brought him to the forefront of media attention. John is frequently quoted in business publications, and has made appearances on television shows ranging from *Louis Rukeyser's Wall Street* to *The Oprah Winfrey Show*.

John graduated in 1980 from Princeton University, where he was also captain of the varsity basketball team.

The Honorable Bobby L. Rush was elected a member of Congress in the U.S. House of Representatives on November 3, 1992. In this role, Rush sits on the powerful House Committee on Energy and Commerce, and serves on the Subcommittee on Commerce, Trade and Consumer Protection; the Subcommittee on Telecommunications and the Internet; and the Subcommittee on Health. He is also a co-chair of the Congressional Biotech Caucus.

Rush has brought nearly $2 billion of federal funding to the First Congressional District of Illinois since his election.

A co-founder of the Illinois Black Panther Party in 1968, Rush operated the Party's Free Breakfast for Children program.

He received a bachelor's degree from Roosevelt University and a master's degree in political science from the University of Illinois at Chicago. He holds a second master's degree in theological studies from McCormick Seminary.

In addition to his congressional duties, Rush is pastor of Beloved Community Christian Church in Chicago. He and his wife, Carolyn, are the parents of six children.

The Honorable Bobby L. Rush

Representative,
1st District of Illinois
U.S. House of Representatives

Since 2004 Carol Sagers has directed McDonald's award-winning national marketing programs targeted at the African-American and Pan-Asian consumer markets. Prior to McDonald's, she was the principal at CHS Marketing Consultants, a company she founded and operated for eight years. CHS Marketing Consultants serviced clients including Kraft Foods, McDonald's, the Chicago Park District, The Federated Group, Soft Sheen Products and Unilever. Carol also worked for Soft Sheen Products in positions ranging from group marketing manager to vice president of marketing.

Carol is the past president of the South Suburban Chicago Chapter of Jack & Jill of America, Inc., and serves as the president of the Chicago Chapter of Carats, Inc. A member of The Links, Inc. and Alpha Kappa Alpha Sorority, Inc., she was named 2007 Trailblazer Working Mother of the Year by *Working Mother* magazine.

With an MBA from Washington University in St. Louis and a bachelor's degree in advertising from the University of Illinois, Carol is an adjunct marketing professor with American Intercontinental University.

She is married to Rudolph Sagers Jr., and has two sons, Ryan and Randall.

Carol Hillsman Sagers

Director, U.S. Marketing
McDonald's USA

Lovie Smith

Head Coach
Chicago Bears

Lovie Smith is in his fourth year as head coach of the Chicago Bears. Smith led the Bears to the 2005 NFC North Division title, earned NFL Coach of the Year honors in his second season, and led the Bears to Super Bowl XLI.

The 13th head coach in Bears history effective January 15, 2004, Smith served three seasons as the defensive coordinator of the St. Louis Rams. He helped the Rams to the Super Bowl in 2001 and became assistant head coach in 2003. He also coached linebackers with the Tampa Bay Buccaneers from 1996 to 2000.

Smith coached 13 years at six different colleges after beginning his coaching career in 1980 at his hometown high school in Big Sandy, Texas. He was a two-time All-American and three-time all-conference defensive back in college at Tulsa.

Smith and his wife, MaryAnne, have three sons, Mikal, Matthew and Miles, and twin grandsons, Malachi and Noah. An active contributor to the American Diabetes Association, he and his wife started a foundation to help qualified high school students from low socio-economic backgrounds afford and attend college.

Thurman Smith

Executive Vice President &
Chief Credit Officer
ShoreBank

Thurman "Tony" Smith heads the commercial credit business lines for ShoreBank, the nation's oldest and largest community development bank. In this capacity, he manages a $1.3 billion loan portfolio through offices located in Chicago, Cleveland and Detroit.

Tony also serves on the board of directors for Community Investment Corporation, one of Chicago's most important conduits for the preservation of affordable housing; the board of trustees for Morgan Park Academy, one of Chicago's top Blue Ribbon schools; and the Committee for Franchise Development and Diversity, an initiative of the Center for Development and Progress aimed at growing minority- and women-owned businesses. Additionally, he serves on various regionally focused advisory groups for the Chicago city treasurer, the Chicago Urban League and the Minority Contractor Development Program (Department of Commerce).

Tony is a graduate of the Naval engineering program and Northern Virginia College. He received a master's degree in finance from the University of Southern California. A native of Chicago, he is a single parent and the proud father of Lawrence M. Smith.

Melody Spann-Cooper is the president of WVON Radio, Chicago's only African-American-owned and -operated radio station, and serves as the chair of Midway Broadcasting Corporation, the station's parent company. She is the only female to hold these positions in the country's third-largest broadcast market.

With its urban talk format, WVON is the oldest black-oriented station in Chicago, and is lauded as a leading source of information and community empowerment.

In August of 2006, Spann-Cooper created a unique relationship with Clear Channel, forging a historic agreement between one of the nation's largest owners of radio stations and one of the oldest African-American-owned radio stations in the country. This agreement is a major upgrade for WVON, previously a 15-hour-a-day broadcasting entity. With this power deal, WVON will now be able to broadcast 24 hours a day, with a wattage increase from 1,000 to 10,000.

Among her accomplishments, Spann-Cooper has been recognized by the *Chicago Sun-Times* as one of the Ten Most Powerful Women in Media, and *Crain's Chicago Business* ranks her as one of the 100 most influential women in Chicago.

Melody Spann-Cooper

President
WVON Radio

As general manager at the LaSalle Bank Building, Nicole Spencer oversees the day-to-day operation of the 1.2 million square-foot landmark property. Leading a team of 80, she manages the building's $30 million budget, identifies and implements process improvements and oversees capital improvement projects. Client satisfaction, tenant retention and service innovations are hallmarks of her management style.

Spencer is a licensed attorney and real estate broker with almost ten years of experience managing Class A office properties in Chicago's central business district. In addition to her property responsibilities, she is a member of the Jones Lang LaSalle Chicago markets regional hiring committee and the Jones Lang LaSalle Americas Diversity Council. Within the Chicago civic community, she is chair of the Building Owners and Managers Association Chicago Diversity Committee and a board member of North Lawndale College Preparatory, a charter high school.

Spencer earned a juris doctorate from Northwestern University and a Bachelor of Arts degree in political science from Bryn Mawr College.

Raised in St. Thomas, U.S. Virgin Islands, and Washington, D.C., Spencer enjoys Chicago's rich cultural and social diversity.

Nicole A. B. Spencer

Vice President &
General Manager
Jones Lang LaSalle

Soul and gospel artist Mavis Staples possesses one of the most recognizable and treasured voices in contemporary music. From her early days sharing lead vocals with her groundbreaking family group, The Staple Singers, to her powerful solo recordings, Staples is an inspirational force in modern popular culture and music.

A 40-plus year veteran of the music scene, Staples is a Rock and Roll Hall of Fame Museum inductee. She is also one of VH1's 100 Greatest Women of Rock and Roll. Staples, both with The Staple Singers and on her own, is responsible for blazing a rhythm and blues trail while never relinquishing her gospel roots.

Her voice has influenced artists from Bob Dylan to Prince, who dubbed her "the epitome of soul." Staples has appeared with several dignitaries, some of which include the Reverend Dr. Martin Luther King Jr.; Bill Cosby; Presidents Kennedy, Carter and Clinton; Janis Joplin; Pink Floyd; Santana; and Tom Petty & The Heartbreakers. She has also recorded with Bob Dylan, Los Lobos, Aretha Franklin, Marty Stuart and many others.

Mavis Staples

National Recording Artist

Commissioner Robert Steele has more than 30 years of experience as a public servant of Chicago and Cook County. Steele is a results-driven county board commissioner who is focusing on making meaningful and measurable contributions to the residents of Cook County. He is also a passionate and outstanding community leader with a history of designing and implementing programs within Chicago communities to benefit local residents and businesses.

Steele graduated with a Bachelor of Science degree in business administration and computer science from Morgan State University in Baltimore, Maryland. He holds certifications from Neighbor Works America, Washington, D.C., and San Francisco, California. Additionally, he is a graduate and fellow of Leadership Greater Chicago.

Steele enjoys spending time with his family, golfing and travel.

The Honorable Robert Steele

Commissioner, 2nd District
Cook County Board of Commissioners

M arshette M. Turner is the national director of the International Trade Bureau (ITB) of the RainbowPUSH Coalition. In this capacity, she oversees a membership base of more than 800 members nationally as well as internationally. The ITB is the business arm of the organization, and members are minority- and women-owned business enterprises seeking inclusion in the corporate community.

Marshette also hosts the live *Saturday Morning Forum* for RainbowPUSH, which airs every Saturday morning at 10:00 a.m. CST. She is a Chicago native and well rooted in the word of God. Marshette is a member of the American Association for Women in Community Colleges, the National Association of Black Journalists and the RainbowPUSH Coalition.

She received an undergraduate degree in English from DePaul University, and is currently considering completing a master's program with a focus on broadcast journalism.

Marshette is the loving wife of Vernal Turner and the cherished and proud mother of Tyler Ben-Franklin.

Marshette M. Turner

National Director
International Trade Bureau
RainbowPUSH Coalition

H ailed as the "Queen of Gospel," Albertina Walker was born in 1929 in Chicago, Illinois. At the age of 4, she began singing.

In 1951 Walker organized her group, the world-famous Caravans. In this legendary group, she discovered and launched the careers of Inez Andrews, Shirley Caesar, Cassietta George, Dorothy Norwood, Delores Washington and James Cleveland.

Since becoming a solo artist in 1973, Walker has recorded 71 albums, and has received a 1995 Grammy Award, 11 Grammy Award nominations, the 2005 Grammy President's Merit Award, five Gold Records, three Stellar Awards, and a 2004 Trumpet Award. Additionally, she was inducted into the Gospel Music Hall of Fame, had a Chicago street renamed in her honor, received an honorary degree from the Chicago Theological Seminary, and received a 2005 National Endowment for the Arts award. In 2002 President Bush honored Walker for her contributions to gospel music at the White House in Washington, D.C.

In 1988 she founded The Albertina Walker Scholarship Foundation for the Creative and Performing Arts, a nonprofit 501(c)3 organization, that offers financial assistance in the form of scholarships.

Albertina Walker

Gospel Music Artist

Roxanne Ward

President
Black Corporate Directors Conference

Roxanne Ward is president of the Black Corporate Directors Conference, a forum for seasoned black directors of publicly traded companies founded in 2002 by Ariel Capital Management, LLC and Russell Reynolds Associates. She is also vice president and corporate liaison of Ariel Capital Management, LLC.

Outside of her distinguished business career, Roxanne has been actively involved with many civic and community organizations. She is a member of the City of Chicago Board of Education, and sits on the board of directors for WTTW and the Safer Foundation. Additionally, she served as a co-chair of the Mayoral Policy Caucus on Prisoner Reentry, and is a former member of the City of Chicago Desegregation Monitoring Commission, and of the boards of the Illinois Facilities Fund and the Congo Square Theatre Company.

A member of Phi Beta Kappa, Roxanne received a Bachelor of Arts degree from The University of Chicago in 1975 and a Master of Arts degree from The University of Chicago in 1976. She graduated from Harvard Law School in 1979.

**The Honorable
Jesse White**

Secretary of State
State of Illinois

The Honorable Jesse White was elected the 37th Illinois secretary of state in November of 1998. In November of 2002, he was re-elected by winning all 102 counties and garnering more than 2.3 million votes, which is the largest vote total by any candidate for Illinois statewide office in 25 years. Recently, White was re-elected on November 7, 2006.

Previously, White was the Cook County recorder of deeds. Before that, he served 16 years in the Illinois General Assembly. White also served as a paratrooper in the U.S. Army's 101st Airborne Division and as a member of the Illinois National Guard. He played professional baseball with the Chicago Cubs and had a 33-year career with Chicago's public school system.

White earned a Bachelor of Science degree from Alabama State College (now Alabama State University) in 1957, where he was a two-sport athlete earning all-conference honors in baseball and basketball. He was inducted into the Southwestern Athletic Conference and the Alabama State University Sports Halls of Fame.

Born in Alton, Illinois, White currently lives on the Near North Side of Chicago.

Anise D. Wiley-Little is chief diversity officer for Allstate Insurance Company, where she is responsible for orchestrating Allstate's enterprisewide diversity strategies. Under her leadership, Allstate has been recognized numerous times for its diversity efforts by many notable organizations. Anise has appeared on television across the country on the subjects of diversity and work life. She has been widely quoted or profiled in many publications including the *Chicago Tribune, Workforce Management, Investor's Business Daily, Diversity Journal* and *HR Magazine.*

An alumna of Illinois State University, Anise holds a master's degree from the University of Illinois. Currently she is a board member for the YWCA of Lake County, where she is president. She is a trustee for Corporate Voices for Working Families and is involved in other significant professional and philanthropic organizations.

Anise is the recipient of the 2006 Freedom Award and the People's Voice Most Influential African American for 2007. She was also selected to receive the 2006 *CareerFOCUS* Eagle Award for Outstanding Leadership Achievement by The National Eagle Leadership Institute and *CareerFOCUS* magazine.

Anise D. Wiley-Little

Chief Diversity Officer
Allstate Insurance Company

Rufus Williams is president of the Chicago Board of Education. He is also president and chief executive officer of Olympus, LLC, a firm that he founded to provide business and financial management to individuals, particularly athletes and entertainers.

Williams, who is from the West Side of Chicago, attended Crown and Dvorak Elementary Schools, Morton Upper Grade Center and Lane Technical High School before playing basketball for and graduating from Orr High School. He graduated, magna cum laude, from Southern University in Baton Rouge, Louisiana, with a degree in accounting.

Williams worked for a decade at Arthur Andersen & Co., and later worked at Baxter Healthcare Corporation. He was also employed at Harpo Entertainment Group of *The Oprah Winfrey Show*, and held several positions during the course of ten years, including controller and chief financial officer.

In addition to serving on the Board of Education, Williams serves on the boards of the Chicago Public Education Fund, the Renaissance Schools Fund, the Children First Fund, After School Matters and the Public Building Commission of Chicago. He is married with two children.

Rufus Williams

President
Chicago Board of Education

CHICAGO'S MOST INFLUENTIAL

Oprah Winfrey

Chairman
Harpo, Inc.

Through the power of media, Oprah Winfrey has created an unparalleled connection with people around the world. As supervising producer and host of the top-rated, award-winning *The Oprah Winfrey Show*, she has entertained, enlightened and uplifted millions of viewers for the past two decades. Produced by her own production company, Harpo Productions, Inc., the show is seen by an estimated 48 million viewers a week in the U.S., and is broadcast internationally in 132 countries.

Oprah began her broadcasting career at WVOL radio in Nashville while still in high school. At the age of 19, she became the youngest person and the first African-American woman to anchor the news at Nashville's WTVF-TV.

Her accomplishments as a global media leader and philanthropist have established her as one of the most respected and admired public figures today. In addition to numerous daytime Emmys, other awards and honors, she was named one of the 100 Most Influential People in the 20th Century by *Time* magazine.

**The Honorable
Karen A. Yarbrough**

Representative, District 7
Illinois House of Representatives

In her first three terms as the 7th District state representative, the Honorable Karen Yarbrough has distinguished herself as an active legislator and a visible and accountable advocate for her district. She chairs the House Appropriations Committee-Public Safety, is vice chair of the House Insurance Committee, and serves on nine other House committees. In March of 2006, Karen was elected Proviso Township Democratic Committeeman. She is also founder and president of Hathaway Insurance Agency in Maywood and a licensed realtor.

Committed to her involvement in the community, Karen has served on the boards of several organizations, including the Proviso Area United Way, the United Way of Suburban Chicago, the Oak Park YMCA and the Fred Hampton Scholarship Fund. She has also been the president of the Maywood Chamber of Commerce for eight years, and is a member of the National Black Caucus of State Legislators and the National Foundation of Women Legislators.

Karen earned a Bachelor in Science degree in business management from Chicago State University and a Master of Arts degree in inner-city studies from Northeastern Illinois University.

interest

limelight

CORPORATE SPOTLIGHT

attention

prominence

highlight

celebrate

headline

focus

recognition

James C. Johnson

Vice President &
Assistant General Counsel
The Boeing Company

Darryl Farrow

Director, Human Resources
The Boeing Company

As vice president and assistant general counsel, Jim Johnson participates as a member of the management team, and provides legal support to the general counsel and the board of directors regarding all matters affecting The Boeing Company. He is responsible for corporate governance, including implementation of the requirements arising out of the Sarbanes-Oxley Act of 2002, legal aspects of company financing activities, compliance with federal securities laws (including matters arising under both the Securities Act of 1933 and the Securities Exchange Act of 1934) and mergers and acquisitions.

Jim has served as corporate vice president, secretary and assistant general counsel at Northrop Grumman Corporation, an associate at Lillick, McHose & Charles in Los Angeles, California, and has served with the United States Securities and Exchange Commission in Los Angeles and Washington, D.C.

Jim is an advisory board member of The Conference Board Global Corporate Governance Research Center, and is on the boards of Ameren Corporation, a public utility holding company registered with the SEC, and the Jazz Institute of Chicago. He received a juris doctorate degree at the University of Pennsylvania.

Darryl Farrow, director of human resources for The Boeing Company, serves as the human resources leader for several senior executive leadership teams. In this role, he partners with the leaders to develop and execute human resources strategies that are aligned with the business requirements.

During his ten-year Boeing career, Farrow has held several leadership positions for corporate and the defense business unit. Prior to his current assignment, he was the senior manager of employee compensation. Other management assignments included equal employment opportunity, affirmative action and staffing.

Before joining Boeing, Farrow worked in human resources for American General Finance, Airborne Express and Gans, Gans & Associates.

Farrow is on the board of directors for the National Industry Liaison Group and serves as the vice chair. He is also on the board of directors for the St. Louis Industry Liaison Group.

A native of Chicago, Farrow received a Bachelor of Science degree in industrial management from Purdue University. He is an active member of Alpha Phi Alpha Fraternity, Inc.

Farrow is married with two children.

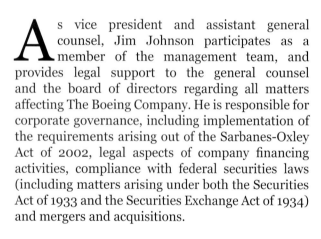

Karen F. Johnson

Director, Employee Rights
The Boeing Company

Denise B. McKinney

Director
Corporate & Strategic Development
The Boeing Company

Karen Johnson is director of employee rights within human resources at The Boeing Company. She is responsible for providing strategic development and alignment of enterprisewide policies and procedures related to employee corrective action and alternative dispute resolution.

Karen's 25-year professional career at the company includes increasing levels of responsibility in several positions. A few of which include staffing representative, senior equal opportunity representative, compensation specialist, manager and director of human resources/communications, ethics advisor, director of regulatory compliance and employee rights. Her corporate social responsibilities include participation in various community events throughout Chicago and other U.S. cities.

A native of Alabama, Karen earned a Bachelor of Science degree in business administration at the University of Alabama in Huntsville. She lived in Houston and Seattle before moving to Chicago.

A member of the Society of Human Resources Management, Karen is also a member of Delta Sigma Theta Sorority, Inc. She enjoys shopping, watching The Learning Channel, social time with family and friends and sharing her cooking skills while testing new recipes.

Denise McKinney is a director of corporate and strategic development at Boeing's corporate headquarters in Chicago, Illinois. In this position, she provides leadership and support to Boeing's business units in the initiation and execution of merger and acquisition, joint venture and divestiture activities.

In addition to her seven years of transaction experience, she has also spent 11 years in business operations with multiyear assignments in product management, including P&L, strategic planning responsibilities and sales.

Denise received a bachelor's degree in chemical engineering from Georgia Tech and a master's degree in business administration from the University of Michigan.

An active member of Jack & Jill of America and the Chicago Chapter, she is a member of Delta Sigma Theta Sorority, Inc. A native of Columbia, Maryland, Denise and her husband, Antonio, have two children, Uriah and Trinity.

CORPORATE SPOTLIGHT

Verett Mims

Assistant Treasurer
The Boeing Company

Lawrence Oliver

Chief Counsel, Investigations
The Boeing Company

As assistant treasurer of Boeing, Verett Mims has many responsibilities, including forecasting and reporting on short-term cash balances, maintaining sufficient liquidity, enhancing return on assets and standardizing cash and banking processes. She provides guidance to address risks related to foreign currency transactions and letters of credit. Previously, she served as Boeing's director of international finance, and was responsible for currency hedging strategy as well as related compliance with applicable accounting standards.

Before joining Boeing, Verett oversaw foreign exchange, interest rate and equity risk management as a senior treasury manager at Sun Microsystems in Palo Alto, California.

A native of Shreveport, Louisiana, she received a bachelor's degree in physics from Southern University and a master's degree from MIT. After completing her master's thesis, she joined Hughes Aircraft. Having completed a Master of Business Administration degree from Stanford University in 1993, Verett spent seven years as a sales trader with Citibank's foreign exchange sales desk in New York. Additionally, she served NationsBank in the Chicago sales desk where she developed new business and advised corporate treasurers and treasury managers on risk management.

In September of 2004, Lawrence Oliver joined The Boeing Company as its chief counsel of investigations, where he manages the company's internal legal investigations. The following month, he received a gubernatorial appointment to the state's first Executive Ethics Commission.

Prior to joining Boeing, Oliver was a partner at the law firm of Perkins Coie in Chicago. During his tenure at Perkins Coie, he was appointed by the mayor of Chicago to investigate the E2 Nightclub tragedy in February of 2003 that left 21 people dead. Oliver also investigated the alleged cover-up of beatings of inmates by guards at the Cook County Jail. He is a former federal prosecutor and federal judicial law clerk.

In 1991 Oliver received a law degree from the Detroit College of Law, and was the Charles H. King Award recipient for graduating first in his class. In 1984 he received a Bachelor of Science degree in industrial engineering from Purdue University.

Oliver is an ordained minister, and he serves on several nonprofit boards.

Ozzie Pierce

Director, EEO Compliance
The Boeing Company

Deborah H. Telman

Assistant Corporate Secretary
& Counsel
The Boeing Company

Ozzie Pierce is director of equal employment opportunity (EEO) compliance at The Boeing Company. He is responsible for providing direction, leadership and guidance for enterprisewide EEO strategies and initiatives. His corporate social responsibilities include participation in diversity events throughout Chicago and other cities where Boeing has employees.

Ozzie's professional career includes private and public sector experience. Previously, he was senior EEO and diversity management consultant with Tucker Spearman and Associates, Inc. Additionally, he served as branch manager of the Opportunity Programs Department at Mitsubishi Motor Manufacturing of America, Inc., and was charge processing assistant manager at the Illinois Department of Human Rights.

Having earned a Bachelor of Arts degree in political science at Valdosta State College in Valdosta, Georgia, Ozzie also holds a Master of Arts degree in legal studies at the University of Illinois at Springfield.

Enjoying sports and music, he appreciates spending time with family and friends.

Deb Telman is assistant corporate secretary and counsel for The Boeing Company. In this position, she is the lead lawyer managing Boeing's mergers, acquisitions, divestitures and joint ventures. She also provides legal oversight for Boeing's pension plan, treasury department and community relations programs.

Prior to joining Boeing, Deb was a partner at Winston & Strawn, and previously worked at Morgan Stanley and Merrill Lynch.

Active in many community and civic affiliations, Deb was named to *Crain's Chicago Business'* 40 Under 40 rising stars in business, government and arts. She is a 1999 fellow of Leadership Greater Chicago, and serves on the board of directors of Jamal Place and Chicago Bar Association Foundation.

Having received a Bachelor of Arts degree from the University of Pennsylvania, Deb holds a juris doctorate from Boston University School of Law. A native of New York, she has lived and worked in Chicago for the last 13 years.

Deb is the wife of Nigel F. Telman and the proud mother of two sons, Nigel II and Nicholas.

BOEING CORPORATE SPOTLIGHT

James R. Turner Jr.

Director, Affirmative Action
The Boeing Company

James R. Turner Jr. is director of affirmative action in the Global Diversity and Employee Rights Department of The Boeing Company. He is responsible for the development and implementation of affirmative action (AA) programs and initiatives designed to ensure compliance with the equal employment opportunity mandates of Boeing's overall diversity goals and the Office of Federal Contract Compliance Programs of the U.S. Department of Labor.

A Boeing employee since 2006, James joined Boeing with more than 30 years' experience in monitoring and directing public and private sector AA programs. Most recently, he was the director of employee solutions for the Public Service Enterprise Group. In 1995 James was appointed to the Senior Executive Service of the U.S. Government, and served as regional director for the U.S. Department of Labor's Office of Federal Contract Compliance Programs-Northeast Region until 2004.

A native of Washington, D.C., James received his Bachelor of Arts degree in psychology from Northeastern University in Boston, Massachusetts. He also serves as a member of the Northeastern University Corporate Governing Board, and is a member of Omega Psi Phi Fraternity, Inc.

interest

limelight

An Exelon Company

CORPORATE SPOTLIGHT

attention

prominence

highlight

celebrate

headline

focus

recognition

Frank M. Clark

Chairman &
Chief Executive Officer
ComEd

John T. Hooker

Senior Vice President, Legislative Affairs
ComEd

As chairman and chief executive officer of ComEd, Frank M. Clark is responsible for the overall strategic direction and operation of the utility that serves 3.8 million northern Illinois customers. One of Chicago's most active civic leaders, he advises and directs resources to community organizations across Greater Chicago.

Before becoming ComEd's first African-American president, Clark held various leadership positions where he was responsible for directing customer service, delivery system operations and regulatory and legislative affairs.

Clark, who earned a bachelor's degree and a law degree from DePaul University, believes education is the great equalizer, and his charitable commitments reflect that credo. In 2007 Clark co-chartered the Rowe-Clark Math and Science Academy for high school students on Chicago's West Side. With more than 40 years of business and leadership experience, he sits on numerous corporate boards and heads several civic boards, including Metropolitan Family Services of Chicago, the Adler Planetarium and Astronomy Museum, and the DuSable Museum of African-American History's $24 million capital campaign.

Fortune magazine named Clark one of America's 50 most powerful black executives.

He and his wife, Vera, have two sons.

As a child growing up on Chicago's West Side, John T. Hooker's mother taught him and his siblings to do a job right the first time because there may not be the opportunity to do it over. Hooker has followed that advice during his 40-year career at ComEd. As senior vice president of legislative affairs, he is responsible for managing relationships with the Illinois General Assembly and state agencies.

Hooker has held management positions in industrial relations, marketing and governmental and regulatory affairs. He is also a founding member of the Exelon African-American Members Association, an employee network group established to empower members to enhance their capabilities and secure career-rewarding opportunities within the company.

Hooker serves on the board of directors of the People's Consumer Cooperative, which provides affordable housing for the elderly, the Safer Foundation, which helps former offenders find the road to lawful and productive living, and Junior Achievement.

Hooker earned a bachelor's degree in marketing from Chicago State University.

He and his wife, Kim, reside in Chicago, and have three children, Felicia, LaToya and Sandor.

Phyllis Batson

Vice President
Customer Contact Center
ComEd

Kevin B. Brookins

Vice President
Work Management & New Business
ComEd

Phyllis Batson, vice president of ComEd's Customer Contact Center, is responsible for managing all call center operations. These duties include developing the overall customer contact strategy for ComEd's 3.8 million customers in northern Illinois.

Batson enjoys setting the strategic direction for the customer organization because it is an evolving process. Technology and customer expectations are always changing, so she believes ComEd must continue to find better ways to ensure a pleasant experience when customers reach out to the company.

The customer contact center's recent achievements include a 23 percent increase in use of customer self-service technology, improved call-handling performance and overall cost reduction by more than $10 million.

Prior to joining the company in 2001, Batson directed customer services at the TeleServices Division of Sears, Roebuck and Company, managing a staff of 3,500 in seven call center locations throughout the country. She also directed customer services at Damark International, and spent 16 years in various front-line and management positions in customer services at Northwest Airlines.

When she is not working, Batson enjoys traveling with her daughter, who lives in Texas.

A versatile electric utility manager with nearly 25 years' experience, Kevin B. Brookins is responsible for the prioritization and scheduling of ComEd's construction and maintenance activities, as well as the design and construction of new and revised service connections. Named to this position in January of 2007, Brookins has served in several key positions since he joined the company in 1983.

His career highlights include achieving the lowest service interruption rate on record for the city of Chicago and, most recently, significantly increasing the customer satisfaction rating for establishing service for new customers.

In addition to his ComEd commitments, Brookins serves on the boards of First Northern Credit Union and Chicago United. He is also a fellow of Leadership Greater Chicago.

Brookins earned a Master of Business Administration degree from Governors State University in University Park, Illinois, and a Bachelor of Science degree in electrical engineering from Howard University.

He resides in Olympia Fields, Illinois, with his wife, Melonese, and his two children, Courtney and Kyle.

CORPORATE SPOTLIGHT

George W. Lofton

Vice President
Economic Development
ComEd

Todd M. Banks

Director, External Affairs &
Large Customer Services
ComEd

Perseverance and personal growth are the hallmarks of George W. Lofton's business philosophy, which helped him ascend to vice president of economic development for ComEd. Lofton is responsible for the company's economic and community development initiatives. In this position, he sets strategies to grow investments and create jobs in northern Illinois, positioning ComEd as an economic development leader.

During his 37-year career with ComEd, Lofton has served in a variety of management roles, including engineering, sales, marketing, public affairs, external affairs, claims and commercial operations. His most recent accomplishment is co-founding and serving as president of the Metro Economic Growth Alliance of Chicago, the state's first regional economic development consortium in northern Illinois.

Lofton serves on several community and corporate boards, including the Chicagoland Entrepreneurial Center, the Illinois Development Council, Illinois State Chamber of Commerce, the Great Bank Corporation of Chicago, the National Utility Economic Development Association, Roosevelt University and the National Brownfield Association.

Lofton holds a bachelor's degree in architectural engineering from Chicago Technical College. He and his wife, Felecia, have three daughters, and reside in Flossmoor, Illinois.

Todd M. Banks, ComEd's director of external affairs and large customer services, is responsible for the leadership and relationship management with the City of Chicago, as well as community and civic organizations within the Chicago service territory. This includes advocating on behalf of ComEd on policy, service and other issues.

Following in the footsteps of his father, Ronald, who fulfilled 28 years of service with ComEd, Banks joined the company in 1991. He began his career in human resources before moving to external affairs. In his current position, he also supervises three external affairs managers who are responsible for the 50 wards throughout the city.

Banks is active in the community, serving on the boards of the Chatham Business Association, Jackson Park Hospital, Greater Southwest Development Corporation and Beloved Community Family Services.

He earned a bachelor's degree in English from the University of Michigan.

Banks resides in Chicago, and has three children, Brandon, 18, Lauren, 13, and Briana, 11.

Michelle M. Blaise

Director, Engineering Planning
ComEd

Tabrina L. Davis

Director, Communications
ComEd

Michelle M. Blaise, director of engineering planning for ComEd, oversees maintenance, reliability and capacity planning. Her team analyzes operating trends and forecasts to develop strategic programs to improve ComEd's reliability performance.

For more than 20 years, Blaise has notably taken positions of increasing responsibility with ComEd. Her career path reflects a relentless pursuit of performance improvement, achievement and commitment to excellence. After beginning her career in energy services, she has held roles in technical support, marketing programs, business planning and strategic planning. Prior to her current position, Blaise served as the manager of construction and maintenance for ComEd's overhead construction group.

Blaise's many civic contributions include membership in the Women's Board of Chicago Urban League. She has also been active in the Midwest Energy Association.

She earned a Master of Business Administration degree in finance from DePaul University and a bachelor's degree in mechanical engineering from the Illinois Institute of Technology.

Blaise resides in Chicago.

Tabrina L. Davis is director of communications for ComEd, the electric utility serving 3.8 million customers across Chicago and northern Illinois. She oversees public/media relations, issues management and employee and crisis/emergency communications.

Davis' leadership earned her department the Silver Anvil Award from the Public Relations Society of America (PRSA) in 2000, the PRSA Skyline Award in 2002, 2006 and 2007 and the Publicity Club of Chicago's Silver Trumpet in 2004.

Before joining the utility in 2000, she served as Chicago Public Schools' deputy chief communications officer, and managed external and internal communications at Cook County Hospital.

Davis has mentored aspiring communicators, previously serving as a member of the boards of the Public Relations Society of Chicago and the Black Public Relations Society of Chicago. She currently serves on the board of directors of the Chicago Children's Advocacy Center.

A lifelong Chicagoan, Davis earned a master's degree in journalism and mass communications from The University of Iowa and a bachelor's degree in journalism and mass communications from Illinois State University.

Davis and her husband, Frank Bello, reside in Chicago.

Kendall C. Hodge

Director
Chicago Region Field Operations
ComEd

Kendall C. Hodge, director of Chicago region field operations for ComEd, oversees nearly 200 first responders responsible for emergent response to ComEd power outages. One of his main objectives is to ensure safe and timely power restoration to the Chicago region's 1.3 million customers.

Hodge enjoys seeing the immediate difference that he and his staff make when outages to customers are restored. He approaches his work and his life with a sense of drive and accountability. Leadership presence and authenticity are two core traits he believes are essential to becoming an effective leader.

Hodge joined ComEd in 1994, and has held various positions including distribution capacity planner, customer design and construction engineer, customer facilities lead engineer and new business manager. Prior to his current role, he was the field operations manager for ComEd's west region.

Hodge has been an active member and the former vice president of the Exelon African-American Members Association. He received a Bachelor of Science degree in electrical engineering from Howard University.

Hodge resides in Bolingbrook with his family.

An Exelon Company

explorer

industrialist

Entrepreneurs

CHICAGO'S
ENTREPRENEURS

pioneer

capitalist

tycoon

proprietor

catalyst

magnate

trailblazer

Jocelyn H. Adams

Owner
Jocelyn H. Adams State Farm
Insurance & Financial Services

Jocelyn H. Adams is the owner of Jocelyn H. Adams State Farm Insurance & Financial Services. Her full-service insurance and financial service agency provides clients with the information they need to make informed decisions regarding their financial futures.

While working as a marketing manager for the National Black MBA Association, Inc. (NBMBAA), Jocelyn received a law degree from Loyola University School of Law in 2002. She also earned a Master of Business Administration degree in marketing and strategic decision making from Loyola Graduate School of Business in 2003. Prior to opening her own agency, Jocelyn worked for retail giant The Home Depot, Inc. in a leadership development program.

Jocelyn is a lifetime member of the NBMBAA. She has been a guest speaker for several high school classes, entrepreneurial conferences and homebuyer expos.

She is married to real estate professional Mani Adams. Jocelyn is the proud mother of two beautiful boys, Mani Jr. and Jaeson Patrick, and loves to travel.

Sheila L. Agnew

President
Mo' Better Publishing

Sheila Agnew established her company, Mo' Better Publishing, to self-publish her debut book, *All About the Vets, A Sharing of Life Experiences for Women of Honor*, which has received rave reviews and inspired women across the country. As a result of the success of *All About the Vets*, she is touring the country for book signings, conducting workshops and speaking on the subject of embracing the aging experience.

A creative and versatile entrepreneur, Sheila also owns Innovative Custom Event Designs, an event management company, and is a partner with Royal Designs, an interior and special event decorating company. In addition, she consults with small businesses, and is a mentor in entrepreneurial programs.

Sheila has a Bachelor of Science in business administration from Chicago State University and several business management certificates in entrepreneurial management.

Sharon C. Allen is the founder and marketing and sales director of Resolutions International, Inc., a small market research, grant writing and business service agency. She is also an adjunct instructor at Columbia College, where she teaches a variety of junior- and senior-level business courses.

A passionate member of the GLM Mentoring Program, Sharon is parliamentarian and past president of the Lambda Nu Omega Graduate Chapter of Alpha Kappa Alpha Sorority, Inc. (AKA). She is a member of the National MBA Association, the American Management Association, the National Association of Women Business Owners and the RainbowPUSH Coalition. Sharon made history in 1990 as the youngest Lake County Urban League board chair at the age of 25.

Her community service awards include StreetWise Volunteer of the Year and AKA Sorority Sister of the Year. She was featured in *Who's Who in Professional Management* in 1998 and 2005.

An honors graduate of Jackson State University, Sharon holds a Master of Business Administration degree from Roosevelt University. She is the mother of a 12-year-old daughter, Imani, whom she considers her pride and joy.

Sharon C. Allen

Founder
Resolutions International, Inc.

Calvin Ashford Jr. is principal and design director of Gilmore-Ashford-Powers Design, which provides a wide range of services for residential and commercial designs. Honored as one of the top interior designers in the country, he is listed in *Who's Who In Interior Design*.

Ashford has clients located in Chicago, New York, Palm Springs, and throughout the United States, Great Britain and Canada.

Among his many awards, Ashford has received the Pioneer Award in Design by the Organization of Black Designers, the J.B. Industry Internationally Design Award, the Steward Award for creative design and the Chicago Design Source Excellence Award. Similarly, Ashford and his work has been profiled in many publications including: *Architectural Digest, Interior Designs, London Design & Interior, Apartment Life, The New York Times, Ebony,* the *Chicago Defender, Chicago Tribune* and *Chicago Sun-Times.*

Receiving a Bachelor of Arts degree from Columbia University, Ashford holds a doctorate from the University of Michigan.

His design philosophy is to focus on designing environments that adapt to people, rather than people adapting to the design.

Calvin Ashford Jr.

Principal & Design Director
Gilmore-Ashford-Powers Design

Phyllis D. Banks

President
P. Banks Communications, Inc.

P hyllis D. Banks is president of P. Banks Communications, Inc., a full-service marketing, communications and public relations entity servicing a broad client mix of Fortune 500 corporations, nonprofit organizations and governmental agencies. Banks conceptualizes, develops and implements marketing communications programs to meet client needs.

She has received numerous awards and honors including the prestigious Publicity Club of Chicago (PCC) Golden Trumpet Award, three PCC Silver Trumpets and an International Association of Business Communicators Spectra Award. She began her career as a newspaper reporter for the *Fort Wayne News Sentinel*, where she shared a Pulitzer Prize awarded to the editorial staff for local reporting excellence.

Banks is a member of Trinity United Church of Christ. In addition, she is a member of the Black Public Relations Society and the Chicago Association of Black Journalists. Likewise, she is an advisory board member of Open Book, and a volunteer for several nonprofit organizations.

Banks has a Bachelor of Arts degree in forensics from Indiana University.

Barbara Ann Bates

Chief Executive Officer & President
Bates Designs

B arbara Ann Bates, the Chicago-based chief executive officer and president of Bates Designs, is a savvy, fashion-smart entrepreneur who designs and creates garments with an affinity to texture.

The urban alternative to traditional couture, Bates Designs not surprisingly attracts people from all walks of life. Bates' mark of quality has caught the eye of many high profile clients such as Oprah Winfrey, Michael Jordan, Mary Ann Childers, Lisa Siracusa, Robin Robinson, Scottie Pippen, Steve Harvey, Whitney Houston, the Winans family and many more.

Established in September of 1986, Bates Designs continues to experience growth. Barbara believes that building a successful business is like constructing a quality garment. Each requires hard work sparked with creativity, respect for valuable resources, the knowledge of how best to use them, unwavering attention to detail, and a clear vision of what the market not only wants, but also what it needs.

Donna Bellinger is co-founder and vice president of PCG International, Inc. In this position, she is responsible for sales, marketing and client services for this growing information technology firm. In addition to her proven track record of success in sales and marketing, she is a leader and a mentor who supports numerous Chicago-area organizations.

Currently, Donna serves on the national board of directors for the National Alliance of Market Developers as director at large, as an advisory board member for Chicago's 1st Black Inventor and Entrepreneurs Organization, and as a technology advisor for the Let's Talk, Let's Test HIV AIDS Foundation.

A native of Chicago, she has a history of community service, and has received much recognition for her contributions from various organizations, including the Fred Hampton Scholarship Fund, Black Data Processing Associates and the Bronzeville Chamber of Commerce.

Donna graduated with honors from American Intercontinental University. She is married to Steve Bellinger, and is also a devoted mother and grandmother whose greatest joy is her family.

Donna Smith Bellinger

Vice President
Business Development
PCG International, Inc.

Joy Management Inc. is an artist management company that grew from the entrepreneurial spirit of Pamela J. Blackman and her quest for excellence. Having achieved five undergraduate and graduate degrees in the areas of education, human behavior and society, psychology and social work, Blackman has a keen perspective on the music industry and its trends, and understands the needs of the artists and how they can flourish.

A consummate entrepreneur with an accomplished business history, Blackman has also been the owner of Kiddie Academy Learning Centers I and II for the past 21 years. It was through her work of nurturing and developing the interest of children and their families that eventually led her to facilitate young, talented artists and behind-the-scene technicians.

Known as a "go to" person, Blackman has helped and advised a diverse group of entertainers, novice entrepreneurs and hard-working families to realize their dreams.

Pamela J. Blackman

President &
Chief Executive Officer
Joy Management Inc.

Clifford L. Bridges

Franchise Owner & Architect
Cartridge World

Clifford Bridges is the franchise owner of Cartridge World in the South Loop neighborhood of Chicago. Cartridge World is an environmentally friendly company that remanufactures inkjet and laser cartridges at a discounted rate to their consumers.

Bridges received a Bachelor of Architecture degree from the University of Illinois at Chicago, and has worked as an architect for 19 years. He has designed several churches, universities, fire stations and daycare facilities in the Chicago area.

In addition to being published in the *Crain's Chicago Business* magazine, Bridges has also won numerous architectural design awards. He has spent many years as an adjunct professor at Triton College in River Grove, Illinois, and has been a successful real estate investor on the South Side of Chicago.

A native of Chicago, Bridges is married to Alifia Bridges, and is the proud parent of his daughter, Patience Rae.

Darius Brooks

President &
Chief Executive Officer
Journey Music Group

After garnering Grammy, Stellar and Dove awards throughout his 25 years in the music industry, Darius Brooks founded Journey Music Group (JMG) in 1999. Located moments outside of downtown Chicago, the entertainment firm houses a state-of-the-art recording studio (DebDash) record label and a music production division. JMG boasts a client list that includes Allstate, Diageo and Pfizer.

Darius, a man who has been one of gospel's greatest driving, creative forces, has an international reach that extends to Great Britain, Scandinavia, Italy, South Africa and Germany.

He has worked with Aretha Franklin, jazz legend Ramsey Lewis, the late Reverend Milton Brunson and the Thompson Community Singers, as well as Shirley Caesar, Stevie Wonder and Avant as a songwriter, singer, accompanist, arranger or producer. Darius has thrived in almost every musical capacity imaginable.

Darius, his wife, Deborah, and their daughter, Dasha, make their home in Chicago where he serves as musical director for the Reverend Jesse Jackson's RainbowPUSH Coalition. He also mentors vocalists and musicians through his SDM Foundation.

Yvonne Brown is chief executive officer of JAD Communications® International, a training, coaching and human potential firm that helps people be more productive and contribute more to the bottom line. She is also president of Ball of Gold® Corporation, a knowledge management consultancy. An international trainer and professional speaker, Brown served as an adjunct professor at the University of Illinois at Chicago for the PDP office in the MBA department and the Business and Professional Institute at the College of DuPage.

Brown is listed in the International *Who's Who Historical Society of Professionals* and the *Manchester Who's Who Among Executive Women*, and is often quoted in technology and business magazine articles. An alumna of the Leadership Illinois Class of 2004, she helps people end self-limiting beliefs and achieve their highest potential.

Brown holds a Bachelors of Arts degree from DePaul University and an Associate of Applied Science degree from the College of DuPage.

Born and raised in Kingston, Jamaica, she resides in Chicago with her husband, Bill, her son, Charles, and daughter-in-law, Amber.

Yvonne Brown

Chief Executive Officer
JAD Communications®
International

Sought after for his uncanny ability to capture the attention of his audience and motivate change, Dwayne Bryant is one of America's most dynamic motivational speakers.

Pursuing his life's purpose of motivating youth, Dwayne, along with his team of experienced educational consultants, designed The Vision™, a highly effective 18-week life management skills curriculum for America's public school system. As a result of its powerful curriculum and trained educational consultants, Inner Vision has proven the direct link between a student's self-esteem and his academic achievement. Since 1999 Inner Vision, along with its team of trained educational consultants, has helped schools increase test scores, attendance and overall student achievement.

Dwayne also serves as the host and keynote speaker for a myriad of teen summits, webcasts, parenting conferences and other high-profile special events sponsored by the Chicago Board of Education and the City of Chicago.

In addition to inspiring audiences both nationally and internationally, Dwayne has appeared as a guest on *The Oprah Winfrey Show*. He also served as the host of the weekly multicultural game show, *Know Your Heritage*.

Dwayne Bryant

President &
Chief Executive Officer
Inner Vision

Elsie Cardell

President
Results Sales & Marketing, LLC

Elsie Cardell, president and owner of Results Sales & Marketing, LLC, is a 20-year industry professional with a history of achievement accomplished with integrity. Elsie is known for accelerated expansion, timely deliverables, sales increases and on-point industry consultation that yields growth. Results Sales & Marketing, LLC provides independent sales representation, creative effective marketing strategies and best-in-class training programs.

Prior to Results Sales & Marketing, Elsie served as assistant vice president and head of national sales for L'Oreal's Mizani Division. She led the business to five consecutive years of double-digit sales growth, more than doubling overall business turnover during her tenure through new customer acquisition, current customer expansion, and effective sales and distribution strategies. Previously, Elsie managed numerous multicultural businesses, consistently delivering sales, share and volume growth.

She was named an industry power broker in 2004, 2005 and 2006 by *Salon Sense* magazine. Elsie is a member of Fellowship Missionary Baptist Church and Delta Sigma Theta Sorority, Inc. She received a Bachelor of Arts degree from The University of Memphis.

Diane Dinkins Carr

Founder & President
DDC Consulting Group

Diane Dinkins Carr serves as an art activist working hard to promote and bring awareness of African Americans in the visual arts. While inspiring, motivating and introducing teens to the fine arts, as well as advising emerging artists on their careers, she believes, "All art must stay alive and flourish, but art by African Americans must be acknowledged and documented by everyone, just like Monet, Picasso and Van Gogh."

Diane is founder and president of DDC Consulting Group, a fine art appraisal and consulting service that provides professional appraisal, advisory and resource services to individuals, collectors, architects, designers, developers, institutions and businesses.

Additionally, she serves as chair and president of South Side Community Art Center, the oldest African-American art center in the country.

Diane and her husband, Louis, are collectors of and philanthropists to the arts.

Roslyn C. Chapman is president of The Chapman Edge, a manufacturers' representative company based in Chicago, Illinois. The Chapman Edge specializes in selling manufacturers' products to drug and discount retail chain outlets at the national account level. She runs the overall operations of the business and oversees client relationship management.

Prior to starting her business in 2000, Roslyn held various national account sales roles with Alberto Culver and Johnson Products. She received a Bachelor of Arts degree in psychology from Hampton University in 1978. She credits her personal and professional mentors as playing a major role in her career development and business success.

Roslyn is involved with various trade organizations, including the NACDS, ECRM, AHBAI and GMDC, and she is often quoted in industry publications.

A travel enthusiast, Roslyn is often called on by her friends as a personal concierge for dining and fun vacation destination recommendations. She enjoys worshipping at several churches and is a member of Trinity United Church of Christ. Her sorority of choice 29 years ago is Delta Sigma Theta Sorority, Inc.

Roslyn C. Chapman

Chief Executive Officer
The Chapman Edge

As a principal with TillmanCarlson, Frank M. Clark III focuses on the recruitment of chief executive, chief finance and chief information officers across industries with a particular emphasis on tracking diversity talent across the country.

Prior to joining TillmanCarlson, Frank spent several years with RR Donnelley as corporate vice president of Alliance Markets Group, where he drove growth across Donnelley's divisions by forging strategic alliances with minority- and women-owned businesses across the country.

His earlier experience includes several years in sales and marketing with Motorola, Ameritech and EDS. He graduated from Northern Illinois University and has a Master of Business Administration from the Illinois Institute of Technology.

A member of the Union League Club of Chicago, Frank is a fellow of the Leadership Greater Chicago organization. He also serves on the board of directors for the Lookingglass Theatre Company and Chicago Communities In Schools.

Frank M. Clark III

Principal
TillmanCarlson

Rev. James I. Clark III

Founder & Managing Principal
EnTrust Realty Advisors

The Reverend James Clark III is founder and managing principal of EnTrust Realty Advisors, one of the few African-American-owned commercial real estate investment brokerage and advisory services companies in the nation. His firm advises institutional and private clients in the recapitalization of investment real estate. He has completed more than $3 billion in investment transactions. He also advises community institutions and churches throughout the country in urban economic and redevelopment projects. An ordained minister, James serves at St. John AME church in Aurora.

James received a Master of Divinity degree from Garrett Theological Seminary at Northwestern University, a Master of Business Administration from Columbia University and a bachelor's degree from New York University. He is also a graduate of the summer leadership institute at Harvard Divinity School. He has been recognized as one of the Stars to Watch in Real Estate by *Commercial Property News*.

James serves on the board and audit committee of Jackson Park Hospital, a nonprofit inner-city hospital, and is a member of the Chicago chapter of the Real Estate Investment Advisory Council.

Delmarie L. Cobb

Owner
The Publicity Works

Delmarie L. Cobb owns and operates The Publicity Works, a Chicago-based public affairs, political consulting and media relations firm. She is also president of Deleco Communications, Inc., which produced the award-winning, national television news-magazine, *Street Life*.

A practicing journalist for almost two decades, Cobb started as a television news reporter on network-affiliated stations throughout the country. Returning to Chicago, she became a WVON radio talk show host, a television producer and a print media columnist.

In 1996 Cobb became the first African-American press secretary to the Democratic National Convention, and in 1988 served as national traveling press secretary for presidential candidate Jesse Jackson. She has advised and served as communications director for several candidates from national and statewide to county and aldermanic races. In 1995 she developed the South Suburban Airport issue for U.S. Representative Jesse Jackson Jr.'s campaign.

Stacia Crawford is the proprietor of African Accents, a cultural store and import business located in Chicago's Austin community. Since 1996 she has worked with importers and designers to offer a unique line of Africentric gifts, clothing, furniture and accessories. African Accents offers classes in African dance, art, belly dancing, jewelry making, quilting and drumming. Members of the community can also drop by to participate in discussions and forums on numerous topics affecting African Americans.

Additionally, Stacia is the founder and executive director of the Sankofa Cultural Arts and Business Center, which offers programs and hosts events centered on African and African-American history, art, culture and entrepreneurship.

Stacia is also the producer of the highest-rated midday news program in Chicago, *ABC 7 News* at 11 a.m. She has received numerous awards, including honors from the National Association of Black Journalists and the Academy of Television Arts & Sciences.

She is a native of Baltimore, Maryland, and a graduate of the University of Pennsylvania. Stacia and her husband, Malcolm, have three sons, Malcolm Jr., Matthew and Emmanuel.

Stacia Crawford

Owner
African Accents

Helen Lawrence Crawley is founder and president of C&L Petroleum and Unicorn Oil Corporation, which is a distributor of oil and gas. She is also a pioneer in an industry dominated by men. Established in 1984, Helen calls her business a gift from God. As an African-American oil and gas distributor in the United States, her mission has been encouraging other African Americans, especially women, to enter the oil and gas industry as entrepreneurs.

Crawley was the pioneer of one of President Clinton's initiatives under the Department of Energy, the Minority Energy Round Table. She was instrumental in creating a program to increase minority business opportunities in the natural gas marketplace under former energy secretary Hazel O'Leary. As a member of the NAACP, Crawley became heavily involved in the Fair Share and Economic Development Program and Policy on Energy and Environmental Justice.

She received a Bachelor of Science degree from DePaul University. She has two children, Deborath and Dontae, and five grandchildren, Erika, Sierra, Ashai, Carmen and Ariel.

Crawley follows God's guidance in the operation of her business.

Helen Lawrence Crawley

Founder & President
C&L Petroleum &
Unicorn Oil Corporation

Gwen C. Duncan-James

President & Chief Executive Officer
Gareda Diversified
Business Services, Inc.

Gwen C. Duncan-James founded Duncan & Associates in 1972, providing accounting services to other local entrepreneurs and individuals. Two years later, Gwen founded Duncan Nurses Registry, Inc., which quickly grew to be the largest African-American nurses' registry in the Chicago area. In 1980 she reorganized her company and formed Gareda Diversified Business Services, Inc.

Through the years, Gareda has provided services ranging from cable television installation to hospital staffing. Today, Gareda proudly reigns as a premier health care agency boasting an employee base of more than 1,100 professional nurses, therapists, homemakers and respite care workers.

Gwen has spent her entire career as a successful entrepreneur. Against the odds, she became one of the first and most successful African-American providers of supplementary staffing in the Chicago area. By daring to venture into uncharted waters, Gwen has bolstered her business savvy, as evidenced by the company's consistent growth.

Throughout her illustrious career, Gwen has received numerous awards for her extraordinary success, including awards in 2004 and 2005 as a finalist for the prestigious Ernst & Young Entrepreneur of the Year.

Janice Fenn

President
Professional Resources
Organization

Janice Fenn is president of Professional Resources Organization, a consulting firm specializing in diversity strategy and diversity training. Fenn has more than 20 years of human resources and diversity experience, and has worked with clients such as American Express, ComEd, DuPont, ING, McDonald's, Microsoft and Northwestern Mutual. Her corporate experience includes positions in human resources, recruitment, succession planning and diversity at Quaker Oats, Sara Lee and Kraft, where she served as senior director of global diversity.

Fenn is co-author of *Do You See What I See? A Diversity Tale For Retaining People of Color*, a board member of African Americans In Insurance and Hubbard Street Dance Chicago, and a trustee at DuPage AME Church. She is a lifetime member of the NAACP, an alumna of Leadership America, and a member of the U.S. delegation to Mexico to discuss women's equity issues related to NAFTA. She has been honored by *Dollars & Sense*, the UNCF and the YMCA.

Fenn holds Bachelor of Science and Master of Science degrees from Tuskegee University and a Master of Business Administration degree from Purdue University's School of Business.

William Hayashi currently serves as chief executive officer for Chiopolis Entertainment, L.L.C., a new movie production house based in Chicago's Humboldt Park neighborhood dedicated to the rejuvenation and promotion of the motion picture industry in Chicago.

William has led his own information technology consulting firm for more than 25 years, specializing in computer-based business solutions. Throughout the last quarter century, he has served clients in government, law enforcement, the Fortune 500 and a wide array of not-for-profits.

As board chair for Cabrini Green Youth and Family Services, William was honored in 2001 by the Illinois Department of Children and Family Services for bringing best business practices to the social service agency model in Illinois.

William is also a writer whose short story, "Your 2 O'clock Is Here," was adapted to film in 2006. He has also completed the first volume of a fictional trilogy about a group of technically advanced African-American separatists. That manuscript is under review for publication and an option as a major motion picture. He is currently completing volume two.

William Hayashi

Chief Executive Officer
Chiopolis Entertainment, L.L.C.

Roosevelt Haywood III is chief executive officer and president of Haywood and Fleming Associates (HFA), a risk consulting, risk management and insurance procurement firm he established in 1984. The firm provides expertise and service to a number of large and complex entities in the private and public sectors. HFA also serves small businesses as well as high net-worth individuals.

Haywood has more than 30 years of experience in the insurance industry, and has served the profession in a number of capacities. He has been chair of the National African-American Insurance Association and board governor of the Chartered Property and Casualty Underwriters Society. Currently, Haywood serves on the advisory board of the International Association of Black Actuaries and on the Emerging Producers Council of the St. Paul Travelers Insurance Company. He received a business degree from Indiana University in 1973.

Haywood has appeared in a number of industry trade publications such as *National Underwriter* and *Independent Agent*. Likewise, his firm has been featured as the Marketing Agency of the Month in *Rough Notes* magazine, the leading publication for the insurance industry.

Roosevelt Haywood III

President &
Chief Executive Officer
Haywood and Fleming Associates

James Hill Jr.

Chairman &
Chief Executive Officer
Hill, Taylor LLC

James Hill Jr. is chairman and chief executive officer of Hill, Taylor LLC, a CPA firm he founded in 1972. The firm specializes in auditing employee benefit plans and nonprofit corporations.

Hill received a Bachelor of Science degree from Central State University, and an MBA from The University of Chicago.

He has served as a board member of various community and nonprofit organizations, and is currently active in various professional organizations, a few of which include principal of Chicago United, The Economic Club of Chicago board member and the Illinois Institute of Technology life trustee. Likewise, he serves on the City of Chicago Economic Advisory Board.

A member of the AICPA, Illinois CPA Society and the National Association of Black Accountants, Hill is also a National Black MBA Association affiliate. Having received numerous awards and honors from both professional and community work, Hill holds the Alumnus of the Year award from The University of Chicago, the Outstanding Young Man of America award, a Certificate of Appreciation award by the comptroller of the State of Illinois, and many others.

Amy Hilliard

Founder &
Chief Executive Officer
The ComfortCake Company

Amy Hilliard is the founder and chief executive officer of The ComfortCake Company, makers of "pound cake so good it feels like a hug." A Harvard Business School graduate, she started her company in 2001 with United Airlines as its first customer. Now a nationally trademarked brand, ComfortCake® is served in the Chicago Public Schools, and in more than 1,000 retail stores, including Jewel (which carries Sugarless Sweetness ComfortCake for diabetics), Dominick's and Walgreens. The company has been featured on CNN, The Food Network, AOL and the Home Shopping Network.

Hilliard's corporate experience includes Bloomingdale's, L'Oreal/Soft Sheen, Pillsbury, Gillette and Burrell Communications Group. She currently sits on PepsiCo's African-American Advisory Board and the Diversity Council of the Premier Auto Group.

An award-winning entrepreneur and proud mother of two young adults, Hilliard is a nationally recognized speaker. She has been profiled in publications including *Fortune, Entrepreneur, Essence, Chicago Tribune, BusinessWeek, Black Enterprise* and *Ebony*. Additionally, she is the author of *Tap Into Your Juice—Find Your Gifts, Lose Your Fears and Build Your Dreams.*

Will Horton is an educator, author, and a leadership and empowerment coach. He has researched and presented lectures on success, and has consulted and worked with adults, families and children for more than 20 years. Dedicated to transforming lives and bringing about greater understanding and change in the world, he is committed to his mission of educating, inspiring and empowering individuals to discover their greatness and reason for being.

Horton is the president of Wisdom Books Incorporated, an educational publishing company. He is also president of the Horton Personal Development Institute, which empowers individuals to give birth to their greatness.

Additionally, Horton is the author of *The 30 Power Principles Workbook*; *Martin Luther King, Jr. Is a Hero*, an inspirational book for children; *Success Guideposts for African-American Children*; *The ABCs of Self-Esteem; Positive Mind Concepts*; and *The Positive Minute*. He is also the editor of *The Success Library*, empowering quotations by great Africans and African-Americans.

Will Horton

President
Wisdom Books Incorporated

Don Jackson is the founder, chair and chief executive officer of 37-year-old Central City Productions, Inc. (CCP), a national television production, sales and syndication company based in Chicago, Illinois.

In 1970 Jackson founded Central City Marketing, Inc., and for more than three decades, the company has specialized in marketing, promotion, sales, and the production of media and television programs for black Americans. Today, CCP is a full-service company that produces, syndicates, and manages advertising sales for all of the company's local and national television programs.

Under Jackson's guidance, CCP has launched many new and unique television programs to black Americans nationwide. Many of these programs have more than 25 years of consecutive airing over local and national television.

He earned his Bachelor of Science in radio, television and film from Northwestern University in 1965. After graduating, he became the youngest and first African-American sales manager at WVON, the top radio station in the Chicago market at the time.

Jackson is married to Rosemary Jackson. The couple has two adult children and two grandsons.

Don Jackson

Founder, Chair &
Chief Executive Officer
Central City Productions, Inc.

Richard James is the owner of an American Family Insurance agency. In this role, he serves his clients as an insurance advisor. He also works with various community organizations to educate the consumers about insurance products in general, and how they impact the consumers in the longterm.

Richard is an active member of his church, Life Changers International Church, where he serves as an usher. He also takes opportunities to serve with other outreach ministries whenever possible.

Richard attended Chicago State University, where he majored in finance. He is a native of Chicago, and still lives in the greater Chicagoland area. He has a wife, Cheryl, and a daughter, Camryn.

Richard James

Agent
American Family Insurance

The internationally traveled A.J. Johnson has covered the world, doing what he does best, pioneering and leading the way with innovative ideas that have made him a highly sought-after professional hair designer and stylist.

How did A.J. become so successful? Simply put, his down-to-earth personality, his passion, enthusiasm and a genuine love for his art. Further, the desire to continuously enhance upon his amazing creativity set a benchmark that is hard for any other stylist to surpass.

A.J. makes sure that each and every client receives the red carpet treatment, celebrity or not. While he provides state-of-the-art services to all his clients, he cares about the condition of his client's hair and can only guarantee healthy growth when they agree to work with him. A.J. will not compromise the high standards he has set for the salon. His staff is hand selected by him, as it is a reflection of him and his work.

A.J is based in Chicago and a stylist to the stars.

A.J. Johnson

Owner & Chief Executive Officer
AJES the Salon

Dominga Cortes Johnson is president and chief executive officer of Mi Spa, Inc., a full-service, 3,000-square-foot Egyptian-inspired spa catering to men and women. Offering more than 100 innovative beauty treatments, Mi Spa is known for its outstanding staff, excellent service and attention to detail, and has been featured on CLTV, WGN, ABC 7 and NBC5.

Dominga opened Mi Spa in December of 2003 after a successful business career in sales, marketing and business development with Fortune 500 companies such as Verizon. She parlayed her more than 20 years of business experience and prodigious work ethic into an entrepreneurial venture that has grown significantly over the past four years. Mi Spa's location in the bustling South Loop is a testament to her business savvy.

Dominga also lends her time to various civic, charitable and business endeavors, including La Rabida Children's Hospital, the South Loop Business Association, the Chicago Urban League and the MLK Memorial Foundation. She is married to renowned make-up artist Landis, and has a son, Carlos, a daughter, Danielle, and five grandchildren.

Dominga Cortes Johnson

President &
Chief Executive Officer
Mi Spa, Inc.

Landis Johnson is one of the most sought-after make-up artists in the world today. His portfolio includes make-up for film, print, television, videos, concerts, infomercials and theater, as well as for politicians, and radio and television personalities.

A small sampling of Landis' client list includes Barack Obama, Queen Latifah, Tavis Smiley, Bernie Mac, Lisa Raye, Brenda Russell, Chaka Khan, George Duke, Kirk Franklin, Common, Angie Stone, Magic Johnson and Debbie Allen. His print work includes shoots for *Vogue*, *Ebony*, *Essence* and *Vibe* magazines. AT&T and Budweiser are among his corporate clients.

In 1986 he founded his own cosmetics and skin care company, Landis Cosmetics, whose products are sold throughout North America and Africa. Landis has extensive training in all aspects of skin care and make-up, including study at the prestigious Bio Elements Laboratories in Illinois. He lives with his wife, Dominga, in Chicago.

Landis Johnson

Founder & Make-up Artist
Landis Cosmetics

CHICAGO'S ENTREPRENEURS

As president and chief executive officer of Johnson Financial Group, Inc. (JFG), Michael A. Johnson has more than 15 years of experience in the financial services industry. Since launching JFG in 2001, Johnson has focused his sights on JFG Capital, the commercial lending side of JFG that assists owners and developers of multifamily, industrial, office, mixed-use and other commercial properties. He balances management, capital market analysis, teambuilding, operations, networking and recruiting to further JFG's growth.

Both *Black Enterprise* and *Metro Chicago Real Estate* magazines have recently recognized Johnson for his accomplishments as an entrepreneur and a loan officer. Johnson was asked to serve on the board of Habitat for Humanity after organizing an annual program where members of the local real estate community volunteer their time to build a home. He also serves on the board of Perspectives Charter School.

A 1998 graduate of Northwestern University's Kellogg Graduate School of Business, Johnson is frequently a guest lecturer for the school's nationally recognized entrepreneurship program. He received a Bachelor of Science degree from Western Michigan University in 1988.

Michael A. Johnson

President &
Chief Executive Officer
Johnson Financial Group, Inc.

Pamela Johnson is the proprietress of the historical Goldblatts Mansion, which was built in 1891. Also known as Bronzeville's 1st Bed and Breakfast Club, the mansion is Chicago's very first black-owned bed and breakfast. Pamela manages a hospitality ministry that hosts overnight guests and special events from all over the world, which she pioneered in the community where the Great Migration took place. She is now president of the Bronzeville Black Chamber of Commerce.

Pamela was also a Cover Girl fashion model and a real estate developer. She is an activist in her community and a born-again Christian, as well as a co-chair of Jazz Unites.

Pamela has received many awards for her accomplishments, such as *Who's Who Manchester New York*, the Hospitality 2006 Award from the National African American Hospitality Museum, the Excellence Award from the Soul Food Museum and many community service awards. Considered a pioneer in her community, she has been featured in the *Chicago Tribune*, *The Washington Post*, *Ebony* and *Essence* magazines and all of Chicago's local television media outlets.

Pamela Johnson

Proprietress
Goldblatts Mansion

S. Jermikko Johnson is the chief executive officer and executive design director of Gamzzo Inc., which was founded in 1966 from a start-up of $50, two tree trunks, a home sewing machine, a metal card table, three yards of fabric and a six-pound dog. Gamzzo, Inc. has grown to become the largest female African-American vertical garment design manufacturer in the nation with employees in the U.S., Africa and China. The clothing lines are carried in 639 retailers nationally and internationally.

Jermikko is a board member for such organizations as Fashion Group International and the Apparel Industry Board. A strong believer in the revitalization of manufacturing, she formed a nonprofit to support artisans in design and manufacturing. She attended The University of Chicago and The School of the Art Institute of Chicago, receiving degrees in fine arts and physiology.

The Chicago Manufacturer Group named her company Manufacturer of the Millennium, making Jermikko the first African recognized in these areas. She was included in *Who's Who in American Women* in 1985, The *HistoryMakers* in 2002, and has made several guest appearances on television.

S. Jermikko Johnson
Chief Executive Officer &
Executive Design Director
Gamzzo, Inc.

Louis Jones formed Louis Jones Enterprises Inc. in 1984 to provide professional construction management, architecture and engineering services.

During his 31-year career, Jones managed large construction projects and programs such as the reconstruction of 56 San Francisco public schools for earthquake safety standards, and served as deputy director of construction-facilities for the O'Hare Airport Development Program. He was also responsible for Provident Hospital's reconstruction, Cook County's new Second District Circuit Court Complex and the Chicago Public Schools Rehab Program.

Receiving a bachelor's degree in architecture from the University of Illinois at Chicago, Jones is a licensed architect and licensed general contractor.

Jones and his wife, Barbara Marie Davenport-Jones, MSW/LCSW, are the parents of adult children Camiria, Eds./Ph.D., Lynnea, interior designer, and Langston, an animator and filmmaker.

The recipient of numerous awards and recognitions, Jones continues to serve his community as president of the Architecture, Construction, and Engineering Technical Charter High School, and as a member of AIA, NOMA and BCU. Jones also serves on the Illinois Capital Development board, the Illinois Employment Security advisory board, and the Governor's Transition Team.

Louis Jones, AIA
President &
Chief Executive Officer
Louis Jones Enterprises, Inc.

Olivet Benbow Jones

Founder & Principal
The Felicity Group, Ltd.

Olivet Jones is a self-described "parallel entrepreneur." As founder and principal of The Felicity Group, Ltd., she provides high-level consulting services in the area of organization development and diversity to executives of the most well known corporations in America. For more than 21 years, she has built her company to a level where she was featured as a subject matter expert on ABC's *20/20* television show.

Her passion for diversity and inclusion stems from early experiences in the corporate world. Born in North Carolina in the era of legal segregation, Jones personally witnessed the impact that strong communities had in the lives of individuals. "We didn't know we were poor. Everybody in my community had a second job or a small business of some kind. That's when I realized economic determination for our people was mission critical."

As an author, consultant and coach, Jones works what she calls the "full spectrum," influencing corporations to institute approaches that fully engage people by supporting the personal and professional development of her individual clients.

Paula Estrada Jones

President
Adartse Productions, Inc.

Paula Estrada Jones is president of Adartse Productions, Inc., a multimedia film and video production company. She was previously president of Black Women in Media Arts and a media executive for Essence magazine.

Her film production credits include *African Americans and Europe, The Ford Family, The Willye White Story, Expeditionary Learning at Harvard University* and *Harvest for the World*, a short film on Hurricane Katrina.

Jones has organized seminars and film series on women and African Americans at the DuSable Museum and the Museum of Science and Industry. She has been a featured moderator and panelist in discussions and workshops, including the Chicago International Film Festival and the Hollywood Black Film Festival.

She has received awards for community service from the mayor of Chicago and the Commission on Human Relations, and is the president of the women's board of the Chicago Urban League.

Jones' educational background includes a bachelor's degree in film and video from Columbia College, a master's degree in theater from the University of Illinois at Chicago and a bachelor's degree from the University of Wisconsin-Milwaukee.

Wilbert Jones is the president of Healthy Concepts, Inc., a food and beverage product development and marketing company founded in 1993. Prior to working for Healthy Concepts, he was a food scientist at Kraft Foods for ten years, working in the biotechnology, product development and culinary departments.

In 2002 Wilbert was the first African American to be inducted into the prestigious Les Amis d' Escoffier Society of Chicago. He is the author of three published cookbooks, *The New Soul Food Cookbook* (1996), *Mama's Tea Cakes* (1998) and *Smothered Southern Foods* (2006). In 1997 the *New Soul Food Cookbook* won the Purple Reflection Award from the National Council of Negro Women, one of the oldest women's organizations in America. He is a contributing editor for *Prepared Foods* magazine and freelance special features writer for Black Entertainment Television's Web site.

Wilbert received a Bachelor of Science degree from Loyola University of Chicago. He studied at the Ecole de Gastronomie Francaise Ritz-Escoffier in Paris, France.

Wilbert Jones
President
Healthy Concepts, Inc.

Barbara Kensey is chief executive officer of Kensey & Kensey Communications, a public relations firm specializing in media relations and event marketing. Her clients have included a variety of local, national and international figures, nonprofit organizations and corporations.

Kensey is also a writer and publisher of *Access Black Chicago*, a resource and visitors guide to black history, culture, education and entertainment in Chicago. Her writings have appeared in a number of national magazines, including *Essence, Emerge, American Visions, Savoy* and *Pathfinders Travel Magazine*, a publication she contributes to regularly as a travel writer. She has also been produced on-stage to critical acclaim.

Kensey is a charter member and former executive vice president of the Black Public Relations Society and recipient of a number of awards, including a Phenomenal Woman Award from Today's Black Woman Expo and a Merit Award from the Publicity Club of Chicago.

A world traveler who has traveled throughout Africa, Europe, Asia, South America, Central America and the Caribbean, she is an active member of Trinity United Church of Christ, where she sings in the choir.

Barbara Kensey
President &
Chief Executive Officer
Kensey & Kensey Communications

CHICAGO'S ENTREPRENEURS

Midge Kimberly

President &
Chief Executive Officer
The Kimberly Group

Midge Kimberly is president and chief executive officer of The Kimberly Group, a promotional entity that provides public relations, marketing and media for an array of clients, including individuals, corporations and nonprofit entities.

Earning a Master in Business Administration degree from DePaul University, her media career began at City Colleges of Chicago in 1980, where she managed the production for the annual U.S. Women and Trades Conference.

With many feathers in her professional cap, Kimberly's passion is mentoring. She was honored as the recipient of the Dr. King Legacy Award in March of 2000.

Kimberly's involvement with major projects include the 1996 U.S. Olympics in Atlanta, Georgia, the National Democratic Convention in Chicago, and serving as director of corporate and media affairs for Donald Trump's 2001 Miss USA Pageant. In 2007 her love for journalism came full circle with the publication of Champagne and Beyond, a celebration of women at the pinnacle of their careers who are inspired to help other women.

She is known nationally for her dedication and commitment to nonprofit organizations.

Cassandra R. Lee

Founder, President &
Chief Executive Officer
SSANEE, Inc.

Cassandra R. Lee, also known as the D.I.V.A. of Dialog™, is one of the most dynamic and electrifying inspirational speakers in the United States. As the founder, president and CEO of SSANEE, Inc. (sawn-knee), an edutainment company, Cassandra provides entertaining theatrical shows and skill-building educational seminars. She offers a unique form of education and entertainment that leaves a long-lasting impression on her audiences. Her seminar topics include communication skills, financial empowerment, goal achievement, leadership and self-esteem.

A former employee of the American Bar Association, Cassandra refined her skills in administration, management, planning and training, which has allowed her to transition into the public speaking arena. She studied English and speech communication at the University of Illinois at Urbana-Champaign. She also holds certifications in diversity training, women's issues and public speaking.

Cassandra is a member of the National Association for Campus Activities, The Professional Woman Network and Toastmasters International.

In her spare time, Cassandra loves to work out and believes that a healthy body is the key to longevity and peace of mind. She resides in Chicago, Illinois.

Frank Christopher Lee is president of Johnson & Lee Architects/Planners. He has 29 years' experience in a variety of architectural areas before and since co-founding the firm in 1983.

Lee has a Bachelor of Architecture degree from the University of Illinois Chicago and a Master of Architecture degree in urban design from Harvard University. He has been a visiting professor, critic and lecturer at a number of universities, including Cornell University, Tuskegee University and Virginia Tech. He has also lectured at the Chicago Architecture Foundation, the Chicago Chapter of the American Institute of Architects, the Graham Foundation and the Chicago Historical Society, to name a few.

A member of the board of overseers at the College of Architecture at the Illinois Institute of Technology, Lee is on the board of directors of the Southeast Chicago Commission. In 2007 the American Institute of Architects elevated him to the College of Fellows.

His selected projects include the new Kennedy-King College, the Northern Trust Company south facility, the James Jordan Boys and Girls Club, Mandrake Park Comfort Station and the Chicago State University Student Success Center.

Frank Christopher Lee

President
Johnson & Lee Architects/Planners

A native of both North Carolina and Minnesota, Faheem Majeed moved to Chicago in 2003. Having learned about the South Side Community Art Center (SSCAC) as a student at Howard University, Faheem was excited to be welcomed into the organization and given a space to work on his art. Although he eventually moved on to his own studio, Faheem continued to volunteer at the SSCAC. In 2005 Faheem became the curatorial consultant for the SSCAC, managing its Margaret Burroughs' Gallery. Recently, his responsibilities have expanded to include facilitating community relationships and fundraising. Faheem also continues to manage his own business, 4th An-Nesu Arts, where he creates steel sculptures.

Faheem is a member of Alpha Phi Alpha Fraternity, Inc. Beta Chapter and Chicago Sculptors International. He is a 2007 recipient of the Abraham Lincoln Fellowship at the University of Illinois at Chicago, and is also a noted speaker whose engagements include the Museum of the Art Institute of Chicago and the Chicago Cultural Center.

Faheem currently resides in South Shore with his wife, LaShana, and two children, Walter and Jackson.

Faheem Majeed

Artist & Curator
4th An-Nesu Arts &
South Side Community Art Center

Doranita Malcom is a registered representative with American Family Insurance. Her agency is proudly designated as a Distinguished Insurance Agency by J.D. Power & Associates.

As a new resident and business owner in the Lynwood community, Doranita's mission is to serve as a positive role model to the young lives she touches through active participation in the local school district and her church.

Doranita received a Bachelor of Arts degree from Columbia College Chicago.

A native of Chicago, Illinois, Doranita is the wife of Andre Tyler, and the proud mother of Daisy and Oliver.

Doranita L. Malcom

Registered Representative
American Family Insurance

Nannette McCullough is an all-lines agent for American Family Insurance. As an agent, she helps customers make the best decisions for their insurance needs.

Nannette sponsored a Little League baseball team in Dolton, Illinois, which allowed her to help the team meet their financial needs in order to carry them through the season. She also sits on the board of directors for Breast Cancer Awareness, a committee that helps keep the residents informed of the reality of breast cancer, and how important it is that women take care of themselves.

Nannette has been a ten-time consecutive All American Winner, and her agency is proudly designated as a Distinguished Insurance Agency by J.D. Power and Associates. Aside from being an agent and a leader in her community, she is a wonderful wife and an excellent mother to her daughter, Misha.

Nannette McCullough

Agent
American Family Insurance

Pepper Miller founded The Hunter-Miller Group, Inc. (HMG), a consumer research and consulting firm, in 1985. Since then, she has been helping Fortune 500 companies understand how to effectively and positively market their products and messages to the African-American market. Some of her corporate clients include American Airlines, Allstate, Ford Motor Company, General Motors, General Mills, Procter & Gamble and the Chicago Symphony Orchestra.

In September of 2005, Pepper and co-author Herb Kemp launched the landmark African-American marketing book *What's Black About It? Insights to Increase Your Share of a Changing African-American Market* (Paramount Market Publishers).

Pepper served as co-research partner and consultant for the first segmentation study on African-American women commissioned by *Essence*, the 2005 Window on Our Women II Study. She established the Ruth C. Hunter Market Research Scholarship Fund to expose and encourage African-American students to consider market research as a career option.

Pepper received the Maxx Award for the 2007 Research Executive of the Year from Target Market News. Additionally, she has been a member of Trinity UCC since 1995.

Pepper Miller

President
The Hunter-Miller Group, Inc.

Sharon Leslie Morgan, a marketing communications consultant, is nationally recognized as a pioneer in multicultural marketing. With more than 20 years of professional experience around the globe, she has had client relationships with international companies, including Wal-Mart, Tyson Foods, Coca-Cola, McDonald's, Mattel Toys, Maybelline, Tribune Entertainment and Beefeater Gin.

Morgan built the communications departments of two major multicultural marketing agencies; executed a survival information campaign after a devastating hurricane in Jamaica; served as managing director of a cellular telephone company in South Africa; supervised communications for a jazz festival in Mexico; and owned a restaurant in France. Along the way, she authored a children's book, researched Pan-African broadcasting, wrote magazine articles for publications such as *Essence*, *Savoy* and Target Market News and worked as a columnist for a Caribbean newspaper. She is also an avid genealogist, having recently created a Web site to assist African-American families discover their family histories.

Morgan is a founder of the Black Public Relations Society, and is a member of the Public Relations Society of America, the Publicity Club of Chicago and Mensa.

Sharon Leslie Morgan

Marketing Communications
Consultant
MORCOMS

Barbara Morris

Partner &
Director of Tour Development
Black CouTours

Barbara Morris founded Black CouTours, a tour operator specializing in black history tours, in 1981. She conducts all of the black historical research, develops tour itineraries for out-of-state tours, and provides destination-planning services for groups planning visits to Chicago.

Barbara has also written booklets and developed special projects to expand the tour's noted educational experiences. Her tours have been featured in the *Chicago Tribune* (April, 1992, February, 1993, 1998 and 2000); *The New York Times* (February, 1998); *Chicago AAA Magazine* (1999); *The Star* (February, 2000); *Chicago Sun-Times* (February, 2002); *Look* (2003); and as the cover story in the February 1997 issue of *Black Meetings and Tourism*.

In 1969 Barbara was the first black teacher hired in Alsip, Illinois. She is a published writer, and is in demand as a speaker. Her work as an entrepreneur has been recognized by the U.S. Minority Business Opportunity Committee in 1996; the Hospitality Advisory Board of Harold Washington College in 1999; the National Black MBA Association in 2000; and the National African American Hospitality Association of Atlanta in 2007.

Yvette J. Moyo

President & Chief Executive Officer
Resource Associates International, Ltd.

Yvette Moyo, president and chief executive officer of Resource Associates International, Ltd., is a marketing authority with nearly 31 years' experience. She is best known for creating two brands, Real Men Cook® and Marketing Opportunities in Business and Entertainment™ (MOBE). She is also co-founder of Real Men Charities, Inc., a nonprofit committed to building healthier families and communities.

Real Men Cook®, the largest annual national urban family-focused Father's Day celebration, generated close to $1 million for nonprofits and has attracted nationwide media coverage. The Real Men Cook® brand product offshoots include Real Men Cook Sweet Potato Pound Cake®, sold in grocery stores nationwide; and the Simon & Schuster published book, *REAL MEN COOK: Rites Rituals and Recipes for Living.*

Moyo co-founded the conference series, MOBE, which generated more than $200 million in business to registrants through associations conceived at MOBE symposiums. In 2000 MOBE created the first White House briefing on African-American business and technology.

Moyo conceived Bonus Living for Families, an initiative renaming blended, adoptive and foster families. She has helped to raise eight bonus children and one biological son.

James Parker is president of GoBlackBiz.com, the first fully advertised Internet directory of black-owned businesses, which also provides seminars and free advertising classes.

James is a member of the metro board of the Chicago Urban League and also volunteers his time and money to many different nonprofits, including H.O.P.E., which stands for Helping Other People Everywhere. He is also the recipient of the Alpha Kappa Alpha Sorority, Inc. Monarch Awards Foundation's Black Businessman of the Year award. He has been featured in the *Chicago Sun-Times* and has been interviewed by the likes of Cliff Kelly of WVON and Dennis Snipe of Focus Radio, 89.3 FM.

James studied business operations at DeVry University before attending DePaul University and focusing on communications and marketing.

A native of Alaska, James lives in Chicago with his wife, Kesha, and their three children, Ciera, Cameron and Connor.

James Parker

President
GoBlackBiz.com

Rick Party entered the radio industry at the age of 15 with his first gig at Chicago Youth Center's radio station, WCYC. Strong mentoring at the start and throughout his career has helped him develop his talent, achieve his goals with success and most importantly, remain grounded and humble.

With a drive to develop his talent and learn more about the technical side of radio, Party enrolled in the Columbia School of Broadcasting, and WCYC appointed him station manager at the age of 19. From there, he went on to hold positions in Wilmington, North Carolina (WBMS); Macon, Georgia (WFXM); and Norfolk, Virginia (WOWI). His stint at WOWI led to the Top 10, and Party caught the attention of a program director at KJMZ in Dallas, where he has attained a No. 1 Arbitron ranking.

Party created Sizzle Productions to take ownership of his voice, which can be heard on more than 50 radio stations across the world. He also created I Rock The Mic, an annual conference committed to the responsibility of preserving the history and shaping the future of urban radio.

Rick Party

Voiceover Artist,
Radio Personality &
Chief Executive Officer
Sizzle Productions, Inc.

Shonda Pierre-Antoine

Agent & Owner
American Family Insurance

S honda Pierre-Antoine is an agent for American Family Insurance in Chicago. Shonda has worked in the insurance industry for 14 years, and has gained expertise in areas of sales, systems and claims. As an agent, her primary goals are to educate her customers on the importance of preserving their assets through insurance and realizing their dreams through estate planning. Shonda has won many sales awards, including the Life Diamond, All-American and Elite All-Lines Leader.

Shonda is very active in the community by working with the Regional Fair Housing Center and local banks hosting new homebuyer seminars. She teaches a class on the importance of homeowners insurance and how to choose the right coverage to protect their investments.

Shonda received a Bachelor of Science degree in accounting from Bradley University, and is a proud member of Delta Sigma Theta Sorority, Inc.

A native of Chicago, Illinois, Shonda is the wife of Dwayne Pierre-Antoine and the proud mother of three children, Alexis, Mason and Asha.

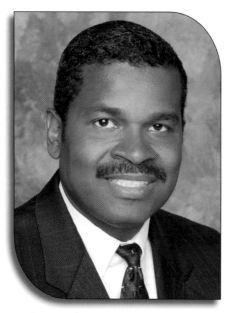

Edward Prentice III

President
Centrax Corporation

E dward Prentice III is the president of Centrax Corporation, which is a custom e-learning solutions company. Ed founded Centrax Corporation in 1985 originally as a video production company, and in 1995 he transitioned to the Internet for program delivery. Early on, Ed recognized that the true value of e-learning would only be achieved if the e-learning engaged, intrigued and captured the attention of learners.

Centrax boasts a who's who list of clients including Ameriprise, Abbott, Harley Davidson, ABN AMRO, Fifth Third Bank, Siemens, Kraft, Allstate, Grainger, Laidlaw, Wrigley, BNSF, and the American Medical Association.

Ed gives his heart and soul to his team and his community. He is on the boards of Concerned Christian Men, Entrenuity and Golden Apple Foundation. He is also on the communications team for Catalyst Lake County. When asked what his long-term goals are, he replies quite simply, "to have the means to be a productive philanthropist." Ed donates time and equipment to local area churches to enlighten youth on the power of the Internet.

Madeline Murphy Rabb is president of Murphy Rabb, Inc., a comprehensive fine art advisory firm founded in 1992 that offers clients the full range of art services to purchase, commission and display artwork for residences and businesses. She is nationally renowned for her expertise in identifying and showcasing artwork created by established and mid-career nationally and internationally acclaimed African-American artists.

Prior to starting Murphy Rabb, Inc., Rabb served as executive director of the Chicago Office of Fine Arts from 1983 to 1991 in the cabinet of Mayor Harold Washington. She was the first African American and professionally trained artist to head this city agency.

Currently, she is a trustee on the board of Columbia College Chicago, and serves on the women's board of the Art Institute and the advisory board of the Illinois Arts Alliance.

Rabb holds a Master of Science degree in visual design from the Illinois Institute of Technology and a Bachelor of Fine Arts degree from the Maryland Institute College of Art in Baltimore, Maryland.

Madeline Murphy Rabb

President
Murphy Rabb, Inc.

Eddie S. Read is the chief executive officer of United Services of Chicago, Inc., where he manages a staff of 15 employees. He implements and directs the company's Community Construction Orientation Program, and he organized an employment placement and retention service for his economically disadvantaged clients. As a worker advocate, Read specializes in construction trades.

As founder and president of the United Independent Workers International Union, Read represents workers in all aspects of business. He is president of the Chicago Black United Communities and manages the various issues and initiatives facing the black community. Serving as an aide to activist Lu Palmer for 23 years, Read was also the campaign manager, consultant, and field director for several independent and progressive candidates.

A few of his outstanding awards and memberships include the Cook County Bar Association; the Harold Washington Award; the South Austin Coalition Service Award; and the Midwest Community Council for Distinguished Community Service in Employment.

Married to Clarice Caul, Read is a father of five and a grandfather of seven.

Eddie S. Read

Chief Executive Officer
United Services of Chicago, Inc.

Cheryl B. Richardson, Ph.D.

President
CBR Consulting, LLC

Dr. Cheryl Richardson is president of CBR Consulting, LLC, specializing in human resources, diversity training and organization development consulting services.

Cheryl has more than 25 years' experience in human resources. She has consulted with human resources professionals and managing directors in the United States, Korea, Thailand, Indonesia, Philippines, Hong Kong, Singapore and Malaysia. She has also had responsibility for several countries in the Caribbean during her 17-year career with McDonald's Corporation.

Cheryl received a Bachelor of Arts degree from Rowan University, a Master of Science degree from Binghamton University, and a Doctor of Philosophy degree in organization development from Benedictine University.

She is a board member for the Dr. Martin Luther King Jr. Boys & Girls Club, and a board member and volunteer for the Naperville Community Career Center. She was honored with the 2006 Dwyer Award by the Community Career Center for her outstanding service to the organization. Cheryl was also honored as one of the 2006 Influential Women in Business by the National Association of Women Business Owners.

A native of Philadelphia, Pennsylvania, Cheryl has two children, Joe and Kailei.

Anthony A. "Tony" Robinson

Principal, Income &
Franchise Tax Services Leader
Ernst & Young LLP

Tony Robinson is a principal and income and franchise tax services leader for Ernst & Young's Midwest region. He also serves as the national leader for state and local tax look-back reviews. He specializes in multistate income and franchise taxation, and has worked on projects dealing with state tax reporting requirements, calculation of income/franchise tax base, apportionment, acquisitions and divestitures, nexus requirements, mergers, restructuring and tax credits.

Tony has presented lectures on state and local tax issues and the accounting profession for audiences in industry and academia, as well as for Tax Executives Institute professionals.

He is a member of the American Bar Association, the National Association of Black Accountants, Inc. and the Illinois CPA Society. He also serves on the Income Tax Advisory Committee of the Taxpayers' Federation of Illinois and on the board of directors of Perspectives Charter School.

Tony received a bachelor's degree from Slippery Rock University, and attended Duquesne Law School and Graduate Business School in their joint juris doctorate and MBA program.

A native of Youngstown, Ohio, he and his wife, Regina, have one daughter, Janay.

Shelomith Yisrael, known as Zelda Robinson of the *N'spirational Conversations* vignette, V103's *Troi Tyler Show*, Inspiration 1390AM, CLTV Traffic and host of her own television show, has taken on new challenges.

Zelda is the founder and life coach of Higher Learning Network, which teaches self-empowerment seminars on a variety of subjects, including how to find free grant money or scholarships. Her passion is assisting others in developing skills to find their purpose in life, as well as behind-the-scenes radio and television production for youth. A Bachelor of Arts degree in broadcast communications from Columbia College prepared her for this dream to help America's youth.

Zelda has expanded her writing career as a screenwriter as well as a columnist for *Noir Woman News* in the weekend edition of the *Chicago Sun-Times*. She is also the host of the hottest new weight loss reality television show, *The Thintuition Competition*.

Recipient of numerous awards including the Ashley Stewart Woman of Style award, Zelda was also nominated for The Pine-Sol Powerful Difference award. A native Chicagoan, her hobbies include bid whist and roller-skating.

Zelda Robinson

Founder
Higher Learning Network

Deborah M. Sawyer is an environmental scientist, certified hazardous materials manager, and president and chief executive officer of Environmental Design International, Inc. (EDI). EDI is a full-service minority- and woman-owned, licensed and professional engineering firm specializing in hazardous waste management and civil engineering.

While completing a master's degree in petroleum microbiology, Sawyer managed a synthetic fuels laboratory. She joined the Ohio Environmental Protection Agency and URS Corporation as a program manager of the toxic and hazardous waste group. In six months, Sawyer booked $1 million in projects. Despite formidable obstacles in a male-dominated field, she founded EDI in 1991. Today, EDI has 65 employees, offices in three midwestern states and annual revenue exceeding $6 million.

Sawyer's recognitions include the U.S. SBA's Minority Small Business Person of the Year at the national level in 1994; and recognitions from Bank of America, the National Association of Women Business Owners, Women of Color in Technology and the Women's Business Development Center awards. EDI, as managing partner of a joint venture, was awarded a $70 million contract for construction inspection on the Dan Ryan Expressway reconstruction.

**Deborah M.
Sawyer, CHMM**

President & Chief Executive
Officer Environmental Design
International Inc.

Erika & Monika Simmons

Designers
Double Stitch Clothing Line

Erika and Monika Simmons are the multitalented twin designers of Double Stitch. What began as a holiday gift-giving tradition, created a demand that rapidly expanded into a line of fun and flirtatious handmade designs that challenge the traditional concept of crochet.

Double Stitch was awarded the 2005 Fashion Group International's Rising Star Award for the 5th Annual Style Makers and Rule Breakers awards gala. Erika and Monika's clothing line has been featured on several television shows and in various nationally distributed publications, a few of which include NBC's *Fashion 5*, *WGN Morning Show*, ABC's *190 North*, *The New York Times*, *Time Out Chicago*, *Chicago* magazine, *Chicago Sun-Times*, *Chicago Defender*, *N'DIGO* magapaper, and *Brides Noir* and *Upscale* magazines.

While the twins have worked with such celebrities as Patti Labelle, they continue to stay focused on uplifting the community through self-esteem workshops and child entrepreneurship programs.

Erica and Monika's favorite quote is, "Pursue the things you love doing, and do them so well that people can't take their eyes off you. All the other tangible rewards will come as a result." – Maya Angelou.

Ken Smikle

President & Founder
Target Market News Inc.

Ken Smikle, president and founder of Target Market News Inc., and editor and publisher of its publications, is considered one of the leading authorities on marketing, advertising and media directed to the African-American market.

For the past two decades, Target Market News has monitored business activities in advertising, marketing and media targeted to black consumers. The company makes its findings available through a number of vehicles that industry professionals have come to rely on for their unique insights.

The company distributes news and information on the latest developments in marketing and media through its Web site, and the online publication is a daily must-read for those tracking African-American marketing and media. Additionally, the 13-year-old annually published report, *The Buying Power of Black America*, analyzes how African-American consumers spend billions of dollars. It has become the bible of black consumer spending.

Target Market News also hosts the annual African-American Research and Advertising Summit and the African-American Magazine Summit, conferences for senior-level executives engaged in marketing to the black consumer market.

In 2000 Shawna Spencer-Kendall founded Alise's Designer Shoe Salon. Rising from an area near the public housing projects in Chicago, Shawna exhibited entrepreneurial promise throughout her adolescent development. As a single parent working full-time as an accounts payable manager and part-time in Marshall Field's shoe department, she honed the skills necessary for life's next phase, "The Ministry of the Soles."

Alise's customer experience is a magical journey for discriminating women who enjoy individual attention when purchasing one-of-a-kind imports while receiving bonus doses of fashion and spiritual affirmation.

Shawna travels internationally to personally select her inventory, and is often sponsored by international footwear agencies in Italy, Spain, Brazil, Germany and Argentina, who respect her opinion on footwear trends and her passion for the industry.

She served on the board of directors of the Central Lakeview Merchants Association, and has been featured by *Crain's Chicago Business*, the *Chicago Tribune*, *Footwear News*, *Morning News with Susan Carlson*, *CBS 2* and *Shop the World*, hosted by fashion guru David Emanuel.

Shawna Spencer-Kendall
President
Alise's Designer Shoe Salon

John D. Sterling is founder and chief executive officer of Synchronous Solutions dba Synch-Solutions. Synch-Solutions delivers services through its three consulting practices of management consulting, enterprise solutions and technology solutions. John ensures that these practices work in concert to provide organizations with the necessary tools to maximize organizational performance and meet the needs of communities served.

Having worked for Fortune 500 companies, including Sears Roebuck & Co., Kraft Foods and CNA Insurance, prior to founding Synch-Solutions in 1998, John developed a strong appreciation for the services most valued by clients. He received a Bachelor of Science degree from Jackson State University.

John is a board member, committee member and supporter of several nonprofit organizations working to promote economic development for minorities, including the Chicago Urban League, Chicago United, Alliance of Black Leaders & Entrepreneurs, Uchlich Childrens' Advantage Network and CEOs for Cities. He is also a member of the Chicagoland Chamber of Commerce.

John enjoys spending time with his family, and is an avid golfer. He resides in Burr Ridge, Illinois, with his spouse and three children.

John D. Sterling
Chief Executive Officer
Synch-Solutions

Kenneth L. Stewart Sr.

President
Stewart Design & Associates

There are two kinds of people that come to this planet: those who hide and those who seek. The desire to create started early with this thrill seeker. After winning a Chicago ad design contest while in high school, Kenneth Stewart knew his path was going to be with the chosen ones in the visual arts industry.

With a Bachelor of Fine Arts degree and a killer presentation, this graphic kingpin is unstoppable.

After a small taste of the nine-to-five, Kenneth started his own design firm in 1990. Stewart Design & Associates is a visual communications firm specializing in promotional advertising. All of Stewart Design's clients want fast results, competitive pricing and quality service. Some of their clients include Anheuser-Busch, Remy Amerique, Mary Kay Cosmetics, the Alpha Kappa Alpha Educational Foundation and the Jane Addams Hull House. Stewart Design has many assignments, such as package design, logo design, I.D. systems, exhibit displays, Web design, collateral graphics, video editing and advertising promotions.

Kenneth's hobbies include anything creative, golf and flying.

Laurel Stradford

Owner
What The Traveler Saw

Laurel Stradford is a renaissance woman whose creativity and achievements have taken her around the world and back again to her roots in Chicago. After a career in private industry and academia, she now owns and operates a gift boutique.

Stradford's professional background includes more than ten years' experience with Revlon. Starting as a district manager, she served as director of special programs for Africa and Europe. Based in London, Stradford wrote a book entitled, *What the Traveler Saw*, which provided the conceptual basis for her Chicago store. She has been a teacher on the university level, a photographer for the White House, lived in Morocco, managed an image consulting business, and served as an arts development and special events director for a Chicago university.

Today, Stradford relies on her "photographer's eye" to select items that enhance the home and gift-giving needs of customers at What the Traveler Saw.

Stradford holds a Bachelor of Arts degree in film and photography. She also holds a double Master of Arts degree from Columbia College and Loyola University in interdisciplinary arts and comparative arts education.

A civil engineering graduate of Northwestern University, Michael Sutton is president and chief executive officer of Infrastructure Engineering, Inc. (IEI), a professional engineering consulting firm providing services in the fields of civil, transportation, construction and traffic engineering along with program and construction management. He has more than 32 years of experience in the civil engineering field with an extensive background focused on transportation projects, particularly mass transit facilities and highways.

Prior to IEI, Sutton further refined his expertise through his diverse work in private and public sectors and by holding positions for local, national and international engineering firms, including ten years of service with the Illinois Department of Transportation. He serves on numerous organizations and boards as director and committee member.

Sutton's firm received the 2007 Regional Minority Construction Firm of the Year Award from the U.S. Department of Commerce Minority Business Development Agency. He was also awarded the Foot Prints in the Sand Award in 2006 by Black Contractors United for having the largest contract awarded by IDOT to a black male or female-owned joint venture.

Michael Sutton

President &
Chief Executive Officer
Infrastructure Engineering, Inc.

Tiffany Taylor-Eastmond is the owner of Taylor Business Solutions, a virtual assistance firm that she founded in 2002. The business is designed to provide off-site administrative support to small businesses and specializes in affordable income tax preparation. As a former personnel security specialist, Tiffany has an administrative background that measures more than 11 years, including eight years working as an assistant to U.S. government executives.

A full-time Realtor, Tiffany is passionate in all that she does as her strong professional communication and negotiation skills make the difference for her clients.

Tiffany is an active member of Trinity United Church of Christ, the Information Technology Ministry and the Order of Eastern Star. Dedicated to giving back to the community, she serves as a mentor in Trinity's Intonjone Ministry, a program for girls ages 8 to 18, intended to nurture and provide support as they experience life.

A native of Chicago, Tiffany is the wife of Marlon Eastmond, and the proud mother of two daughters, Nikayla and Aniyah.

Tiffany Taylor-Eastmond

Owner
Taylor Business Solutions

Patricia A. Walton

President
Walton's Urban Retreat

Patricia A. Walton is a nationally certified-licensed massage therapist, an active member of the American Massage Therapy Association, a Reiki master, and a meditation and yoga instructor (Temple of Kriya Yoga – Meridian Touch, Chicago, Illinois).

In 1995 Patricia's experience as an on-site therapist in the corporate community inspired the birth of Walton's Urban Retreat (WUR) in the Ford City Shopping Mall, the first shop of its kind in a Chicago mall. WUR is now located in Hyde Park and specializes in body-mind therapy. Her hope is that WUR will provide an environment to experience peace and relaxation, and to gain knowledge with skill that can be practiced in an urban lifestyle to bring one back to self and wholeness.

Patricia earned a Bachelor of Arts degree from Columbia College Chicago. Additionally, she studied at the Chicago School of Massage Therapy and received additional training in deep tissue, yoga therapy massage, acupressure, aromatherapy, hot stone massage, Reiki and the Palmer's Method of seated massage. She also developed her spa skill at Mario Tricoci, Urban Oasis and the world-renown Elizabeth Arden Salon.

Rodney D. Weary

President &
Chief Executive Officer
RCM Group

Rodney D. Weary is the founder, president and chief executive officer of RCM Group, a real estate development company, and its affiliate, RCM Investment Group. His vision is to provide a comprehensive turnkey operation that encompasses general contracting, construction management and property management services. RCM Group has successfully performed construction projects throughout the Chicago metropolitan area, and has actively launched its business in the southwest region.

Weary is a St. Louis native who received an undergraduate degree in economics and consumer affairs from the University of Missouri-Columbia and a master's certificate from the Urban Developers Program at the University of Illinois at Chicago. He has been featured in *Urban Living* as a successful urban developer.

In addition to his duties at RCM Group, Weary is an active member of 100 Black Men of Chicago and a supporter of the Let's Talk, Let's Test Foundation. Weary has also completed The Runners' Club, which is an executive entrepreneur program. He and his wife, Mica Owens-Weary, have a 19-month-old son, Caleb Bryce Alexander.

Helen Y. West is the founder and curator of Neleh Galleries Internationale. She manages day-to-day business operations, curates fine art exhibits, and in 2005, after a 25-year hiatus, she successfully re-established the Lake Meadows Art Fair. The Lake Meadows Art Fair, originally organized in the early 1950s by Dr. Margaret Burroughs, was a venue for African-American artists to exhibit and sell their art.

Helen is an astute businesswoman and risk taker. She enjoyed a successful management career spanning 24 years in sales, marketing and product management at Lucent Technologies. After early retirement in 2001, she embraced entrepreneurship.

In just four years of business, Helen relocated the gallery to a Frank Lloyd Wright home built in 1894, which was designated as a historic landmark. Featured in the March of 2007 issue of *Chicago* magazine and the May of 2007 issue of *Hemispheres* magazine, she has also received numerous awards, including one from her local chamber of commerce.

Helen received a Bachelor of Science degree from DePaul University. Born in Chicago, Illinois, she is the proud mother of one daughter, Crystal.

Helen Y. West
Proprietor & Curator
Neleh Galleries Internationale

If ever there was an unlikely combination of careers, it is with Tony Williams, a board-certified physician assistant specializing in orthopedic surgery and an interior designer specializing in kitchens and baths. Just as skillful with a knife as he is with a table saw, Tony creates designer-styled kitchens and baths with the precision of a surgeon. In the operating room, he realizes there is no room for error. With this same philosophy, he works tirelessly to ensure his designs meet this same criteria. In the end, functional and beautiful is paramount.

In the spring of 2008, his company will launch a state-of-the-art kitchen, bath and closet showroom. The product line will feature upscale cabinet designs and state-of-the-art faucets for those who seek the unique.

His career as a designer shocks most of his friends and family. Why would an accomplished medical professional want to embark upon such an unparalleled career? He answers them with this quote, "Every man has but one destiny." This is his.

Tony Williams
Kitchen & Bathroom Designer
CRI Construction and Designs

Charisse Witherspoon

President &
Chief Executive Officer
Witherspoon Marketing Group, Inc.

Charisse Witherspoon is president and chief executive officer of Witherspoon Marketing Group, Inc., a marketing and management consulting firm established in 1993. Witherspoon was unanimously elected president of the Publicity Club of Chicago (PCC), the nation's largest organization of independent public relations practitioners. She became the first African American elevated to that position in the organization's 63-year history.

Before founding her firm, Witherspoon directed public relations for the *Chicago Defender* newspaper and WBEZ radio. That media experience, in addition to radio and television work in Illinois and New York and a degree in journalism, laid the foundation for the effective, strategic campaigns that are hallmarks of her firm.

Her event management acumen was demonstrated while she was a coordinator of three Bud Billiken® parades, the second-largest parade in America. Witherspoon also hosted and produced an award-winning business issues public service program that aired on WGCI-AM for more than a decade.

Witherspoon has been saluted by WMAQ-TV and featured by CNNfn. She remains on the board of directors of PCC and the Tony award-winning Victory Gardens Theater.

Nikki Woods

President
360° Entertainment and
Media Corp.

Nikki Woods is president of 360° Entertainment and Media Corp., a company that specializes in media imaging for companies and individuals as well as artist development.

Nikki has more than 13 years of media experience, having been the morning show co-host of WILD Boston for almost three years and spending nearly ten years at WGCI Chicago. In that time, she won numerous community and service awards for her dedication to children and the community.

Nikki is a published author. Her novel, *Easier Said Than Done*, was released in September of 2005. Her second novel is due to be released in January of 2008.

Nikki is the Chicago chapter president of Just Between Girlfriends, a women's philanthropic group. She also oversees The Nikki Woods LeadHerShip Academy, which mentors young women between the ages of 13 and 18.

Nikki graduated, summa cum laude, from the University of St. Francis with a bachelor's degree in journalism. A native of St. Louis, Missouri, she is the proud mother of two sons, Tyler and Willis Jr.

interest

limelight

CORPORATE SPOTLIGHT

attention

prominence

highlight

celebrate

headline

focus

recognition

JoAnn K. Adams

Vice President, Human Resources
Global Turnkey Solutions Business
RR Donnelley

Jerry Carpenter

Vice President of Sales
Premedia Technologies
RR Donnelley

JoAnn K. Adams was named vice president, human resources with the Global Turnkey Solutions Group in January of 2006. She was part of Banta Corporation's senior leadership team prior to the January 2007 acquisition by RR Donnelley. Adams maintained her role after the acquisition. In this role, she is responsible for the global human resources function and plays a significant role in shaping the organization's growth strategies and business plans from a human capital perspective.

Before joining RR Donnelley, Adams was a group vice president, human resources, at Rockwell Automation, one of the world's largest industrial automation companies. Prior to that, she was with Westinghouse Electric Corporation, where she held positions of increasing responsibility.

Adams earned a Bachelor of Arts degree from Bowdoin College in Brunswick, Maine, and a Master of Science degree from Duquesne University in Pittsburgh, Pennsylvania.

She is a member of the Society for Human Resource Management and the Human Resources Planning Society, and a former member of the Milwaukee Chapter Cream City Links and Milwaukee United Negro College Fund Steering Committee.

Jerry Carpenter is vice president of sales in the premedia technologies business unit of RR Donnelley. Jerry is charged with developing sales strategies and directives that drive positive profit and loss as well as with the integration of recently acquired Banta Corporation. He has successfully increased sales, year after year, as his business unit has exceeded its annual quota.

Born and raised in Philadelphia, Jerry graduated from Indiana University of Pennsylvania in 1987 and began a lengthy sales career with Johnson & Johnson. From there, Jerry went to Ameritech, where he managed solution consultants in corporate accounts. He was recruited from SBC/Ameritech to Advo, where he served as area sales manager. In 2004 Jerry moved to RR Donnelley, North America's largest printer. He was hired as director of sales and promoted to vice president of sales in 2005.

Jerry is married with three children, and serves as treasurer and trustee board member at Greater Open Door Baptist Church. He is a lifetime member of Alpha Phi Alpha Fraternity, Inc., and serves as a mentor for Big Brothers Big Sisters.

Gilbert Carson

Programmer Analyst Manager
RR Donnelley

Eva Chess

Vice President
External Affiars
RR Donnelley

Gilbert Carson is a programmer analyst manager at RR Donnelley, where his main focus is managing data warehousing and data mart initiatives. Carson is responsible for managing a team of project managers and business analysts to drive integrated reporting solutions for the analytical and strategic needs of the entire enterprise.

He has experience managing global information technology projects that enable the organization to determine computer solutions that will support global order to cash operations. His long-term experience includes roles as a manager, project manager, systems analyst, systems integrator and mainframe developer.

Carson is also chairman of the RR Donnelley Inclusion Council – Downers Grove. For the past two years, he has been responsible for leading his team to provide inclusion awareness to the workplace through programs and other initiatives.

Eva Chess is vice president of external affairs at RR Donnelley, where she is responsible for overseeing minority business development initiatives, and for managing corporate community relations and the RR Donnelley Foundation. A lawyer by training, she also had careers in investment banking and corporate social responsibility.

A lifelong equal rights advocate, Chess is a frequent commentator on minority business development issues, and specializes in promoting women's equality and advancement. She is well connected among women's rights advocates and has worked professionally and at the grassroots level to develop programs that recognize women and their achievements.

Chess holds a Bachelor of Arts degree from the University of North Carolina and a juris doctorate from the University of Virginia, where she is a member of the Alumni Council board. She is active in the nonprofit community and serves on the Chicago board of the Jackie Robinson Foundation and on the advisory board of Leadership Illinois. Her professional affiliations include the Senior Businesswomen's Forum, Leadership America and the American, National and Virginia bar associations.

Monica Guillory

Regional Human Resources Manager
RR Donnelley

Pamela Griffith Valderrama

Vice President,
Associate General Counsel
RR Donnelley

Monica Guillory is a regional human resources manager with 15 years of experience in organizational development and project management. For the last ten years as a senior generalist with RR Donnelley, she has led organizational development, leadership succession planning, workplace diversity and inclusion, compensation and staffing.

Guillory's recognitions include being named an Outstanding Woman of RR Donnelley and a multiyear Mentor of the Year for consistent and effective efforts to build and sustain inclusion and employee development.

Guillory is a graduate of The University of Houston with a bachelor's degree in business communications and certification from the Society of Human Resources Management (SHRM). Her professional memberships include the American Association of University Women, SHRM and Empowering Women's Network.

Pamela Valderrama is currently vice president, associate general counsel for RR Donnelley, where her primary responsibilities include handling labor and employment issues for the company on a national basis. She manages a wide variety of state and federal employment litigation, including discrimination and harassment claims brought under Title VII, the Americans with Disabilities Act, the Family and Medical Leave Act and other state and federal statutes. Valderrama provides advice and counseling to management regarding employment practices and policies. She also advises on traditional labor matters, including arbitration, collective bargaining and union avoidance.

Prior to joining RR Donnelley in 1998, she spent seven years at Waste Management, Inc., as labor and employment counsel. Valderrama also spent three years as an associate with the law firm of Seyfarth, Shaw, Fairweather & Geraldson in Chicago, specializing in management labor and employment law.

She has a Bachelor of Arts degree from the University of Virginia, and she received a juris doctorate from the University of Pennsylvania Law School. Valderrama currently lives in Oak Park with her husband and three children.

interest

limelight

CORPORATE SPOTLIGHT

attention

prominence

highlight

celebrate

headline

focus

recognition

CORPORATE SPOTLIGHT

Kerri-Simone Adedeji

Midwest Communication &
Change Management Consultant
Hewitt Associates L.L.C.

Nikel Cleaves

Sales & Account Executive
Hewitt Associates L.L.C.

Kerri-Simone Adedeji is a communication and change management consultant in Hewitt Associates' Midwest Communication business. In recent years, she has worked with organizations across a variety of industries to develop and execute communication strategies around employee benefits, specifically health care and retirement, as well as other workforce-related issues. Her client relationships have included a broad range of companies, including Kraft Foods, SUPERVALU and Goldman Sachs.

Prior to joining Hewitt Associates, Kerri-Simone managed health care marketing communications for the National Rural Electric Cooperative Association in Arlington, Virginia, and worked as an analyst in the change management practice of Accenture, LLP in Chicago. She received a Bachelor of Science degree in education from Northwestern University, where she concentrated her studies on learning and organizational change.

Kerri-Simone lives in the South Loop with her husband, Dapo. They are both active in the community, and attend Trinity United Church of Christ.

Nikel Cleaves is a human resources advisor who supports several internal multiprocess human resources outsourcing clients, acting as a business partner to leaders and their respective teams. She is also a lead for Hewitt's affinity group for African-American associates. Prior to Hewitt, she held several human resources management and sales positions, including training and organizational development, recruiting, and call center management for Knight/Williams Corporation in St. Louis, Missouri.

Nikel has a Bachelor of Arts degree from the University of Missouri–Columbia and a dual master's degree in human resources management/training and development from Webster University in St. Louis. She has held memberships with the Society of Human Resource Management and the National Association of African Americans in Human Resources, and is a member of Alpha Kappa Alpha Sorority, Inc.

For more than ten years, Nikel has volunteered in support of various organizations and ministries, such as the Mathews-Dickey Boys Club in St. Louis, and most recently, as coordinator of the Precious Lambs Children's Ministry at Rock of Ages Baptist Church in Maywood, Illinois.

Linda DeLavallade

HRO Diversity Talent Program Manager
Executive Staffing Consultant
Hewitt Associates L.L.C.

Sharon Hidalgo

Sales & Account Executive
Hewitt Associates L.L.C.

L inda DeLavallade is a seasoned professional within both the corporate and not-for-profit arenas. She has worked for Hewitt Associates for the past nine years, and serves in two roles for Hewitt's Human Resources Outsourcing Segment. She is diversity talent program manager, responsible for the global delivery and implementation of firmwide diversity programs and curriculum for more than 15,000 associates, and executive staffing consultant, responsible for executive and sales professionals' on-boarding process.

Previous roles Linda has served are talent retention manager, talent manager and staffing manager. Prior to Hewitt, her corporate experience spans the pharmaceutical and banking industry in various senior staffing roles.

Linda started her career in the not-for-profit arena as assistant director of cooperative education at Truman College and as an internal auditor for the IDPA. Linda serves on the human resources board for UCAN, a Chicago-based organization for abused and neglected children, and is a volunteer for the Court Appointed Special Advocates For Children of Lake County.

S haron Hidalgo is a sales and account executive for Hewitt Associates, a global human resources consulting and outsourcing firm located in Lincolnshire, Illinois. In this position, she identifies, cultivates, and leads human capital management business development opportunities. Her efforts allow clients to augment and enhance their ability to deliver effective and efficient benefit programs to their employees, while increasing return on investment and clients' ability to maintain or reduce costs relative to net profit achievement.

Sharon is actively involved in corporate diversity initiatives at Hewitt Associates. She serves on the Governance Council for Women in Leadership at Hewitt. Sharon is a member of the Multi-Cultural Leadership Advisory Council, and she serves as the co-business sponsor to Hewitt's Latino and Hispanic Associates affinity group. She is also an executive board member of Changing Worlds in Chicago.

Sharon received graduate and postgraduate degrees from Indiana University. She is a member of the National Association of African Americans in Human Resources and Alpha Kappa Alpha Sorority, Inc.

CORPORATE SPOTLIGHT

CORPORATE SPOTLIGHT

Kerri S. Lindsay

Listening Project Coordinator
Hewitt Associates L.L.C.

Tony McClendon

Assistant Treasurer
Hewitt Associates L.L.C.

Kerri Lindsay is a listening project consultant in the Global Employee Listening Practice for Hewitt Associates. She supports the execution of listening studies by coordinating the logistics of U.S. and global projects, ensuring proficient implementation and profitable delivery of engagement employee research projects. She is experienced in research assignments, including managing smaller quantitative projects or segments of larger projects, survey procedures and the execution of survey write-in comments, as well as handling translation coordination.

Prior to joining Hewitt Associates, Kerri was a resources communications specialist at Mather LifeWays, a nonprofit firm. She has more than six years of experience in the marketing industry. Her recent clients include Rich Food Products, Hilton, BIC, Wal-Mart and Holcim.

Kerri is a native of Jamaica, and now resides in Zion, Illinois. She holds a business degree in management, and is pursuing a Bachelor of Science degree in psychology from Columbia College.

The wife of Gregg and proud mother of Phileisa and Brian, Kerri enjoys reading, traveling and gardening.

Tony McClendon is assistant treasurer for Hewitt Associates, the Lincolnshire, Illinois-based benefits and consulting firm. McClendon joined Hewitt in March of 2007 after leaving a seven-year career with Fortune Brands, Inc., most recently as manager of international finance. His prior work experience includes Banc One Capital Markets and Sears.

Tony holds a Master of Business Administration degree from the University of Notre Dame and a Bachelor of Arts degree from The University of Chicago. He is also an alumnus of A Better Chance, graduating from Mount Greylock Regional High School in Williamstown, Massachusetts.

Born and raised in Dayton, Ohio, Tony now lives in Libertyville, Illinois. He is married, and has two daughters and a son, with another son on the way.

Jocelyn Moore

Human Resources Business Consultant
Hewitt Resources L.L.C.

Breanna L. Speed

Database Administrator
Hewitt Associates L.L.C.

Jocelyn Moore is a human resources business consultant supporting global business services at Hewitt. In her current role, she is responsible for overall human resources initiatives for global business services and day-to-day human resources support for client support services, associate services, supplier management and strategic sourcing, and real estate planning and strategy.

Prior to becoming a human resource business consultant, Jocelyn held the position of national campus recruiter for Hewitt for five years, recruiting mainly for Hewitt's outsourcing business. During her time as a national campus recruiter, she designed and implemented Hewitt's first National Diversity Campus Recruiting Program.

Jocelyn joined Hewitt eight years ago, shortly after graduating from Northern Illinois University with a degree in management with an emphasis in human resources. She received a professional in human resources certification in November of 2004.

Currently, Jocelyn serves on the advisory board for the Hewitt Career Center at Waukegan High School. She is also active in her church and community.

Breanna Speed is an information technology professional at Hewitt Associates, located in Lincolnshire, Illinois. In this position, she manages Oracle and SQL Server databases, which belong to more than 2,300 companies with human resources, health care, payroll and retirement programs on behalf of more than 300 companies located in 35 countries.

Breanna is an active volunteer in community efforts to help maintain and improve the appearance of Chicago Public Schools and parks through Chicago Cares. She has also been a key supporter and motivator for gay, lesbian, bisexual and transgendered employees' rights and privileges across America, and was featured in the September 2006 issue of *The Advocate*.

Breanna received a Bachelor of Science degree from DeVry Institute of Technology in Addison, Illinois. She is currently preparing to attend Kellogg University for a master's degree in business administration. A proud native of Waukegan, Illinois, Breanna is the spouse of Em and proud parent of four children, Wendell, Cory, Dominique and Dereene, and has five beautiful grandchildren.

CORPORATE SPOTLIGHT

Tyronne Stoudemire

Global Director
Diversity & Inclusion
Hewitt Associates L.L.C.

Robert Thomas

North America Operations Leader
Benefits Division
Hewitt Associates L.L.C.

Tyronne Stoudemire is global director for diversity and inclusion at Hewitt Associates. He partners with the chief executive officer, vice president of human resources and chief diversity officer to drive the overall operation and optimization of diversity programs. He also leads the development of competencies, skills and relationships required for recruiters and hiring managers to source, attract and recruit diverse talent across Hewitt's landscape.

Tyronne develops strategic plans for local and national events and coordinates recruiting efforts. He also manages external relationships with key community partners, such as the National Black MBA Association, Black Data Processing Associates, Out and Equal, Diversity Best Practices, Working Mother Media and the League of Black Women.

Tyronne is a member of the advisory board for Diversity Best Practice and the National Black MBA Association, and a member of the board of trustees of the Music Institute. He received the 2006 Chicago United Benefactor Award and 2007 National Golden Eagle Award. He also received the Monarch Award for outstanding African-American male and the People's Voice Award for most inspirational African American in Lake County.

Robert Thomas is the North America operations leader for the Benefits Division. He focuses his efforts on organizational excellence and strategic leadership of a multimillion-dollar business, workforce diversity, increased profitability and strategic change management. He has consistently delivered superior performance, and as a progressive business executive, he is widely recognized for driving results and being a strategic thinker and leader of change.

Previously, Robert was division vice president for ADP, and held various senior leadership roles while at Bank of America. Robert is a Vietnam-era veteran who served in the U.S. Marine Corps as a non-commissioned officer with honors, and trained in all phases of combat, military intelligence and computer science.

Robert was part of ADP's special recognition programs, and has received numerous awards, including the ADP President's Y2K Special Recognition Award, the Best in Class Award for Best Overall Profits in North America, Most Improved Operation in the Western Division, and the ADP President's Special Performance Achievement Award.

Robert's postgraduate work includes an MBA in technology management with a focus on leadership from Harvard Business School.

proficient

excel

Corporate

CHICAGO'S

CORPORATE BRASS

outshine

surpass

transcend

enhance

surmount

master

triumph

Mark Allen

Area Vice President
City of Chicago
Comcast

M ark Allen is the area vice president for Comcast's City of Chicago area. In this position, he is responsible for providing Comcast digital cable, high-speed Internet and digital voice to Chicago's 77 neighborhoods. Mark manages all aspects of the business, including finances, sales and marketing, government and community affairs, operations and human resources.

Mark was named one of the Top 100 Minorities in Cable and Media by *CableWorld Magazine* for 2006, and a Next Generation Leader by the National Association for Multi-Ethnicity in Communications (NAMIC) for 2006. He is also a member of several organizations, including the NAMIC, the Wharton Alumni African-American MBA Association and the Emerging Venture Network.

He received a Bachelor of Arts degree in business administration from Morehouse College in Atlanta, and a Master of Business Administration degree in strategic management and entrepreneurial management from the Wharton School of the University of Pennsylvania. Mark is also a graduate of the National Executive Leadership Development Program at UCLA's Anderson School of Management.

Patricia Andrews-Keenan

Vice President
Communications and
Community Affairs
The Nielsen Company

P atricia Andrews-Keenan is vice president of communications and community affairs for The Nielsen Company. Her responsibilities include community outreach, education, advertising, government relations, philanthropic initiatives and the continued successful implementation of Nielsen's Local People Meter services across the U.S.

An award-winning PR executive, Andrews-Keenan has spent 19 years in the telecommunications industry.

Andrews-Keenan holds a bachelor's degree in journalism from Grambling State University in Louisiana. She is a Walter Kaitz Foundation fellow, and in 2002 she graduated from the prestigious Executive Leadership Development Program at UCLA.

Andrews-Keenan serves on the board of the Chicago Children's Choir and the National Association for Multi-ethnicity In Communications, where she was national president. She is also a member of The Economic Club of Chicago, Women in Cable Telecommunications and the Association of Cable Communicators. Past board affiliations include the Volunteers of America, Quad County Urban League, Naperville Area Chamber of Commerce and DuPage County Girl Scouts. Her recognitions include *Chicago Defender*'s 2007 Women of Excellence Award, honoree at the 100 Black Men of Chicago Gala and Influential Women in Business honors from NAWBO.

Peggy Austin is vice president of Danielle Ashley Communications, a full-service advertising and public relations firm. In this position, she oversees the day-to-day operations as well as client services for the firm's many clients. She also manages several of the firm's top accounts, such as Walgreens, Illinois Lottery, the Chicago Foundation for Women, Blue Cross Blue Shield of Illinois, Proviso Township School District 209 and others.

An 18-year communications and advertising strategist, Peggy joined the Danielle Ashley staff from WBBM-TV in Chicago. Prior to WBBM-TV, she had an extensive career in African-American consumer marketing with Clear Channel Communications in St. Louis, Missouri; Richmond, Virginia; Jacksonville, Florida; Milwaukee, Wisconsin; and Chicago, Illinois.

Peggy holds a Bachelor of Arts degree from the University of Missouri-Columbia. She is a past recipient of the National Sales Network's Outstanding Achievement in Sales Award. She sits on the board of the National Sales Network and American Women in Radio and Television. Additionally, Peggy is an active member of the Black Public Relations Society of America and a member of Delta Sigma Theta Sorority, Inc.

Peggy Austin

Vice President
Danielle Ashley Communications

Ernest L. Baker is senior vice president and chief financial officer of E. Morris Communications, Inc. (EMC), and is responsible for managing the company's finance organization, including corporate accounting, finance, operations and information technology. He serves on EMC's board of directors, and is a key member of the senior management team, providing financial and operational perspective on all business matters.

Before joining EMC in 1992, Baker gained extensive experience through several years in various positions of increasing responsibility. Baker was vice president and controller of The Combined Fund, Inc. (CFI). Before CFI, he was a corporate tax accountant with Peoples Energy, and served for four years as a U.S. auditor. He was also chief financial officer for Stratford Safety Products, and has held various positions in banking.

Baker is a certified public accountant and a member of the Illinois CPA Society, National Association of Black Accountants, The Executives' Club of Chicago and the finance committee of the AAAA.

Baker earned a bachelor's degree from Roosevelt University in Chicago. He and his wife, Cherie, have three children, Ernest III, Cherish and Chelsea.

Ernest L. Baker

Senior Vice President &
Chief Financial Officer
E. Morris Communications, Inc.

Heidi M. Barker

Senior Director of
Corporate Media Relations
McDonald's Corporation

Heidi M. Barker is senior director of corporate media relations for McDonald's Corporation. In this role, Barker helps to manage some 15,000 media inquiries a year to the world's largest restaurant chain. She is responsible for creating key messages to enhance and protect the McDonald's brand. Barker also specializes in crisis communications, prepares top management for press events and serves as a spokesperson.

Prior to joining McDonald's, Barker worked for ten years as a network producer for NBC News, contributing stories for *NBC Nightly News with Brian Williams*, the *Today* show, and MSNBC. Barker was based in the Chicago bureau and traveled nationally and internationally. She also frequently filled in as a senior producer for *NBC Nightly News* in New York.

Barker has garnered two Emmy nominations, several Edward R. Murrow Awards and National Headliner Awards, the Mongerson Prize Award of Distinction for Investigative Reporting, and a National Association of Black Journalists Award.

Barker began as an anchor and reporter for the ABC affiliate in Decatur, Illinois. She is a 1991 graduate of the Medill School of Journalism at Northwestern University.

Talethea M. Best

Director
U.S. Learning & Development
Aon Corporation

Talethea M. Best heads talent development for all operations in the Americas for Aon Corporation. With 16 years of diversified business experience, her special areas of expertise include talent and employee engagement, improving organizational effectiveness, developing corporate leadership strategies and executing succession management processes.

Committed to helping organizations work better, faster and smarter, Best has project-led Aon's first global employee engagement survey to drive culture change, launched a Web-based mentoring tool to support retention, and implemented high potential leadership programs to build common skills. "To ensure high performance," said Best, "enterprise learning must operate efficiently and rigorously, with one eye on the bottom line and the other on the value being created for the company."

Talethea has been a speaker for a number of groups, including Princeton, Rutgers University, the National Black Caucus, the Finance and Insurance Workforce Summit, and the Human Resources Management Association of Chicago.

As a graduate of Drexel University with honors and a Bachelor of Science degree in marketing and communications, Talethea is a current master's candidate at Northwestern University's Learning and Organizational Change Graduate Program.

Greg Bins began his career with Harris N.A. in 1980. Today, he serves as vice president and market manager of the institutional market. In this role, Greg manages a team of commercial bankers who specialize in governments and nonprofit organizations.

Greg received an undergraduate degree from Stanford University. He also earned a master of business administration degree from Northwestern University. He is an active volunteer, serving as a Harris Bank tutor at a local elementary school and participating in the bank's Mentoring Program. Greg also works with the bank's African-American affinity group, the African-American League of Professionals. He recently received the Daryl Grisham Award, the highest honor presented by this affinity group for outstanding achievement and commitment to the greater community.

Greg serves as treasurer and board member of Windows of Opportunity, a nonprofit organization dedicated to serving the needs of public housing residents. He has been a longtime participant in the Chicago Public Schools Principal for a Day Program. Additionally, Greg is a longstanding supporter of the UNCF and a member of the Chicago Urban League.

Gregory Bins

Vice President & Market Manager
Institutional Market
Harris N.A.

Julian E. Brown is corporate contributions manager for Nicor Gas. He is responsible for corporate contributions, memberships, volunteerism, scholarships, matching gifts and community programs.

Julian currently serves on the advisory boards of Clear Channel Radio Chicago and the James F. Jordan Foundation. He is also chair of the United Way's Strength Through Diversity initiative, and serves as a board member for Illinois Dollars for Scholars. The Office of the Governor recently appointed Julian to the Illinois Commission on Volunteerism and Community Service, and for the third time he was selected as Someone You Should Know in Philanthropy by *The Business Ledger*.

He is one of the founding members of the Corporate Volunteer Council of Metropolitan Chicago, and is one of the founding fathers of the African American Management Network, known at Nicor Gas as "En Rapport."

Julian holds a bachelor's degree in business administration from Bradley University in Peoria and a master's degree in business administration from Benedictine University in Lisle.

He also coaches Special Olympics basketball, and he and his wife, Carla, have two sons, Darren and Andrew.

Julian Brown

Corporate Contributions Manager
Nicor Gas

Phoegina Brown

Manager of Strategic Analysis
Ernst & Young LLP

Phoegina Brown is a manager of strategic analysis within Ernst & Young's Center for Business Knowledge. In this capacity, she is responsible for operations oversight, customer relationship management, baseline competencies development, as well as creating vehicles to transfer knowledge across the firm. She also has a proven track record of project management, strategic planning, and international market and business development.

Phoegina is a lifetime member of the National Black MBA Association and is actively involved with the local Chicago chapter. Most recently she worked with the Partnerships Committee, where she had responsibility for securing strategic partnerships and funding from Chicago-area corporations.

A member of Delta Sigma Theta, Inc., Phoegina is a charter member of the Schaumburg-Hoffman Estates Alumnae Chapter. Additionally, she is a board member of Profit Through Knowledge, Inc., a newly formed not-for-profit corporation created for the purpose of providing charitable, socially conscious programs and activities for underserved youth, families and individuals in the northwest suburban areas of Chicago.

Phoegina earned a Master of Business Administration degree from Clark Atlanta University and a bachelor's degree in finance from Northern Illinois University.

Jeff A. Carroll

Senior Account Executive
Siemens Building Technologies

Jeff Carroll is senior account executive for Siemens Building Technologies in Chicago. In this position, he delivers energy and environmental solutions to state and local government and manages strategic accounts in the Chicagoland area and Gary, Indiana.

A seasoned energy professional, Jeff has worked in the energy sector for more than 14 years. During his career, his responsibilities have included engineering, sales, natural gas product development, and natural gas and electricity supply management. He is also a co-founder of East Gate Energy, Inc., a Chicago-based, certified minority business enterprise.

Jeff is professionally certified with the Association of Energy Engineers and the Gas Technology Institute, and he earned a Bachelor of Science degree in mechanical engineering from the Illinois Institute of Technology. He is the current president of the Chicagoland chapter of the Association of Professional Energy Consultants, a trustee at Chicago's Hales Franciscan High School, and a board member of CHA's Windows of Opportunity.

A native of Chicago, Jeff is a regular volunteer with Chicago Cares and Chicago Public Schools. He also enjoys music.

rlene Carruthers-Williams is senior vice president of lending for Seaway National Bank. In that capacity, she oversees the entire business development, negotiating, underwriting, and management of the bank's diverse loan portfolio.

A seasoned financial and managerial professional, Williams began her career as an auditor for a local public accounting firm in Chicago and was later recruited by General Electric Credit Corporation to join their Audit Department. She also managed the Audit Department of the Chicago office of Bankers Trust Corporation of New York, until her promotion to relationship manager in 1987. Moreover, Williams held several leadership positions in the lending department at Seaway prior to her promotion as senior vice president and senior loan officer in 1998.

Williams serves as a board member for the National Bankers Association and the Chatham Business Association. In addition, she is a member of the National Association of Black Accountants, the Chicago State University Mentoring Program, the Lincoln's Challenge Mentoring Program and the Neighborhood Housing Association.

Williams received a Bachelor of Science degree in accounting from the University of Illinois at Chicago.

Arlene Carruthers-Williams

Senior Vice President of Lending
Seaway National Bank

andi Castleberry-Singleton is vice president of global inclusion and diversity at Motorola. She is responsible for developing and implementing a One Motorola strategy that reflects Motorola's commitment to inclusion in the marketplace, workforce and workplace.

Formerly the chief diversity officer at Sun Microsystems, Candi created and implemented The Global Inclusion Model™, a systems integration model she used to transition Sun from compliance and diversity processes led by human resources, to integrated global activities that made inclusive behavior and cultural acumen the responsibility of every Sun employee.

Prior to moving to Sun Microsystems, she worked in sales, product marketing, training and sales management at the Xerox Corporation for 12 years.

A recipient of the 2004 Women of Color in Technology Award, Candi holds a Master of Business Administration degree from Pepperdine University, a bachelor's degree in legal studies from the University of California at Berkeley, and is a graduate of the Stanford University Human Resources Executive Program. Her board memberships include Diversity Best Practices, the Linkage Diversity Summit, the League of Black Women and the Women of Color in Technology Alumni Association.

Candi Castleberry-Singleton

Vice President
Global Inclusion & Diversity
Motorola, Inc.

Allan Cave

Senior Vice President
Northern Trust

Allan Cave is a senior vice president at Northern Trust in Chicago. He is assistant general counsel of human resources and employee relations manager. Allan joined Northern Trust in July of 2005 as a senior attorney in the Corporate Legal Department. In July of 2006, he was promoted to his current role.

Prior to joining Northern Trust, Allan was an attorney at Connelly Sheehan Harris LLP. From 1998 to 2004, he held a number of positions with The Stop & Shop Supermarket Company, including vice president of employment and regulatory law and vice president of associate relations. From 1993 to 1998, he was an associate at Day, Berry & Howard LLP.

Allan received a Bachelor of Arts degree from Duke University and a juris doctorate from the Georgetown University Law Center.

Titilope Cole

Senior Vice President
Retail Banking and Investor Services
Harris N.A.

Titilope "Titi" Cole began her career with Harris in 2004. She currently serves as a senior vice president of retail banking and investor services.

In this role, Cole works with Harris sales, marketing and operations teams to grow the bank's retail banking and investment services business. Her responsibilities include overseeing all retail banking and mortgage product teams, Harris Investor Services and branch operations teams. Prior to joining Harris, Cole spent five years with McKinsey & Company in Chicago.

After earning a Bachelor of Science degree in economics, with honors, from the University of Ibadan in Nigeria, Cole went on to receive a Master of Business Administration degree, with honors, from Northwestern University's Kellogg Graduate School of Management.

Cole sits on the board of directors of the DuSable Museum of African American History.

Angela L. Coley is chief operating officer and vice president of sales for AlMae Publisher's Representatives, Inc., an independent advertising sales rep company for nationally distributed magazines. These magazines include *American Legacy, American Legacy Woman, Being Single, Sophisticate's Black Hair Styles* and *Care Guide*, and the book publication, *Who's Who In Black Chicago*®.

As a business partner with her sister, Beverly A. Coley, Angela is responsible for the daily operations of the company. She also manages AlMae's national sales accounts and marketing activities for *Sophisticate's Black Hair Styles* and *Care Guide*.

Angela enjoys singing and she is an active member of the Trinity United Church of Christ Women's Chorus and a member of Alpha Kappa Alpha Sorority, Inc.

Attending Chicago State University, Angela received a Bachelor of Science degree in business administration. She earned a certificate in the Lawyer's Assistant program at Roosevelt University.

Angela L. Coley

Chief Operating Officer &
Vice President, Sales
AlMae Publisher's Representatives, Inc.

Chadwick Cunningham is a manager within Jones Lang LaSalle's Markets Group. Until recently, he served as property manager at Hyatt Center, a 49-story Class A office high-rise in downtown Chicago and the city's 2006 Office Building of the Year recipient for buildings larger than 1 million square feet. Awarded by peers, the honor recognizes excellence in property management, operational efficiency, tenant relations, emergency preparedness and community impact. In his new role with the firm, he is working with the group's senior management on defining and executing growth strategies.

Cunningham attended the University of Louisville on full academic scholarship, and was the recipient of the 2001 Mr. Cardinal award. This distinction is awarded to one senior male based on academic achievement, extracurricular activities and overall contributions to the university.

Cunningham received a Bachelor of Science degree in civil engineering and a Master of Engineering degree from the University of Louisville. He also earned a Master of Business Administration degree from Harvard Business School.

A native of Frankfort, Kentucky, Cunningham is the husband of Shawntay Cunningham.

Chadwick M. Cunningham

Manager
Jones Lang LaSalle

Clark Delanois

Senior Vice President &
Managing Director
Schaumburg Financial Center
Northern Trust

Clark Delanois is senior vice president and managing director for the Schaumburg Financial Center, where he manages trust, investment services and private banking. He is also a member of the Northern Trust Illinois West Region leadership team.

Clark earned a bachelor's degree in business from the University of Illinois at Chicago (UIC). He received his trust certificate from the Cannon Financial Institute and holds the designation of CTP with the Association for Financial Professionals.

A commissioner for the Village of Schaumburg, Clark is on the board of directors for the Harper College Educational Foundation and the Cenegenics Education and Research Foundation. He is an advisory board member for The Chicago Community Trust Professional Advisory Committee, Roosevelt University (CAB), Destiny Outreach and Women in Need Growing Strong (WINGS). Clark is also a member of the Union League Club of Chicago and the National Association of Securities Professionals.

In 2001 Clark was voted Distinguished Alumnus by the Business Alumni Association at UIC and inducted into the Alumni Leadership Academy at UIC College of Business.

Amina J. Dickerson

Senior Director
Global Community Involvement
Kraft Foods

As senior director of global community involvement, Amina J. Dickerson is responsible for Kraft's philanthropic strategy worldwide, including programs in health and wellness, hunger and employee engagement.

Previously, Dickerson held executive posts with the Chicago Historical Society and the National Museum of African Art at the Smithsonian Institution. She was also president of Chicago's DuSable Museum of African American History. Named Distinguished Visitor by the John D. and Catherine T. MacArthur Foundation, Dickerson was appointed a Class XVI Kellogg fellow and a Newberry Library fellow.

Dickerson is an advisor for Chicago's African American Legacy Fund, Department of Cultural Affairs, and for the Harris Theater at Millennium Park. She was also named to the International Committee of the Council of Foundations in 2005. Dickerson has received numerous honors for her work, including Chicago's Professional Grantor of the Year.

She studied theater and arts management at Emerson College and Harvard University, and holds a master's degree in arts management from the American University in Washington, D.C. She resides in Chicago's South Shore community with her husband, Julian Roberts.

Troy Dickerson is director of diversity strategy and development for Ernst & Young. Her responsibilities include developing national strategies that support initiatives focused on training, mentoring, pipeline development and networking. She also provides direction to senior leaders in support of regional diversity and inclusion programs.

Prior to Ernst & Young, Troy was vice president of diversity and community affairs for Coors Brewing Company. Her responsibilities included the Office of Inclusion, workforce and supplier diversity functions, corporate relations, corporate philanthropy and volunteerism. She also acted as the company's lead liaison for the Hispanic and African-American coalitions. Additionally, Troy served as human resources director for the West Region sales organization, director of ethnic markets, and vice president of diversity and community affairs.

A native of Chicago, Troy sits on the corporate board of advisors for the National Council of La Raza, the corporate advisory council for the National Hispana Leadership Institute, and is a member of the Society of Human Resource Management.

She earned a master's degree in human resource management and a bachelor's degree in business administration from the University of Illinois.

Troy Dickerson

Director, Diversity Strategy & Development
Ernst & Young LLP

Deirdre Drake is senior vice president of human resources for Harris N.A. She is responsible for creating business strategies and operational priorities that focus on people and a higher performing culture. Deirdre builds and drives human resource strategic plans, measures and metrics for Harris, and is instrumental in the planning and development of annual goals and objectives for the division. A native of Michigan, she was appointed to the role in January of 2006.

Deirdre brings more than 18 years of experience and leadership in human resources from Marathon Oil, Kraft General Foods, MCI Telecommunications and ARAMARK Corporation. She serves on the board of the American Red Cross of Greater Chicago and is a lifetime member of the National Black MBA Association.

Deirdre has a Master of Business Administration degree from St. Joseph's University and a Bachelor of Science degree in business administration from Central Michigan University.

Deirdre Drake

Senior Vice President
Human Resources
Harris N.A

Jason Few

Corporate Vice President &
General Manager
Global Accessories, Retail &
Distributors Business
Motorola, Inc.

J ason Few has more than 19 years of experience in marketing and sales management. As the corporate vice president and general manager of global accessories, retail and distributors business, he drives global retail and distributor sales as well as the product development for mobile devices accessory products.

Prior to this role, Jason served as vice president of Motorola's Global Quality and Customer Advocacy Organization. He joined Motorola as vice president and chief marketing officer of North America mobile devices business.

Before joining Motorola, Jason worked for SBC as vice president of Wi-Fi implementation, and prior to SBC, he held various senior marketing and sales positions at AT&T and NCR.

He earned a Master of Business Administration degree from Northwestern University's J.L. Kellogg Graduate School of Management and a bachelor's degree in business administration in computer systems from Ohio University.

Additionally, Jason serves on the board of directors for Syniverse Holdings, Inc., Notebaert Nature Museum Chicago and AIDSCARE Chicago.

Michael A. Foster

Director of Sales & Marketing
Seneca Hotel and Suites &
The Belden-Stratford

M ichael A. Foster has been the director of sales and marketing at the Seneca Hotel and Suites and the Belden-Stratford for the past eight years. He is a seasoned 35-year veteran of the hospitality industry.

His focus is on the international, corporate and entertainment industries. Michael's expertise is working with the multicultural segments of the hospitality industry.

Michael was with The Hilton Corporation for 20 years before joining the Seneca Hotel. Although he received extensive training and experience in various management capacities with The Hilton Corporation, he prefers the intimacy of a boutique hotel concept.

Michael is on the board of the Better Boys Foundation, the American Red Cross and the Mexican Tourism advisory board, and is a member of several international organizations. He is very involved with the film industry in Chicago, and has traveled extensively to the film capitals, where he has built exclusive relationships. Michael has a passion for selling, and enjoys every facet of the hospitality industry.

A native of Jamaica, Michael has resided in Chicago for 38 years. He is married, and has four adult children.

D eborah Gray-Young is vice president and director of media services for E. Morris Communications, Inc. (EMC), a full-service advertising agency specializing in connecting premium brands and services to African-American consumers. Relying on more than 26 years of experience, she is responsible for overseeing the planning and placement of advertising budgets for EMC's Fortune 500 clients.

Deborah, who is currently the chair of the Multicultural Media Committee for the Association of American Advertising Agencies, is frequently quoted in business and trade publications including *Black Enterprise*, *USA Today*, *The Washington Post*, and *Advertising Age*. She is also a frequent presenter at industry conferences including the Target Market News African-American Research Summit, The Power of Urban Radio, and the Multicultural Media Expo. Likewise, she contributed to the Cabletelevision Advertising Bureau's annual Multicultural Marketing Guides.

A member of Christ Universal Temple, Deborah is a facilitator of spiritual empowerment classes. She also serves on the board of directors of the Universal Foundation for Better Living.

A published author of inspirational booklets, Deborah is an avid reader and amateur photographer.

Deborah Gray-Young

Vice President &
Director of Media Services
E. Morris Communications, Inc.

B obbie Gregg is vice president and global chief compliance officer of Aon Corporation. She is responsible for compliance risk management and business conduct across the Aon enterprise. She also oversees compliance with the requirements of the Aon Regulatory Settlement Agreement, which requires Aon to implement certain business reforms in the United States and abroad. Prior to joining Aon, Bobbie held similar positions at Sears, Roebuck and Co. and Bank One.

Bobbie was identified as a leader to watch in "Minority Corporate Counsel Association Spotlights In-House Women-of-Color: 15 Leaders to Watch," published in the March/April 2003 edition of *Diversity and The Bar*. She was also recognized for her leadership role at Sears in "Women at the Top in Corporate America," published in the March 2001 edition of *Ebony* magazine.

Bobbie earned a juris doctorate degree, cum laude, from Northwestern University School of Law in Chicago and a Bachelor of Arts degree from the University of Illinois. She is married to David Gregg, and they are the parents of three lovely daughters.

Bobbie Gregg

Vice President &
Global Chief Compliance Officer
Aon Corporation

CHICAGO'S CORPORATE BRASS

Jason Gumbs

Director, Customer Care
Comcast

Jason Gumbs is the director of customer care for Comcast's Tinley Park Call Center. In this position, Jason oversees Comcast's largest Chicagoland call center, which provides 24/7 support and service to customers who have Comcast digital cable, high-speed Internet and digital voice products. He is responsible for managing direct customer contact with millions of Comcast customers each year, and is helping to drive a "think customer first" focus for the organization dedicated to assisting people with billing and service issues in a friendly, timely fashion. In his previous role as director of sales and marketing, he helped propel the Chicago West Area to recognition as Comcast's Midwest Division System of the Year in 2005.

Jason received a Bachelor of Science degree from Northwestern University in Evanston, Illinois. He is also a 2005 graduate of the Comcast Executive Leadership Forum, and served as co-vice president of the National Association of Multi-Ethnicity in Communications (NAMIC) in 2006.

Jason lives in the Wicker Park neighborhood with his wife, Sue.

Darrel Hackett

Senior Vice President
Acquisition Integration Office
Harris N.A.

As senior vice president of the Acquisition Integration Office, Darrel Hackett is charged with leading the expansion strategy and business integration efforts in Harris N.A.'s pursuit to become the leading bank in the Midwest.

Prior to his current role, Hackett was regional president of Harris Community Banking, where he was accountable for the overall financial performance of the bank's northern Chicago region.

Hackett joined Harris in 2004 as vice president to help launch the Acquisition Integration Office. On a concurrent basis, he supported the chief executive officer in developing and managing the bank's strategic agenda.

Hackett has a Master of Business Administration degree from Stanford University's Graduate School of Business and a Bachelor of Science degree in mechanical engineering from the University of Tennessee-Knoxville.

Hackett is a 2007 Leadership Greater Chicago fellow, and was recently recognized as a 2007 Business Leader of Color by Chicago United. He is on the Black Ensemble Theater's board of directors, is a member of The Executives' Club of Chicago, and serves as an active alumni interviewer for Stanford University's Graduate School of Business.

Charles Horn III began his career with BMO Financial Group, parent company of Harris, 19 years ago. Today, he serves as managing director and head of the direct business development team for the U.S. cash management sales division of BMO's investment banking arm, Harris Nesbitt.

Charles leads a specialized team of professionals that cover the global insurance industry, securitization and equity sponsors, and diversified financial services market segments. He has an ongoing mandate to develop new revenue sources for the bank, targeting the above industries, as well as managing several of the firm's largest clients.

Charles earned a bachelor's degree from the Illinois Institute of Technology, with concentrations in information technology management and accounting. Additionally, he serves on the executive board of the Have a Heart for Sickle Cell Anemia Foundation.

Charles Horn III

Managing Director
Harris Nesbitt/BMO Nesbitt Burns

Anthony Hoskins became the plant manager at Chicago Assembly Plant on November 3, 2004. Subsequently, the plant was awarded the Mercury Montego J.D. Power Best-in-Class; the Highest Ford NA Plant in Customer Satisfaction; the 2005 Safety Innovation Regional Winner; the *Consumer Reports* Recommended Buy for Ford 500, Mercury Montego and Freestyle; the J.D. Power/Harbour 2nd Best-in-Company; and the Energy Star Award for North America's most efficient assembly plant.

Previously, Hoskins was lean manufacturing manager at Atlanta Assembly Plant when that plant earned the title of Most Improved North American Assembly Plant in Lean Manufacturing Implementation and the Bronze Award from J.D. Power & Associates.

Joining Ford in 1990 as a supervisor at Dearborn Assembly, Hoskins has held various positions, including final body superintendent at Dearborn Assembly, and assembly and stamping area manager at Dearborn Frame. His notable achievements include $1.2 million in total cost and labor improvements at Dearborn Framing and the Presidential Award for Most Improved TGW Plant in Ford.

Hoskins earned a bachelor's degree in industrial technology from Iowa State University and a master's degree in science from Central Michigan University.

Anthony L. Hoskins

Plant Manager
Chicago Assembly Plant
Ford Motor Company

CHICAGO'S CORPORATE BRASS

Andre Jackson

Senior Vice President
Jones Lang LaSalle

A ndre Jackson is a senior vice president and chief counsel of construction for Jones Lang LaSalle. He has primary responsibility for legal support of Jones Lang LaSalle construction.

Jackson earned a Bachelor of Business Administration degree and a Master of Business Administration degree from the University of Iowa. He is also a graduate of the University of Michigan Law School.

A native of Chicago, Jackson and his wife, Camille, have three daughters, Corinne, Colette and Jasmine.

Oscar Johnson Jr.

Senior Vice President &
Division Manager
LaSalle Bank

O scar Johnson Jr. has worked as a commercial banker with LaSalle Bank in Chicago, Illinois, since March of 1998. He is a senior vice president and division manager, and is responsible for managing a group of lenders that source and underwrite commercial loans to mid cap companies throughout the country.

Oscar obtained a Bachelor of Business Administration degree from Howard University in Washington, D.C., and a Master of Business Administration degree from Marquette University in 1999.

In addition to his job at LaSalle Bank, Oscar teaches commercial banking courses through the Illinois Bankers Association, and serves as a volunteer with Big Brothers Big Sisters. He also serves on the board of directors of Big Brothers Big Sisters of Chicago; Resurrection Hospital/ West Suburban in Oak Park, Illinois; Urban Prep Charter Academy for Young Men (a new charter school created in 2006 in Chicago's Englewood Community); and the Scenemakers Council at the Goodman Theatre.

Elliott Jones is managing director of Aon's Chicago Service Center, located in Glenview, Illinois. He is responsible for a staff of more than 350 people whose job it is to provide service to Aon offices throughout the United States in support of their clients.

Before joining Aon in 1999, Elliott was employed by Willis and Alexander & Alexander, where he managed brokerage operations specializing in casualty insurance and alternative risks programs. He began his career in 1971 as an underwriter for CNA Insurance Company and later joined Zurich Insurance Company, where he managed a national account team focused on large corporate clients. While at Willis, he was named president and chief executive officer of the Chicago office of Willis' wholesale broker, Stewart Smith.

Elliott is vice president of the Chicago chapter of the National African-American Insurance Association. He received a bachelor's degree in economics and business administration from Wheaton College in 1969, and earned an associate in risk management designation in 1988.

A native of Chicago, Elliott has six children, ranging in age from 19 to 32.

Elliott Jones

Managing Director
Aon Client Services
Aon Risk Services, Inc.

Lorna Jones is director of human resource technology for Aon Corporation. She is responsible for enabling global technology solutions that allow Aon colleagues to effectively manage the company's talent. Lorna has led several major projects, including acquisitions, divestitures and the redesign of Aon's payroll system that resulted in a savings of $9 million.

Lorna has been selected for Aon's Catalyst Program, which places emerging leaders in increased responsibilities, to leverage her expertise. This high impact program is designed to help Aon leaders make strategic business decisions and leverage talent in a way that grows the business.

Consistently, Lorna has encouraged her team to engage in philanthropic giving. For the past five years, she and her team have collected toys for the Jane Addams Hull House Association's foster care program granting wishes to those who may not otherwise experience the true meaning of the season.

Lorna is the wife of Kenneth and the proud mother of two sons, Marcus and Vincent. She enjoys the theater, concerts and sporting events, and has been active on a number of civic committees.

Lorna Jones

Director
Human Resource Technology
Aon Corporation

CHICAGO'S CORPORATE BRASS

Nicole Lawson-Travis

District Sales Manager
American Family Insurance

Nicole Lawson-Travis is the district sales manager/recruiter of district 829 for American Family Insurance in Chicago. In this position, she manages agents, sales production, profit, growth, retention and recruits new talent into the agency field force.

Nicole is on the board of directors for the Neighborhood Housing Services of Chicago, which educates soon-to-be and existing homeowners about mortgages, insurance and safety concerns. She is active in several communities throughout the Chicagoland area, facilitating educational insurance seminars and offering agency career opportunities.

Nicole is currently enrolled at the University of Phoenix, completing a Bachelor of Arts degree in business management. She has received several insurance licenses and industry accolades for exceptional sales production as an agent and manager.

A native of Chicago, Illinois, Nicole is recently married to her inspirational husband, Dana Travis, and is a proud new mother of Dayna Lawrence Travis Jr., and 13-year-old daughter Sarah Lawson.

Cindy Lazard-Hunt

Chicago Location Manager
Ernst & Young LLP

Cindy Lazard-Hunt is the location manager for Ernst & Young's Chicago office. In this capacity, she has overall responsibility for administrative operations and facilities management for more than 1,600 employees. She leads a management staff of five and has overall accountability for more than 100 people. Additionally, she manages the office's annual operations and capital expenditure budget, and works closely with Ernst & Young leadership to align people and processes and to identify workplace efficiencies.

Prior to her recent career change in February of 2007, Cindy spent 12 years with Ernst & Young's technology organization, where she managed both operations and infrastructure.

Cindy received her Bachelor of Science degree from California State University–Dominguez Hills in Carson, California. She is also very active in the Girl Scouts of America, Chicago chapter.

A native of Los Angeles, Cindy and her husband, Greg, have one child.

Spencer Leak Jr. is senior vice president of Leak and Sons Funeral Chapels. He has earned a reputation for being a compassionately relentless driving force, who has forged the business principles of sound aptitude, integrity and unbridled community vision throughout the organization.

Leak works diligently with chairman Spencer Leak Sr., the Leak and Sons policy committee and the board of directors. He received an Associate of Science degree in mortuary science from Southern Illinois University. A board member of OperationPUSH and the Better Boys Foundation, Leak is a member of Liberty Baptist Church, Kappa Alpha Psi Fraternity, Inc. and 100 Black Men of Chicago. Additionally, he is a Cook County Board of Elections deputy registrar.

Leak has served as the campaign chairman for Jesse Jackson Jr. for U.S. Congress, and has hosted fundraisers for several public service luminaries. He has also served on the steering committees for Barack Obama for U.S. Senate and Kwame Raoul for Illinois State Senate.

Leak is married to Dr. Donna Simpson Leak. They have two children, Spencer Leak III and Emma Sophia.

Spencer Leak Jr.

Senior Vice President
Leak and Sons Funeral Chapels

Adorn Lewis has worked in various management positions for Flowers Communications Group (FCG) since 1994. As senior vice president, she is responsible for agency client services.

Prior to joining FCG, Lewis was the national director of the National Council of Negro Women's Black Family Reunion Celebration. Before this position, she was the president and chief executive officer of ALD Communications, a Chicago-based public relations and special events firm. She previously served as an account group supervisor at Burrell Public Relations. Lewis has also worked as a brand public relations supervisor at Milwaukee-based Miller Brewing Company. She launched her public relations career in 1985 as an associate editor at ShopTalk Trade Publication.

With a bachelor's degree in mass communications from Drake University, Lewis currently serves as a board member for Muntu Dance Theater of Chicago and Little Brothers – Friends of the Elderly. She is a member of the National Association of Black Journalists, the Chicago Association of Black Journalists and Alpha Kappa Alpha Sorority, Inc.

She has garnered more than 25 industry awards for excellence in communications and public relations.

Adorn L. Lewis

Senior Vice President
Flowers Communications Group

Darlene Lewis, Ph.D.

Vice President &
Chief Human Resources Officer
The University of Chicago
Medical Center

D r. Darlene Lewis is vice president and chief human resources officer at The University of Chicago Medical Center. She has 55 members on her human resources staff who service the 9,300 employees of the medical center by providing labor/employee relations, compensation, benefits, human resources information systems, selection and recruitment, training and development, workers compensation, and occupational medicine services. Approximately one-quarter of the medical center employees are represented by five unions.

In her human resources experience, Lewis has worked in both the private and public sector. She has directed human resources functions for the Cleveland Public Library, Tandon Corporation, Johnson and Higgins, Tokyo, and the Massachusetts Department of Employment Security. Her last 17 years of senior human resource officer experience have been in academic health care, when she was employed at Magee-Womens Hospital of the University of Pittsburgh Medical Center and Vanderbilt University Medical Center.

A native Californian, Lewis received a bachelor's degree from San Diego State, a master's degree from the University of Illinois, Champaign-Urbana, and a doctorate degree in organizational development from Benedictine University in Lisle, Illinois.

J. Corey Lewis

Senior Vice President
Jones Lang LaSalle

J . Corey Lewis is a senior vice president in the Corporate Capital Markets Group at Jones Lang LaSalle. He is responsible for developing and executing financial strategies that incorporate occupancy and financial objectives for the firm's major clients. Prior to his current role, Lewis was the chief financial officer for the corporate solutions business, where he was responsible for financial and business matters for a diverse group of global real estate service lines, including tenant representation, facility management, project management and strategic consulting.

Lewis is a member of the National Association of Black Accountants and an active participant in the Executive Leadership Council, an organization providing African-American executives in Fortune 500 companies with a networking and leadership forum. He also serves on the board of directors of the Partnership for Quality Childcare, a nonprofit organization improving childcare for Chicago's low-income families.

Lewis earned his Master of Business Administration degree from The University of Chicago and a Bachelor of Science degree from Hampton University. A Milwaukee native, he and wife Raishon have two children, James Bryton and Raina Devyn.

Entering his 15th season as a member of the Chicago Bulls front office, Bob Love is the director of community affairs. Serving as the Bulls' "goodwill ambassador," Bob represents the organization at various functions throughout the Chicago community. He makes more than 300 appearances every year at schools, charity events, clinics, nonprofit groups and youth programs. Bob is a member of the Bulls' All-Star Reading Team, and assists in fundraising for their charity arm, CharitaBulls. As a motivational speaker, he also travels to schools and social agencies to deliver his inspirational message about overcoming a speech handicap and his life as a professional athlete.

Bob played 11 seasons in the NBA, including eight with the Bulls. On January 14, 1994, he became the second Chicago Bull to have his jersey retired.

Bob is an honorary spokesperson for the National Stuttering Federation of America, and has been awarded honorary doctoral degrees from Carthage College and the University of Rhode Island. He also serves on the boards of the Chicago Abused Women Coalition and the American Cancer Federation.

Bob Love

Director of Community Affairs
Chicago Bulls

William L. Lumpkin is the regional vice president of hotel accounting North America for the Hyatt Hotels Corporation based in Chicago, Illinois. In this capacity, he oversees the accounting operation for more than 30 hotels located along the east coast and in the Caribbean.

Lumpkin began his career with Hyatt 26 years ago at the Hyatt Regency Memphis, holding positions such as night auditor, night manager, chief accountant/payroll supervisor and assistant controller. From there, he became controller, regional controller and information technology manager of software development. Additionally, he worked as the information technology manager of software development for a major airline, and was manager of business process design for a major consulting and accounting firm.

Graduating from the University of Memphis with a Bachelor of Business Administration degree in accounting, Lumpkin is a certified public accountant and a certified hospitality technology professional.

A native of Memphis, Tennessee, he currently resides in Carol Stream, Illinois, and is married to Linda Lumpkin, vice president of human resources for the Midwest division of Cadbury Schweppes Bottling Group.

William L. Lumpkin

Regional Vice President
Hotel Accounting
Hyatt Hotels Corporation

CHICAGO'S CORPORATE BRASS

La Rue Martin Jr.

Community Services Manager
UPS

L a Rue Martin Jr. is the community services manager for UPS in the Metro Chicago District, which employs approximately 4,500 people and covers the Chicago metropolitan area, extending into northwest Indiana.

While in this position, La Rue has received a Leadership in Community Relations Award from the Human Resources Development Institute, a Chicago Urban League Beautiful People Award, a Dr. Martin Luther King Jr. Legacy Award and a Black Heritage Award. He was most recently identified by UPS corporately as one of 86 exceptional employees being honored in 2007 during the company's centennial celebration.

La Rue's board memberships and civic affiliations include the Westside Association for Community Action, Athletes Against Drugs, the City Club of Chicago, the YMCA Mentoring Program, the Cook County State's Attorney's Office and the African American Advisory Council.

A native of Chicago, La Rue graduated from De La Salle High School and earned a bachelor's degree from Loyola University. In 1972 he was selected as the number one overall pick in the NBA draft by the Portland Trail Blazers.

Anthony McCain

Vice President, Field Operations
Nicor Gas

A nthony McCain is vice president of field operations for Nicor Gas. In this role, he is responsible for the distribution of natural gas throughout the company's 32,000-mile pipeline system, which serves more than two million customers across the upper third of Illinois.

Anthony is a member of the American Gas Association, the Will County Center for Economic Development, the American Association of Blacks in Energy, and Leadership of Greater Chicago. He also serves on the board of directors of Voices for Illinois Children and the Midwest Energy Association.

Anthony earned a bachelor's degree from Benedictine College in 1984 and a Master of Business Administration degree from Benedictine College in 1993.

Darren McQueen is a member of the Global Cellular and Broadband Networks Group senior leadership team, and serves as vice president of global product management, IMS, cellular and broadband access technologies for the home and networks mobility business.

Darren has recently been given the responsibility of Motorola's second big bet in wireless broadband. He is also responsible for leading Motorola's global CDMA cellular technology, IMS (IP multi media subsystem), UMA (unlicensed mobile access), seamless mobility, messaging and converged core product management organizations. He is currently responsible for driving more than $400 million in research and development as well as maintaining a $2 billion-plus product portfolio.

Prior to joining Motorola, Darren was director of CDMA and common platform product management for new global product introduction for Lucent Technologies mobility solutions radio access network organization.

He holds a Master of Business Administration degree from The University of Chicago, a master's degree in management information systems from Stevens Institute of Technology and a bachelor's degree from Fairleigh Dickenson University.

Darren and Angella, his wife, have three children, daughter Samantha, and twin boys Christopher and Aaron.

Darren McQueen

Vice President
Global Product Management
Motorola, Inc.

Roosevelt Moncure is the catering marketing director at Hyatt Regency Chicago, Hyatt and Chicago's largest hotel. He is responsible for overseeing all aspects of catering functions, from sales and planning to execution and retention, with a primary focus on the social market.

Roosevelt began working at Hyatt Regency Chicago in 1984. He has been named Hyatt Regency Chicago's Manager of the Year three times, and has received the prestigious honor of being named a Hyatt Master for the past eight years. Roosevelt achieved Hyatt's highest catering honor, being named Hyatt's Catering Manager of the Year in 2000 and again in 2005. His accomplishments, dedication and service have set an entirely new standard at Hyatt Regency Chicago.

Roosevelt is an active member of 100 Black Men of Chicago, the Urban League, the RainbowPUSH Coalition and the Chicago Assembly. In his spare time, he enjoys spending time with his wife, Shari, and daughter Brooke.

Roosevelt Moncure

Catering Marketing Director
Hyatt Regency Chicago

Daryl Newell

Senior Vice President
ShoreBank

Daryl Newell is a senior vice president at ShoreBank, the first community development and environmental bank in the country with $2 billion in assets. He is responsible for the Retail Banking Department's $15 million annual budget and the management of more than 100 full- and part-time employees in the bank's Chicago offices serving consumers and small businesses.

Daryl was honored with the 2006 Friend of the Continental Africa Chamber of Commerce U.S. Award; a 2003 Monarch Award in the business category; inclusion in *Who's Who Among African Americans, 15th Edition*; and an Illuminati Award from the Institute for Positive Living's Open Book Program. His volunteer efforts with the Big Ten Conference Advisory Committee, the National Football League Retired Players Association and 100 Black Men of Chicago, Inc. are preparing hundreds of youth for a better future.

Daryl attended the Kellogg School of Management's KMI14 Program, and received a master's degree from the Keller Graduate School of Management and a bachelor's degree from Northwestern University. A Gary native, he and his wife, Verlena, are raising two sons, Daryl and Grant.

Linda M. Nolan

Senior Vice President
Northern Trust

Linda Nolan is a senior vice president at Northern Trust. She is a managing director in the Private Banking Group with responsibility for private banking teams as well as employee banking. Her responsibilities include financial management, business development and client servicing for the Consolidated Group, which generates more than $25 million in annual revenues. Linda chairs the Personal Financial Services-Illinois Deposit Rate Setting Committee, and manages emerging markets initiatives. She assumed her current responsibilities in September of 2004.

Prior to assuming her current role, Linda served as managing director of the State Street Financial Center. She received her Bachelor of Science degree in marketing from Florida A&M University, and is a certified cash manager.

Linda serves on the boards of Family Focus Englewood, Horizons for Youth, the New City YMCA and the Alpha Kappa Alpha Educational Advancement Foundation advisory council. She has served as chair for the signature fundraising event for Women Changing Our World for the past three years.

Al Orendorff is director of U.S. public relations for Aon, the world's largest commercial insurance brokerage. In this capacity, he manages relationships with the news media throughout the United States, working to ensure Aon's marketplace strategies, goals and business objectives are understood and accurately reported.

Orendorff has worked in public relations for 25 years. Prior to coming to Aon, he was a media relations vice president at a financial communications firm, the Financial Relations Board, and he managed media relations for Allstate Insurance Co. In 1982 he was featured in *Jet* magazine as Bradley University's first African-American media relations director.

Orendorff began his communications career as a television and radio journalist. During those years, he won numerous awards for reporting.

He earned a Bachelor of Science degree in communications from Illinois State University in Normal. In 2002 he was named a Distinguished Alumnus.

A native of Lincoln, Illinois, Orendorff is married to Murrieal Orendorff. They have one son, Alex.

Al Orendorff

Director, U.S. Public Relations
Aon Corporation

Debra Parker is a senior banker in the Government, Nonprofit and Health Care Department of JPMorgan Chase (formerly First National Bank of Chicago). She is responsible for marketing commercial banking services to governmental and not-for-profit entities, as well as managing several key municipal relationships. She joined the company as an operations analyst in the Control Department, and later worked in the Government and Public Banking Division as a marketing associate, industry analyst, client services team leader and senior corporate finance associate.

Prior to joining Chase, Debra was a management consultant for Alexander Proudfoot, where she conducted productivity measurement studies and change training for mid-level managers at Fortune 500 companies.

She holds a Master of Business Administration degree from Northwestern University and a Bachelor of Science degree from Illinois State University.

Debra is active in youth education-related activities, and has been involved with numerous education organizations and programs, including Junior Achievement, the United Negro College Fund, The Black Star Project, Jessie Owens Academy Readers and Donors Choose. She is a mentor and sponsor with LINK Unlimited.

Debra R. Parker

Vice President
JPMorgan Chase Bank, N.A.

CHICAGO'S CORPORATE BRASS

Bill Payne

Vice President
Networks Advanced Technologies
Motorola

Bill Payne is vice president of the Networks Advanced Technologies (NAT) organization within Motorola's $5 billion Networks business. NAT is chartered with the development of roadmap technologies for the lines of business within Networks. This includes new wireless technologies for video over wireless and mobile high speed Internet access over wireless.

Since joining Motorola in 1996, Bill has directed engineering operations in cable, broadband wireless and cellular infrastructure. Previously, he spent 16 years at AT&T Bell Laboratories.

Bill has six patents awarded and several pending. He received a Bachelor of Science degree in electrical engineering from Purdue University, a Master of Science degree in electrical engineering from Georgia Institute of Technology, and a Doctor of Philosophy degree in electrical engineering from Illinois Institute of Technology.

Bill is a member of the Institute of Electrical and Electronics Engineers, and a past member of the Sigma Xi and Eta Kappa Nu Engineering Honoraries. He is also a life member of Alpha Phi Alpha Fraternity, Inc.

A graduate of Chicago's Leo High School, Bill is a past member of Leo's Governing Board.

Cheryl Pearson-McNeil

Senior Vice President
of Communications
ACNielsen U.S.
The Nielsen Company

Cheryl Pearson-McNeil is senior vice president of communications for ACNielsen U.S., where she leads the company's external and internal communications activities across its businesses in the U.S.

Cheryl joined The Nielsen Company in 2004 as vice president of communications and community affairs for Nielsen Media Research. An award-winning executive with more than two decades of public relations, communications and writing experience, she has worked in television, community relations and politics. Before joining The Nielsen Company, she was director of station relations for NBC5 Chicago.

Cheryl is a member of The Executives' Club of Chicago and The Economic Club of Chicago, and has served on several boards including Girl Scouts of Chicago and the Chicago Foundation for Women. She has won numerous industry awards and was recently named one of America's 25 Influential Black Women by *The Network Journal*. She has also been featured in *Jet*, *Ebony*, *Black Enterprise*, *SELF* and *Today's Chicago Woman* magazines. Cheryl has a Bachelor of Arts degree and a Master of Business Administration degree, and is currently working on a Master of Fine Arts degree.

Grace Ratliff is vice president of payroll for Jones Lang LaSalle Americas. In her current position, she manages a payroll of 9,000 employees. Ratliff brought to her current role a broad payroll background. Previously, she managed payroll for more than 40,000 employees at Montgomery Ward, where she received the President's Choice Award for her role as payroll manager.

In 2005 Ratliff was highlighted in the Who's Who registry publication for her dedication and hard work at Jones Lang LaSalle, and in 2006 she was recognized and honored with the Jones Lang LaSalle Club Award for her efforts in securing financial assistance for Hurricane Katrina victims in New Orleans. However, her humanitarian efforts did not begin there. A native Chicagoan, Ratliff has a long-standing affiliation with the Starlight Starbright Children's Foundation, which grants wishes to sick underprivileged children, and she is a member of Grant Memorial AME Church.

Ratliff is the mother of two sons, Myron and Tavaris.

Grace Ratliff

Vice President of Payroll
Jones Lang LaSalle

Art Redmond is currently chief marketing officer for Chicago Sun-Times News Group. In this capacity, he is fully responsible for leading the company's strategic marketing, new product development, circulation, sales and service, branding and market research activities. Sun-Times News Group is the largest local news company in the nation focusing on a single geographic market with a dominant portfolio of more than 100 publications.

Before joining Sun-Times, Redmond served as a senior vice president of marketing for Aetna, where he established the corporate marketing function. Earlier in his career, Art served in senior marketing and strategy capacities for PepsiCo, Bristol-Myers Squibb, Citibank and Ford Motor Company. During his 14-year stint with PepsiCo, he traveled extensively while designing and executing marketing programs across more than 120 countries.

Redmond is a graduate of the University of Wisconsin where he received both a bachelor's degree and a master's degree in marketing. He is a board trustee of the Marketing Science Institute and an advisor to the U.S. Census Bureau.

His personal interests include biking, hiking and listening to contemporary jazz.

Art Redmond

Chief Marketing Officer
Chicago Sun-Times News Group

CHICAGO'S CORPORATE BRASS

Wynona Redmond

Public Affairs Director
Dominick's Finer Foods

Wynona Redmond is public affairs director for Dominick's Finer Foods. She oversees the operations of the public affairs office, including public relations, local and state government relations, community relations, special events and the Dominick's Children's Foundation.

Wynona has strengthened Dominick's connection to the community through special events, including the Dominick's annual Ministers' Breakfast. She participates in food drives with the Greater Chicago Food Depository, and awards scholarship dollars to the United Negro College Fund and to Dominick's employees.

Prior to Dominick's, Wynona served in a public affairs management capacity for the Illinois Department of Children & Family Services, the Chicago Housing Authority and Cook County Hospital.

Active in the North Lawndale community, Wynona is a member of St. Agatha Catholic Church, and serves as supervisor of the Lawndale Civic and Educational Jr. Girls and Boys Club. She is the elected president of the National Black Public Relations Society and a member of several distinguished boards, councils and committees.

A resident of Oak Park, Illinois, Wynona graduated from Loyola University Chicago with a bachelor's degree in communications.

Kevin J. Rocio

Managing Director
The KJR Group
National City Mortgage

Kevin J. Rocio is "Chicago's Mortgage Specialist" as named by *Chicago Social* magazine. He serves as managing director at National City Mortgage, and has received numerous awards, including the Bruce Abrams Award, which is the Chicago Association of Realtors' highest award; and the Association's Good Neighbor Award, which he won with his business partner for their new homes initiative for the Englewood Project.

Kevin entered the mortgage industry 17 years ago, and has been recognized as a rising star and top producing loan officer. He is often consulted and quoted for news stories on credit and finance, and frequently speaks to companies on the same topics. The *Chicago Defender* newspaper has also referred to Kevin as half of the "Dynamic Duo of the Mortgage Industry," further demonstrating his strong financial acumen.

He received an undergraduate degree in finance and international economics at Elmhurst College of Illinois. Kevin's unique marketing style has enabled him to build an impressive list of clients and successfully close more than 4,200 residential mortgages.

LaTonya Seanior is manager of corporate supplier diversity for Smurfit-Stone Container Corporation. In this capacity, she is responsible for developing strategies that promote the utilization of diverse suppliers through effective supply chain integration and cultural change. As a member of the senior level diversity council, she also assists in the development and implementation of workforce diversity and community affairs.

Prior to joining Smurfit-Stone, LaTonya worked for RGMA, Inc., a leading expert in supplier diversity program development. While there, she developed strategic plans and training modules for many Fortune 100 companies. Before RGMA, LaTonya was a management consultant with Ernst & Young LLP.

She is a board member of the Chicago Minority Business Development Council and a corporate partner of the Women's Business Development Council. She is also an advisory member of the Chicago Minority Business Opportunity Center and the Minority Business Development Agency (MBDA).

LaTonya is a graduate of Northern Illinois University and a proud member of Alpha Kappa Alpha Sorority, Inc.

LaTonya Seanior

Manager
Corporate Supplier Diversity
Smurfit-Stone Container Corporation

Omar L. Simmons has spent his career working with leading private equity firms and executives. He brings experience in later-stage private equity and leveraged buyout transactions.

Prior to joining Reliant Equity Investors LLC as managing director, Simmons was a senior associate in New York at McCown De Leeuw & Co., a middle-market buyout firm with $1.2 billion in assets under management. There, he focused on growth and leveraged equity investments, including recapitalization and buy-and-build acquisitions, identified potential investments, negotiated with sellers, and structured and arranged debt financing. Post-acquisition, he played an active role in the financing and strategic direction of portfolio companies and participated at board meetings.

Prior to McCown, Simmons served as an associate in Boston for Summit Partners, a later-stage private equity firm where he was responsible for evaluating and analyzing potential acquisition opportunities, and supporting deal teams with business due diligence, deal structuring and analysis.

Simmons earned a Bachelor of Arts degree from Princeton University's Woodrow Wilson School and earned a Master of Business Administration degree, with honors, from Harvard Business School, where he was a Toigo Fellow.

Omar L. Simmons

Managing Director
Reliant Equity Investors LLC

CHICAGO'S CORPORATE BRASS

Warren M. Smith

Director &
Midwest Human Resources Leader
Ernst & Young LLP

Warren M. Smith is a director and the area human resources leader for Ernst & Young's Midwest region. In this capacity, he oversees the enterprise human resource function and is responsible for the development and deployment of strategic human resources initiatives for more than 3,400 employees in the Illinois, Indiana, Iowa, Minnesota, Missouri, Nebraska, western Michigan and Wisconsin offices.

Prior to transferring to the Chicago marketplace in the fall of 2005, Warren spent three years with Ernst & Young's Strategy and Operations Group, where he managed both strategy development and resource management for the Americas People Team.

Warren received a Bachelor of Arts degree from the University of Virginia, and is a member of the Alpha Phi Alpha Fraternity, Inc. and the Society of Human Resources Management. Prior to moving to Chicago, he served on the board of directors of the Washington Technical Professional Forum, a leading human resources association, as the vice president of programs and professional development.

A native of northern Virginia, Warren and his wife, Tasha, have three children.

Lyndon A. Taylor

Executive Director
Russell Reynolds Associates

Lyndon A. Taylor is a member of the Russell Reynolds Associates' Corporate Officers and Financial Services Sectors and Diversity Practice. Within the Corporate Officers Sector, Lyndon focuses on searches for finance professionals, including chief financial officers and finance function leaders. His financial services search work focuses on recruiting professionals in alternative asset and wealth management, commercial finance and global and investment banking.

Lyndon began his executive search career in 2000. Prior to his executive search career, he worked in both the financial services and energy industries. He previously held investment-banking positions with UBS Warburg LLC and Merrill Lynch, and worked in corporate development for Enron.

Lyndon is a member of the National Black MBA Association and The University of Chicago Graduate School of Business Alumni Association. He received the Rising Star Award from The University of Chicago African American MBA Association in 2004. He also served in the U.S. Navy.

Lyndon received bachelor's degrees in history and ethnic studies from Southern Methodist University. He received a Master of Business Administration degree from The University of Chicago Graduate School of Business.

Rita Taylor-Nash is vice president of corporate diversity for Health Care Service Corporation (HCSC), which includes Blue Cross and Blue Shield of Illinois, Texas, New Mexico and Oklahoma. She is responsible for the development, oversight, review and implementation of diversity strategies and initiatives. Through Rita's leadership, HCSC has received several major recognitions, including the 2005 Corporate Diversity Award from the Chicago Council on Urban Affairs; *Diversity-Inc*'s Top 50 Companies for Diversity, Top 10 Companies for Latinos and African Americans, and Best Companies for Blacks in Technology; and Chicago United's Changing How Chicago Works diversity award.

She is a member of the South Suburban Chicago Chapter of Jack & Jill and a board member for the South-Southwest Suburban United Way. She also serves on the executive committee of the Blue Cross and Blue Shield Association Diversity Alliance.

Rita earned a bachelor's degree in sociology from The University of Chicago and a master's degree from the University of Michigan.

She and her husband are proud parents of one daughter. Rita has also served as a mentor to many throughout her career.

Rita Taylor-Nash

Vice President, Corporate Diversity
Health Care Service Corporation

Shundrawn A. Thomas serves as senior vice president and head of corporate strategy for Northern Trust. His primary responsibilities include supporting the Executive Management Group with strategic planning initiatives and coordinating the strategic planning process for each of the four business units.

Prior to joining Northern Trust, Shundrawn served as a vice president at The Goldman Sachs Group. As senior relationship manager in the equities division, he co-managed a team that serviced several of the firm's largest institutional clients. Before that, Shundrawn worked as a fixed income analyst at Morgan Stanley. His product experience includes high-yield research, corporate bond trading, and futures and options sales.

In addition to his corporate experience, Shundrawn is the co-founder of two knowledge-based companies, Adelphos Holdings LLC and Tree of Life Resources LLP. Shundrawn received a Bachelor of Science degree in accounting from Florida A&M University and a Master of Business Administration degree from The University of Chicago Graduate School of Business. Shundrawn, his wife, Latania, and their two sons, Javon and Micah, reside in Flossmoor, Illinois.

Shundrawn A. Thomas

Senior Vice President &
Head of Corporate Strategy
Northern Trust

Jason J. Tyler

Senior Vice President
Portfolio Management
Ariel Capital Management, LLC

Jason Tyler is a member of the portfolio management team for Ariel Capital Management, LLC. More specifically, he leads the firm's research analysis of banks, information services, office equipment and supplies, office furnishings and fixtures, and telecommunications industries. He also oversees the team's daily activities, including the supervision and development of Ariel's research associates and administrative staff.

In 2006 Jason was appointed to oversee Ariel's client restriction monitoring. In this capacity, he manages the team that ensures adherence to specifications for client contracts. Prior to joining Ariel in 2003, he worked at Bank One/American National Bank for ten years, most recently as a finance manager in the Planning and Analysis Group.

Jason received a Master of Business Administration degree from The University of Chicago and a Bachelor of Arts degree in politics from Princeton University. He serves as president of the board of directors for the Emergency Fund for Needy People and the After School All Stars. In addition, he serves as treasurer of the board of directors for the Joffrey Ballet.

Mark Urquhart

Vice President, Facilities,
Design & Construction
The University of Chicago
Medical Center

Mark Urquhart is vice president for facilities, design and construction at The University of Chicago Medical Center, where his team oversees more than six million square feet of space, including dry and wet research laboratories in academic buildings and clinic space in the Medical Center. The department also includes security, operations and maintenance, parking, institutional safety and environmental services.

Prior to joining the Medical Center in 2000, Mark was resident regional director for Crothall, Sodexho and Marriott Management Services. He has worked in the facilities management field around the country at Children's of Philadelphia, Children's of Pittsburgh, Northwestern Memorial Hospital and University of Illinois at Chicago Hospital. A Philadelphia native, Mark earned a bachelor's degree from Indiana University in Pennsylvania and a Master of Business Administration degree from The University of Chicago in 2006.

Mark's unwavering commitment to the utilization of minority- and women-owned businesses and hiring and promoting a diverse management team has earned him numerous awards. Most notably, he was named a 2007 Chicago United Business Leaders of Color for outstanding success in business diversity and promoting multicultural leadership.

Emmett Vaughn developed Exelon initiatives that have resulted in $250 million of business to minority- and women-owned business enterprise (MWBE) suppliers in two years. Exelon has received several Corporation of the Year awards from nationally recognized business advocacy organizations for its leadership in diversity.

Before Exelon, Emmett managed a consulting practice that focused on diversity and business development strategies for the retail, manufacturing and small businesses serving clients in Chicago, Dallas and Los Angeles.

He worked as a senior consultant for RGMA Management Consulting, concentrating on supplier diversity and economic development projects. While employed at RR Donnelley in 2000, Emmett worked a loaned executive assignment as the chief operating officer with the Reverend Jesse Jackson's RainbowPUSH Coalition, assisting management with corporate outreach and minority business projects.

He holds a Master of Business Administration degree from Northwestern University and a bachelor's degree from Northeast Missouri State University.

Emmett's community interests include serving on the boards of the Chicago Minority Business Development Council, NMSDC, UCAN Social Services and the House of Blues Foundation, and ministering at Salem Baptist Church.

Emmett T. Vaughn

Diverse Business Enablement Leader
Exelon Corporation

Cynthia Washington is an associate director at the American Hospital Association (AHA), where she manages a diversity initiative to advance relationships and increase involvement with ethnic minority hospital chief executive officers. She manages the Hospital Awards for Volunteer Excellence, which recognizes outstanding hospital volunteer programs, and serves on the AHA's Eliminate Racial and Ethnic Disparities in Healthcare Committee.

Cynthia was re-elected to a third term as the first female board chair of Habilitative Systems, Inc., a health and human services organization. She is a founding member of the Sistuh Fund Giving Circle, which is Illinois' first African-American women's giving fund. Cynthia served on the board of trustees of Trinity United Church of Christ for more than 15 years.

Cynthia received an undergraduate degree from North Carolina A&T State University and is a certified meeting professional. She is the recipient of the American Society of Association Executives' Diversity Executive Leadership fellowship and a member of Delta Sigma Theta Sorority, Inc.

A native of Charlotte, North Carolina, Cynthia enjoys gardening, step aerobics and golfing. She is the proud mother of one son, Brooks.

Cynthia M. Washington

Associate Director
American Hospital Association

Mark David Welch

Vice President
Global Diversity Director
Northern Trust

Mark David Welch is vice president and global diversity director for Northern Trust. In this role, he is responsible for the development and execution of Northern Trust's global strategy for diversity and inclusion.

Prior to his current position, Mark served as vice president and director of marketing for the Western Region of Northern Trust's Personal Financial Services. In that role, he was responsible for all marketing activities, including advertising, public relations, graphic design, sales generation, project management, demographics, and economic and market analysis in the states of California, Nevada, and Washington. Before joining Northern Trust in 1999, Mark served as marketing officer of the Private Client Group at Jurika & Voyles LLP, a boutique investment management firm that managed more than $7 billion in assets.

He earned Bachelor of Arts degrees in economics and environmental studies (policy and planning) from the University of California. In 1996 Mark was named an Irvine fellow in urban policy and planning at Stanford University.

He is actively involved in several community organizations, including Alpha Phi Alpha Fraternity, Inc.

Chareice White

Corporate Director of
Community Relations
Majestic Star and
Fitzgeralds Casino Hotel

Chareice White is the corporate director of community relations for Majestic Star and Fitzgeralds Casino Hotel. She is responsible for corporate and local sponsorship, charitable and in-kind donations and corporate community-related events. She is also responsible for overseeing special events for Don H. Barden, the owner, chair, CEO, and first and only African American to own and operate a national casino company.

Under the direction of White, the company has donated thousands of dollars to various organizations. Additionally, she is the vice president of the Barden Gary Foundation, and a board member for the Boys and Girls Club of Northwest Indiana, American Heart Association, Northwest Indiana Sickle Cell Foundation, Gary Chamber of Commerce, and the Lake County Convention and Visitors Bureau. She is also a member of the National Coalition of Black Meeting Planners and the Northern Indiana chapter of The Links, Inc.

White was instrumental in forming a prestigious group of select company team members known as Community Ambassadors. The purpose is for individuals to serve as goodwill ambassadors on behalf of the company, being "committed to the community."

Diane White is the vice president of operations at the Field Museum. She is responsible for the strategic planning and oversight of guest relations, protection services, housekeeping, the mailroom, the print shop, and food and vending services.

Diane joined the museum in December of 1990 with more than ten years of progressive management experience in customer-oriented, labor-intensive environments.

Diane has a Bachelor of Science degree in management from Northeastern Illinois University and a Master of Business Administration degree from Benedictine University. She teaches a course in customer service at National-Louis University in Chicago.

Diane is married and has two children.

Diane White

Vice President of Operations
Field Museum

Wayne White is vice president of global consumer services and GTM strategy, responsible for accelerating Motorola's growth in the consumer services space. He has global go-to-market responsibility for customer care, e-commerce, application services, business development and strategy. Prior to his current role, Wayne was vice president and general manager of the iDEN Go-To-Market, where he was responsible for managing Motorola's multibillion-dollar push-to-talk handset business in North America, South America, Asia and the Middle East. Prior to joining Motorola, he held leadership positions at Verizon Wireless, AT&T and General Electric.

Wayne is a former board member of Gleaner's Food Bank and the National Kidney Foundation of Southeast Michigan. He is a 2002 recipient of *Crain's Detroit Business* 40 Under 40 Award, and is currently a big brother in the Big Brothers Big Sisters program.

Wayne holds a Bachelor of Science degree in mechanical engineering from the University of Pittsburgh, and a Master of Business Administration degree from Case Western Reserve University in Cleveland.

Wayne White

Vice President
Global Consumer Services &
GTM Strategy
Motorola

W. "Bill" Williams Jr., CMP

Vice President, Diversity & Sales
Chicago Convention & Tourism Bureau

W. "Bill" Williams Jr. serves as vice president of diversity and sales for the Chicago Convention and Tourism Bureau (CCTB). Bill has been with the CCTB for three decades, covering the SMERF Market, and has more than 40 years in the hospitality industry.

Bill is a founding member of the National Coalition of Black Meeting Planners and a founding board member of the Chicago Chapter of the Society of Government Meeting Professionals.

A former marine, Bill is a lifetime member of Kappa Alpha Psi Fraternity, Inc., and is a 33rd degree Mason Shriner. He also holds memberships in numerous organizations, including the Religious Conference Management Association, the NAACP, Christian Meetings & Convention Association, the Urban League, RainbowPUSH Coalition, the International Rat Pack Organization, and the Improved Benevolent Protective Order of Elks of the World. Additionally, he served as vice chair of the Westside Association for Community Action, and a board member of Shoop School 49ers and the Chicago Public Schools Academy of Travel and Tourism.

Born in Chicago, Bill is a graduate of Chicago State University with a business degree.

Michael Woods

Regional Director
Marketing Communications
Comcast

Michael Woods is regional director of marketing communications for Comcast's largest market. In this position, she manages marketing and advertising campaigns for all products, including Comcast digital cable, high-speed Internet and digital voice.

Michael has been recognized for her expertise in urban target marketing and ability to reach key niche markets. She has managed brand and acquisition promotional campaigns with organizations including the Chicago Bears, the United Negro College Fund, the Greater Chicago Food Depository, the Greenhouse Shelter for women and children, and several prominent Chicago sports professionals.

justice

protect

CHICAGO'S

COUNSELORS AT LAW

serve

equality

freedom

dedicated

wise

law

honorable

Melvin L. Brooks

Partner, Attorney at Law
Cochran, Cherry, Givens,
Smith & Montgomery

Melvin L. Brooks is a partner in the law firm of Cochran, Cherry, Givens, Smith & Montgomery. Prior to joining the Cochran firm in 2003, Brooks was associated with the personal injury firm of Costello, McMahon & Burke, Ltd., handling cases involving construction negligence, police misconduct, products liability and medical negligence. He has extensive experience as a civil litigator from serving with the City of Chicago Law Department as deputy corporation counsel handling complex multimillion-dollar cases. Brooks' litigation skills have been recognized by legal publications such as *The National Law Journal* and *Chicago Law Bulletin*.

Brooks is a member of the American Trial Lawyers Association and the Cook County Bar Association. He is admitted to practice before the Federal District Court for the Northern District of Illinois, and is a member of the Federal trial bar. Brooks regularly lectures at seminars for the Illinois Institute of Continuing Legal Education, and was published in the Summer 1997 edition of the *Legal Defense Manual*.

Brooks is a 1985 graduate of the University of Iowa College of Law.

Andrea M. Buford

Managing Member
Buford Law Office, LLC

Andrea M. Buford is the managing member of Buford Law Office, LLC. As such, she manages and practices civil defense litigation for Fortune 500 companies as well as many government entities. A past president of the Cook County Bar Association, she serves as a vice chair of the National Bar Association, Commercial Law Section. Buford has been appointed a federal foreclosure commissioner and a special assistant attorney general. Additionally, Buford was named an Illinois Super Lawyer and One of the Most Influential Chicagoans. She is the recipient of many awards and recognitions, including The National Black Expo Presidential Award and the Women at the Top of the Game Award.

Serving as a mentor and volunteer attorney, Buford has donated countless hours to assisting lawyers in establishing practices. She has served on the boards of the National Bar Association, the Cook County Bar Association and Positive Anti-Crime Thrust, to name a few.

Buford earned a Bachelor of Science degree from Northwestern University and a juris doctorate from IIT Chicago Kent College of Law.

Peter C.B. Bynoe is a senior partner in the Chicago office of DLA Piper, a global law firm with 3,400 attorneys. Bynoe serves on the firm's executive committee. He also serves as the chair of Telemat Ltd., a project management and financial services firm that he founded in 1982. Bynoe is a director of Rewards Network and Covanta Holding Corporation. He is a life trustee of Goodman Theater, a trustee of the Rush University Medical Center and a director of The CORE Center for the Prevention, Care and Research of Infectious Diseases.

In 2005 Bynoe was named by *Fortune* magazine to the Fortune Diversity list of the most influential African Americans, Latinos and Asian Americans. He was designated an Illinois Super Lawyer in both 2005 and 2006. Prior to joining DLA Piper, Bynoe oversaw the development of the Olympic Stadium and its conversion to Turner Field, and he owned the NBA's Denver Nuggets from 1989 to 1992.

Peter C.B. Bynoe
Partner, Attorney at Law
DLA Piper, LLP

Dorothy Capers is the deputy corporation counsel for the City of Chicago Department of Law. Her areas of focus include licensing, ordinance prosecution, zoning and building-related matters. Dorothy has handled many high-profile media cases in her position. Her division produces more than $50 million in annual revenue. Dorothy is also the chair of the hiring committee for the Department of Law. She has greatly improved the diversity of the department.

Dorothy is the president of the Black Women Lawyers Association of Greater Chicago. She dedicates her time to service organizations, including Jack and Jill of America, Delta Sigma Theta Sorority, Inc. and Trinity United Church of Christ, where she serves on the Board of Long Range Planning.

Dorothy received a Bachelor of Arts degree from the University of Illinois, and obtained a juris doctorate from Howard University School of Law.

A native of Pine Bluff, Arkansas, Dorothy is married to Steven Capers, and has two daughters, Mariah and Mackenzie.

Dorothy G. Capers
Deputy Corporation Counsel
City of Chicago Department of Law

Demetrius E. Carney

Partner, Attorney at Law
Perkins Coie LLP

Demetrius E. Carney, a partner at Perkins Coie LLP, is a member of the firm's Government Relations and Public Finance Practice groups. His practice focuses on structuring relationships between local government agencies and private sector clients in an effort to create private/public partnerships to simulate economic development through incentive programs, public finance, land use and structured financings (debt and equity). He regularly counsels clients on local government procurement contracting and on federal and local government regulations governing minority, women's and disadvantaged business enterprise programs.

Carney received a bachelor's degree from Loyola University Chicago and graduated with a juris doctor degree from DePaul University College of Law.

A member of the Cook County, American and National bar associations, Carney is also involved in the Alliance of Business Leaders & Entrepreneurs, Inc. and The Economic Club of Chicago. He is currently president of the Chicago Police Board.

Eric P. Dunham

Senior Partner
E. Powell Dunham & Associates

Eric Dunham is the senior partner for E. Powell Dunham & Associates and of counsel with the firm of Bourgeois & Klein. In his position as senior partner, he serves as chief trial counsel and oversees day-to-day operations of the law firm, concentrating in criminal and real estate law.

Although Eric's major concentration is now criminal law, he is listed in *Who's Who in Environmental Law* for his work as an attorney with the U.S. Environmental Protection Agency and the Cook County State's Attorney's Office.

Eric received a Bachelor of Science degree in business administration from Lakeland College, where he also served as president of the Black Student Organization and the Campus Center Board, and served on the alumni board of directors. In 1977 he received a juris doctorate from Northwestern University School of Law.

Eric, a native Chicagoan, is the widowed father of two boys, Justin and Jeremy.

Jeanne M. Gills is a partner in Foley & Lardner LLP's Chicago office. She is vice chair of Foley's national Intellectual Property (IP) Litigation Practice, which is consistently ranked among the top ten for IP litigation and top five for patent litigation. Her trial experience includes such "bet the company" cases as *DeKalb v. Pioneer*, a patent case concerning genetically engineered corn where more than $500 million was at stake.

Gills regularly counsels clients on the procurement and enforcement of IP rights worldwide. She has been regarded as a leading patent and trade secrets litigator by Legal 500 U.S. (2007), a Top Minority IP Partner by AIPLA and MCCA (2003), and an Illinois Super Lawyer® (2005, 2006).

Gills serves on Foley's Diversity Committee, formerly chaired its African-American Affinity Group, and served seven years on its Recruiting Committee. She is also a board member of the Evening Associates of the Art Institute of Chicago.

Holding an electrical engineering degree (with honors) from Michigan State University and a juris doctorate degree from The University of Chicago Law School, Gills is a registered USPTO patent attorney.

Jeanne M. Gills

Partner, Attorney at Law
Foley & Lardner LLP

Graham Grady, a partner at Bell, Boyd & Lloyd LLP, concentrates on zoning, land use and government relations matters. A noted figure in Chicago's private, public and civic sectors, he is an experienced advocate for his clients.

Among his zoning victories are land use approvals for McCormick Place's $582 million expansion, the Shakespeare Theater at Navy Pier, the Admiral at the Lake senior community, Evanston Hospital and Highland Park Hospital's expansions and numerous Chicago-area residential, commercial and industrial projects.

Graham served in the administration of Mayor Richard M. Daley as acting commissioner of economic development, zoning administrator, buildings commissioner and chief executive of the Chicago Housing Authority. He was the first African American elected president of both the ABA Retirement Funds and the Lawyers Club of Chicago.

He has been honored by Northwestern University, *Ebony*'s "30 Leaders Under Age 30," *Crain's Chicago Business*' 40 Under 40, the Aspen Institute and as a fellow of Leadership Greater Chicago and the American Bar Foundation.

Graham is a graduate of the University of Illinois at Urbana-Champaign and Northwestern University School of Law.

Graham C. Grady

Partner, Attorney at Law
Bell, Boyd & Lloyd LLP

Martin P. Greene

Co-Founder &
Co-Managing Partner
Greene and Letts

Martin P. Greene is founder and co-managing partner of Greene and Letts, a nationally respected law firm he founded with Eileen M. Letts in 1990. Greene's primary practice is in labor, employment law and other civil litigation. He represents such clients as Sara Lee, Eastman Kodak, ITW, Northwestern Memorial Hospital, the University of Illinois and The University of Chicago, where he received his juris doctorate in 1977.

Greene serves on the board of visitors for the University of Illinois at Chicago, where he is a 1974 alum, and is president of the National Minority Law Group. He has served on transition teams for Mayor Harold Washington and President Ronald Reagan, where he worked under the direction of the late Jewel S. LaFontant in preparing a study on the U.S. Commission on Civil Rights.

Raised on Chicago's west side, Greene graduated from St. Ignatius College Prep. He is a member of the American, National and Cook County bar associations.

Greene is a frequent speaker on labor and employment matters, and on the need for greater diversity in business and education.

Philip L. Harris

Partner, Attorney at Law
Jenner & Block LLP

Philip L. Harris is a litigation partner in Jenner & Block's Chicago office. Harris focuses his practice on the defense of substantial and complex product liability, mass tort and commercial cases for large corporate entities. He serves as national and regional trial counsel for General Motors Corporation in a variety of product liability and commercial disputes.

In addition, Harris has served as national, regional and generic defense counsel for companies facing repetitive exposure issues. He has extensive experience in early resolution and case management techniques.

Harris serves on the board of trustees and executive committee for Northwestern University and the Chicago Zoological Society board of trustees. He is chair of the board of trustees of the Student Affairs Committee for Northwestern University. Harris is also a fellow of The Aspen Institute's Henry Crown Leadership Program and a fellow of Leadership Greater Chicago.

Harris received a Bachelor of Arts degree in political science from Northwestern University in 1980 and a juris doctorate from The University of Chicago Law School in 1983.

onita L. Hatchett is a partner at Bell, Boyd & Lloyd LLP, one of Chicago's oldest law firms. As a member of the ERISA Practice, she advises employers on the laws that govern tax-favored qualified and nonqualified employee benefit plans. Hatchett also represents employers in connection with regulatory audits and corporate transactions, and provides fiduciary advice to both employers and investment advisors. She serves on several firm committees, and is licensed to practice in Illinois and New Jersey.

Hatchett has published several articles in her area of practice. In 2004 the Law Bulletin Publishing Company named Hatchett a Leading Lawyer in Employee Benefits Law.

Hatchett received an undergraduate degree from the University of Michigan and a law degree from the Rutgers University Law School. She also received a Master of Laws degree and a certificate in employee benefits law from the Georgetown University Law Center.

A resident of Flossmoor, Illinois, Hatchett enjoys playing golf and hosting social events in her spare time.

Bonita L. Hatchett, Esq.

Partner, Attorney at Law
Bell, Boyd & Lloyd LLP

aVon M.J. High is a partner with Pugh, Jones, Johnson & Quandt, P.C. and the manager of the Real Estate Practice Group. For more than 12 years, she has represented clients in multimillion-dollar commercial real estate transactions, including acting as lead real estate counsel in the privatization of the Chicago Skyway toll bridge for $1.8 billion and the Millennium Park parking garage system.

In 2004 High was named one of 40 Illinois Attorneys Under Forty to Watch by Law Bulletin Publishing Company. In 2006 she was designated an Illinois "Super Lawyer" by *Law & Politics* and *Chicago* magazines. She is a member of Women in Planning & Development, the American Bar Association, Alpha Kappa Alpha Sorority, Inc., and Top Ladies of Distinction. Recently, she was inducted into Lambda Alpha International.

High received a bachelor's degree from Creighton University and a juris doctorate degree from Northwestern University School of Law in 1996.

A native of Chicago, LaVon is the wife of Archie High and the proud mother of a son, Luke.

LaVon M.J. High

Partner, Attorney at Law
Pugh, Jones, Johnson &
Quandt, P.C.

Reginald J. Hill

Partner, Attorney at Law
Jenner & Block LLP

Reginald J. Hill is a partner in Jenner & Block's Chicago office. He represents clients in intellectual property litigation involving patents, copyrights, trademarks and trade secrets. His trial experience includes bench and jury trials, and arbitration.

Prior to practicing law, Hill spent ten years as an engineer in R&D with AT&T Bell Laboratories and Motorola. Based on his contributions to the AT&T computer family, he was awarded the Distinguished Member of Technical Staff Award. Additionally, Hill managed his own law firm before rejoining Jenner & Block in 2002.

He is a member of the American, Illinois and Cook County bar associations, as well as the American Intellectual Property Law Association. In 2003 he was named by *Diversity & The Bar* as one of the top intellectual property lawyers of color in the country.

A 1984 graduate of Tuskegee Institute, Hill holds a bachelor's degree in electrical engineering. He also earned a master's degree in electrical engineering from Georgia Tech in 1985 and a juris doctorate from John Marshall Law School, cum laude, in 1994.

He is married and has three daughters.

Patricia Brown Holmes

Equity Partner
Schiff Hardin LLP

Patricia Brown Holmes is an equity partner in the Chicago office of Schiff Hardin LLP. Holmes, a former state court judge, is an experienced trial lawyer who concentrates her practice in general litigation, including contract disputes, shareholder derivative actions, securities fraud and other commercial litigation. She also conducts internal investigations and counsels corporations and individuals in matters involving the federal government, particularly those pertaining to regulatory and compliance issues and white collar criminal cases.

Prior to taking the bench in Cook County, Holmes honed her skills as a chief assistant corporation counsel for the City of Chicago, assistant U.S. attorney for the Northern District of Illinois and assistant state's attorney for Cook County. She has extensive experience teaching and lecturing in the legal community, and is a leader in several professional and service organizations. She has received numerous awards and recognitions.

Holmes, a member of Delta Sigma Theta Sorority, Inc., received both an undergraduate degree and a law degree from the University of Illinois at Urbana-Campaign. She is married to Michael Holmes and has three children.

A registered patent and trademark attorney, John S. Kendall represents clients regarding intellectual property law matters. As an electrical engineer for Northrop DSD, he tested U.S. Air Force F-15 and F-16 aircraft fighters' electronic countermeasure systems. He chairs the Metropolitan Reclamation District of Greater Chicago Civil Service Board.

John received a juris doctorate degree from The Ohio State University School of Law in 1990 and a Bachelor of Electrical Engineering degree from the University of Dayton in 1985. He is admitted to practice law in the states of Ohio (1990) and Illinois (1991), and the U.S. Patent and Trademark Office (1993).

He is a founding board member and past president of 100 Black Men of Chicago, as well as a national board member for ten years and the current national vice chair of development.

Recent awards include Allstate Insurance Company's From Whence We Came (2007), Connection Enterprise, Inc.'s Men of Excellence Award (2005), and the Cook County Bar Association's J. Earnest Wilkins Award (2004).

Born on Chicago's westside, he is a proud father of two and grandfather of three.

John S. Kendall, Esq.

Managing Partner
Davis & Kendall, P.C.

A lan S. King is vice chair of Drinker Biddle Gardner Carton's Human Resource Law Department and co-chair of its Labor and Employment Practice Group. His practice is concentrated in the area of employment litigation and counseling. King has extensive experience on behalf of both private and public employers in virtually all types of employment-related litigation. He is a frequent lecturer to bar associations and employer groups, with recent topics including the Americans with Disabilities Act, workplace harassment, violence in the workplace, employee handbooks and at-will employment issues.

King is a member of Mayor Richard Daley's 21st Century Leadership Council, and serves on the board of directors of the Leadership Council for Metropolitan Open Communities, the Ounce of Prevention Fund, and the Chicago Public Schools' Children First Fund.

King was named to Law Bulletin Publishing Company's prestigious list of 40 Illinois Attorneys Under 40 to Watch in 2003. In 2004 he was named a Leading Lawyer in management employment by the Leading Lawyers Network, and in 2005 he was selected as an Illinois Super Lawyer by *Chicago* magazine.

Alan S. King

Partner, Attorney at Law
Drinker Biddle Gardner Carton

CHICAGO'S COUNSELORS AT LAW

Gregory L. Lacey

Partner, Attorney at Law
Dykema Gossett PLLC

Gregory L. Lacey is a partner in the Chicago office of Dykema Gossett PLLC, a full-service law firm. His practice areas include employment, commercial litigation and entertainment law. He also serves on the firm's Recruiting and Diversity committees.

Gregory was named one of the 40 Under 40 Illinois Lawyers to Watch, and was selected as one of the Illinois Super Lawyers. He serves as a mentor/sponsor of a high school student through LINK Unlimited and with the prison ministry through his church.

He received a Bachelor of Arts degree from Washington University in St. Louis. Gregory also obtained a juris doctorate degree from the University of Iowa, where he was a member of the *Iowa Law Review*. He is a member of the National and American bar associations, Life Changers International Church, and Kappa Alpha Psi Fraternity, Inc.

Gregory is a native of New Orleans, Louisiana. He is married to Dr. Cereesa Longest Lacey, and is the father of three amazing children, Zoë, Ian and Eli.

Eileen M. Letts

Co-Founder &
Co-Managing Partner
Greene and Letts

Eileen M. Letts is founder and co-managing partner of Greene and Letts, a nationally respected law firm she founded with Martin P. Greene in 1990. The primary focus of Letts' practice involves defending a wide range of personal injury cases for corporations and governmental entities. A few cases include Wal-Mart; Travelers, State Farm, Liberty Mutual and General Casualty insurance companies; City of Chicago; and Daimler Chrysler Financial.

Letts maintains a prominent role in the development of the legal profession by serving on numerous committees for the American, National, Cook County and Chicago bar associations. She is a member of the Black Women Lawyers Association and The Economic Club of Chicago, and is past president of the Chicago Bar Foundation, which provides financial support to pro bono legal service organizations. She also served on the transition team for Mayor Harold Washington.

A 1975 graduate of The Ohio State University, Letts graduated from Chicago-Kent College of Law in 1978. A member of New Faith Baptist Church and Alpha Kappa Alpha Sorority, Inc., Letts is a frequent speaker and contributor on diversity and professional development.

Joseph McCoy is a partner at Schwartz Cooper Chartered, a practice that includes the representation of banking institutions, real estate developers, landlords and tenants. He is certified to represent professional athletes by the National Basketball Players Association, the Women's National Basketball Players Association and the National Football League Players Association. McCoy also serves as the firm's hiring partner.

McCoy received a Bachelor of Arts degree in public policy and a Master of Arts degree in educational policy studies from The University of Chicago in 1994. In 1998 he received a juris doctorate degree from Northwestern University School of Law.

McCoy is an active alumnus of Northwestern University School of Law serving as an admissions interviewer, an instructor in the Introduction to Legal Learning Program and a guest lecturer for the student body on various topics. The board chair of Urban Prep Academy, he is a board member of Big Brothers Big Sisters of Metropolitan Chicago and Leadership Greater Chicago.

A native of Little Rock, Arkansas, McCoy is the husband of Jamenda A. McCoy and father of Quentin J. McCoy.

Joseph Q. McCoy
Partner, Attorney at Law
Schwartz Cooper Chartered

Samuel Mendenhall is a partner in the Chicago office of the international law firm Winston & Strawn LLP. He concentrates his practice in commercial litigation, insurance coverage litigation and product liability defense. Mendenhall's clients include Fortune 500 companies, governmental entities and nonprofit agencies.

Before joining Winston & Strawn, Mendenhall served in the United States Army, where he graduated first in his training class. He was awarded the Army Achievement Medal for his leadership abilities and the Good Conduct Medal for exemplary conduct and discipline.

Mendenhall founded the Giveback Foundation, a nonprofit organization devoted to providing college scholarships, mentoring and internship opportunities to inner-city high school students. He is a member of The Economic Club of Chicago, a fellow of Leadership Greater Chicago and serves on the board of visitors of his alma mater, the University of Illinois College of Law. He was chosen as an Illinois Super Lawyer for 2005 and 2006, and was selected by the Law Bulletin Publishing Company for its 2001 edition of *40 Illinois Attorneys Under 40 to Watch*.

Mendenhall is married, and has two children.

Samuel Mendenhall
Partner, Attorney at Law
Winston & Strawn LLP

Leslie D. Minier

Chief Diversity Partner
Katten Muchin Rosenman, LLP

L eslie Minier is a corporate partner at Katten Muchin Rosenman, LLP, concentrating her practice in the areas of mergers and acquisitions, private equity and general corporate matters. She is the firm's chief diversity partner and co-chair of its diversity committee.

Minier is a member of the executive committee and co-chair of the Chicago Bar Association's Alliance for Women. She is a member of the board of directors for the Joffrey Ballet, the Make-a-Wish Foundation of Illinois and the Chicago Committee on Minorities in Large Law Firms. Minier is also a member of The Economic Club of Chicago, the Black Women Lawyers Association, the ABA's Business Law Section and Delta Sigma Theta Sorority, Inc. She has been selected to participate in the Leadership Greater Chicago 2008 Fellows Program.

Minier received a juris doctorate and a master's degree in management from Northwestern University Kellogg Graduate School of Management in 1994, a master's degree in electrical engineering from Georgia Institute of Technology in 1988 and a bachelor's degree in electrical engineering from Tuskegee University in 1987.

Stephen S. Mitchell

Partner, Attorney at Law
Harris, Mitchell & Dinizulu, LLC

S tephen S. Mitchell practices personal injury and medical malpractice law. He serves on the board of directors for the Cook County Bar Association, and is a hearing officer for the Illinois Supreme Court Attorney Registration and Disciplinary Commission.

Mitchell graduated from Florida A&M University with a Bachelor of Science degree in business economics, magna cum laude, along with a master's degree in public finance. In addition, he received his Doctor of Law degree from the University of Wisconsin, where he was a member of the *Wisconsin Law Review* and the Wisconsin Moot Court board.

A former member of the board of directors for the Legal Assistance Foundation, Mitchell was selected as one of 40 Illinois Attorneys Under 40 To Watch in 2006. He is a member of Kappa Alpha Psi Fraternity, Inc. and the H.E. Daniels Lodge #532.

An art collector, Mitchell is on the board of directors of Diasporal Rhythms, an association of collectors. He is also an owner of Gallery Guichard, a prominent art gallery in Chicago that specializes in art of the Diaspora.

James D. Montgomery Jr. was born in Chicago, Illinois, in 1957. He received a Bachelor of Science degree from Stanford University in 1979, and in 1982 he received his juris doctorate from the University of Illinois College of Law.

Montgomery is admitted to the practice of law in the state of Illinois, the Federal District Court for the Northern District of Illinois and the Seventh Circuit Court of Appeals. He is a member of the Cook County Bar Association and the Illinois Trial Lawyers Association.

Montgomery began his professional career with Coopers & Lybrand, specializing in federal and state tax consulting. He later practiced with James D. Montgomery & Associates for five years, concentrating in civil and criminal litigation. He continued his professional career with the McDonald's Corporation in the legal department as senior and managing counsel until moving into the management ranks of the company.

Since June of 2004, Montgomery has been a partner with Cochran, Cherry, Givens, Smith & Montgomery, concentrating in major plaintiff's litigation. His most recent trial resulted in a verdict of $7.5 million against a defendant hospital.

James D. Montgomery Jr.

Partner, Attorney at Law
Cochran, Cherry, Givens,
Smith & Montgomery

James D. Montgomery Sr., a 1956 graduate of the University of Illinois Law School, is no stranger to the battle for civil rights. He has litigated in the area of civil rights, criminal law and personal injury for more than four decades, including serving as lead counsel in the 18-month trials arising from the murders of Fred Hampton and Mark Clark.

In 1983 Montgomery was appointed corporation counsel for the City of Chicago under Mayor Harold Washington as the city's chief legal officer. He was also named a fellow in the prestigious International Academy of Trial Lawyers that same year. In 1999, he was presented to the Illinois Supreme Court as one of 12 laureates of the Academy of Illinois Lawyers in its inaugural class.

Montgomery formed a Chicago partnership with the late Johnnie L. Cochran Jr., specializing in catastrophic permanent personal injury, medical malpractice, wrongful death, police misconduct and product liability cases. He has attained verdicts and settlements in excess of $100 million on behalf of his clients, including most recent verdicts of $6.7 million and $23.5 million.

James D. Montgomery Sr.

Principal, Attorney at Law
Cochran, Cherry, Givens,
Smith & Montgomery

CHICAGO'S COUNSELORS AT LAW

Marian E. Perkins, Esq.

Attorney at Law
Law Office of Marian E. Perkins

Marian E. Perkins is a trial attorney in private practice with a concentration in criminal defense in the state courts of Illinois. She is also a professor in the Criminal Justice Department at Chicago State University. She has published in the area of incarcerated women, and presented at conferences on current issues in criminal and juvenile law.

Marian is second vice president of the Cook County Bar Association (CCBA), the oldest association of black lawyers and judges in the nation. As the coordinator and a pro bono attorney with the CCBA Expungement Project, she has trained the attorney volunteers and assisted hundreds of indigent ex-offenders in the preparation of petitions to clear their criminal records.

Marian has received numerous plaques for outstanding service to the legal profession and the community, including the 2007 Outstanding Pro Bono Service Award from the Illinois State Bar Association. Born and raised in Chicago, Marian is a graduate of Howard University School of Law and a member of Delta Sigma Theta Sorority, Inc. She is the wife of Darrell L. Phillips. They have one daughter, Imani.

Adrienne B. Pitts

Litigation Partner
Sidley Austin LLP

Adrienne B. Pitts, a litigation partner in Sidley Austin LLP's Chicago office, concentrates her practice in antitrust, complex commercial litigation and white-collar defense matters. She has tried several white-collar cases in federal court, and has counseled clients through several federal grand jury investigations. More recently, she was a member of the trial team that defended former Governor George H. Ryan in his federal corruption trial.

Adrienne is vice president of the board of directors for L.E.A.R.N. Charter School in North Lawndale, and a member of the board of directors for the Chicago Urban League, High Jump and the Chicago Committee on Minorities in Large Law Firms. She is also a member of Alpha Kappa Alpha Sorority, Inc., and was honored this year by the Chicago Bar Association's Alliance for Women for exemplary professional achievement and promoting women in the legal profession.

Adrienne received a bachelor's degree in economics from the University of Pennsylvania in 1990, and a juris doctorate, with honors, from Boston University School of Law in 1995. She is married with two children.

Tracie R. Porter is principal of the Law Offices of Tracie R. Porter, LLC. Her practice concentrates on a broad variety of real estate law matters, including transactional and litigation cases, corporate law and probate proceedings. She has handled a broad range of transactions from a $4,000 vacant lot purchase, to a $15.3 million commercial acquisition. Her real estate litigation practice includes investors, developers and individuals.

Porter is an adjunct professor at IIT Chicago-Kent College of Law teaching business-related law courses. At The John Marshall Law School, she teaches commercial real estate law and legal drafting courses.

Porter is affiliated with the American Bar Association, the Chicago Bar Association, the Cook County Bar Association, the Illinois Real Estate Lawyers Association and the Black Women Lawyers Association. She was published in the *Chicago Bar Association Journal,* and has been quoted and featured in various news media, including the real estate section of the *Chicago Tribune* and the *Citizen Newspaper.* She has been seen on several television programs discussing topics related to real estate.

Tracie R. Porter

Principal, Attorney at Law
Law Offices of Tracie R. Porter, LLC

Stephen Pugh is a graduate of Loyola University Chicago School of Law and a Woodrow Wilson fellow. Previously, he was a law clerk to the Honorable James B. Parsons, U.S. District of Illinois, special trial attorney in the honors program for the U.S. Department of Justice and partner with Chapman and Cutler.

Since founding Pugh, Jones, Johnson & Quandt, Pugh has practiced real estate litigation, director and officer liability cases, general and complex commercial litigation, and has represented local government entities. He tried the first civil RICO jury trial in the Northern District of Illinois, and is currently a hearing officer for the Chicago Board of Education in contractor debarment proceedings. A member of the bar of the U.S. Supreme Court, Pugh has extensive trial experience and has argued before the U.S. Circuit Courts of Appeals and the Illinois Supreme Court.

Pugh has authored several articles and has received numerous awards, including the prestigious Francis J. Rooney/St. Thomas Moore Award from Loyola University School of Law. He serves on many boards, including Columbia College Chicago and the Emergency Fund.

Stephen H. Pugh

President
Pugh, Jones, Johnson & Quandt, P.C.

Timothy Ray

Partner, Attorney at Law
Neal, Gerber & Eisenberg LLP

Timothy Ray is a partner with Chicago-based law firm Neal, Gerber & Eisenberg LLP's Litigation Practice Group, where he concentrates in complex commercial litigation. Tim is admitted to practice in Illinois, before the U.S. District Court for the Northern District of Illinois and before the U.S. Court of Appeals for the Seventh Circuit. He has tried more than 30 jury trials to verdict in both federal and state courts.

Tim obtained his juris doctorate from the University of Iowa College of Law. He is a member of his firm's hiring and diversity committees, and co-chair of its minority initiative. He is AV® peer review-rated by Martindale Hubbell, the highest rating.

Named one of 40 Attorneys Under 40 to Watch in 2004, Tim is a member of the State of Illinois Supreme Court Committee on Professional Responsibility, The Economic Club and the University of Iowa College of Law board of directors. He is also a member on the board of directors of the Illinois Sports Facilities Authority, the developer, owner and operator of U.S. Cellular Field, home of the Chicago White Sox.

Gail Saracco

Partner, Attorney at Law
Mayer, Brown, Rowe & Maw LLP

Gail Saracco is a partner at the law firm of Mayer, Brown, Rowe & Maw LLP in Chicago. She was the first black female attorney partner of this international law firm. Gail is a partner in the Corporate Group where she advises sponsors in structuring and negotiating private investment funds and represents investors in connection with their investments in private investment funds. Her practice also includes the representation of corporations in mergers and acquisitions. Gail is a member of the firm's Committee on Diversity and Inclusion, the Women's Initiatives Committee and the Pro Bono Committee.

Gail was a 2003 Leadership Greater Chicago fellow. She is a member of the board of trustees of the Lawyers' Committee for Civil Rights Under Law and a member of the Leaders Council for Chicago United.

Gail is a 1987 graduate of Yale University and a 1990 cum laude graduate of the University of Michigan Law School where she was a member of the *Michigan Law Review.*

A native of Jamaica, she currently resides in River Forest with her husband and two daughters.

Lisa T. Scruggs is a litigation partner in Jenner & Block's Chicago office. In addition to an active business litigation practice, she maintains a public policy practice that focuses on advising public sector clients, including school districts and individual schools, on how to achieve their policy goals. She also has experience counseling nonprofits and schools on a variety of governance, municipal and school law issues.

Between 2004 and 2006, as part of an innovative executive loan arrangement, Scruggs served as senior policy advisor to the chief executive officer of the Chicago Public Schools. She currently serves on the boards of the Young Women's Leadership Charter School, the Just the Beginning Foundation, the Chicago Foundation for Education and the Mikva Challenge advisory board.

Scruggs attended Georgetown University and earned a Bachelor of Arts degree in 1993, cum laude, with honors in English. She earned a Master of Arts degree in 1994 from The University of Chicago, and a juris doctorate from The University of Chicago Law School in 1998, where she was awarded the Beale Prize for Legal Writing.

Lisa T. Scruggs

Partner, Attorney at Law
Jenner & Block LLP

Lewis Steverson is corporate vice president of Motorola's Law Department and has responsibility for managing the legal affairs and the legal teams for Motorola's Home and Networks Mobility, Government and Public Safety, and Enterprise Mobility businesses. He joined Motorola in 1995 and was promoted to vice president in 2001 and corporate vice president in 2005. During his tenure at Motorola, Lewis has progressed through numerous roles of increasing responsibility, including head lawyer roles for the Energy Systems business; the Iridium Handset business; the North American Cellular Sales Group; and Corporate Product Safety, the Connected Home Solutions business, and the Government and Enterprise Mobility business.

Prior to joining Motorola, Lewis was in private practice at the law firm of Arnold & Porter in Denver, Colorado, and Washington, D.C., where he concentrated on commercial litigation, product safety and bankruptcy. He graduated summa cum laude from Siena College in Albany, New York, with a degree in English, and from Harvard Law School, in Cambridge, Massachusetts, with a juris doctorate degree.

Lewis Steverson

Corporate Vice President
Law Department
Motorola

CHICAGO'S COUNSELORS AT LAW

Nigel F. Telman

Partner, Attorney at Law
Sidley Austin, LLP

Nigel F. Telman is a partner in the Chicago office of the international law firm Sidley Austin, LLP. He concentrates his national law practice on litigating single and class action disputes arising out of the employer-employee relationship, including claims of workplace harassment and employment discrimination. He also advises, counsels and trains the firm's clients on compliance with federal, state and local employment laws.

Nigel was appointed by the mayor of Chicago to the Chicago Metropolitan Agency for Planning and serves on that agency's executive committee. He is a member of the board of directors of the Chicago Committee on Minorities in Large Law Firms, Just The Beginning Foundation, Project Match, and Jamal Place. He also sits on the Chicago State University Foundation board and the Leadership Committee of the Art Institute of Chicago, and is a fellow of the 2004 class of Leadership Greater Chicago.

Nigel received an undergraduate degree from Cornell University and a law degree from Boston University School of Law. He lives in Chicago with his wife, Deborah, and their twin sons, Nigel II and Nicholas.

Juan R. Thomas

Founder
The Thomas Group

Juan R. Thomas is founder of The Thomas Group. Thomas practices in the areas of labor and employment, real estate, and governmental relations on behalf of the firm's clients.

In April of 2005, he was elected Aurora Township clerk, becoming the first African American to win a township-wide office in Aurora, Illinois, the second largest city in Illinois. In 1995 Thomas became the youngest person elected to the West Aurora School Board, and he became the first African American re-elected to the board in 1999.

Thomas has been featured in *Ebony* and the *Chicago Sun-Times* as a leader to watch in the 21st century. His civic affiliations include numerous local, state and national organizations. He currently serves as chair of the board of directors of the African-American Chamber of Commerce serving suburban Chicago counties.

Thomas graduated from Morehouse College, and earned a law degree and a master's degree in educational policy from the University of Illinois. He is currently completing a master's degree in religious studies at The University of Chicago, and attends Trinity United Church of Christ.

Gordon K. Walton is a partner at the law firm Clausen Miller P.C. Walton devotes a significant portion of his practice to complex tort and environmental litigation. He has extensive experience in toxic tort defense litigation and resolving a wide range of coverage issues that arise under general liability, pollution legal liability, professional liability and excess and umbrella liability policies, in addition to many specialty coverage policies. He frequently speaks on emerging general litigation and insurance coverage issues as he is at the forefront of new developments in these areas.

Walton received a Bachelor of Arts degree from The University of Chicago in 1990. He obtained a juris doctorate degree from The John Marshall Law School in 1994, where he received numerous awards.

Walton is a member of the Cook County Bar Association, Chicago Bar Association and the American Bar Association, and has been actively involved in volunteer programs. He is also a member of the Chicago Inns of Court, a society of prominent lawyers and judges that addresses current issues in the legal community and significant court decisions.

Gordon K. Walton

Partner, Attorney at Law
Clausen Miller P.C.

Everett S. Ward is a partner in the Chicago office of Jenner & Block LLP. He is a member of the firm's real estate practice, and serves on the firm's Diversity Committee, Hiring Committee and Business Services and Transactions Committee.

A graduate of Princeton University and Harvard Law School, Everett has practiced real estate law for more than 20 years. He represents clients in the acquisition, disposition, development, financing and leasing of commercial, industrial and multifamily properties and the formation and financing of joint ventures.

Everett is a member of the ABA's Section of Real Property, Probate and Trust Law, and chairs that section's Real Estate Investment Trust Committee. He is also a member of the American College of Real Estate Lawyers, and was twice named an Illinois Super Lawyer.

Everett is a member of The Economic Club of Chicago and the Facilities and Administrative Services Committee of The Field Museum board of trustees, and serves on the board of directors of Thresholds. Everett is also an active Princeton alumnus and a past member of the executive committee of Princeton's Alumni Council.

Everett S. Ward

Partner, Attorney at Law
Jenner & Block LLP

Char Whitaker

Corporate Vice President
Law Department
Motorola

Char Whitaker is a corporate vice president of the Law Department, responsible for Motorola's Intellectual Property Transactions and Licensing organizations. She has provided IP counsel for various Motorola business units, including Motorola's networks business unit, as well as the former Motorola semiconductor business. Prior to joining the Motorola Law Department, Char worked with the law firm of Spensley, Horn, Jubas & Lubitz, and was an engineering manager with Motorola's Semiconductor Product Sector.

Char received an undergraduate degree in electrical engineering from California State University in San Francisco, and a law degree from The University of Texas at Austin. She is admitted to practice before the U.S. Court of Appeals for the Federal Circuit, the U.S. Patent and Trademark Office, and in the states of Texas and Illinois.

Allison L. Wood

Principal, Attorney at Law
Bellows & Bellows, P.C.

Allison L. Wood is a principal with the firm Bellows & Bellows, P.C., where she specializes in commercial and employment litigation. She has extensive trial experience representing corporate clients in various industries, including pharmaceuticals, electronics, manufacturing and transportation. She also counsels executives and senior level managers relative to employment disputes, and negotiates severance and compensation agreements. Prior to entering private practice, Wood was of counsel at Peoples Energy Corporation, and began her career as an assistant public defender, where she tried numerous jury trials.

For more than a decade, Wood has been an adjunct faculty member at DePaul University College of Law, teaching pre-trial and trial courses. She has published numerous articles on trial practice, and is often invited to teach in trial programs throughout the city.

Wood is a past treasurer of the Cook County Bar Association, past hearing chair for the Attorney Registration and Disciplinary Commission, and past chair of the board for a social service agency, Centers for New Horizons.

Wood received a law degree from DePaul University College of Law.

interest

limelight

CORPORATE SPOTLIGHT

attention

prominence

highlight

celebrate

headline

focus

recognition

Ronald E. Daly

Board Member
U.S. Cellular®

Elliot Rawls

Senior Director, Strategic Planning
U.S. Cellular®

Ronald Daly is a private investor and serves on the board of directors at U.S. Cellular. He is also a director of SuperValu, a major distributor, wholesaler and retailer in the food service industry.

Daly was the president and chief executive officer of Océ-USA Holding, Inc. from November of 2002 to September of 2004. Océ-USA Holding, Inc. is the North American operations of the Netherlands-based Océ-N.V., a publicly held company, and a global supplier of document management and delivery solutions. Prior to joining Océ-USA Holding, Inc., he served as president of RR Donnelley Printing Solutions.

Daly holds a Master of Business Administration degree from Loyola University and a Bachelor of Arts degree from Governors State University. His numerous civic activities include serving as a fellow of Leadership Greater Chicago and as a member of the Metropolis 2020 board, the Chicago Symphony Orchestra board of trustees, the Business School Advisory Board of Loyola University Chicago and the Conference Board Council of Operating Executives.

Elliot Rawls is senior director of strategic planning at U.S. Cellular. He leads the strategic and financial evaluation of more than $1 billion in proposed and/or executed acquisitions and divestitures. His responsibilities also include corporate level strategic analysis and telecom industry analysis.

Prior to this position, Rawls held director-level positions at U.S. Cellular in pricing strategy, intercarrier business, intercarrier revenue and networking, and corporate research and communications. His responsibilities included business development, decision and risk analysis, pricing strategy, negotiation strategy and market research. Before joining U.S. Cellular, he was president of The Cambaire Corporation, a consultancy that provided market research, and financial and general management services to a variety of clients.

Rawls received a bachelor's degree in architecture and a Bachelor of Architecture degree from Rice University. He also received a Master of Business Administration degree from Stanford Business School.

Additionally, Rawls serves on the board of Marwen, a Chicago-based organization for arts education and youth development.

He and his wife, Susan, live in Chicago with their daughter. A pianist, Rawls counts jazz and architectural drawings among his many interests.

Noel Hornsberry

Director, Diversity Strategy
U.S. Cellular®

Lamart Clay

District Sales Manager
U.S. Cellular®

Noel Hornsberry is director of diversity strategy at U.S. Cellular. He is responsible for the successful design and implementation of the diversity and inclusion initiatives.

Prior to joining U.S. Cellular in 2001, Hornsberry held positions in retail sales management with emphasis on training, hiring and team building. He has received recognition for his outstanding performance as a leader and his commitment to driving the "Dynamic Organization" by winning the U.S. Cellular Expect It! Award, the West Region All-Star Award and the coveted Midwest Region Leadership Award.

Hornsberry earned a Bachelor of Science degree in criminal justice from Loyola University Chicago. He is a member of the corporate advisory committee of the Black Data Processing Association, the RainbowPUSH Coalition, the United Way Diversity Alliance and the Cosmopolitan Chamber of Commerce.

A resident of the Plainfield area, Hornsberry enjoys spending quality time with his family. In his free time, he enjoys landscaping, bowling, bicycling and attending sporting events.

Lamart Clay is a district sales manager at U.S. Cellular. In this position, he manages corporate-owned and agent locations in the greater Chicagoland area. A consistent top performer, Clay has received several professional accolades. Most recently, he was honored with a Director's Club Award and the Midwest Vice President's Excellence Award.

Additionally, Clay serves on the board of directors at Faith's Place, a transitional shelter for women, and is an active member of the community through his involvement with youth programs in Chicago. An avid proponent of self-empowerment, he volunteers at several employment agencies to teach employment training, job retention and interviewing skills.

Clay received a Bachelor of Arts degree in organizational management from North Park University. A native of Chicago, he is married with three children.

US.Cellular

US.Cellular

David Malone

Director, Supply Chain Services
U.S. Cellular®

Chawn Jackson

Manager, Talent Strategies
U.S. Cellular®

David Malone is director of supply chain services at U.S. Cellular, and is responsible for leading strategic sourcing, national logistics, accounts payable and travel services. He has more than 25 years of management experience within municipal and Fortune 500 organizations, specializing in supply chain management and process improvement.

Prior to joining U.S. Cellular, Malone served as principal of David Malone & Associates, providing business development and consulting services to both public and private sector clients. He also previously served as senior vice president of Mesirow Financial, and from 2000 to 2004, he served as chief procurement officer for the City of Chicago.

Before joining the City of Chicago, Malone served as director of worldwide procurement for RR Donnelley & Sons Co., and as director of purchasing and supplier development for Avery Dennison Corporation. He has also worked for Xerox Corporation and Digital Equipment Corporation.

Malone is married with three beautiful children.

Chawn Jackson is manager of talent strategies for U.S. Cellular, the sixth largest wireless communication company in the United States. In this position, she sets the course for new and improved staffing strategies, processes and procedures to carry the company forward as a center of excellence and an employer of choice.

Prior to joining U.S. Cellular, Chawn worked in a senior level human resources capacity with the Chicago Transit Authority, which is Chicago's mass transit system and the second-largest in the country. Additionally, she has been committed in her career and in her personal endeavors to mentoring young professionals. She has worked with organizations such as the Chicago Urban League's Metropolitan Board and the League of Black Women, which focus on the professional development of up-and-coming leaders.

While pursuing a psychology degree at Southern University A&M in Baton Rouge, Louisiana, Chawn volunteered her time to work with several organizations that focused on the academic and personal development of abused, neglected and underprivileged children.

A native of Chicago, she is the proud mother of Nayah.

Gloria Cannon

Manager
Equal Employment Opportunity
Planning & Analysis
U.S. Cellular®

Sharon L. Gardner-Crowe

Diversity Strategist/Supplier Diversity
U.S. Cellular®

Gloria Cannon is manager of equal employment opportunity (EEO) planning and analysis at U.S. Cellular. In this role, she develops strategies and implements the company's EEO and affirmative action policies and programs. Her leadership and guidance in creating compliance strategies supports the important goal of building a more inclusive workplace.

Cannon is a dynamic human resources professional with more than 30 years of progressive leadership and managerial experience. Prior to joining U.S. Cellular, her experiences included working for International Harvester, J.I. Case and Keebler Company. At Keebler Company and later Kellogg Company, Cannon provided executive and leadership coaching to ensure EEO compliance. She developed initiatives to ensure that the company could attract, retain and promote a diverse workforce.

Holding a degree from Eastern Illinois University, Cannon is a member of several organizations, including the Society for Human Resource Management (SHRM) and the League of Black Women. She is married and has two children.

Sharon Gardner-Crowe is a diversity strategist responsible for implementing programs and processes to execute U.S. Cellular's supplier diversity strategy.

In this position, she identifies and screens potential minority and women suppliers, and maintains knowledge of government regulations and agency developments. She also works with other areas of diversity, including project management, affinity groups, inclusion councils, and affirmative action and equal employment opportunity (EEO) programs.

Gardner-Crowe has more than 25 years of experience in affirmative action and EEO programs. Prior to joining the company, she was a senior compliance officer with the Chicago Park District, and has served in affirmative action positions with Stein & Company and the Chicago Urban League. Her interest in minority business development began with employment at the Chicago Economic Development Corporation (CEDCO), where she consulted with at-risk high school students on becoming entrepreneurs.

Holding a bachelor's degree in special education from Chicago State University, Gardner-Crowe is a member of the American Contract Compliance Association, the Chicago Minority Business Development Council and the Women's Business Development Center. She has one child, Anita, who resides in Las Vegas.

Kelly Jackson

Senior Manager
Operational Standards &
Asset Inventory Management
U.S. Cellular®

Laté Lawson

Director, Information Management
U.S. Cellular®

Kelly Jackson is a senior manager of operational standards and asset inventory management at U.S. Cellular. He is responsible for operational policy, standards and quality for more than 6,000 cellular telephone sites across 26 states. Additionally, he oversees the development, testing and implementation of U.S. Cellular's engineering and network operations database, which is used for managing and tracking cellular network assets.

A transplant from Milwaukee, Wisconsin, where he served two-and-a-half years as a network operations manager, Kelly was responsible for managing cellular telephone sites in the Milwaukee market.

He earned a Bachelor of Arts degree in communications from the University of Wisconsin Oshkosh and an AASEET from ITT Technical Institute in Greenfield, Wisconsin. He has a lovely wife, LaShaun.

Laté Lawson is director of information management at U.S. Cellular. He is responsible for leading companywide business intelligence as well as data-movement and integration efforts.

In 1986 Lawson earned a Bachelor of Science degree in business administration from Bénin University in Lomé, Togo. He also holds a master's degree in management information systems from Northern Illinois University.

Additionally, Lawson is a founding member of the Kishwaukee Valley Habitat for Humanity in DeKalb, Illinois. He is active in the Togolese Diaspora, promoting cultural exchanges and advising on educational matters.

A native of the Republic of Togo, Lawson is married to Dogbovi Lawson, and they are the proud parents of three daughters, Nadou, Koko and Kayi.

Karen Taylor

Manager, Associate Relations
U.S. Cellular®

Toni L. Williams

Manager, Associate Relations
U.S. Cellular®

Karen Taylor is manager of associate relations in U.S. Cellular's Midwest region, supporting associates in Illinois and Indiana. She is responsible for human resources leadership in planning, designing and executing companywide initiatives, business strategies and programs. She also advises and coaches leaders on complex associate relations issues, and provides policy and procedure interpretation and consulting.

Taylor has 16 years of human resources experience with a diverse background in employee relations, salary administration, variable pay programs, compensation strategy development and administering welfare benefits programs.

She currently resides in Glen Ellyn, Illinois, with her husband and their three children.

Toni L. Williams is an associate relations manager in U.S. Cellular's Midwest region, supporting associates in Illinois and Indiana. She is responsible for human resources leadership as well as partnering with call center leaders in planning, designing and executing companywide initiatives, business strategies and programs.

Prior to joining U.S. Cellular in March of 2007, Williams spent 14 years with Ameritech, SBC and AT&T, where she held various positions within call center management and human resources.

Williams holds a Bachelor of Arts degree in management and leadership from Judson University, and is currently pursuing a senior professional of human resources certification.

She enjoys gardening, traveling and spending time with her family.

interest

limelight

Corporate Spotlight

attention

prominence

highlight

celebrate

headline

focus

recognition

Linda Artope

Local Sales Account Executive
CBS 2 Chicago

Steve Baskerville

Meteorologist
CBS 2 Chicago

Linda Artope is the longest-tenured African-American female sales account executive in the Chicago market. Transitioning from the CBS 2 newsroom as a field producer in 1987, she broke the sales barrier in 1988.

Linda's success in sales is reflected in her personal style with clients. When designing media plans for companies, she focuses on long-term goals. This has resulted in tremendous success for many Chicago retailers, more than quadrupling the sales of many clients and garnering more of the available media dollars in the marketplace.

Linda is the proud mother of two sons, both graduates of the University of Southern California in film and music. George has edited a film, *Cuttin Da Mustard* featuring Sinbad, the comedian. William, a jazz trumpeter, recently performed with Mariah Carey at the Grammy Awards.

Linda's professional life is based upon a strong personal sense of self, evolving around her activities for world peace. As a member of the SGI-USA, an American Buddhist Association, Linda is involved in promoting world peace and individual happiness through culture, education and music.

Viewers know Steve Baskerville as Chicago's most accurate weather forecaster. He is chief meteorologist for CBS 2 Chicago's 5 p.m., 6 p.m. and 10 p.m. newscasts.

Steve's achievements as lead meteorologist for CBS 2 have resulted in numerous industry honors, including eight local Emmy Awards. He earned an Emmy for Outstanding Achievement for Individual Excellence in 2006, and one in 2005 for the news feature, "Steve's Getaway Guide."

The Illinois Broadcasters Association acknowledged Steve's work in 2001 and again in 2006 for Best Weathercast. His breaking news coverage of the deadly tornado in Utica, Illinois, in 2004 also earned him an Emmy Award, as did his 1999 news feature series, "Best of Chicago."

Off the air, Steve has been a longtime champion for several local organizations such as the eta Creative Arts Foundation, the Illinois Fatherhood Initiative, the National Kidney Foundation, the Leukemia Society and the National Runaway Switchboard (based in Chicago).

Derrick Blakley

General Assignment Reporter
CBS 2 Chicago

Diann Burns

News Anchor
CBS 2 Chicago

D errick Blakley, who was raised in Chicago, has reported from all corners of the globe. Since joining CBS 2 Chicago in 2003, he has received three local Emmy Awards and one national Emmy for his work as a news reporter and anchor.

In 2005 Derrick was honored for his role as news anchor during CBS 2's spot news coverage of the death of Pope John Paul II. In addition, Derrick received a prestigious national Emmy award for his work on the same broadcast. His reporting contributions were recognized with two Emmys for a 2003 live sports special covering the LaSalle Bank Chicago Marathon and a 30-minute news special on the 2004 tornado in Utica, Illinois.

Derrick worked for CBS News for seven years, based in Chicago, London and Bonn, Germany.

Derrick graduated from Hales Franciscan High School in Chicago, and now serves on the school's board of trustees. He has a Bachelor of Science degree in journalism from Northwestern University and a master's degree in communications from the University of Illinois.

V eteran Chicago broadcaster Diann Burns is co-anchor of CBS 2 Chicago's 5 p.m., 6 p.m. and 10 p.m. newscasts. One of Chicago's most recognized journalists, she joined CBS 2 in October of 2003, and 2007 marks her 13th year in the anchor chair for the 10 p.m. newscast.

Diann was the first African-American woman to serve as lead anchor of a 10 p.m. Chicago newscast, and she is currently the only woman of color serving in that role. She has earned eight local Emmys throughout her career, including one in 2004 when she was recognized as the Outstanding News Anchor.

In August of 2007 she anchored CBS 2's three-and-a-half hour live coverage of the devastating Chicago rainstorm. Diann also anchored the station's coverage from Houston when the White Sox won the World Series.

Diann has donated her time to several groups and has mentored young women of color. She has established three journalism scholarships: the RainbowPUSH Coalition, the Indigo Foundation and the Museum of Broadcast Communications scholarships. Additionally, Diann maintains an active membership with the National Association of Black Journalists.

Pamela Jones

Reporter & Northwest
Indiana Bureau Chief
CBS 2 Chicago

Suzanne Le Mignot

News Anchor & General
Assignment Reporter
CBS 2 Chicago

Pamela Jones serves as the Northwest Indiana bureau chief and as a reporter for CBS 2 Chicago. Pamela is based at the station's news bureau in Northwest Indiana, headquartered at the *Post-Tribune*, CBS 2's news partner. She covers stories and issues important to viewers in that region. Pamela, who was born and raised in Gary, Indiana, made a personal choice to invest in that community; she purchased her current home there because of her deep commitment to help the area rebuild.

Since joining the station, she has become a strong CBS 2 representative, supporting many important local organizations and events including the Lake County Indiana Animal Adoption and Control Center, the American Red Cross "Go Red" Fundraising Dinner, Calumet College's Law Enforcement Training Seminar, the Delaney Housing Project Christmas Celebration and Northwest Indiana Sports Charities. This year, Pamela was nominated to become part of Northwest Indiana's first FBI Citizens' Academy class.

Pamela started at CBS 2 in early 2005. However, she actually became part of the CBS family back in college, when she interned for the *CBS Evening News*.

Suzanne Le Mignot is CBS 2 Chicago's weekend morning news anchor and general assignment reporter during the week. Suzanne, who has worked at CBS 2 since 1995, has been recognized for excellence in broadcasting throughout her career.

In 2007 the Associated Press honored her for her investigative report entitled "Tracking Your Security." Suzanne's investigation uncovered that bomb sniffing dogs at Chicago's Metra train stations could not detect explosives. Following her report, state legislation was drafted requiring all dog security firms in Illinois to meet standards so dogs will be trained to find explosives on command and by scent. The report also earned Suzanne and CBS 2 a Peter Lisagor award and an award from the Chicago Bar Association.

She has served as a mentor and volunteer at Bunche Elementary School in Chicago's Englewood community. Additionally, she is an advocate for several important philanthropic organizations throughout the community, including board memberships with the Girl Scouts of Chicago, PAWS Chicago, the Better Boys Foundation and the Lifeline Humanitarian Organization, a group that provides aid for war orphans throughout the former Yugoslavia.

Shawnelle Richie

Director of Public Affairs
CBS 2 Chicago

Dorothy Tucker

Reporter
CBS 2 Chicago

Shawnelle Richie is the director of public affairs for CBS 2 Chicago and is responsible for the station's public outreach to local non-profits and civic organizations. Her job is to develop strategic events and sponsorship opportunities that showcase the commitment CBS 2 has to its viewing community.

She joined the station in 2003, becoming part of a team of television industry leaders whose mission it is to present local stories and issues on CBS 2, both for and about the people of Chicago, its suburbs and Northwest Indiana. As the primary liaison to the viewing community, Shawnelle is responsible for involving the station and its on-air personalities in a myriad of local events and activities.

CBS 2 has developed numerous on-air and in-community campaigns designed to build awareness for organizations doing important work in the community. Under Shawnelle's leadership, the station has partnered with several organizations, including the American Red Cross, the Chicago Public Schools and PUSH.

She is personally dedicated to many important local organizations such as the Parkways Foundation, which provides private support for the Chicago Park District.

For more than 20 years, reporter Dorothy Tucker has been a strong station representative in the African-American community. Today, she reports for CBS 2 Chicago's 5 p.m. and 6 p.m. weekday newscasts and is the station's consumer reporter, helping viewers save money, time and avoid scams. She has also distinguished herself with "Tucker's Tips," a consumer column featured on CBS 2's Web site.

Dorothy has been awarded some of the industry's highest honors: eight local Emmys, including two for her work on CBS 2's 2003 and 2004 broadcasts of the LaSalle Bank Chicago Marathon; the Chicago Association of Black Journalists' annual award for Outstanding Television Reporting; and a national UPI Spot News Award.

Dorothy scored a major coup when she secured U.S. Senator Barack Obama's visit to CBS 2 in support of UNITY, the journalists of color convention that will be held in Chicago in 2008.

She is on the board of the National Association of Black Journalists' Chicago Chapter and was co-chairman of their Katrina fundraiser, which raised money for hurricane survivors who are making Chicago their new home.

Ron Vasser

Director
CBS 2 Chicago

Deidra White

News Planning Manager
CBS 2 Chicago

Ron Vasser is a CBS 2 Chicago Emmy winner who has directed news, sports and entertainment programs for the station since 1979. Under his direction, many of the programs have earned CBS 2 impressive local and national industry honors.

In 1970 Ron started working at WSNS-TV Chicago, Channel 44, as a production assistant. He was promoted to crew chief and then producer and director of the Chicago Bulls, Chicago White Sox, Chicago Blackhawks and NCAA Basketball television broadcasts.

Ron is a member of the National Association of Black Journalists and has held a part-time faculty position for more than 14 years, instructing television classes at Columbia College Chicago. In 2006 he was inducted into Chicago's Wendell Phillips High School Hall of Fame.

Ron's profession is television but his passions are music, horses and being a cowboy. As a horse owner, he enjoys training and riding horses on the trail, in the Bud Billiken Parade® and competing in the Black Rodeo and other events.

Deidra White is the news planning manager for CBS 2 Chicago. With more than 20 years of newsroom experience, she is part of the management team responsible for editorial content for the daily news broadcasts. She is also responsible for generating story ideas and tracking developing stories. Additionally, Deidra is involved in long-range planning for special events and news coverage.

Before CBS 2, Deidra worked for WBBM Newsradio 780, where she served in several management roles such as assistant news director and managing editor. A longtime mentor, Deidra manages the internship program for the CBS 2 newsroom. Recently, she was selected to be a CBS 2 mentor for an annual program sponsored by the Emma Bowen Foundation, a national minority internship program that is supported by all of the major broadcast networks. A native Chicagoan and South Sider, Deidra is a graduate of the University of Illinois at Chicago.

CORPORATE SPOTLIGHT

J im Williams, a native Chicagoan, is the co-anchor of CBS 2 Chicago's weekend evening newscasts. He also serves as a general assignment reporter during the week. Jim, who has worked at CBS 2 since December of 2002, previously served as weekend morning news anchor for the station. He has more than 30 years of journalism experience.

He was a correspondent for ABC News, based at the network's Chicago bureau, from 1997-2001. Jim reported from around the world for *Good Morning America*, *World News Tonight* with Peter Jennings and *Nightline*.

From 1992 to 1997 Jim was Mayor Daley's press secretary. In this capacity, he supervised media relations throughout city government and worked with news organizations from around the world on such significant stories as the 1996 Democratic National Convention, the mayor's takeover of the board of education, his 1995 re-election campaign and the 1994 World Cup soccer tournament. Jim also created the city government's first television magazine show, *Chicago Works!*

Jim supports many local community organizations and is a board member for the Mercy Home for Boys and Girls.

Jim Williams

News Anchor & General
Assignment Reporter
CBS 2 Chicago

See What's New

About EBONY

About YOU!

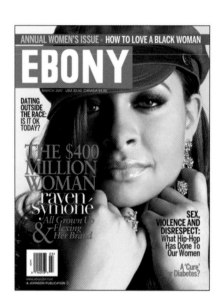

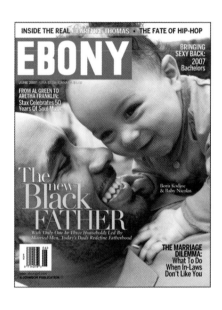

Telling Our Stories Like No One Else

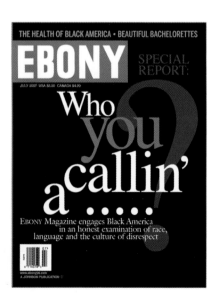

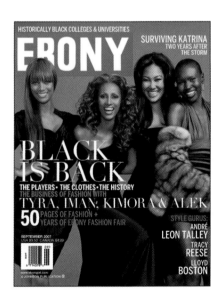

Subscribe Today!

Visit us online at **www.ebonyjet.com** or pick up
EBONY magazine today for a special subscription deal!

enliven

recreate

Media MEDIA PROFESSIONALS

inspire

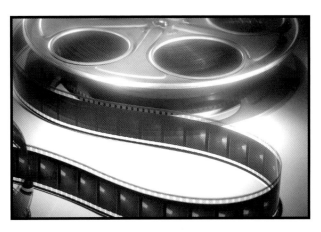

captivate

delight

imagine

amuse

illuminate

innovative

Mark S. Allen

Associate Editor
South Street Journal

Mark S. Allen is the new associate editor of the *South Street Journal* newspaper. He is also a nationally known political and community organizing consultant with people such as U.S. Senator Barack Obama and Congressman Jesse L. Jackson Jr., who called Mark "one of the greatest organizers of grassroots people in the country."

Most recently, Mark became a community relations consultant for Cheryle Jackson, who is the new president of the Chicago Urban League. The League engages Chicago's black grassroots community into projectNEXT, an economic empowerment agenda.

His hard-hitting weekly commentaries on the next stages of black leadership have caught the eye of many, including the Reverend Al Sharpton, who asked Mark to also play a role in getting Chicago's black grassroots community to support his new Chicago Chapter of Sharpton's National Action Network. He has more than 30 years in public service, including seven years as a national staff member to the Reverend Jesse L. Jackson Sr.

Mark has a Bachelor of Arts degree in communications from Western Illinois University. He has two children, daughter DaNia and son Markus.

Helen Bailey

Editor-in-Chief
Urban Livin' Home

When ABC 7 wants their viewers to decorate like *Desperate Housewives*, or CBS 2 needs to give their viewers some budget-minded decorating tips, when Wal-Mart needs to decorate the ultimate dorm room, or *Upscale* magazine needs to quote a decorating expert, when *Essence* magazine wants to spotlight a fabulous bathroom, or *Ebony* magazine needs decorating tips for the holidays or wedding layouts; they all give a shout-out to decorating dynamo Helen Bailey.

Helen has even spread her message on Chicago's airwaves for Clear Channel's WGCI-FM radio with her "Make Your Home a Haven" spots. She has presented and paneled numerous seminars, including her popular Keeping Up with the Jones', While Decorating on a Budget.

As editor-in-chief of a chic new publication, *Urban Livin' Home*, she has created a media outlet to help urban readers create exceptionally beautiful, yet affordable living spaces.

Helen is also responsible for creating Harvest at Home, an annual expo that brings an abundance of home decorating, home improvement, home buying and in-home entertaining information to the public through visually exciting displays and inspirational seminars.

Bonita Bennett is the president of HarBon Publishing, a publishing company she founded in 1982. She is also publisher of *Being Single*, a national lifestyle magazine for singles, which just celebrated its 25th year.

Bonita is a best-selling author who has written two books, *How To Catch and Keep The Man Of Your Dreams* and *The Coming Of Dawn*, a mystery novel that has received rave reviews.

Bonita's monthly column, "As I Look Out," is popular with thousands of readers nationwide who read *Being Single*. Her widely known training manual on management principles has made her a much sought-after speaker at business and leadership conferences nationwide. She is also a former television and radio personality who had her own talk show on major radio stations in Chicago, and her show, *Tips on Single Living*, was syndicated nationally and internationally.

Bonita conducts monthly rehabilitative sessions with female inmates at Cook County Jail in Chicago and monthly self-improvement workshops for area women at the Chicago Public Library.

Bonita Bennett

Publisher
Being Single Magazine

In 2006 Deborah Olivia Brown was named director of station relations for NBC5 Chicago, serving as the liaison between the station and the community. Under her leadership, NBC5 sponsors several health- and literacy-focused initiatives, including the recent Tri-Masters Triathlon for kids, fulfilling NBC5's objectives to combat childhood obesity.

Deborah spearheaded NBC5's first Women's History Month clothing drive, benefiting the Women's Resource Assistance Program (WRAP) and The Primo Center for Women and Children. She sits on the NBC Universal Community Affairs Council, where NBC5 recently awarded $100,000 to four organizations making a difference in the community.

Deborah is a board member of Africa International House and a member of Rotary International, living out the motto "Service above Self." She is a mentor and former board president of WRAP. Deborah also sits on the Black Perspectives board of the Chicago Film Festival, and serves on the Walgreens Community Advisory Task Force.

Additionally, Deborah is a member of Delta Sigma Theta Sorority, Inc. and St. Mark's Missionary Baptist Church in Harvey, Illinois, where she started an AIDS ministry, assisting individuals afflicted with the disease.

Deborah Olivia Brown

Director of Station Relations
NBC5

Earl Calloway

Fine Arts and Travel Editor
Chicago Defender

Earl Calloway has served as a journalist for more than four decades. An alumnus of Oakwood College, he graduated from Chicago Musical College of Roosevelt University, and studied at Chicago State and Governors State universities.

Calloway is fine arts and travel editor at the *Chicago Defender*. He was also a journalist for Claude A. Barnett's Associated Negro Press. As a singer he sang in *Die Fledermaus, Carmen, Aida, The Ordering of Moses* and the operas of Puccini.

Calloway organized the Black Esthetics Festival, now known as Black Creativity, at the Museum of Science and Industry, the Philharmonic Youth Choir and the Oratorio Society at Shiloh SDA Church. He also directed the Umbrian Glee Club, hosted the Artist Circle, and co-founded the Fine Arts Academy and Children Adolescent Forum.

Calloway received Kuumba Theater's Media Award, the Charles P. Browning Journalism Award, and the Cultural Citizens Foundation Arts Lifetime Achievement Award. Additionally, he received an honorary Doctorate of Philosophy degree in music from Faith College in his hometown of Birmingham, Alabama.

Denise D. Campbell

Executive Director
Advertising Sales
Chicago Defender

Denise D. Campbell is the executive director of advertising sales for the *Chicago Defender*. She has been a media executive for BET, Cox, ABC Disney, Infinity and Tribune.

Her passion for coaching fuels her life's mission to be a "visionary agent of change," whose work will be a catalyst impacting the lives of others and helping them elevate the power of their own personal brands. Denise has authored her soon-to-be-published, first book, "The Preferred Brand… Creating A Mirror Reflection That Is Uniquely You." Additionally, she has created an executive leadership development company of the same name, which specializes in keynote speaking and leadership development.

Denise lives life with a commitment to timeless core values. She has a Bachelor of Arts degree from the University of Illinois in Chicago, a Master of Education degree from the University of Illinois in Champaign, and a Master of Arts degree from Northwestern University in Evanston.

A Chicago native, Denise is the daughter of parents Ernest and Florence Jones, and has three brothers and two sisters. She has one son, Ryan (Trina), and one granddaughter, Ryauna.

William C. "Bill" Campbell is host and producer of WSL-TV ABC 7's *Chicagoing*, a weekly program showcasing Chicago's "I Will" spirit. Now in its 18th year, *Chicagoing* is the longest-running public affairs program of its kind. Campbell also co-hosts various local parades and specials for the station, and serves as a spokesperson for ABC 7's Holiday Food Drive each winter.

A three-time Emmy winner, he was ABC 7's director of community services from 1980 until 2001. He was named a William Benton fellow in broadcast journalism in 1988-1989, as part of a select group of journalists chosen to participate in academic study at The University of Chicago.

Campbell's many honors include a Dr. Martin Luther King, Jr. Freedom Award from St. Sabina Church and a Communications Leadership award from the Westside Branch NAACP. His alma mater, Harlan High School, made him the first inductee in their Hall of Fame. *Dollars & Sense* magazine named him one of America's Best and Brightest.

Campbell volunteers at many Chicago-area charities. He is a graduate of Carleton College in Minnesota.

William C. "Bill" Campbell

Host & Producer
Chicagoing
WSL-TV ABC 7

Muriel Clair belongs to that first-rate group of journalists whose reports represent a clear, balanced set of facts.

Clair joined the WGN-TV news team in 1978, and has developed a solid track record as its principal trial reporter. The depth of coverage she brings to the courtroom is carried to the general assignment beat.

Clair taught English in Detroit and Kansas City public schools before she began working at the NBC Kansas City affiliate, WDAF-TV. While there, she won the kind of praise that earned her a spot on the NBC-owned and -operated news operation in Chicago, WMAQ-TV, where she covered the education beat from the vantage point of an ex-teacher and an experienced, award-winning journalist.

In 2002 the Northwestern University School of Law's Center on Wrongful Convictions awarded Clair for her journalistic integrity and work to improve the criminal justice system. She has also received several awards for her highly acclaimed For Kids' Sake series and the Illinois Broadcasters Association recognized her for Best Spot News Reporting. The Detroit, Michigan, native lives in a Chicago suburb.

Muriel Clair

Reporter
WGN-TV

Dee Daniels

Publisher &
Chief Executive Officer
NoirWoman News

Dee Daniels is the publisher and chief executive officer of *NoirWoman News*, a professional, African-American woman's publication. Her duties include creative concept, editorial management and business operations.

After a career in radio and print media in Chicago, Dee decided it was time to go out on her own, and she created the publication *NoirWoman News* in 2004 as a stand-alone, which was distributed throughout local businesses in Chicago. Later in May of 2007, the publication launched as a monthly insert in the *Chicago Sun-Times* weekend section, distributed in the south city and suburban zones.

Dee is active as a mentor to youth and supports women's causes on issues of health, business and education through her numerous affiliations. She attended college in Los Angeles, where she studied English and broadcast journalism.

Dee is a member of the Chicago chapter of the National Association of Black Journalists, and enjoys playing golf. She also has a daughter attending DePaul University and majoring in law.

Richard M. Deal

Programming Assistant &
On-Air Personality
WSRB Soul 106.3 FM

Richard M. Deal is an on-air personality for Soul 106.3 "The Best Mix of R&B" of Crawford Broadcasting. Prior to his career in radio, Richard interned at NBC Channel 5 for *The Jenny Jones Show* during the 1996-1997 season. His start in radio began as "Shawn Knight" in 1997 under the leadership of Elroy Smith at Clear Channel's WGCI AM and FM.

In March of 2001 Jay Alan invited Shawn Knight to join WPWX Power 92. Shawn has been a part of the Power 92 family for four years. Subsequently, Richard was promoted by Jay to join WSRB Soul 106.3 for the morning drive in February of 2005. He then became known as "The Real Deal." Currently, Richard is programming assistant for WSRB Soul 106.3 and an on-air personality.

Richard was included in *Who's Who In Black Chicago®*, and was honored on May 4, 2007, for his work with the Let's Talk, Let's Test Foundation in Chicago, Illinois.

He is a graduate of Kennedy-King College in Chicago, Illinois, and the proud father of 11-year-old twin boys, Jacob and Jacolby.

Merri Dee is one of Chicago's great treasures. For the past 30 years, she has been with WGN-TV serving as a news anchor, talk show host and director of community relations.

Dee is an on-camera host for the *SINGSATION!* Gospel Awards, the National United Negro College Fund and hundreds of other worthy charitable organizations. This includes her lobby, orchestration and passage for the Illinois victims Bill of Rights legislation, and national adoptions of special needs children.

Dee holds many awards, including the Lifetime Achievement Award from the Academy of Television Arts and Sciences and the United Negro College Fund. Considered an amazing and charismatic keynote speaker, panel moderator and emcee, she is in demand for appearances around the country.

The story of her challenges to reach the great success she has obtained showcases her incredible will and inner strength, as she survived kidnapping and attempted murder at the hands of a crazed stalker. She turned her survival ordeal into an example of what motivation and depths of inner spirit can conquer.

Merri Dee is an icon and inspiration.

Merri Dee

Director of Community Relations
WGN-TV

Camille Edwards is the news director at NBC5 in Chicago. She is responsible for managing the day-to-day operations of a top-rated news department. Her duties also include community outreach for the station.

Before joining NBC5, she was the assistant news director at WPVI-TV in Philadelphia. Prior to Philadelphia, Camille was at WLS-TV in Chicago for more than four-and-a-half years.

Camille started her career as a reporter in Toledo, Ohio. She made the jump to producing while in Toledo. She moved to Baltimore and was the 6 p.m. producer at WBAL-TV. In 1993 Camille moved to Chicago as a weekend producer at WBBM-TV.

She was born in Delaware but spent much of her childhood in suburban Detroit. She is a graduate of the University of Michigan in Ann Arbor.

Camille is a member of the National Association of Black Journalists and a member and former vice president of broadcast for NABJ-Chicago. She is also a member of RTNDA, the Chicago Urban League, The Economic Club of Chicago and Alpha Kappa Alpha Sorority, Inc.

Camille Edwards

News Director
NBC5 Chicago

Renee Ferguson

Reporter
NBC5 News

Award-winning investigative reporter Renee Ferguson brings more than 30 years of reporting experience to NBC5 News. She has covered major stories locally, nationally and internationally with insight and expertise.

Ferguson has received some of the nation's most prestigious journalism awards, including the duPont Award, given by Columbia University in New York; the Goldsmith Award, given by the Kennedy School of Government at Harvard; the Gracie Award, given by American Women in Radio and Television; and the Associated Press Award for Best Investigative Reporting. She has received seven Chicago Emmys as well as reporting awards from the National Association of Black Journalists and its local Chicago chapter. In 2006 she was awarded one of journalism's most coveted honors, the Nieman Fellowship at Harvard University.

Ferguson's investigation into allegations that minority women were unfairly targeted as drug couriers and strip-searched at O'Hare Airport by United States Customs led to a GAO (Government Accountability Office) study, congressional hearings, a major change in Customs personal search policies nationwide, and a law requiring that Customs report the number and reasons for strip-searches to Congress every year.

Bioncé Foxx

Radio Personality
WGCI-FM Chicago (107.5)

When Bioncé Foxx speaks, people listen. Between the hits, the vivacious radio personality captures the attention of thousands of listeners with topics and issues that anybody can relate to. Bioncé is definitely a household name in Chicago, returning to WGCI-FM (107.5) after a stint as midday host at KVGS-FM (V108) in Las Vegas. Before transitioning into midday at WGCI, she hosted the highly rated *Whispers in the Dark* show, also at WGCI, and garnered international fame with the *Foxx on the Box* show in Bermuda at WHT-FM (Hott 1075).

In addition to the *Foxx on the Box* show at WGCI, this radio star also hosts the *Foxx on the Box* show in Tyler, Texas. And that's not all; Bioncé winds down the day as host of *The Quiet Storm* at WKKV-FM (V100.7) in Milwaukee.

Bioncé is also a music vocalist and voiceover talent. She is actively involved in the community through volunteer work with several organizations, and she enjoys traveling around the world.

onya Francisco joined CLTV in December of 2002. She can be seen each weekday morning anchoring the CLTV *Morning News*.

In 2006 Tonya was nominated for an Emmy for her work on the documentary *Englewood Speaks*. She also earned a Michigan Broadcasters Association Award of Merit and a National Association of Black Journalists second-place finish for a documentary on Idlewild. She has served as mistress of ceremonies for a number of community events, and has helped to raise funds for area nonprofit organizations.

Tonya began her television career as a desk assistant for WLS-TV in Chicago. She moved on to WOOD-TV in Grand Rapids, Michigan, to become a reporter/associate producer. After a year, it was on to WJRT-TV in Flint, where she worked her way up from general assignment reporter to weekend anchor.

Born and raised on Chicago's West Side, Tonya is a graduate of Whitney M. Young Magnet High School, and has a degree in mass communications from the University of Illinois at Chicago. Tonya is a member of Alpha Kappa Alpha Sorority, Inc. and the National Association of Black Journalists.

Tonya Francisco

Morning News Anchor
CLTV News

---

endra "G" Gilliams is the morning show co-host of *Trey the Choklit Jok Morning Jump-Off* heard weekday mornings on WPWX Power 92.3. As the morning show co-host, one of her many responsibilities is informing the city of Chicago on all the latest information in the entertainment world. Kendra G. has also broken several major entertainment stories first which have been written about on numerous Web sites such as, allhiphop.com, eurweb.com and mediatakeout.com.

Before moving to Chicago to become the morning show co-host on Power 92, she hosted her own radio show in Buffalo, New York, and Hartford, Connecticut.

Kendra G. was born and raised on the east coast in Waterbury, Connecticut. She received a Bachelor of Science degree in marketing from Hampton University.

Currently, Kendra G. is writing her first book and working on an "Ab" workout tape.

Kendra "G" Gilliams

Morning Show Co-Host
WPWX Power 92.3

Evelyn Holmes

Reporter
ABC 7 News

Evelyn Holmes is a general assignment reporter for ABC 7 News, the top-rated news station in Chicago. She joined the station in May of 2003 from Chicagoland Television News (CLTV), where she served as a weekday morning news anchor.

Holmes has worked in Chicago broadcasting for the past 13 years. She started at CLTV as a traffic reporter in June of 1996. While there, she also served as a weathercaster, a general assignment reporter, a fill-in news anchor and a weekend news anchor.

Before moving to television, Holmes was a part of both the Bob Collins and the Spike O'Dell shows on WGN Radio. Recently, she has served as a fill-in show host on WVON-AM radio.

Holmes is a Chicago native and a graduate of Northwestern University. She is a member of the Chicago Association of Black Journalists and the National Association of Black Journalists.

Holmes is involved in numerous charitable and community projects.

Jonathan Hood

Sports Talk Show Host
ESPN Radio AM1000

Jonathan Hood is the co-host of *The Show* and *Chicago Baseball Tonight* weeknights on ESPN AM1000. Currently, he is the only full-time African-American sports talk host in Chicago. Every night, "J-Hood" runs the gamut on sports talk and entertainment, and he has covered various events, including Chicago Bulls playoff games, the White Sox World Series, NCAA tournaments, the Arena Bowl and the Top of the World Classic college basketball tournament in Fairbanks, Alaska. He also authors *The Wrestling Ringpost*, a professional wrestling column on espnradio1000.com.

Jonathan attended Kennedy-King College in Chicago where he honed his on-air, production, play-by-play and television skills. A radio veteran since 1990 and two-time Chicagoland A.I.R. Award winner, his passion for sports talk is evident through his various innovations that Chicago sports fans know and love. He lends his knowledge as a substitute host and contributor for *The 2 Live Stews*, a nationally syndicated sports show on Radio One.

When off the air, Jonathan heads the media ministry at Victory Christian International Ministries in Markham, Illinois, where he and his wife, Michelle, are members.

Theresa Fambro Hooks ("Teesee") is a columnist/journalist for the *Chicago Defender*, a newspaper serving the African-American community. A 46-year veteran in her field, she pens a daily column, "Teesee's Town," reporting on arts, theatre, and the comings and goings of business, community and social leaders. She covers special events in a regular feature, "Seen on the Scene," for which she takes photos. Previously, Theresa was a *Defender* public relations vice president and president of Chicago Defender Charities, Inc.

Theresa's previous professional positions include regional community relations manager, Coors Beer; marketing/communications director, Parker House Sausage Co.; special assistant to the president for public information/community services, Olive-Harvey College; and community/public affairs manager, Philco-Ford Job Corps Center. She was also president of Theresa Fambro Hooks & Associates, a public relations, communications and marketing firm.

Some of her many honors include Phenomenal Woman, V-103 FM; Lifetime Achievement, Black Public Relations Society; Russ Ewing Legacy Award of Excellence from the Chicago Association of Black Journalists; Phenomenal Woman, Alpha Phi Alpha Fraternity, Inc.; Woman Making History, National Council of Negro Women; and Outstanding Media Woman, Chicago Urban League.

Theresa Fambro Hooks ("Teesee")

Columnist/Journalist
Chicago Defender

Leah Hope is a general assignment reporter for ABC 7 News, Chicago's top-rated news station. She is an award-winning reporter who focuses on special investigations and other important stories affecting the lives of Chicagoans. She joined ABC 7 in 1997.

Hope's work covering important issues in the African-American community has been honored on both national and local levels. She has won two awards from the National Association of Black Journalists, as well as the prestigious Russ Ewing Excellence in Journalism Award and the Excellence in Enterprise Journalism Award for her series on affirmative action. Her work has also been honored with an Emmy award, a Gracie Award and four Peter Lisagor Awards from the Society of Professional Journalists for excellence in covering breaking news.

Hope is a member of the Investigative Reporters and Editors Association, the National Association of Black Journalists, American Women in Radio and Television, and the National Academy of Television Arts and Sciences.

A graduate of New York's Syracuse University, she is the great-granddaughter of John Hope, the first African-American president of Morehouse College in Atlanta, Georgia.

Leah Hope

General Assignment Reporter
ABC 7 News

CHICAGO'S MEDIA PROFESSIONALS

Zondra Hughes

Editor
N'DIGO

Zondra Hughes is the editor of *N'DIGO* magapaper, the largest urban weekly newspaper in the nation. She is also the editorial director of the companion Web sites for *Savoy* and *N'DIGO*, both of which are properties of Hartman Publishing.

Hughes, formerly an associate editor at *Ebony* magazine, is the author of a well-received novel, *The M.O.O.D. Lounge.*

Hughes received a Master of Arts degree in journalism, with honors, from Iowa State University. Her background includes marketing and public relations. She has been cited as one of the 30 Under 30 Leaders in Business by the *Chicago Sun-Times* and 100 Women Making a Difference by *Today's Chicago Woman*.

Hughes is the protégée of the late Chicago media icon, journalist Vernon Jarrett, a founding member of the National Association of Black Journalists.

Santita Jackson

Host
WVON 1690AM

Santita Jackson brings her worldly perspective on current events and contemporary issues from behind the scenes to behind the mic. She is the eldest of the Reverend Jesse Jackson Sr.'s five children, and has traveled nationally and internationally as a performer.

As the producer of *Upfront with Jesse Jackson*, she has been instrumental in coordinating informative, sometimes controversial programming, and will bring her provocative style to *The Santita Jackson Show.*

Iman A. Jefferson is the assistant editor of *N'DIGO* magapaper, where she began as a summer intern and worked her way up the editorial ladder. In her current position, Iman assists in the day-to-day editorial operations of the publication. While at *N'DIGO*, she has interviewed a wide array of celebrities from Ben Gordon to Jennifer Hudson. She has also written for *Black Enterprise*, *Savoy* and *Time Out Chicago* and has done marketing communications on behalf of Flowers Communications Group. Iman also completed a student journalism institute for *The New York Times* in New Orleans as well as covered the post-Katrina rebuild.

Iman received a Bachelor of Arts degree in journalism from Lincoln University of Missouri. Born in Chicago and raised in Flossmoor, she is a member of the National Association of Black Journalists and the National Association of Black Journalism – Chicago Chapter. She cites Ronald Childs, Monroe Anderson and Zondra Hughes-Riyaz as her mentors.

Iman A. Jefferson

Assistant Editor
N'DIGO

Lauren Jiggetts joined NBC5 Chicago as a general assignment reporter in January of 2007. Prior to joining NBC5, Jiggetts served as a general assignment reporter and fill-in anchor for WLVI-TV, Boston's CW.

Before joining Boston's CW, she worked as an anchor and reporter for the award-winning *Channel One News* in Los Angeles, California. The daily 12-minute newscast is sent via satellite to 12,000 middle and high schools nationwide.

Jiggetts began her broadcasting career in the public affairs office at MTV Studios in New York City, where she worked on its Emmy Award-winning anti-discrimination campaign, Fight for Your Rights. She also interned in the newsrooms of WFLD-TV and Chicagoland's Television.

A member of the National Association of Black Journalists, Jiggetts graduated, cum laude, from Harvard University.

Lauren Jiggetts

General Assignment Reporter
NBC5 Chicago

Karen Jordan

Co-Anchor
ABC 7 News

Karen Jordan co-anchors ABC 7 News' No. 1-rated weekend newscast in Chicago. Jordan, who grew up in Evanston, joined ABC 7 in 2003. Previously, she served as weekend anchor and general assignment reporter for WPHL-TV in Philadelphia, Pennsylvania.

Jordan began her career as a general assignment reporter for WIFR-TV. She also gained early experience at WMAQ-AM in Chicago, where she worked through the Medill News Service as a radio reporter.

Recognized for excellence throughout her career, Jordan was named a 2003 Rising Star in *Today's Chicago Woman*. She received the YMCA Black Achiever Award in 2000 and the Bethune Recognition for women in the media from the National Council of Negro Women in 1999. Additionally, she is a member of the National Association of Black Journalists.

Jordan graduated from Spelman College in Atlanta, Georgia, with a Bachelor of Arts degree in English in 1994. She also earned a master's degree in broadcast journalism from Northwestern University in 1995.

Born in Nashville, Tennessee, Jordan is married to broadcast journalist Christian Farr. Her father, Robert Jordan, is a longtime anchor and reporter at WGN-TV.

Cliff Kelley

Host
WVON 1690AM

Cliff Kelley has distinguished himself as a popular talk show host, who brings a wealth of knowledge on local, national and international affairs to WVON's vast listening audience. A native Chicagoan and attorney, he has been in active in Chicago's political arena for more than 30 years, including 16 years on Chicago's City Council.

Kelley has been a featured guest on issue-oriented programs on local, national and international television and radio, and is a frequent contributor to *Chicago Tonight*, which airs on Chicago's public television station, WTTW11. He has also traveled extensively to Africa, the Middle East, Asia and Europe.

Herb Kent is an urban radio pioneer. He is a voice of the community, a father, a friend and a living history lesson. To many Chicagoans, Herbert Rogers Kent, also known as "the Cool Gent," "the King of the Dusties" and the Honorary Mayor of Bronzeville, stands for all these things and more.

As one of the most important figures in Chicago radio history, Herb has not only been able to entertain and inform listeners for more than 60 years on the radio, he has also opened up many doors for African Americans. Simply put, Herb Kent is a Chicago treasure and a bankable commodity.

Herb Kent

On-Air Personality
V103
Clear Channel Radio

Lisa Lenoir is travel and society editor for the *Chicago Sun-Times*. She writes travel features, and manages freelancers and staffers who submit stories to the weekly "Sunday Travel" section. She also covers the city's vibrant philanthropic community in a weekly column called "In Society." Prior to these appointments, Lisa was the paper's fashion editor.

Lisa attended Indiana University, graduating in 1989 with a Bachelor of Arts degree in journalism and a minor in graphic design. She has served in many organizations, including the African-American Leadership Advisory Committee for the Art Institute of Chicago, Alpha Kappa Alpha Sorority, Inc., the North American Travel Journalists Association, the Apparel Industry Board of Chicago and Fashion Group International of Chicago.

Her awards include the Chicago Association of Black Journalists' Award of Excellence in Commentary in 1998, the 2003 Peter Lisagor Journalism Award (team project) and the 2002-2003 Lowell Thomas Silver Award for the *Sun-Times* "Travel Section" (team project).

In addition to her media work, Lisa teaches fashion journalism and writing for managers at Columbia College Chicago, and creates handmade greeting cards for private clients.

Lisa Lenoir

Editor, Travel & Society
Chicago Sun-Times

Roland S. Martin

Host
WVON 1690AM

R oland S. Martin, a nationally award-winning journalist and syndicated columnist with Creators Syndicate, is the founding editor of BlackAmericaWeb.com. He is a frequent guest commentator on TV One, CNN, MSNBC, Fox and Black Entertainment Television (BET), and is also the author of *Speak, Brother! A Black Man's View of America*. Additionally, he is a member of the National Association of Black Journalists (NABJ), the American Society of Newspaper Editors and Alpha Phi Alpha Fraternity, Inc.

Micah Materre

Anchor
WGN-TV

W GN's Micah Materre has been a broadcast journalist for more than 20 years. She joined Chicago's WGN-TV in January of 1998 as a *WGN Morning News* anchor and medical reporter. While at WGN, Materre has covered entertainment news and special assignment stories. She is currently an anchor for the *WGN News at Noon*.

Before working in Chicago, Materre spent eight years at WJBK-TV in Detroit, where she was a main anchor and general assignment reporter. While at WJBK, her work garnered numerous awards and accolades. Prior to moving to the Motor City, Materre worked in Cedar Rapids, Iowa, as a general assignment reporter and weekend anchor. She began her career in broadcasting in 1983 at NPR affiliate WBEZ radio in Chicago, producing and reporting for four years. In addition, she taught radio production at Columbia College.

Materre is an Emmy Award-winning reporter, and she has been honored by the Michigan Association of Broadcasters. She has also been featured in several national publications, including *The New York Times Magazine, Glamour, Ebony* and *Good Housekeeping*, and locally in *Today's Chicago Woman*.

"He's got it!" That is all one can say when they meet the media savvy Matt McGill. The native Chicagoan's charismatic charm brought him to WVON Radio after a one-time meeting with the station's president.

McGill attended Santa Monica College, where he majored in broadcasting, and hosted a radio talk program for two years. Upon his return to Chicago, he provided media services and public relations for area radio stations. McGill is a single father of two girls and a boy.

Perri R. Small is a veteran print and broadcast journalist. During the height of the City of Chicago's "Council Wars," she was hired to join Mayor Harold Washington's press office.

After leaving city government, Small relocated to Atlanta, Georgia, and worked for the *Atlanta Daily World*, the APEX museum, and two of the South's leading African-American-owned and -operated advertising and public relations firms. She returned to Chicago, and was hired as a producer for WVON 1450 AM and eventually became executive producer and host.

McGill and Small are the hosts of *Matt & Perri* on WVON 1690 AM.

**Matt McGill &
Perri R. Small**

Hosts, *Matt & Perri*
WVON 1690 AM

Mary Mitchell is an editorial board member and columnist for the *Chicago Sun-Times*. Her column appears Sundays, Tuesdays and Thursdays.

Mitchell is the recipient of numerous journalism awards, including the prestigious Award of Excellence from the National Association of Black Journalists, the Studs Terkel Award from the Community Media Workshop and the Peter Lisagor Award from the Chicago Headliner Club. Likewise, she is the recipient of the Phenomenal Woman Award by the Expo for Today's Black Woman and the Humanitarian Award from 100 Black Men of Chicago. In 2004 *Crain's Chicago Business* honored her as one of the 100 Most Influential Women in Chicago.

Named "courageous" and "compassionate" by readers who trust her, Mitchell gives them a voice on issues ranging from police misconduct to the tragedy of black-on-black violence.

Mitchell earned a bachelor's degree in journalism at Columbia College Chicago. She is the mother of four children, the grandmother of three, and resides in Maywood, Illinois.

Mary Mitchell

Editorial Board Member &
Columnist
Chicago Sun-Times

Allison Payne

Anchor
WGN-TV

Allison Payne joined WGN-TV News in March of 1990 as co-anchor of the *WGN News at Nine*. She is the five-time Emmy Award-winning anchor of the *WGN News at Nine* and co-anchor of WGN's bi-weekly program, *People to People*, with Steve Sanders. Previously, Payne anchored the nightly news for WNEM-TV in Saginaw, Michigan. Her career as a television journalist began at WNWO-TV in Toledo, Ohio.

In August of 2005, Payne joined the *The Real Show* with Ramonski Luv and Joe Soto on V103 102.7 FM as headline reader. In her role, she delivers the weekday news updates for the popular radio show in studio from 3 to 5 p.m.

Payne was recognized by *Today's Chicago Woman* in the 1999 special edition of 100 Women Making a Difference in the City. She has also been featured in *Essence* magazine for her work as an anchor.

Payne grew up in Detroit, Michigan, where she graduated, magna cum laude, from the University of Detroit. She also has a Master of Arts degree from Bowling Green State University in Ohio.

Harry Porterfield

Feature News Reporter
ABC 7 News

ABC 7's veteran feature news reporter, Harry Porterfield, joined the station in September of 1985 after 21 years in Chicago television. He is a local icon known for his continuing series of human-interest "Someone You Should Know" reports, which he created in 1977. Having profiled more than 2,000 subjects, "Someone You Should Know" is one of the most popular series in Chicago television, and was honored with the 2007 American Scene Award from the American Federation of Television and Radio Artists.

Porterfield has received 11 Emmy awards for news and feature reporting, among countless other honors. He was inducted into the Chicago Television Academy's Silver Circle in 1998, recognizing 25 years of excellence in journalism.

Porterfield is a board member of the Jazz Institute of Chicago, an honorary board member of the Merit Music Program and a member of the Chicago Federation of Musicians. A violinist, he is a member of the annual Do-It-Yourself Messiah Orchestra and the Chicago Bar Association Orchestra.

Porterfield holds a degree in chemistry from Eastern Michigan University and a law degree from DePaul University in Chicago.

Marcus Riley is NBC5's manager of Web development. He is responsible for integrating new online technology and content onto NBC5.com and guiding the site's long-term vision. As the line between on-air and online content continues to shrink, Marcus is involved in creating and seeking original and exclusive Web content, including working closely with the other nine NBC-owned and -operated station Web sites in the country on projects such as the 2008 Summer Olympics. In 2004, he spent a month in Athens working for nbcolympics.com.

Marcus hosts several podcasts (www.nbc5.com/podcast), and won a regional Emmy for Media Interactivity in 2005. He is also a contributor for NBC's *Nude Hippo*, and is a board member for the Afrocentric theater group, MPAACT.

He has more than 15 years of experience in television, including stints as reporter, weatherman and Web manager at stations in Clarksburg and Wheeling, West Virginia; Tallahassee, Florida; Lexington and Louisville, Kentucky; Cincinnati; and Indianapolis.

Marcus grew up near Toronto, Canada, and graduated from West Virginia University, where he was also the captain of the track and field team for three years.

Marcus Riley
Manager of Web Development
NBC5

Since joining ABC 7 News in 1982, Jim Rose has become a major force in Chicago sports broadcasting. He currently serves as sports anchor and reporter for the station's top-rated 4 and 6 p.m. newscasts. A contributor to ABC 7's Emmy Award-winning *People, Places & Things*, Rose also co-hosts the station's annual broadcast of one of the largest parades in the country, the Bud Billiken® Parade and Picnic.

He began his career in sports broadcasting while serving in the U.S. Army, acting as sports director for AFN-TV in Berlin, West Germany (1973-1975). He has won several awards for his work, including the 1981 Best Sports Story Award and Best Reporting Under Deadline Pressure.

After four-and-a-half years of sweat equity, Rose recently gave away the "Swan House" he helped build to a Chicago-area single mother who had achieved academic excellence in college. He considers this one of his life's crowning achievements.

Rose participates in many Chicago-area charities and serves as a mentor to the Chicago Public Schools and Harold Washington College.

Jim Rose
Sports Anchor & Reporter
ABC 7 News

Hosea Sanders

Morning News
Co-Anchor & Reporter
ABC 7 News

Hosea Sanders plays a major role at ABC 7 News, both in the news and programming areas. In addition to anchoring the station's top-rated 5 to 7 a.m. newscasts, Sanders hosts such important local specials as Operation Save-A-Life, the station's fire safety program credited with helping decrease fire fatalities, and a salute to John Johnson, honoring Chicago's iconic black publisher. He is a featured reporter on ABC 7's Emmy Award-winning *People, Places & Things* program, focusing on Chicago's African-American community.

Sanders won six Emmys, gaining honors for live coverage, spot news, entertainment reporting, news writing and overall news achievement. He has received more than 100 awards from various civic and community organizations for his community outreach.

A nationally sought-after motivational speaker, Sanders is dedicated to mentoring and helping young people. He is active in the Alpha Phi Alpha Fraternity, Inc. Big Brothers Program, the Chicago Public Schools Mentoring Program and the NAACP Mentoring Program.

He is a member of the National Association of Black Journalists, the Chicago Association of Black Journalists and the National Academy of Television Arts and Sciences.

Art "Chat Daddy" Sims

Entertainment, Nightlife &
Travel Columnist
Chicago Defender

Art "Chat Daddy" Sims is an entertainment, nightlife and travel columnist, and is the brainchild behind "Dear Chat Daddy," his relationship advice column. He is also the travel expert for *Desirable Destinations Travel Show*, which can be heard on WVON 1690 AM.

Sims is a familiar and welcomed face in many diverse communities in Chicago and around the world. He is the founder and host of "The Real Deal Relationship Chats," which is an engaging, informative, down-to-earth relationship forum that is now in its 11th year. His chat touches on real issues, especially those concerning African-American relationships.

Sims is a member of the National Association of Black Journalists and the metropolitan board of the Chicago Urban League. He is in the process of starting a nonprofit organization that will educate youth about HIV and AIDS. He is a proponent of HIV education and speaks to groups globally, while encouraging the importance of getting tested and knowing one's status.

The native Chicagoan lives his life by his personal motto, "if you believe in change, it shall happen."

David Smallwood is a veteran journalist and author with more than 30 years of print experience in Chicago. He has more than 400,000 of his own words in print, and has edited more than one million words that have been published by other writers.

A founding member of *N'DIGO* Magapaper, David was its editor for six years, and has written more than 80 cover stories for the paper since its inception. He has worked as a *Chicago Sun-Times* reporter, a *Jet* magazine editor, a *Dollars & Sense* magazine head writer, and a *Chicago Reporter* investigative reporter. He has also served as a journalism instructor at Columbia College and communications director at Olive-Harvey College. Co-author of *The Cool Gent*, radio legend Herb Kent's autobiography scheduled for release by Chicago Review Press in October of 2008, Smallwood currently has two other books in development.

A product of Lindblom High School, he was a National Achievement scholar who graduated from the University of Illinois at Chicago in 1976, and began his journalism career with the legendary Lu Palmer.

David Smallwood

Writer, Editor &
Media Consultant
3-Much Communications, Inc.

Keenan Smith has been a member of the WGN-TV Weather Center team since December of 2003. Prior to joining WGN, he worked for CLTV, NBC Network News and television stations in Peoria, Illinois; Lancaster, Pennsylvania; Trenton, New Jersey; and Raleigh, North Carolina.

Keenan graduated from Franklin & Marshall College in Lancaster, Pennsylvania, and later earned a dual master's degree in domestic policy and urban and regional planning from Princeton University in Princeton, New Jersey. He also completed meteorology course work from the College of DuPage, Pennsylvania State University, Portland State University and Oklahoma State University.

Born in Philadelphia, Keenan is a member of the American Meteorological Society and the National Weather Association. In 2005 he was nominated for a Midwest Regional Emmy for Outstanding Achievement in Weathercasting, and previously received an Illinois Associated Press Award for Investigative Reporting. Awarded the American Meteorological Society Seal of Approval in 2005, he now serves on the AMS Board on Woman and Minorities.

Keenan and his wife live in Chicago.

Keenan Smith

Meteorologist
WGN-TV

Charles Thomas

General Assignment Reporter
ABC 7 News

Charles Thomas joined ABC 7 News in September of 1991 as a general assignment reporter, following several years as a Midwest correspondent for ABC News in the Chicago and St. Louis Bureaus. He has worked as a professional journalist since 1973, after his graduation from the University of Missouri's School of Journalism.

While working at the network, Thomas traveled to all 50 states and to five continents. Despite his extensive travel, Chicago remained the most intriguing city for him, personally and professionally. So when ABC 7 offered him a position on its staff covering Chicago on a daily basis, it was a dream come true.

Thomas remains one of ABC 7's most well-traveled reporters, adding a Chicago perspective to many stories of national interest. As an ABC 7 reporter, he has covered the O.J. Simpson and Rodney King trials, the Oklahoma City bombing story, major airline crashes, natural disasters, and the 2005 White Sox World Championship run, among other assignments. He also reported for ABC 7 from Europe and Asia, and in 2006 accompanied U.S. Senator Barack Obama to Africa.

La Donna Tittle

Producer & Host
The La Donna Tittle TV/Radio Show

La Donna Tittle is producer of her own show on CAN TV 19, *The La Donna Tittle TV/Radio Show*, featuring "Cookin' Wit' Tittle." She is an on-air talent and mentor at Kennedy-King College Radio, WKKC 89.3 FM.

As a professional model, she launched her radio career with WBEE in 1970, and was Chicago's number one disc jockey in 1973 with WBMX. Tittle went on to join Johnson Publishing Company's WJPC in 1978. In 1983, she received Arbitron's highest ratings for middays and the Black Radio Exclusive Air Personality Award.

Her versatile career includes noteworthy theatrical performances with ETA, the Gospel Repertory Theater Company, Goodman, Steppenwolf and Organic Theaters. She was also in the movies *Ali* and *The Relic*, and has done national television voiceovers and commercials.

Tittle graduated from Dunbar Vocational High School, where she is an inductee of the Alumni Hall of Fame. Earning a Bachelor of Arts degree from Chicago State University, she currently writes a column in *NoirWoman*, a supplement distributed monthly in the *Chicago Sun-Times*, called "Tittle's Cosmopolitan World, Arts, Entertainment & Beyond."

For 11 years, Trey has succeeded in producing and hosting dynamic Chicago radio. His passion for radio has superseded anything he could imagine. Trey's career began as a high school sports reporter at age 16 on WGCI.

Trey currently hosts the only local and most popular urban morning show in Chicago on Power 92 WPWX. His mission every morning is to enrich the community through building awareness on the issues that affect us daily as well as entertain. He focuses on covering real life topics and politics with a touch of humor that keeps the listeners tuning in.

In 2004 Trey founded The Choklit Jock Foundation, which enables him to bless Chicago high school and college students with opportunities.

Trey has also gone beyond his radio persona and shifted to television by co-hosting *Know Your Heritage* and nationally with the annual Bud Billiken® Parade. He is also an esteemed member of the Masonic Lodge Malachi No. 9. Trey is living proof that if you trust God and put your mind to it, anything is possible.

Trey the Choklit Jok

On-Air Personality
Power 92 WPWX

LeeAnn Trotter is NBC5's entertainment reporter, and covers everything from celebrities to what's happening around town. This Chicago native joined WMAQ-TV in December of 2005, after working at CLTV for eight years. There, LeeAnn anchored the weekend news and hosted the award-winning entertainment show, *Metromix: The TV Show*, which earned her a local Emmy and several nominations for Best On Camera Performance.

Prior to working at CLTV, LeeAnn was the news and public affairs director at WUSN-FM, where she reported news on the morning show and hosted *Chicago Up Close*, a weekly public affairs show. She also worked briefly at Fox News and WGN Radio. LeeAnn began her broadcasting career at WBBM Newsradio 780, where she held numerous positions, including production manager and traffic reporter.

LeeAnn graduated from the University of Illinois at Champaign, with a degree in broadcast journalism, and attended high school at the Latin School of Chicago.

LeeAnn Trotter

Entertainment Reporter
NBC5

David "D-Nice" Walker

On-Air Personality &
Executive Producer
WSRB-FM Soul 106.3

David Walker, known to Chicago as "D-Nice," is an integral part of the Crawford Broadcasting Family, working with both Soul 106.3 and Power 92 radio stations. His many contributions to both stations include serving as on-air personality, executive producer for *The Michael Baisden Show* and production assistant. When tuning in to either Crawford station, his attention-grabbing voice is sure to be heard.

David is also host and executive producer of *In the Mix Magazine*, a music entertainment show that can be seen in the Chicagoland and Northwest Indiana areas. A native of Gary, Indiana, he has been in the entertainment industry since 1995, starting as a personality with WLTH radio station.

David and his lovely wife, Towanna, are members of Living Word Christian Center in Forest Park, Illinois. He believes that God has placed him in the industry to make a positive impact. "Staying positive and grounded is the key to success," says David.

Valerie Warner

Anchor
WGN-TV

Valerie Warner joined WGN-TV in July of 2005 as anchor of the 5 a.m. news hour. She also serves as traffic reporter for *WGN Morning News* from 6 to 9 a.m.

Prior to WGN-TV, Warner served as evening anchor and reporter for WEYI-TV in Flint, Michigan, for five years. From 1998 to 2000, she anchored and reported the morning newscast at KSNT-TV. She also spent a year as fill-in anchor and reporter at KRQE in Albuquerque and KBIM in Roswell, New Mexico.

Warner received a Bachelor of Arts degree from the University of California, San Diego.

Carl West is chief executive officer of MIDWEST GAP Enterprise, a ten-year-old publishing and promotional company focusing and celebrating the multibillion-dollar business of hip-hop culture.

MIDWEST GAP is the publisher of *The TRUTH magazine: Hip-Hop Culture At its Best*, which highlights Chicago's emerging hip-hop industry, and *Hip-Hop IMAGEMAKER*, a monthly Q&A profiling personalities delivering positive images within hip-hop culture. MIDWEST GAP also produces The TRUTH Awards, which salutes and awards the best and brightest Chicagoan in television, radio, music, sports, comedy and business; and it is responsible for the TRUTH 4 Literacy Program, a not-for-profit after-school mentoring program teaching at-risk youth reading, writing and communication skills.

In 2006 Carl established the CHI brand label to represent Chicago and all who wear the apparel. He also contributes a weekly column to Citizen Newspaper Group's five periodicals, and sits on the board of several civil, social and business organizations. He is often asked to speak at conferences on business and youth culture.

Carl's most rewarding project is 5-year-old Karly Olivia West, future leader of hip-hop's next generation.

Carl West
Chief Executive Officer
MIDWEST GAP Enterprise

Terri Winston is the chief executive officer of Hush Media Group (HMG) and the publisher of *SalonSENSE* magazine. As owner of the only African-American industry trade magazine, Winston now joins an elite list of African-American female-owned publishers.

HMG is a publishing medium established to empower urban salon professionals with business, management and marketing tools for economic growth and inspire more to become salon entrepreneurs through its *SalonSENSE* magazine. HMG maintains its pulse on the beauty industry online and through its events. Winston oversees the company's marketing initiative that helps advertisers and brand managers build a bridge into the beauty industry by removing the veil of misinformation concerning the ethnic salon and grooming professional market.

Winston is sought after for her views on political, social and beauty-related issues. She speaks regularly at trade shows and is often a featured expert on articles and radio shows that address the market. Winston's reception of the 2006 Beauty Entrepreneur ICON Award and nomination for a Black Enterprise Innovator of the Year Award uncovered ethnic salon business as the fastest-growing sector of small business.

Terri Winston
Chief Executive Officer
Hush Media Group

CHICAGO'S MEDIA PROFESSIONALS

EACH ONE REACH ONE

"What they see, they will be."

As we launch the Second Edition of *Who's Who In Black Chicago*®, we want this book to be a source of inspiration for the boys and girls in Chicago schools and other youth development programs. Our goal is that you move beyond reading to reaching. Reach beyond the pages of this publication to touch others by purchasing an additional book and passing the dreams on.

We are asking you to join the list of individuals, community organizations, and businesses who are purchasing books, either for 'adopting' schools, or donating to organizations as a tool of encouragement for African-American girls and boys in your community.

What they see, they will be. Let them see achievement at its best in *Who's Who In Black Chicago*®. Buy one, or several; Sunny Martin, the CEO of Who's Who Publishing, has agreed to make these books very affordable for bulk purchase, and any donation will be made in your name. Please contact Paula Gray at Who's Who corporate office at 614-481-7300 or paula@whoswhopublishing.com. Together we can uplift and inspire the next generation of leaders.

1650 Lake Shore Drive, Suite 250 • Columbus, OH 43204 • (614) 481-7300 • www.whoswhopublishing.com

perform

elevate

Academia

CHICAGO'S
ACADEMIA

phenom

scholar

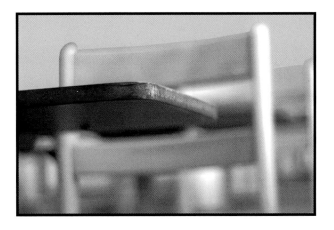

prodigy

mentor

merit

value

attain

Joan Archie

Executive Director
Construction Compliance
The University of Chicago
Medical Center

Samuel Attoh, Ph.D.

Dean, Graduate School
Loyola University Chicago

Joan Archie is executive director of construction compliance for The University of Chicago Medical Center. In this position, she is responsible for implementing and managing the Medical Center's Construction Compliance Initiative to establish and attain or exceed its minority and women contracting, procurement and workforce goals.

Joan has won numerous awards, including Compliance Officer of the Year from Black Contractors United for her dedication to the marketing, promotion and continued development of minority- and women-owned businesses.

Joan received a Bachelor of Arts degree and a Master of Arts degree from Roosevelt University. A native of Chicago, Illinois, she is married and the proud mother of one son.

Dr. Samuel Attoh is dean of the graduate school at Loyola University Chicago. As leader of the school, his research and teaching interests lie in urban and regional planning, housing and community development and the geography of international development.

Most recently, Attoh served as professor and chair of geography and planning at The University of Toledo. He served as a fellow of the American Council on Education in 2003-2004, and completed his administrative internship at Carnegie Mellon University. Attoh also received the College of Arts and Sciences Master Teacher Award for two consecutive terms in 1993-1995 and 1995-1997.

Along with editing a book, *Geography of Sub-Saharan Africa* (Prentice Hall, 2003), and contributing chapters in *Global Change in Local Places* (University of Cambridge Press, 2004), *World Regional Geography* (Prentice Hall) and the *Columbia Gazetteer* (Columbia University Press), he has published more than 30 journal articles and technical reports and presented more than 40 papers at national and international conferences.

Attoh received a Doctor of Philosophy from Boston University and a Master of Arts degree from Carleton University, Ottawa.

Sharonda T. Benson

Chemistry Professor
City Colleges of Chicago

Dawoud Bey

Professor & Photographer
Columbia College Chicago

Sharonda T. Benson is a faculty member at Kennedy-King College in Chicago, Ilinois. As a chemistry professor teaching organic and general chemistry, she actively supports and leads students to high academic achievement and success.

Founder of an on-campus student-based organization, Project Discovery, Benson inspires students to focus on careers in the sciences, which are underrepresented by minorities. To increase minority representation in the science field, she integrates seminars, career workshops, shadowing projects, science-related field trips and research opportunities into the curriculum.

Benson is an independent consultant for Arbonne International, and is a member of Alpha Kappa Alpha Sorority Inc., the National Organization of Black Chemists and Chemical Engineers, the American Chemical Society, and the United States Bowling Congress. She received a Bachelor of Science degree in chemistry in 1997 from Norfolk State University and a Master of Science degree specializing in organometallic chemistry, and co-published two articles in the *Journal of Organic Chemistry* and *Tetrahedron Letters.*

Currently pursuing a doctorate degree in education focusing on educational leadership at Argosy University, Benson plans to continue her pursuits in education.

Renowned photographer Dawoud Bey is a professor of photography at Columbia College Chicago, where he has taught since 1998. He holds a Master of Fine Arts degree from Yale University.

Bey was born in New York in 1953. Inspired by the "Harlem on My Mind" exhibition at the Metropolitan Museum of Art when he was 16, he began his career with a series of photographs, "Harlem, USA," that were exhibited in his first one-person exhibition in 1979. He has since had numerous exhibitions worldwide in galleries and museums from Los Angeles to London. The Walker Art Center organized a mid-career survey of his work that traveled throughout the United States and Europe.

Bey has received numerous fellowships, including those from the John Simon Guggenheim Memorial Foundation and the National Endowment for the Arts. His works are included in the permanent collections of numerous museums, both here and abroad. Additionally, his critical writings have been widely published, and he has curated exhibitions internationally.

Aperture is publishing his latest project, "Class Pictures," in 2007, and is mounting a traveling exhibition of this work.

CHICAGO'S ACADEMIA

Cynthia E. Boyd, M.D.

Associate Vice President &
Chief Compliance Officer
Rush University Medical Center

Lisa Brock, Ph.D.

Chair
Department of Liberal Education
Columbia College Chicago

Dr. Cynthia Boyd is associate vice president and chief compliance officer at Rush University Medical Center. She oversees implementation and operation of the Corporate Compliance Program, including HIPAA Privacy and Security. She is also an assistant professor of medicine at Rush Medical College, and serves as director of medical staff operations at Rush. She is a member of the Health Care Compliance Association's board of directors, a fellow of the American College of Physicians and the national chair-elect of the Association of American Medical Colleges' Group on Student Affairs Minority Affairs Section.

Cynthia has lectured and written widely on Medicare, health care reform, medical research compliance and health disparities.

A native of Detroit, Michigan, Cynthia received a Bachelor of Arts degree in biology from the University of Colorado in Boulder, a Doctor of Medicine degree from the George Washington University School of Medicine and Health Sciences, and a Master of Business Administration degree from The University of Chicago, with certification in health administration and policy.

She is the wife of Dr. William Gradishar and the mother of two sons, Zachary and Nicholas.

Dr. Lisa Brock is chair of the department of liberal education and a professor of African history and Diaspora studies at Columbia College Chicago. Her articles on South Africa, Mozambique, African Americans, Cuba and blacks in the Diaspora have appeared in such journals as *Cuban Studies*, *Contributions in Black Studies* and *Issue: A Journal of Opinion*. Her book, *Between Race and Empire: African-Americans and Cubans Before the Cuban Revolution* (Temple University Press), was published in 1998, and her writings are regularly a part of the Web site AfroCubaweb.

Brock has lectured and served as visiting professor at numerous institutions, including the University of New Mexico, Clemson University and Columbia University. She has given papers at the Latin American Studies Association, the American Historical Association and the National Association of Black Journalists, among others.

Brock has served on the planning committees of the African Studies Association, and is on the editorial collective of the *Radical History Review*. She is working on a second book, entitled "Black in Two Americas: Comparative Identity, History and Struggle in Cuba and in the United States."

Tony Burroughs

Professor
Chicago State University

Art T. Burton

Instructor, History
South Suburban College

Tony Burroughs teaches genealogy at Chicago State University, and has presented more than 80 lectures at national conferences. His research qualified him for six lineage societies, and led to discovering instructions to the census index, thereby correcting a 40-year National Archives error. He also consulted on the Al Sharpton/Strom Thurmond genealogy and Oprah Winfrey's genealogy.

Burroughs served as an expert in *Oprah's Roots*, *African American Lives*, *Ancestors*, six episodes of *Ancestors 2* on PBS, and was the featured genealogist in *The Real Family of Jesus* on the Discovery Channel. His expertise has also led to his participation in national and international news programs and publications.

Burroughs' book, *Black Roots*, was No. 1 on *Essence* magazine's best-seller list. He also has chapters in *The Experts' Guide to 100 Things Everyone Should Know How to Do*, *The Source* and *African American Genealogical Sourcebook*.

A fellow of the Utah Genealogical Association, Burroughs received the Distinguished Service Award from the National Genealogical Society. He is a former president of the Afro-American Genealogical and Historical Society of Chicago, and served on the board of the Association of Professional Genealogists.

Art T. Burton teaches American history, African-American history, and African-American arts in the social and behavioral science department at South Suburban College.

Art is an expert on the Old West, and has written three history books on the African-American experience on the western frontier. His most recent book, *Black Gun, Silver Star: The Life and Legend of Frontier Marshal Bass Reeves*, won a Spur Award as a finalist for Best Biography for 2007 from the Western Writers of America. Art has been featured on the History Channel four times and was a panelist on BET's Teen Summit.

Art graduated from Governors State University with a bachelor's and master's degree in cultural studies. He was recognized by *Who's Who Among Students in American Universities and Colleges* in 1976–1977 for outstanding accomplishment as a student.

Art is a trustee of the Village of Phoenix, Illinois, and school board member of High School District 205. He is secretary of the Association for the Advancement of Creative Musicians.

A native of Phoenix, Illinois, Art is proud of his wife, Patrice, and daughter, Aisha.

Sharon E. Byrd, M.D.

Professor of Radiology &
Attending Neuroradiologist
Rush University Medical Center

Dr. Madie M. Cannamoré

Professor
City Colleges of Chicago

Dr. Sharon E. Byrd is a full-time member of the Radiology Department at Rush University Medical Center (RUMC) in the section of neuroradiology. She is fellowship director of the service, and maintains quality assurance of neuroimaging at RUMC for magnetic resonance imaging and computed tomography. Byrd performs daily interpretation of clinical neuroimaging studies. She is a member of numerous radiological professional organizations, including fellow of the American College of Radiology, senior member of the American Society of Neuroradiology and National Medical Association. She has served on many national professional committees and local community committees.

Byrd received her undergraduate education and medical degree from Wayne State University in Detroit, Michigan. She completed diagnostic radiology training at the University of California at Los Angeles (UCLA), with additional neuroradiology training at the Hospital for Sick Children in Toronto and UCLA.

She was chief of the section of neuroradiology at King/Drew Medical Center in Los Angeles for eight years, and chief of the section of neuroimaging at Children's Memorial Hospital in Chicago for 14 years.

She is the wife of gourmet chef Richard Hadden.

Dr. Madie Cannamoré is a computer science professor at Kennedy-King College, where she has taught for 35 years. She has served as an educator for more than 42 years. She is an honorary member of Phi Delta Kappa, Phi Theta Kappa and Kappa Delta Pi.

Cannamoré holds seven college degrees and four master's degrees: one from Northeastern, two from Chicago State University and one from Governors State University. She also holds Certificate 75 for principalship.

Cannamoré is affiliated with many organizations and has received many awards, including Outstanding Woman of the Year from the American Association of Women in Community Colleges, Chicago State University Alumna of the Year, The Kathy Osterman Award, Distinguished Professor, Educator of the Year, and the Trailblazer Award. She was inducted into Englewood High School's Premiere Hall of Fame and serves as principal for a day. She was also featured several times in *Who's Who Among America's Teachers*. Additionally, Cannamoré is the queen mum of the Red Hat Society-Virtuous Women and a designer of CUZ-2 jewelry.

She is the proud mother of Dr. Pamela C. Cannamore.

Dr. Pamela Cannamore

Assistant Professor
Speech/Communications
Kennedy-King College

Isiaah Crawford, Ph.D.

Dean, College of Arts and Sciences
Loyola University Chicago

Dr. Pamela Cannamore has more than 20 years' experience from corporate, nonprofit and educational organizations. Her Illinois teaching certificate is endorsed in business and computers. Pamela was a cooperative work-study coordinator for Chicago Public Schools, and taught communications/speech and computer classes for City Colleges of Chicago, Triton College and Elgin College. She has taught teacher, business and multicultural education at Concordia and Chicago State University. Currently, she serves as an assistant professor at Kennedy-King College.

She holds two master's degrees from Governors State and Chicago State. Her doctorate and bachelor's degrees are from Northern Illinois University.

Pamela is affiliated with many organizations, and has received many awards, including Educator of the Year from Phi Delta Kappa, Kappa Delta Pi and the Living Word Christian Center Scholarship. She was also featured in *Who's Who Among America's Teachers*.

Pamela is the first African-American female to win the Impromptu Speaking Contest D30 Toastmasters International. She has won Miss Goddess, Ashley Stewart Woman, Miss Chicago+, Miss Figure+ Illinois and was a Ms. Plus USA Finalist. Additionally, she is a motivational speaker and volunteer.

Isiaah Crawford, Ph.D., dean of the College of Arts and Sciences at Loyola University Chicago (LUC), leads the college's 600-member full- and part-time faculty and more than 7,000 students. Crawford's scholarly work focuses on human sexuality, HIV/AIDS prevention and health promotion and professional practice issues in clinical psychology.

He served as director of the Clinical Psychology Ph.D. Program at LUC from 1993-1997 and as chair of the department of psychology from 1997-2002. He is the former president of the board of directors of the AIDS Foundation of Chicago, and is the former president of the Clinical Psychologists Licensing and Disciplinary Board of the Illinois Department of Financial and Professional Regulation.

Crawford has published more than 40 professional papers and a co-edited book, and has delivered numerous conference presentations. To date, his work has been nationally recognized with several awards, including two from the American Psychological Association.

Crawford received a bachelor's degree in psychology in 1982 from Saint Louis University, and earned master's and doctorate degrees in clinical psychology from DePaul University in 1985 and 1987, respectively.

Addie L. Davis, Ph.D.

Associate Professor
Mathematics Department
Olive-Harvey College

Thomas Fisher, M.D., MPH

Instructor of Medicine
Section of Emergency Medicine
The University of Chicago

Dr. Addie L. Davis is an associate professor of mathematics at Olive-Harvey College, where she engages and encourages students to overcome their math anxieties. She is the senior faculty advisor for the Lambda Iota Chapter of Phi Theta Kappa International Honor Society of two-year colleges. Addie participates in numerous community activities and annual cancer walks in the city and suburbs.

Addie is Olive-Harvey's 2003-2004 Distinguished Professor. She has also received the 2003-2004 Phenomenal Woman Award for the American Association of Women in Community Colleges and the 2005 Paragon Award for her outstanding achievements in Phi Theta Kappa. Additionally, she has been featured repeatedly in *Who's Who Among America's Teachers* and *Who's Who of American Women*. As a member of Little Mountain of Hope Ministry, she serves in an evangelical capacity, and has delivered many speeches. She also served as a mentor to 11 university students for LeaderShape, Inc.

Addie received a bachelor's degree from Roosevelt University and a master's degree in education from Chicago State University. In 2006 she was awarded a Doctor of Philosophy degree in education from Capella University.

Dr. Thomas Fisher is an instructor of medicine in the section of emergency medicine at The University of Chicago. In this position, Fisher practices emergency medicine in the neighborhood where he grew up.

Fisher's research and advocacy work is organized by a social justice agenda, and is focused on revealing the underpinnings of racial disparities in health and health care. He studies the complex roles of race, socio-cultural structures, stereotyping and physician contributions to racial disparities in health and health care. Fisher participated in the founding of Project Brotherhood, and has engaged Chicago Public Schools students in various contexts.

Fisher serves as faculty affiliate to the Center for the Study of Race, Politics and Culture; the Center for Interdisciplinary Health Disparities Research; and Finding Answers: Disparities Research for Change. He holds degrees from Dartmouth College, Harvard School of Public Health and The University of Chicago's Pritzker School of Medicine. His medical training at The University of Chicago includes a year as chief resident and a fellowship in the Robert Wood Johnson Clinical Scholars Program.

Robert Higgins, M.D., MSHA

Mary & John Bent Professor &
Chairman of Cardio-Thoracic Surgery
Rush University Medical Center

Preston Jackson

Artist & Professor of Sculpture
School of the Art Institute of Chicago

Dr. Robert Higgins joined Rush University Medical Center in February of 2003 as the Mary and John Bent professor and chairman of cardio-thoracic surgery.

Higgins earned a bachelor's degree from Dartmouth College in 1981 and a medical degree from the Yale University School of Medicine in 1985. He completed a general surgery residency at the university hospital in Pittsburgh and a fellowship in cardio-thoracic surgery at Yale University. In 1993 he was a senior registrar in transplantation at Cambridge University's Papworth Hospital in England.

Higgins has written more than 100 peer-reviewed papers and book chapters and has made dozens of presentations throughout the United States. He has provided high-level leadership skills, combining proven expertise in administration, education and research as one of the country's few African-American academic chairman in cardiac surgery.

In June of 2007, Higgins was elected as vice president of the Organ Procurement and Transplant Network, and the United Network for Organ Sharing, the organization that oversees the nation's transplant programs for the U.S. government. He is the first African American to hold this prestigious position.

Preston Jackson is a professor of sculpture at The School of the Art Institute of Chicago, and an artist who specializes in bronze and stainless steel sculptures and creating paintings and prints. Preston's "Fresh from Julieanne's Garden" series, which continues to grow, has been widely exhibited.

His recent commissions include a stainless steel and cast bronze wall relief for McCormick Place West; a nine-foot cast bronze sculpture of Irv Kupcinet on Wacker Drive near Wabash; a bust of Fred Hampton for the village of Maywood, Illinois; and a freestanding, two-sided stainless steel and cast bronze relief for the CTA's 69th Street Station.

Preston was designated a 1998 Laureate of the Lincoln Academy of Illinois, the highest honor given to individuals in the state. He was selected as a HistoryMaker in 2007.

Preston received a Bachelor of Fine Arts degree from Southern Illinois University and a Master of Fine Arts degree from the University of Illinois. A native of Decatur, Illinois, he is the husband of Melba Jackson, father of two daughters, Natalie and Alice Jackson, and grandfather of Blake, Natalie's son.

Marva Lee Pitchford Jolly

Artist & Professor
Chicago State University

Aldon Morris

Leon Forrest Professor of Sociology
Northwestern University

In 1982 Marva Lee Pitchford Jolly decided to become a professional artist after having spent more than 20 years in teaching and social service careers. Self-taught as a potter, such a decision might have seemed audacious. However, today she is a professor at Chicago State University, sharing her talent with students since 1987.

Marva's earlier work was heavily influenced by African hand-building techniques. Ranging from stick figures to abstraction, her personal style communicates and depicts the energy of the black people in the Mississippi cotton fields where she grew up. Marva's background as a social activist provides further exploration of the beauty and pain of the urban black experience. Her current work has progressed to use an assortment of objects, including nails, rags, beads and glass.

Marva is influenced by her mother, Aretha Franklin's music and spiritual creativity, Elizabeth Catlett's sculpture, Georgia O'Keefe's uses of color and eye for beauty in the unexpected, and black women's spiritual energy and transcendence. Her pottery and sculpture are an expression of the diversity, unity and spiritual quest that forms her life as an African-American woman.

Aldon Morris is the Leon Forrest professor of sociology at Northwestern University. Before coming to Northwestern, he was a professor at the University of Michigan.

Currently, Morris is completing a four-year term as the associate dean of faculty. He is the author of *The Origins of the Civil Rights Movement: Black Communities Organizing for Change*, which won numerous awards including the Distinguished Contribution to Scholarship Award of the American Sociological Association. He is also co-editor of *Frontiers in Social Movement Theory* (1992) and *Oppositional Consciousness* (2001). Additionally, Morris has published extensively in major outlets on topics that include the civil rights movement, racial inequality, African-American religion and W. E. B. DuBois. He recently authored "Sociology of Race and W. E. B. DuBois: The Path Not Taken" in *Sociology in America: A History*, published by The University of Chicago Press. He is currently researching a book on DuBoisan sociology.

Morris was a consultant for the acclaimed documentary *Eyes on the Prize*, and has lectured extensively both nationally and internationally. Throughout his career, Morris has mentored many students, many of whom have become major scholars.

Olufunmilayo I. Olopade, M.D.

Professor
Medicine & Human Genetics
The University of Chicago

Terry Peterson

Vice President, Government Affairs
Rush University Medical Center

D r. Olufunmilayo Olopade is an oncologist, who translates her research on individual and population cancer susceptibility into clinical practice for treating breast cancer among high-risk women. This would include African and African-American women with early research identification of a tumor suppressor locus on the short arm of the ninth chromosome. This demonstrates distinct biological characteristics, including a high level of aggressiveness and resistance to treatment. Olopade first described recurrent BRCA1 mutations in extended African-American families with breast cancer reporting BRCA1 and BRCA2 mutations in pre-menopausal breast cancer patients from West Africa.

Olopade received a Doctor of Medicine degree from the University of Ibadan in Nigeria as a medical officer at the Nigerian Naval Hospital. She completed an internship and residency at Cook County Hospital in Chicago, and trained in hematology/oncology as a postdoctoral fellow at The University of Chicago. Olopade is a professor of medicine and human genetics and director of the Center for Clinical Cancer Genetics at The University of Chicago, where she has been on the faculty since 1991.

T erry Peterson is Rush University Medical Center's new vice president of government affairs. In this role, he serves as the primary contact for the hospital and university staff regarding governmental issues, and as a liaison for elected officials, government agencies and advocacy organizations. He promotes legislative and public policy priorities that will enable the medical center to maintain its high-quality services to the community.

Terry has had a long and successful career in public service. Most recently, he was the campaign manager for Mayor Richard Daley's successful re-election. He was chief executive officer of the Chicago Housing Authority from 2000 to 2006, and played a central role in the agency's $1.5 billion housing program, transforming Chicago's public housing from unsafe, high-density developments into safe, low-rise mix-income communities.

In his role as alderman of the 17th Ward, Terry assisted in generating more than $200 million in development in his ward. He has held other positions in city government including executive assistant for Mayor Daley, assistant commissioner in the Department of Planning and Development, and chief of staff for his predecessor, the 17th Ward alderman.

Alexis Pride, Ph.D.

Professor, Creative Writing
Columbia College Chicago

Nadia M. Quarles, Esq.

Director, Business Diversity
The University of Chicago

Dr. Alexis Pride is a professor of creative writing and the programs coordinator for teacher training and outreach in the fiction writing department at Columbia College Chicago.

At Columbia, Pride teaches advanced fiction writing, critical reading and writing, and practice teaching and tutor training. She is a volunteer coordinator for Story Week: Festival of Writers, and serves on the Educational Issues, Student Affairs and the Fiction Writing Department Curriculum committees. She is also a member of the International Leadership Association and presented a paper, "Teaching Artists as Civic Leaders," at its 2005 world conference.

Pride's novel, *Where the River Ends,* was recently published by UTOUR Press, while her short stories and novel excerpts have appeared in *F Magazine* and *Ink Stains Magazine.* Her stage play, *Wives,* has been performed in several venues. She is also the founder and chief executive officer of the AJ Ensemble, a professional theatre company with a mission of youth outreach.

Pride earned a bachelor's degree in broadcast communication and a master's degree in writing at Columbia, and a doctorate in English from the University of Wisconsin–Milwaukee.

Nadia M. Quarles is director of business diversity for The University of Chicago. In this position, she is responsible for building the business diversity process and increasing the utilization of minority- and women-owned business enterprises within university procurement activities.

Prior to her position at the university, Quarles served as manager of business diversity for Chicago Public Schools. She also worked for the City of Chicago Department of Procurement Services, where she created contracting opportunities specifically targeting minority- and women-owned business enterprises. Additionally, she has served as an adjunct professor at Northeastern Illinois University, where she taught justice studies courses.

Quarles holds a juris doctorate degree from Hamline University School of Law in St. Paul, Minnesota, and has several years of legal experience preceding her roles in procurement and supplier diversity. She also holds a bachelor's degree from Northeastern University in Boston.

Quarles serves on The University of Chicago Diversity Leadership Council, and is a member of the Minnesota Bar Association, the American Bar Association, Delta Sigma Theta Sorority, Inc. and Trinity United Church of Christ.

Steven Rogers

Professor, Entrepreneurial Finance
Kellogg School of Management
Northwestern University

Larry E. Ross

Assistant Professor & Coordinator
Kennedy-King College

Professor Steven Rogers is the Gordon and Llura Gund Family Professor of Entrepreneurship at the Kellogg School of Management. He teaches entrepreneurial finance and authored *The Entrepreneur's Guide to Finance and Business.*

In 2005 Rogers was selected as Chicago United's Business Leader of Color. *BusinessWeek* named him one of the top 12 entrepreneurship professors in 1996, and Ernst & Young recognized him with the Entrepreneur of the Year award. Kellogg students have awarded him the Outstanding Professor Award 14 times, and the Lawrence G. Lavengood Outstanding Professor of the Year award an unprecedented two times in 1996 and 2005.

Rogers serves as a board member for Supervalu, Oakmark Mutual Funds, AMCORE Financial and SC Johnson. He is also on the boards of A Better Chance and Urban Prep High School, a trustee of Williams College and a former member of the Harvard Business School Visiting Committee.

He received a Master of Business Administration degree from Harvard Business School and a Bachelor of Arts degree from Williams College.

Larry E. Ross is assistant professor and coordinator of the Addictions Studies program at Kennedy-King College in Chicago, Illinois. There, he developed and continues to maintain the program while also teaching addictions studies and social service courses. Larry served as president of faculty council from 2002 to 2004, and is currently advisor to the Student Social Work Club.

Larry has received numerous awards, including Outstanding Alumnus from Governors State University's Bachelor of Social Work program and the Distinctive Imprint Award from the National Association of University Women. He was selected to *Who's Who Among America's Teachers* from 2002 to 2006, and he holds the honor of Distinguished Professor for 2004-2005.

Larry serves on college and university advisory boards and boards of directors for social service agencies; he is chair of two different boards. He attained a Master of Social Work degree from Aurora University, and he has completed 30 postgraduate credit hours.

William Alfred Sampson, Ph.D.

Professor of Public Policy
DePaul University

Dyrice Garner Stewart

Principal
Ludwig Beethoven Academic Center

Dr. William Alfred Sampson is a professor of public policy studies at DePaul University in Chicago. He is also the author of more than a dozen scholarly articles and four books, including *Black Student Achievement* and the recently published *Race, Class, and Family Intervention*. Both books focus on the role of the family in the education of poor, non-white students.

Additionally, Sampson has served as the president of Chicago United, one of the preeminent business organizations in the city, and as a professor at Northwestern University. He has won Teacher of the Year awards, and his research has been widely praised by scholars such as Dr. James Comer of Yale and Dr. Thomas Cook of Northwestern.

Sampson received a Bachelor of Arts degree from Howard University, a Master of Arts degree from the University of Wisconsin-Milwaukee and a Doctorate of Philosophy degree from The Johns Hopkins University. He is not married, and is an avid runner and tennis player.

Dyrice Garner Stewart started her teaching career at Piccolo Elementary School. She then transitioned to Jamieson Elementary School, and enjoyed teaching at both schools. Stewart offered children many wonderful educational experiences that taught them to think critically, and prepared them for advanced learning. She later became a part of the Skinner Classical School Team, where she served as a testing and admissions coordinator for children who qualify for classical testing.

Stewart furthered her horizons by applying and being accepted into the LAUNCH Program (Leadership Academy and Urban Network for Chicago). The LAUNCH Program prepared her for another rewarding professional achievement: to become principal of Ludwig Beethoven Academic Center. Stewart has embraced the Beethoven culture, and has taken the school to greater heights. She is preparing children to become productive citizens who are ready to compete in a highly competitive society.

Born and raised in Chicago, Illinois, Stewart attended Chicago Public Schools, where she received a full, comprehensive education. She is married to Carlos Stewart, and they have enjoyed rearing four beautiful children together.

Dr. Howard T. Strassner Jr.

Professor & Chair
Department of Obstetrics & Gynecology
Rush Medical College
Rush University Medical Center

D r. Howard T. Strassner Jr. received an undergraduate degree and a medical degree from The University of Chicago's Pritzker School of Medicine. His postdoctoral residency in obstetrics and gynecology was at the Columbia-Presbyterian Medical Center and The Sloan Hospital for Women in New York. Strassner's postdoctoral fellowship was in maternal-fetal medicine at The Women's Hospital, University of Southern California/Los Angeles County Medical Center.

In addition to being professor and chair of the department of obstetrics and gynecology, Strassner is also director of maternal-fetal medicine and co-director of Rush's perinatal center and of the Rush Regional Perinatal Network. He has received gubernatorial appointments to statewide bodies, including the Infant Mortality Reduction Advisory Board and the Governor's Task Force on AIDS in Healthcare. He chairs the State of Illinois' Perinatal Advisory Committee, and he is the past chair of the Illinois Section of the American College of Obstetricians and Gynecologists. In 2001 *Chicago* magazine featured Strassner as one of Chicago's top doctors.

His clinical and research interests include preterm delivery, prenatal diagnosis, medical complications in pregnancy and preconception counseling.

Natatia M. Trotter-Gordon

Director, Business and Industry Services
Kennedy-King College

N atatia M. Trotter-Gordon is director of business and industry services at Kennedy-King College, one of the City Colleges of Chicago. As director, she is responsible for being a liaison for local businesses as well as offering customized contract training to businesses as a way to increase employee competency on the job.

The business and industry department's best program has been the Entrepreneurship Certificate Program. This assists aspiring individuals who would like to open a business or maintain their current business. Gordon has partnered with several community agencies to sponsor students for this program.

Gordon is an executive board member of the Georgia Doty Health Education Fund, chief financial officer of the Great Black Music Project and a member of Alpha Kappa Alpha Sorority, Inc.

She received a Bachelor of Science degree in chemistry from Spelman College in 1991, a Bachelor of Science degree in biology from National College of Chiropractic in 1995, and a Master of Science degree in chemistry from the University of Illinois at Chicago in 1999.

CHICAGO'S ACADEMIA

Laura S. Washington

Ida B. Wells-Barnett
University Professor
DePaul University

William H. (Bill) Watkins

Professor
College of Education
University of Illinois at Chicago

Laura S. Washington, the Ida B. Wells-Barnett university professor at DePaul University, is an award-winning journalist who has served as a contributing columnist for the *Chicago Sun-Times* since 2001. She is also a senior editor and columnist for *In These Times* and a regular commentator on National Public Radio and Chicago Public Radio.

She is the former editor and publisher of *The Chicago Reporter*, and served as deputy press secretary to Mayor Harold Washington, Chicago's first black mayor. Washington earned her bachelor's and master's degrees in journalism from the Medill School of Journalism at Northwestern University.

Washington has been honored with more than two dozen awards for her work, including two Emmys, the Peter Lisagor Award for Outstanding Journalism, the Studs Terkel Award for Community Journalism and the Racial Justice Award from the YWCA of Metropolitan Chicago. *Newsweek* named Washington one of the nation's 100 People to Watch in the 21st Century. *Newsweek* said, "Her style of investigative journalism has made [*The Chicago Reporter*] a powerful and award-winning voice."

William H. Watkins is an author, lecturer and professor in the College of Education at the University of Illinois at Chicago. His books include *The White Architects of Black Education* (2001), *Race and Education* (lead editor, 2001), and *Black Protest Thought and Education* (editor, 2005). Additionally, Bill has written and published more than 100 conference papers, essays in academic journals, book chapters, encyclopedia entries, book reviews and articles in the mass media. He has lectured on education, race and politics throughout the United States, Asia, Africa, Europe and Central America.

Bill is a member and has held leadership positions in the American Educational Research Association, the American Educational Studies Association, the World Council for Curriculum and Instruction, Professors of Curriculum, the Association for the Study of Afro American Life and History, Research Focus on Black Education and the National Council for Black Studies.

Bill received a Bachelor of Arts degree from the California State University at Los Angeles. He also received a Master of Education degree and a Doctor of Philosophy degree from the University of Illinois at Chicago.

John H. White
Professor, Photography
Columbia College Chicago

James S. Williams Jr.
Business Diversity Manager
The University of Chicago
Medical Center

Pulitzer Prize-winning photojournalist John H. White has been a *Sun-Times* photographer and a photography professor at Columbia College Chicago since 1978. White, who bought his first camera at age 13 for 50 cents and ten bubble gum wrappers, has photographed history being made all over the world—the first trip John Paul II made to Mexico as Pope, Nelson Mandela's release from prison, Elvis Presley's funeral, the administrations of at least six United States presidents and Jesse Jackson's peace mission to the Middle East. He has also covered smaller events, such as the births of New Year's babies and the Chicago River being dyed green for St. Patrick's Day.

A North Carolina native and the son of a reverend, White was the first photographer inducted into the Chicago Journalism Hall of Fame in 1993, and has won more than 300 awards from international, national and local organizations. Additionally, White has worked on several book projects, including *The Final Journey of Joseph Cardinal Bernardin*, a look at Cardinal Bernardin's final days; and *Glimpses of My Journey*, a year captured in 365 photos.

James Williams Jr. came to The University of Chicago Medical Center in 1988 as a member of the patient accounts and admission services departments. In admission services, he was a transplant coordinator before eventually managing the department. In 1999 Williams joined purchasing as a specialty buyer for information services, planning, design and construction, and all of senior management. In 2002 the Medical Center formed the Business Diversity Department, and Williams was appointed its first manager.

Williams' commitment to developing relationships with minority- and women-owned businesses is exemplary. In his current role as business diversity manager, he co-leads the Medical Center's initiative, specifically focusing on procurement and professional services. For his efforts, the Chicago Minority Business Development Council named him an Outstanding Buyer in 2005.

In the last few years, Williams participated in identifying opportunities for diverse businesses in all aspects of the Medical Center's supply chain. Due to his efforts and the support of the Medical Center's senior management, tens of millions of dollars are spent with diverse firms annually.

A Chicago native, Williams is a married father of three.

CHICAGO'S ACADEMIA

Eric V.A. Winston, Ph.D.

Vice President
Institutional Advancement
Columbia College Chicago

Dr. Eric V.A. Winston joined Columbia College Chicago in 2005 as interim vice president for institutional advancement, and was named vice president in May of 2006.

His career in higher education began in 1969 at Michigan State University, where he served as an assistant dean and assistant professor of urban development. From 1975 to 1978, he served as a vice president, dean and faculty member at Chicago State University. Winston then served as vice president for development and university relations at Wilberforce University from 1983 to 2002. Under his leadership, the university's endowment increased from $1.5 million in 1990 to more than $12 million in 2002.

Winston earned a doctorate in administration and higher education from Michigan State University. He also holds a master's degree in library science from Atlanta University and a bachelor's degree from Morehouse College.

Winston served as a city council member in Xenia, Ohio, from 1992 to 2006, and has chaired the Planning and Zoning Commission for the last five years. In June of 2006, he was elected to the Illinois Chamber of Commerce board of directors.

The positive effect of being yourself is too great to measure.

At Ernst & Young, we want you to grow and succeed. That's why we've created an environment that values all aspects of diversity, including ethnicity, gender identity, and expression. This fact has not escaped *Fortune* magazine, *Working Mother* magazine, DiversityInc., or the National Association for Business Resources who named us "Chicago's Best of the Best" for three consecutive years among "Chicago's 101 Best & Brightest Companies to Work For."

Visit us at ey.com/us/careers and see how we measure up.

Audit • Tax • Transaction Advisory Services

ERNST & YOUNG

Quality In Everything We Do

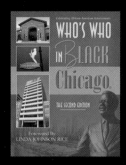
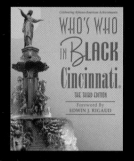
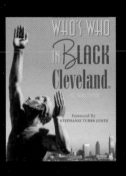
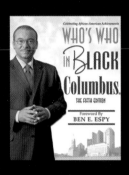
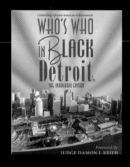

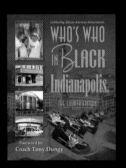
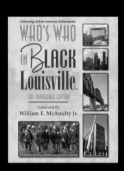
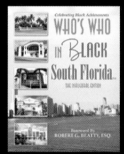

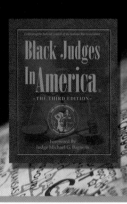
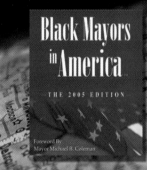

noble

caring

CHICAGO'S
COMMUNITY LEADERS

self-sacrificing

generous

empowering

heroic

philanthropic

humanitarian

altruistic

Andrea C. Adams

Center Director
South Shore Cultural Center

For the past three years, Andrea Adams has been responsible for all programming and special events planning, including weddings, receptions, dance classes and conferences, in the vintage South Shore Cultural Center (SSCC).

After many years with a national nonprofit and other community organizations, Andrea joined the Chicago Park District. The first part of her career was spent downtown overseeing grants and donations. Having an extensive background in special events, she eventually became center director.

Under Andrea's leadership, revenues have doubled. SSCC has played host to Rev. Jesse Jackson's birthday party, *VIBE* magazine's Black Chef Series finale, Real Men Cook Father's Day, WVON's PreKwanzaa, BMOA's Write to Achieve, and appearances by actress Vivica A. Fox, Senator Barack Obama and Ellen Johnson-Sirleaf, president of Liberia. Her passion now is selling people on the newest addition to the building, Parrot Cage Restaurant, which is part of City Colleges of Chicago.

Andrea continues her sense of community in church and other local organizations. She is a graduate of Lincoln University and the proud mother of Alicia, an economics and theatre major at Spelman College.

Patrice Ball-Reed

Deputy Attorney General
Child Support Enforcement
Office of the Illinois Attorney General

Patrice Ball-Reed graduated from Trinity College in Hartford, Connecticut, with a Bachelor of Arts degree in economics in 1980. Upon graduating from The John Marshall Law School, she began working as an associate in a small general practice law firm.

Patrice learned to practice law in the private sector and moved on to the public sector. Her first position was as an assistant state's attorney for Cook County, where she served for 14 years. She spent seven years in the child support enforcement division as a supervisor and senior trial attorney, and seven years in the real estate property tax unit as a deputy supervisor. She then became the first African-American female to hold the position of deputy attorney general for child support enforcement at the Office of the Illinois Attorney General in April of 2003.

An attorney, wife, mother, and grandmother, Patrice has enjoyed her career. During her 20 years as an attorney, she has received numerous awards, held leadership positions, and participated in many organizations. She is a member of multiple bar associations and Delta Sigma Theta Sorority, Inc.

Ken Bedford is an Emmy Award-winning photojournalist for ABC-TV in Chicago. In his 30-year career, he has worked with Oprah Winfrey, Max Robinson, Peter Jennings and Phil Donahue, just to name a few.

Since the death of his wife, Anaia, in April of 2004 to breast cancer, Bedford has devoted much of his time to helping underserved women to become better educated on the importance of being screened for the early detection of the disease. He formed ABCAP, Inc. (Anaia's Breast Cancer Awareness Program), a not-for-profit organization named after his wife.

Bedford tries to attract women at the events he produces, such as a concert or dance, and once they have assembled, he tells them about how important it is to get screened with mammograms, ultrasound and MRIs. His mission is to make sure that as many women as possible understand the importance of early diagnosis.

Ken Bedford

Founder
ABCAP, Inc.

Fran Bell is vice president of government and community relations for the YMCA of Metropolitan Chicago. Bell, formerly vice president of operations for the YMCA, is responsible for advancing city, state and community partnerships with the YMCA and enhancing programs and services offered to members and community residents.

As a member of the executive committee of the African American Leadership Forum, she is dedicated to the recruitment, retention and development of black professionals in the YMCA, which led to the creation of the YMCA of the USA's Minority Executive and CEO Development Program.

Her background as an education major at West Chester University fueled her passion for teaching and mentoring youth. Bell's dedication is further demonstrated by serving as a board member for the Support Group, an organization helping youth achieve academic goals through athletics, and as a member of the Teen Advisory Council of Apostolic Church of God, where she worships.

The mother of two adult children, Bell is one of the voices of world-traveled gospel recording artists, JourneySong, an extension of her lifelong desire to serve.

Fran J. Bell

Vice President of Government &
Community Relations
YMCA of Metropolitan Chicago

Ingrid E. Bridges

Administrative Assistant
Office of the Mayor

As administrative assistant to the honorable Mayor Richard M. Daley of Chicago, Ingrid E. Bridges serves as liaison to the entire ecumenical community. Pegged as a renaissance woman of religion, this journalist is heavily sought out for her impeccable oratorical skills and profound ability to create award-winning stories about the humanistic journey.

Formerly the religion editor of the *Chicago Defender* newspaper for 15 years, Ingrid earned the Merit Award for best church page from the National Newspaper Publishers Association.

An author of the book *The Choices We Make - a days journey*, Bridges remains devoted to her ultimate calling, writing.

Born in Chicago, Illinois, she graduated from Columbia College, earning a Bachelor of Arts degree in journalism, an honorary doctorate of humanities from the Chicago Baptist Institute in 1998 and an honorary doctorate of humanities from GMOR Theological Institute of Northeastern Indiana in 2003.

Bridges loves cooking, jogging and praising God as a member of Apostolic Church of God, where Bishop Arthur M. Brazier is pastor. She has one son, Brian Jr., a graduate of Florida A&M University.

Deborah L. Dangerfield

Executive Director
Alpha Kappa Alpha
Educational Advancement Foundation, Inc.

Deborah L. Dangerfield is the executive director for the Alpha Kappa Alpha Educational Advancement Foundation, Inc. in Chicago. Deborah is responsible for overseeing the operations, fundraising, membership and fiscal management of the foundation. The foundation's mission is to provide financial support to individuals and organizations engaged in lifelong learning. Deborah strives for excellent scholarly performance as she manages more than 60 endowment funds, investments of more than $3.4 million, and annually distributes more than $150,000 in scholarships and community service awards.

Deborah has been a member of Alpha Kappa Alpha Sorority, Inc. since 1972. She has received many awards for her leadership with many organizations, including the President's Award from the Marcy Newberry Association of Chicago for outstanding leadership and service, the Joy of Serving Award in recognition of distinguished leadership and service across the United Methodist Church, and the Trailblazer Certificate from the Central Region of Alpha Kappa Alpha Sorority, Inc.

Deborah received a Bachelor of Arts degree from Fisk University and a master's degree from Governors State University. She is a native of Chicago, and enjoys bowling and traveling.

ollis Dorrough Jr. is a college graduate of Calumet College of St. Joseph (Whiting, Indiana) with a degree in law enforcement management. He currently serves as deputy police chief for the Village of South Holland, Illinois. He has served in this capacity for five years.

After 33 years of service, Dorrough retired from the City of Chicago Police Department. His last position there was sergeant of police, serving on the security team for Mayor Richard M. Daley. Dorrough's years of police service included seven years as a supervising sergeant at the Chicago Police Training Academy where he was instrumental in creating the first domestic violence program, which is still being used today. He also received Governor Jim Edgar's award for working with numerous outside agencies that assisted abused women and children, the homeless and residents of shelters.

Dorrough is looking forward to retirement and the chance to fulfill his dreams of writing music, singing and teaching.

Hollis Dorrough Jr.

Deputy Police Chief
Village of South Holland

ona Fourté is executive director of the Chicago Minority Business Opportunity Center program offered by the Chicago Minority Business Development Council, Inc. She oversees staff providing brokering services and development assistance to minority business enterprises that impact economic growth and empowerment.

Rona received formal training in supplier diversity in the early '90s as a senior consultant with Ralph G. Moore & Associates. During her six-year tenure, she led many visible projects including the Boeing World Headquarters relocation and the Chicago Department of Transportation South Lake Shore Drive Reconstruction project. Her experience also includes technical assistance to businesses in the Illinois Department of Transportation DBE and the Chicago Transit Authority Business Development programs.

A graduate of DePaul University with a major in business administration and accounting, Rona served in management accounting for ten years before transitioning to supplier diversity. Additionally, she is an ordained minister and holds a master's degree in pastoral ministry, graduating with honors.

A Chicago native, Rona is the wife of Darnell Fourté and the proud mother of four children, Brittanie, Alex, Dominae and Trinity.

Rona Fourté

Executive Director
Chicago Minority Business
Opportunity Center

Quin R. Golden

Chief of Staff
Illinois Department of Public Health

Since 2003, Quin Golden has been chief of staff for the Illinois Department of Public Health (IDPH). She is responsible for formulating policy and objectives for IDPH's more than 200 programs, managing day-to-day operations including administration of the agency's $400 million budget, oversight of its 1,100 employees and management of all offices and laboratories. Golden is the principal investigator for the agency's $40 million emergency preparedness and response activities. In 2006 she was appointed co-director for the Illinois Regenerative Medicine Institute, which distributed $10 million in stem cell research grants.

Golden has served on the Joint Commission Accreditation Hospital Organization task force at Cook County Hospital and the Institutional Review Board for Rush Medical Center in Chicago. In 2005 she was selected as a Public Health Leadership Institute fellow. Golden was instrumental in organizing the 2006 Pandemic Flu Summit for the Secretary of Health and Human Services in Illinois. She has a Master of Business Administration degree from DePaul University.

Golden is married to Victor Golden, is the mother of Victor Jr., and lives in a suburb of Chicago.

Frances Guichard

Director, Food Protection Program
Department of Public Health
City of Chicago

Frances Guichard received an undergraduate degree in dietetics, nutrition and food science and a master's degree in public health with a focus on health policy. She works as a director of the Food Protection Program for the City of Chicago's Department of Public Health, and manages up to 90 employees in the food safety and sanitation program. Their mission is to prevent food-borne illness, and ensure good sanitation in retail and wholesale food establishments that serve more than four million citizens and another four million tourists visiting Chicago.

Frances' intimate knowledge of food and safety programs is a great asset in building successful food operations. She is a member of the Illinois Environmental Health Association, the North Central Association of Food and Drug Officials and the Mid-America Regional Public Health Leadership Institute.

Frances is also co-owner, along with her husband, Andre Guichard, and day-to-day manager of Gallery Guichard Fine Art Gallery, located in Chicago. Frances is responsible for artist relations, and provides gallery administrative services.

She has two children, Brittany Patch and Milton Patch, and one stepson, Miles Guichard.

Robert F. Harris is the Cook County public guardian in Chicago, Illinois. His law office represents abused or neglected children and elderly persons as their guardian, as well as children in divorce cases. His office is one of the largest offices to represent children, and the only office that represents both children and the elderly in the United States.

Harris has received awards and honors from DePaul University College of Law, the Cook County Juvenile Court and Illinois child welfare agencies. He is a board member of the AIDS Legal Council of Chicago, Coordinated Advice and Referral Program for Legal Services and the Little Black Pearl Arts Foundation. He has been featured in *N'DIGO* magazine, and has appeared in local and national print and broadcast media.

Harris received a Bachelor of Science degree in industrial engineering from the University of Illinois-Urbana, Champaign and a juris doctorate degree from DePaul University College of Law. Previously, he worked as a manufacturing, quality and sales engineer.

Robert F. Harris

Public Guardian
Cook County

As founder and executive director of Chicago-based Little Black Pearl Workshop, Monica Haslip has combined her entrepreneurial spirit and passion for the arts into an innovative, inner-city non-profit organization. Created in 1994, the organization's mission is to create an avenue for exposure to art and culture, while teaching the profitable connection between art, education and business.

Monica was born in Birmingham, Alabama, where she began her love affair with visual arts while attending Alabama School of Fine Arts and Atlanta College of Art.

Beyond her entrepreneurial endeavors, her professional career has included Johnson Publishing Company and Black Entertainment Television.

Monica contributes her time to various boards and committees, such as the Greater Chicago Food Depository board of directors and the Women's Policy Board for Jane Adams Hull House Association. She has received accolades from individuals and organizations, including Hilary Rodham Clinton, *Essence* magazine, *Crain's Chicago Business* and *UPTOWN Chicago* magazine. Additionally, she was voted one of six 2004 Chicagoans of the Year by *Chicago* magazine and one of 50 Women of Excellence by the *Chicago Defender*.

Monica Haslip

Founder & Executive Director
Little Black Pearl

Georgina E. Heard-Labonne

Deputy Director, Strategic Planning
Illinois Department of
Employment Security

Georgina E. Heard-Labonne is the deputy director of strategic planning for the Illinois Department of Employment Security. She develops and implements strategic plans and community engagement initiatives for the agency.

Before joining state government, Georgina was the director of government and public affairs at United Airlines, where she directed external affairs in Washington, D.C., and Illinois, and created the nationally recognized mentor program published as a Harvard Business School case study and recognized by former President Clinton. She co-founded Chicagoland Business Partners with Mayor Daley's Welfare Reform Task Force, and served as its president and executive director.

Georgina serves on the board of trustees for Bradley University, Youth Guidance and the Heartland Alliance. She was featured in "Women to Watch" in the March 2003 issue of *Today's Chicago Woman*. She was also a member of Governor-elect Rod Blagojevich's transition team in 2002.

Georgina holds a master's degree in clinical psychology from DePaul University and a bachelor's degree in psychology from Bradley University. A native of Chicago, she is married to Paul Labonne and has one son, Marc, who attends Elmhurst College.

Shelia C. Hill

President
Chicago Minority Business
Development Council

Shelia C. Hill was appointed president of the Chicago Minority Business Development Council, (CMBDC) on September 20, 2006. In this capacity, she oversees the day-to-day operations of one of the nation's oldest and largest agencies devoted to increasing corporate and government purchasing from minority-owned businesses.

At CMBDC, Hill's charge is to continue to forge strategic alliances between its membership through innovative programs, activities and outreach efforts, including the highly successful Chicago Business Opportunity Fair, which serves as a prototype for similar trade fairs nationwide.

Hill is a seasoned business diversity veteran, whose blend of talent crosses several major Fortune 500 corporations and a plethora of agencies dedicated to diversity business development. She has built local and national supplier diversity initiatives from the bottom-up and top-down.

Hill has earned numerous awards and citations, and has been recognized nationally for her work in the diversity business development arena. Her accomplishments have been detailed in publications, including *Minority Business News USA*, TMSDC's *inBusiness* magazine, *Chicago Minority Business News*, *Who's Who in Corporate America* and more.

Frederick Hobby is president and chief executive officer at the Institute for Diversity in Health Management. He has developed tools and resources to enhance diversity in our nation's hospitals, and has helped health care organizations with diversity activities.

Before joining the institute, Fred spent ten years with the Greenville Hospital System, a 1,086-bed acute care teaching hospital system. As administrator and chief diversity officer, he developed and implemented a systemwide diversity initiative that is nationally recognized for its comprehensiveness and success.

Fred is a member of the American College of Healthcare Executives, and was founding president of the SC Chapter of the National Association of Health Services Executives.

Fred received a bachelor's degree in history and political science from Kentucky State University in Frankfort and a master's degree in sociology from Washington University in St. Louis. He served as a clinical administrator with the Portsmouth General Hospital, and is the former chief executive officer of the Newport News General Hospital. *Modern Healthcare Magazine* listed Fred as one of the 100 Most Powerful People in Healthcare.

Frederick D. Hobby

President &
Chief Executive Officer
Institute for Diversity in
Health Management

Calvin Holmes is the executive director of the Chicago Community Loan Fund (CCLF), a certified Community Development Financial Institution providing low cost, flexible financing and technical assistance to community development organizations conducting neighborhood revitalization projects throughout metropolitan Chicago. Holmes has worked for the loan fund for more than 12 years, having been promoted to executive director in 1998. Under his leadership, CCLF's capitalization has more than quadrupled from $3.7 million to more than $18 million in total capital under management.

In 2001 Holmes was honored as one of *Crain's Chicago Business* journal's 40 Under 40 young leaders, and was a 2002-2003 Leadership Greater Chicago fellow. He holds a master's degree in urban and regional planning, with a concentration in real estate development, from Cornell University and a bachelor's degree in African-American studies from Northwestern University.

Holmes currently serves on a number of nonprofit and for-profit boards. He is a director of the Opportunity Finance Network, secretary of the Interfaith Housing Development Corporation, and treasurer for both the Parkland Condominium Association and the Supportive Services Development Corporation.

Calvin L. Holmes

Executive Director
Chicago Community Loan Fund

Jann W. Honoré

Illinois Area Development Director
United Negro College Fund

J ann W. Honoré held her first professional fundraising position in 1976, and knew immediately that she would dedicate her career to helping the cause of minority education. Since joining the United Negro College Fund (UNCF) in 1980, she has held various development positions with UNCF across the country. She has vast experience in strategic fundraising, most notably as a staffer on the team that created the now famous UNCF *Lou Rawls Parade of Stars*® telethon.

In her current role as Illinois area development director, Honoré manages a development and administrative team responsible for an annual campaign to achieve a $6.2 million goal.

Recognized for her achievements, Honoré has received several leadership, excellence and meritorious service awards from UNCF through the years. Most recently, she has proudly accepted awards from Clear Channel Radio Chicago, the *Chicago Defender*, Hewitt Associates and God First Ministries.

Honoré is an alumna of Spelman College, and is married to Morris Honoré. She and her husband have a daughter, Michele, who will enter Spelman College as a freshman in the fall of 2007.

Eboni C. Howard, Ph.D.

Director
Herr Research Center for
Children & Social Policy

D r. Eboni C. Howard is director of the Herr Research Center for Children and Social Policy at Erikson Institute, where she also holds the Frances Stott chair in early childhood policy research. At Erikson Institute, she leads and oversees several policy research projects in the areas of children's mental health, social-emotional development, foster care and state-funded, pre-kindergarten programs.

Howard has extensive experience in program evaluation in the areas of childhood education, early childhood intervention, welfare reform and family functioning, family support and child welfare. She has also served on several advisory committees, including the National Academy of Sciences National Research Council Committee on Developmental Outcomes and Assessments for Young Children.

Prior to joining Erikson Institute, Howard was a senior researcher at Chapin Hall Center for Children at The University of Chicago, and a research associate at the Joint Center for Poverty Research at Northwestern University and UCLA.

She earned a Bachelor of Arts in psychology from The University of Chicago, and a Master of Arts and a Doctorate of Philosophy in human development and social policy from Northwestern University.

Hattie Johnson is the president of the Chicago-Midwest chapter of the National Association of Health Services Executives, a nonprofit association of health care executives founded in 1968 for the purpose of promoting the advancement and development of black health care leaders.

In her role as president, Hattie is charged with leading the chapter in meeting national goals that include professional programs and workshops, educational programs, scholarships and community service projects. She took office on January 1, 2007, and will lead the chapter for two years.

Hattie received a Bachelor of Administrative Studies degree and a Master of Public Administration degree from Roosevelt University in Chicago, where she is also a lifetime alumna.

A native of Chicago, Illinois, Hattie is single.

Hattie Johnson

President
Chicago-Midwest Chapter
National Association of Health Services Executives

As director of special events for the Chicago Minority Business Development Council, Cynthia Jordan oversees the execution of events, meetings and programs during the year. She ensures that leading corporations and minority business enterprises have an opportunity to meet and network for the purpose of global supplier diversity. Under her leadership, the prestigious annual Chicago Business Opportunity Fair has become one of Chicago's premier business expos, which showcases minority businesses, corporate buyers and government agencies.

Cynthia is also the principal and owner of Royal Affair, an event planning and management company, servicing clients that have included fantasy weddings for NBA players and philanthropic events hosted by Hollywood A-listers. She has recently expanded her creative enterprise to include Royal Designs, a high-end interior design company.

Cynthia attended Graham College in Massachusetts, Boston University, where she studied business and fashion merchandising, and Ray Vogue Art School, where she studied interior design. She is also the proud mother of two young entrepreneurs, Erika Janeé and Marcus Scott.

Cynthia L. Jordan

Director of Special Events
Chicago Minority Business
Development Council

Gwendolyn Kenner-Johnson

Associate Director
Office of Family Support Services
Illinois Department of Human Services

Gwendolyn Kenner-Johnson is associate director of the Office of Family Support Services for the Illinois Department of Human Services. With a budget of more than $280 million, she is responsible for the Bureaus of Homeless Services and Supportive Housing, Refugee and Immigrant Services, Title XX Social Services and the Illinois Katrina Assistance Relief Efforts.

Gwendolyn's commitment to enhancing the lives of individuals and families is also evident in her civic activities. She is immediate past president of the Lake Shore chapter of The Links, Inc. She is also a member of Delta Sigma Theta Sorority, Inc. and the sanctuary choir of Trinity United Church of Christ. Gwendolyn has received awards from the YMCA, UNCF and the Spelman Alumnae Association, and appeared in the inaugural edition of **Who's Who In Black Chicago**®.

Gwendolyn, a Spelman graduate, has a Bachelor of Arts degree in psychology and a Master of Education degree from Northeastern Illinois University.

She is married to Martin G. Johnson, a retired executive, and is the mother of Dr. Michele Jolivette, a college professor, and grandmother to Teal and Aubrey.

Carl W. Latimer

President
Coalition for United Community
Action-O.R.T.C., Inc.

Carl W. Latimer, president of Coalition for United Community Action-O.R.T.C., Inc. (CUCA), formed the coalition in 1969 in response to the glaring lack of African-American participation in construction jobs and the growing tensions arising in various neighborhoods throughout Chicago. Led by Latimer, CUCA has grown from protest to programs. The coalition is credited with developing and implementing programs that have integrated the construction ranks from apprentices to management.

Two of the coalition's successful union-affiliated programs, the Apprenticeship Preparedness Training Program and Project Upgrade, have made it possible for African Americans, females and other minorities to gain status in the construction industry.

Latimer is very well known among the Chicago political elite, and serves on a number of trade, civic and advisory boards. He has been honored many times throughout his nearly 40-year career.

Latimer is a graduate of Chicago State University. His hobbies include basketball, bid whist and dancing. He has one daughter, two sons and seven grandchildren.

The Reverend Rae Lewis-Thornton is a renowned AIDS activist. She rose to national acclaim when she told her story of living with HIV/AIDS in a cover story for *Essence* magazine. In the past 14 years, she has traveled worldwide in an unending crusade challenging stereotypes and myths around HIV/AIDS.

Rae has been featured in countless newspapers and magazines, such as *The Washington Post*, *Chicago Tribune*, *Chicago Defender*, *Jet*, *Ebony*, *Life Line* and *Emerge*. She has also appeared on numerous national television specials, documentaries and news shows, including *Nightline*, *Dateline* and *The Oprah Winfrey Show*. She received an Emmy for an ongoing series of first-person stories on living with AIDS for WBBM-TV, a CBS-owned and operated television station.

Rae is a licensed Baptist minister. She received a master of divinity degree from McCormick Theological Seminary, and is currently a doctorate of philosophy candidate at the Lutheran School of Theology in Chicago. Rae is a member of Delta Sigma Theta Sorority, Inc.

Rev. Rae Lewis-Thornton

AIDS Activist
Rae Lewis-Thornton, Inc.

William E. Lowry Jr. is the senior advisor to the president of the John D. and Catherine T. MacArthur Foundation. He joined MacArthur in 1994 as vice president for human resources and administration, and served in that position until October of 2005. Prior to MacArthur, Lowry was chief operating officer at James H. Lowry & Associates, a management consulting firm, and corporate director of personnel and recruitment for Inland Steel Industries. He retired from Inland in 1993.

Lowry also worked in television where he hosted the Emmy and Peabody award-winning show *Opportunity Line* on WBBM-TV. The show ran for 24 years.

Lowry currently serves on the boards of the Rehabilitation Institute of Chicago and the Children's Home and Aid Society of Illinois. He is also a trustee of Kenyon College. In addition, he served as chair of the City/County Task Force on Welfare Reform.

Lowry, a native of Chicago, earned a bachelor's degree in history from Kenyon College and a master's degree in industrial relations from Loyola University Chicago.

William E. Lowry Jr.

Senior Advisor
John D. and Catherine T.
MacArthur Foundation

Peggy A. Montes

Founder & President
Bronzeville Children's Museum

Peggy A. Montes is founder and president of the Bronzeville Children's Museum, the first and only African-American children's museum in the country.

Previously, Peggy served as a volunteer for 27 years at the DuSable Museum of African American History where she became the first female chair of its board of trustees and building committee. Moreover, she co-founded Leadership Illinois and was selected as one of the top 100 women leaders in the U.S. by Leadership America. Currently, Peggy is chair of the board of trustees for Chicago State University and commissioner and chair of the Cook County Commission on Women's Issues.

Former President Clinton appointed her to the White House Women's Conference over which First Lady Hillary Clinton presided. Governors Jim Edgar, George H. Ryan and Rod Blagojevich have given her appointments and Secretary of State Jesse White has reappointed her to serve on the Illinois Literacy Advisory Board.

Peggy lives in Chicago with her husband and is the proud mother of a son, an attorney, and a daughter, an educator. She is the doting grandmother of three delightful grandchildren.

Missouri Myers

Secretary
North Chicago Community
School Board, District 187

Missouri Myers is a lifetime resident of North Chicago, Illinois, and is the proud mother of three children, five grandchildren and a great-granddaughter. In September of 2005, after 28 years of employment, Missouri retired from the Waukegan Township Supervisor's Office to care for a sick daughter and brother, who both have cancer.

She is currently serving as secretary to the North Chicago Community School Board, District 187, which she has been a member of since April of 1999, and has also served as board president and vice president. To Missouri, helping the children of her community receive an excellent education is a very rewarding experience.

In 1999 she received a certificate of appreciation from the Honorable John Porter of the United States House of Representatives for not supporting the re-downsizing of North Chicago Veterans Administration Medical Center. Additionally, in 2002 she received a Woman In the Spirit Award, and in 2004 she was recognized as one of the Most Influential African Americans for Education.

Missouri attends First Corinthian Missionary Baptist Church, where Eugene Roberson is the pastor.

Malik S. Nevels is the executive director for the Illinois African American Coalition for Prevention (ILAACP), a statewide membership-based organization strengthening early intervention and prevention systems, policies and strategies in African-American communities through culturally competent research, training and advocacy.

Prior to joining the ILAACP, Malik served in various senior executive capacities for the Illinois Center of Violence Prevention, Duncan YMCA and the Chicago Urban League. He has also worked for U.S. Representative Jesse Jackson Jr., Mayor of Chicago Richard M. Daley and U.S. Senator Carol Moseley-Braun.

Additionally, he is active in various civic organizations and professional associations, including Leaders United, Healthy Schools Campaign, Public Allies and 100 Black Men of Chicago.

Malik earned a juris doctorate degree from the University of Illinois College of Law. He also holds a Bachelor of Arts degree in political science from the University of Illinois at Chicago and a certificate in strategies in nonprofit management from The University of Chicago.

Malik S. Nevels

Executive Director
Illinois African American
Coalition for Prevention

David A. Northern Sr. serves as deputy director of the Lake County Housing Authority. David assists with the administration of an agency with annual resources of roughly $27 million and an inventory of more than 3,800 properties servicing more than 10,000 citizens throughout Lake County.

David's educational background includes a master's degree from Indiana University and a bachelor's degree in accounting from Ball State University. He also holds a certificate from the University of Maryland for completion of the executive education program in housing, a graduate certificate in public management and a certificate from the Institute for Innovative Leadership Development Program.

Dedicated to giving, his civic affiliations include serving as vice president of housing for Illinois NAHRO and on the board of the Affordable Housing Commission.

David has received numerous honors, including the Graduate of the Last Decade Award from Ball State University, a profile in *Ebony* magazine's 2004 editorial "30 Leaders Under 30," ***Who's Who In Black Chicago®*** 2006, and the Most Influential African-Americans of Lake County Award. He shares his life with his wife and two kids.

David A. Northern Sr.

Deputy Director
Lake County Housing Authority

Wendell B. O'Neal Sr.

Executive Director
Alliance of Business Leaders
& Entrepreneurs

For the past four years, Wendell B. O'Neal Sr. has served as executive director of the Alliance of Business Leaders & Entrepreneurs (ABLE). ABLE is a 15-year-old business organization that is made up of 55 African-American business leaders in the Chicago area. ABLE members represent nine business categories, and collectively generate approximately $1.5 billion in annual revenues.

Assisting companies and organizations in the achievement of strategic objectives for more than 30 years, O'Neal has provided business development and organizational development consulting services to small, mid-sized and Fortune-listed organizations. Additionally, major health care systems have benefited from his expertise. He has consulted with senior executives in the development and implementation of employee satisfaction and customer satisfaction processes, continuous quality improvement processes, strategic thinking and strategic planning approaches.

O'Neal completed undergraduate studies at Roosevelt University and received a master's degree in cultural studies from Governors State University. He has served as adjunct professor of business communications at Roosevelt University.

Bonita Parker

Chief of Staff, 7th Ward
City of Chicago

Bonita Parker is a respected visionary leader with more than 20 years of exemplary achievement who has demonstrated success in organizational leadership obtained in the financial service, not-for-profit and public service industries. She currently serves as the chief of staff to Alderman Sandi Jackson.

Bonita has held positions as director of financial education for The Office of The State Treasurer; chief operating officer and national director of 1,000 Churches Connected for the RainbowPUSH Coalition; director of investments and economic empowerment for Salem Baptist Church; and various management positions at The Northern Trust Company, including second vice president of worldwide operations.

Her professional memberships and affiliations include V.I.P. membership in Cambridge's Who's Who, *Marquis Who's Who of Emerging Leaders*, the RainbowPUSH Coalition board of directors, the NAACP, the Urban League and the National Association of Urban Financial Services. She has also appeared in *Crain's Chicago Business*, *Money* magazine and *Black Enterprise*.

Bonita is an active volunteer at her church, Salem Baptist Church of Chicago. She has a strong passion for economic empowerment, advocacy and civil rights.

Lisa M. Rollins is chief development officer of Ada S. McKinley Community Services, Inc. (ASMCS), headquartered in Chicago, Illinois. She directs all fundraising efforts including philanthropic, corporate, civic and governmental giving. She is the first woman to hold the position.

As chief fundraiser on behalf of ASMCS, Lisa manages a variety of programs and campaigns and oversees all aspects of development and communications. An expert in fundraising for nonprofit organizations, she is part of a new vanguard of professionals bringing innovative ideas, strategies and systems to the development field.

Lisa holds a Bachelor of Science degree in biology education from Bethune-Cookman College and a Master of Business Administration degree from Hampton University in Hampton, Virginia. She is a member of the National Academy of Volunteerism and Alpha Kappa Alpha Sorority, Inc. She has received numerous awards and honors and is a recent Black Pearl recipient.

A native of Brunswick, Maine, Lisa lives in Matteson, Illinois, with her husband, Larry, and three children.

Lisa M. Rollins

Chief Development Officer
Ada S. McKinley
Community Services, Inc.

Retired Colonel Eugene F. Scott is the president of the Chicago Defender Charities, organizers and sponsors of the Bud Billiken® Parade and Picnic.

Scott, a native of Miami, Florida, graduated in 1962 from Florida A&M University with a Bachelor of Science degree in political science. Additionally, he was commissioned as a second lieutenant in the Armor Branch of the U.S. Army. A graduate of the Armed Forces Staff College, he has also completed graduate studies in human relations at the University of Oklahoma. Scott was a combat officer who served two tours of duty in the Republic of Vietnam, Germany and numerous stateside assignments.

In 1990 he joined the *Chicago Defender* newspaper and Sengestacke Enterprises as executive assistant to the chair of Sengestacke Enterprises. In 1993 he assumed the position of general manager of the *Chicago Daily Defender* and later became publisher in April of 2000.

Scott has served on the executive boards of the Boy Scouts of America, Red Cross, YMCA and the United Way. He is a Rotarian and a member of the Omega Psi Phi Fraternity, Inc.

Col. Eugene F. Scott, Ret.

President
Chicago Defender Charities

Charles R. Sherrell II

Founder & President
drumsHORNS&Voices, Inc.

Charles R. Sherrell II is the founder and president of DHV (drumsHORNS&Voices, Inc.), a fine arts service institution dedicated to the development, preservation and general support of classic black jazz music, literature, photography, theatre and dance.

For more than 35 years, Sherrell was president and owner of Chicago's real jazz radio station, where he began sponsoring and promoting music and arts concerts, seminars, clinics and workshops.

Currently, Sherrell sponsors and promotes art shows and jazz concerts in the Miami/Fort Lauderdale, Florida, areas. He is a supporter of black dance troupes and theatre in both cities. As an avid snow skier, scuba diver, and golf and chess player, he vigorously challenges black youth to develop skills in these disciplines. He also strongly encourages students to study the literature of black writers, philosophers and historians, and to support black cultural fine arts.

Sherrell's education includes a bachelor's degree in philosophy and letters, and a master's degree in modern romance languages. He is married to Trutie Thigpen Sherrell, a retired business professor from City Colleges of Chicago.

Leslie Brown Simmons

Founder & Director
Leslie's Place &
Support Advocates for Women

Leslie Brown Simmons is the founder and director of Leslie's Place and Support Advocates for Women, a transitional housing facility for women released from prison and on parole. Simmons founded Support Advocates for Women in 1992, and opened Leslie's Place in 1994. Since that time, more than 600 women, many with their children, have lived at Leslie's Place. The facility has an overwhelming 97 percent success rate of women not returning to prison. In addition, scores of women have been empowered by Simmons' motivational and self-esteem programs presented inside prison walls.

Simmons has appeared on many shows, including *The Oprah Winfrey Show*, *Donahue* and *The Naomi Roberson Show*. *Crain's Chicago Business* recognized Simmons as one of the 100 Most Influential Chicago Women.

Simmons is the mother of six children, one girl and five boys. She is a former battered woman and former prisoner who served seven years at Dwight Correctional Center. Former Governor Jim Thompson granted her clemency in 1988. Since her release, Simmons has dedicated her life to helping women who are incarcerated or recently released from prison.

D r. Ann Smith is president of the Gamaliel Foundation, a multifaith organizing network of 61 affiliates that represents more than one million people working together on campaigns for social justice.

Gamaliel is a challenge Smith undertook after a career in academia and business. She was associate chancellor and director of community relations at the University of Illinois at Chicago. At Northeastern Illinois University, she was interim vice president for academic affairs. Additionally, Smith was sales manager for the Prudential Insurance Company, director of marketing for Cook, Stratton & Company and vice president of Endow, Inc.

In 1985 she became the first black woman in Illinois to win a statewide election, taking a seat on the board of trustees at the University of Illinois. Smith has served on numerous boards including The American College and Business and Professional People for the Public Interest.

Smith earned a Doctor of Philosophy degree from Union University, a master's degree from the University of Iowa, and received bachelor's and honorary doctorate degrees from Lincoln University. She is a noted lecturer and interpreter of African-American poetry.

Ann E. Smith, Ph.D.

President
Gamaliel Foundation

D eirdre Joy Smith is the founder of the Women's Networking Community (WNC), an innovative not-for-profit organization committed to helping women transcend the traditional boundaries of the workplace by establishing personal and professional connections through networking.

POWER: Opening Doors for Women, WNC's flagship event held in May, includes a kick-off reception, followed by 16 simultaneous topic-based dinners held in private homes and venues, hosted by some of the city's most influential women leaders.

Deirdre is also principal of DJS Events, an event planning and fundraising management firm with an extensive list of clients across the nation, including Chicago. She served as the deputy Midwest finance director for the Al Gore 2000 presidential campaign, the Democratic National Committee's finance director for the Midwest region for the 2000 presidential election cycle, and the deputy finance director for Carol Moseley Braun's 1998 senatorial campaign.

Deirdre also worked for the U.S. Department of Commerce in Washington, D.C., and the Women in International Security at the University of Maryland's Center for International and Security Studies.

She received a Bachelor of Science degree from Purdue University.

Deirdre Joy Smith

Founder
Women's Networking Community

Priscilla Stratten

Director of Special Events &
Individual Giving
United Negro College Fund

Priscilla Stratten is the development director of special events and individual giving for the United Negro College Fund (UNCF). She is responsible for producing five major events each year in the Chicago area, including the Black & White Ball, the Chicago Public Schools Kick-Off Reception, the Annual UNCF Walkathon, the Annual UNCF Mayor's Reception and the viewing party for *An Evening of Stars* television special. Additionally, Priscilla is responsible for raising scholarship dollars through the individual giving society A Mind Is.

The events have become extremely important for the organization nationally, and locally, they stand out as some of Chicago's finest fundraisers. The Black & White Ball has raised more than $6 million in its seven-year history.

Holding a Bachelor of Science degree in business education from Chicago State University, Priscilla has received various awards, including the Black Pearl Award in 2005, the Leadership Award from Dr. Mildred Harris and God First Ministries in 2006, and the National Special Recognition Award from UNCF for the Black & White Ball in 2007.

She is the proud mother of Tracy and Michael.

Alana Yvonne Wallace

Founder & Artistic Director
Dance>Detour

Alana Yvonne Wallace, a lifelong disability advocate, was recently awarded the crown of Ms. Wheelchair America 2008. The first African American to be crowned in the 35-year history of the program, she will serve as a national spokesperson for people with disabilities advocating the need to eliminate architectural and attitudinal barriers.

Since 1995 Wallace has served as founder and artistic director of Dance>Detour, Chicago's first professional dance troupe that fully integrates dancers with and without disabilities.

Wallace, who contracted polio at the age of five, is a professional wheelchair dancer, actress and vocalist. She has been featured in dance pieces with Mikhail Baryshnikov's White Oak Dance Project and The Joffrey Ballet of Chicago. In 1998 she appeared in the Emmy-winning PBS documentary, *Dance From the Heart*.

A graduate of Columbia College with a Bachelor of Fine Arts degree in theater/music, Wallace was named one of the 100 Women Making a Difference in *Today's Chicago Woman* magazine in 1997.

She resides in Chicago with her husband, Cornell, and is the proud mother of four children, Natasha, Nicholas, John and Nadia.

Debra Wesley-Freeman is president and chief executive officer of Sinai Community Institute, a community-based, not-for-profit health-and-wellness resource center. Established in 1993 by Sinai Health System in Chicago, the institute serves more than 22,000 adults and children each year. With a master's degree in social work from the University of Illinois at Chicago, she joined Mount Sinai Hospital in 1987 as director of family planning. She later took on full responsibility for Sinai's wide range of community health programs, which expanded further with the creation of the institute.

Debra has received national recognition for developing innovative, community-based programs that address the unique health and psycho-social needs of urban residents. She is the founding president of the North Lawndale Employment Network board of directors and a board member for the Legacy Charter School and Westside Association for Community Action. She is also a Denali Initiative Class II Harvard University Social Entrepreneurial fellow.

Debra is the president of Healthy Feet, Inc. d.b.a. Wesley's Shoe Corral, one of Chicago's oldest African-American family-owned shoe businesses, founded by the late Reverend Dr. Alvin J. Wesley.

Debra Wesley-Freeman

President &
Chief Executive Officer
Sinai Community Institute

Robert L. Wharton is president and chief executive officer of the Community Economic and Development Association of Cook County, Inc. (CEDA). With an annual budget in excess of $150 million, CEDA is the nation's largest community action agency and the second-largest charitable organization in the Chicago area.

Wharton has received numerous awards for outstanding public service, most recently the prestigious Don Sykes Leadership award from the African-American Community Action Leaders. He has authored several articles in major and community newspapers advocating economic empowerment for low-income families. He appears on Chicago-area television and radio, and serves on several local and national boards.

Wharton began his career in 1969 at the Great Lakes regional office of the United States Office of Economic Opportunity and the United States Community Services Administration. He earned a bachelor's degree in English and French at Kentucky State University and a master's degree in public administration at Roosevelt University. He has completed major course work for the Doctor of Public Administration degree at Nova University.

Wharton lives in suburban Crete with his wife of 41 years, Shirley Wharton.

Robert L. Wharton

President & Chief Executive Officer
Community Economic and
Development Association of
Cook County, Inc.

Dollie M. Williams

Executive Director
Primo Center for Women and Children

Spanning 45 years, Dollie M. Williams' life's work has centered on positively impacting the lives of others. A veteran community activist, she has been on the forefront of the civil rights movement. Today, Dollie is helping young women and children get their lives back on track as the executive director of Primo Center for Women and Children.

Dollie has a history of supporting the efforts of black leaders, including the late Lutrelle "Lu" Palmer, a community activist and journalist during his run for Congress, and the Reverend Jesse Jackson Sr. for Operation Breadbasket which later became Operation PUSH. She was also a member of special projects under the Reverend Willie T. Barrow and a campaigner for Chicago's first black mayor, the late Harold Washington.

Dollie is a graduate of Daniel Hale Williams University, with a Bachelor of Arts degree in sociology. She has received many humanitarian awards and recently had her name added to the Wall of Tolerance in Montgomery, Alabama.

Dollie is the wife of Elvert Williams Sr. and the proud mother of Anthony, Kevin, Stanley and Angela.

Victoria Wilson

Founder &
Chief Executive Officer
New Vision of Hope Foundation

Victoria Wilson is founder and chief executive officer of New Vision of Hope Foundation, a nonprofit organization focusing on HIV/AIDS education and prevention in a resale store. In this position, she manages the administration, marketing, advertising, HIV/AIDS education and testing, and all cause-related fundraising events. She also writes, produces and directs theatre productions on HIV/AIDS and other matters, providing edutainment (education through entertainment) for Chicago public high schools, colleges and universities.

Victoria's current affiliations include the Society for Arts in Healthcare, the National Association of Women Business Owners and the Chicago Foundation for Women. She received certifications as an HIV educator, tester and counselor from the American Red Cross and the Illinois Department of Public Health.

A native of Chicago, she is the proud mother of one daughter, Cicely Wilson, who is also an educator in the Chicago Public School system. Victoria enjoys theatre, music, traveling and staying fit, but more importantly, teaching HIV prevention and showing people how they can live safe and happy lives.

Antoinette D. Wright is president and chief executive officer of the DuSable Museum of African American History. She also acted as deputy director of the museum from 1990 to 1993, and returned to the Museum in 1997, with a focus on expanding the museum's dynamic and varied programming and collection development.

Antoinette attended DePaul University and Mundelein College for undergraduate studies, and earned a Bachelor of Arts degree in business administration. She has a certificate of museum management from the University of Colorado, and served as an Arts Midwest arts administration fellow at the Columbus Museum of Art and the Cincinnati Museum of Natural History in Ohio.

Antoinette is a board member for the Association of African American Museums and After School Matters. She also serves on the Illinois State Historical Records advisory board, and is a member of The Economic Club of Chicago.

Antoinette is a former board member of Hales Franciscan High School, PUSH for Excellence, Inc., the Duke Ellington Society, Chicago Youth Centers, Greer Residential Center, Kids Voting-Illinois, Little Black Pearl and the Chicago Junior Association of Commerce and Industry.

Antoinette D. Wright

President & Chief Executive Officer
DuSable Museum of
African American History

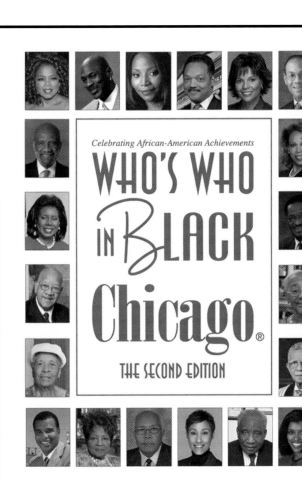

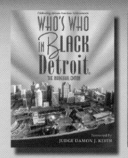   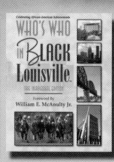  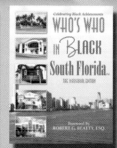
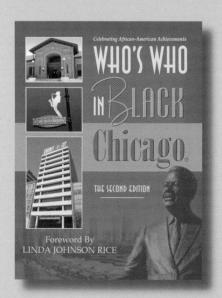

earnest

merciful

CHICAGO'S

Spiritual

SPIRITUAL LEADERS

faithful

consecrated

virtuous

dedicated

wise

benevolent

honorable

Bishop D. Rayford Bell

Senior Pastor
Christ Temple Apostolic
Faith Church, Inc.

B ishop Dennis Rayford Bell was born on July 9, 1923 in Mississippi. In April of 1949, he first heard the gospel of Jesus Christ, and began a new life.

Bell is a firm believer of education being the road to true freedom and success. Attending LaSalle University, he completed his high school requirements. He earned a bachelor's degree in religious studies from Southwestern College in Oklahoma. At American Bible College in Florida, Bell was a straight "A" student pursuing a master's degree in theology. In August of 1979, Bell received doctorate degrees in theology and philosophy from Toledo Bible College, where he was the first in the school's history to achieve two doctorate degrees in one year.

As senior pastor of Christ Temple Apostolic Faith Church for 48 years, his motto is: "I'm apostolic across the fence, behind the barn and everywhere." Bell's life has been one of serving the church and community. He is a chaplain for the Chicago Police Department, and his primary joy is sharing the life and saving grace of Jesus Christ with others.

John Leland Belser Sr.

Pastor
First Baptist Church
of Melrose Park

P astor John Leland Belser Sr. is a native of Maywood, Illinois. Belser has earned two bachelor's degrees, a Master of Arts degree and two teacher certificates from the State of Illinois.

Belser served as a public school educator for 18 years prior to becoming a pastor. He was honored by *Who's Who Among American High School Teachers* for four consecutive years, 2001–2005. Additionally, he received the Most Inspirational Teacher Award from Western Illinois University.

Belser became the eighth pastor of the First Baptist Church of Melrose Park in 2002. He also serves as chief executive officer of the H. McNelty School, a private, nonprofit school operated by First Baptist Church for grades pre-school through eight.

Happily married to the former Kimberly Cherisse Ivy of Chicago, Belser and his wife are the proud parents of four children.

Columbus F. Bland

Founder & Pastor
Glory To Glory Family
Christian Center

A postle Columbus F. Bland is founder and pastor of Glory To Glory Family Christian Center. He has been married for 40 years to Katie Bland, and is the father of three and grandfather of five. Born in Charleston, Mississippi, Bland is one of 15 children. Because his family was very poor, he had to forego a formal education to help support his family.

His life has been transformed by the power of God, from an alcoholic and a gambler to a new man of peace, integrity and holiness. Bland has ministered in the Cook County correctional system for more than 14 years. His evangelistic ministry has traveled throughout the United States, including Hawaii and the Bahamas.

Bland is a man that loves and obeys God. He has shared his home with several, and disciples many to Christ. After prevailing with principalities and winning over depression, he is an effective marriage and family counselor. Bland is a role model to many men who find him approachable and down to earth.

Minister Epluribus Cornelius Cunningham received his calling to preach the gospel in November of 1989 at the age of 19. He was licensed to preach in 1990 under the ministry of Pastor Napoleon Davis of Christ First Baptist Church of Harvey, Illinois, where he served as an associate minister and minister of music for seven years.

Cunningham joined the staff of Salem Baptist Church of Chicago in 1998 under the leadership of the Reverend James T. Meeks, senior pastor. He currently serves as pastor of K2B (Kid's Kingdom Building) Children's Ministry.

Cunningham has been instrumental in helping hundreds of children and adults find faith, hope and purpose through a relationship with Jesus Christ. His main goal in ministering to children is to help them become active, productive and kingdom-minded students and citizens in today's society. Cunningham accomplishes this goal each week as he leads Salem's Children Church, consisting of more than 700 children, in what both parents and children consider an exuberant and captivating time of praise, worship and Bible study.

Epluribus C. Cunningham

Children's Pastor
Salem Baptist
Church of Chicago

A native of Milwaukee, Wisconsin, the Reverend Alexis L. Felder graduated, with honors, from Garrett-Evangelical Theological Seminary at Northwestern University in Evanston, Illinois, with a Master of Theological Studies degree in New Testament. Currently, she is pursuing a Doctor of Ministry degree in preaching at McCormick Theological Seminary.

As the minister of ministry operations at New Faith Baptist Church International, Felder is completing her first book entitled, "Preparing to Hear His Voice." Additionally, her sermons were featured in *The African American Pulpit's* Fall 2005 edition, where she was recognized as an emerging voice among women preachers.

She is the founder of Triumphant Living Ministries International, which helps women and men in discovering their true identity and accessing their authority in Jesus Christ. She is also the co-founder of The Joseph Assignment Global Initiative, a Christian global relief organization.

She is married to the Reverend Dr. Trunell D. Felder, senior pastor of New Faith Baptist Church International in Matteson, Illinois, a thriving worship center with 6,000 members and five churches in Ghana, West Africa. The couple has one son, Andrew.

Rev. Alexis L. Felder

Minister of Ministry
Operations
New Faith Baptist
Church International

Dr. Trunell D. Felder was born in Los Angeles, California. He earned a Bachelor of Arts degree in marketing from Michigan State University in East Lansing, Michigan. In 1990 he matriculated to Candler School of Theology at Emory University in Atlanta, Georgia, where he received his Master of Divinity degree with a concentration in pastoral care in May of 1993.

In 2000 Felder graduated, summa cum laude, from Interdenominational Theological Center in Atlanta, Georgia, with a Doctor of Ministry degree. His dissertation, entitled, *An Inward-Outward Journey: A Paradigm for the Spiritual Formation of the African American Male Disciple*, addresses the challenges and provides solutions for the spiritual formation of Christian African-American men in the church.

Presently, Felder is the senior pastor of New Faith Baptist Church International in Matteson, Illinois, a thriving church with 6,000 members, as well as five churches in Ghana, West Africa. He is also the founder of The Joseph Assignment Global Initiative, a Christian global relief organization.

Felder is married to the former Reverend Alexis L. Brinkley of Milwaukee, Wisconsin, and they have one son, Andrew.

Dr. Trunell D. Felder

Senior Pastor
New Faith Baptist
Church International

Rev. Dr. William H. Foster Jr.

Pastor
Providence Missionary
Baptist Church

The Reverend Dr. William H. Foster Jr. is pastor of Providence Missionary Baptist Church (PMBC), a congregation consisting of more than 1,200 members. Some of Foster's goals are to meet the needs of people, to win souls to Christ and to feed his flock the word of God. His principal commitment is the spiritual growth and development of people.

He has continued to move PMBC forward, implementing several new ministries and capital improvements, including a youth church service, a computer technology center, the Providence Employment Resource Ministry, a marriage ministry, an early morning worship service and a transitional housing facility.

Foster received a Bachelor of Science degree in business from Montana State University and a Master of Business Administration degree from The University of Chicago. He received a master's degree in religion from Trinity Evangelical Divinity Seminary and a doctorate degree in ministry from United Theological Seminary.

Foster was drafted by the Chicago Bulls in 1980, and played for the Montana Golden Nuggets in the CBA. He has been featured in several publications, including *Dollars & Sense* and *Crain's Chicago Business*.

Rabbi Capers C. Funnye Jr.

Spiritual Leader
Beth Shalom B'nai Zaken
Ethiopian Hebrew Congregation

Rabbi Capers C. Funnye Jr. is chief rabbi and spiritual leader of Beth Shalom B'nai Zaken Ethiopian Hebrew Congregation, located in Chicago, Illinois. He also serves as a senior research associate for the Institute of Jewish and Community Research, located in San Francisco, California.

Funnye earned a Bachelor of Arts degree in Hebrew literature and rabbinic ordination from the Israelite Board of Rabbis, Inc. in Queens, New York. He also earned a Bachelor of Arts degree in Jewish studies and a Master of Science degree in human service administration from Spertus Institute of Judaica in Chicago. Funnye has lectured at several institutions throughout the United States and Africa. He has also served as a consultant to several institutions throughout the United States.

Funnye is a member of several boards in the Jewish community, including The Chicago Board of Rabbis and the Jewish Council on Urban Affairs, and is vice president of the Israelite Board of Rabbis.

He and his wife, Mary, have four children and are the proud grandparents of five grandsons and one granddaughter.

Rev. Rosemarie Green

Chicago Chapter Director
National Consortium of Black
Women in Ministry, Inc.

The Reverend Rosemarie Green is a founding member and Chicago chapter director for the National Consortium of Black Women in Ministry, Inc. (NCBWIM), a professional organization founded in September of 2005. NCBWIM supports women in ministry across the United States, mobilizing them to impact issues affecting the African-American community. Rose leads continuing education and relevant socio-political initiatives to empower African-American women in ministry.

Rose is a pharmacist currently employed at Takeda Pharmaceuticals as a senior project manager, where she is responsible for managing cross-functional global teams in drug development efforts.

Rose is a three-time recipient of the Outstanding Young Women in America Award. She was recognized for her outstanding community service by The North Shore – Chicago Chapter of the Top Ladies of Distinction in 2004.

She is a graduate of Purdue University School of Pharmacy, and in 1997 was awarded a Master of Divinity from Garrett-Evangelical Theological Seminary. A member of Alpha Kappa Alpha Sorority, Inc., Rose is a native of Savannah, Georgia. She enjoys spending time with her nieces and nephews, traveling, fine dining and attending theatre performances.

The Reverend D. Darrell Griffin is the senior pastor of the Oakdale Covenant Church of Chicago, Illinois.

Previously, he served as the assistant pastor of the Abyssinian Baptist Church of Harlem, New York, pastored by Dr. Calvin O. Butts III. In 1997 he became the fourth pastor of the Antioch Baptist Church in Brooklyn, New York.

A graduate of Morehouse College in Atlanta, Georgia, Griffin received a bachelor's degree in marketing and completed a Master of Divinity degree at the Harvard Divinity School in Cambridge, Massachusetts. Additionally, he earned a Doctorate of Ministry in homiletics from North Park Theological Seminary.

Griffin is chair of the executive board of the Evangelical Covenant Churches of America, and a member of the advisory board at North Park University School of Business and Nonprofit Management. He also sits on the boards of the Chicago State School of Business and the department of social work at Trinity Christian College, and is a member of Alpha Phi Alpha Fraternity, Inc.

Griffin is married to Chereese Newton, and they have two sons, Miles Spence and Bryce Langston.

Rev. D. Darrell Griffin
Senior Pastor
Oakdale Covenant Church

The Reverend Dr. Glenn A. Harris Jr. is an associate minister of Bread of Life Missionary Baptist Church. A native of Chicago, Harris was born the second child of two to Angelique and Glenn Harris Sr.

Harris graduated from the public schools of the District 63 and District 207 education systems. He also attended Columbia College in Chicago for oral communications in public speaking. Harris then went on to pursue pastoring his own church, which began in October of 1999. After being ordained in the ministry in January of 1999, he received an honorary doctorate degree in theology for his merit on his thesis.

Later, wanting to learn from Universal Ministries School of Theology in Milford, Illinois, Harris received an Associate of Divinity degree in theology in August of 2004. In that same year, he also earned a diploma as a pharmacy technician from the Professional Career Development Institute in Atlanta, Georgia. Earning a bachelor's degree in biblical studies in 2006, Harris also received a High Honors Achievement Award for a GPA of 7.0.

Rev. Dr. Glenn A. Harris Jr.
Associate Minister
Bread of Life Missionary
Baptist Church

Dr. Mildred C. Harris is founder and chief executive officer of God First Church and Ministries of Chicago, with chapters in Georgia, Indiana, Ohio and New York. For 20 years, the ministry has sponsored the largest community breakfast in Chicago with thousands in attendance.

In 1999 Mayor Richard M. Daley appointed Harris commissioner for the Chicago Housing Authority with a Plan for Transformation budget of $1.5 billion. She refurbished 57 sitting rooms in CHA Senior Buildings, raising more than $200,000.

Harris received the Dominick's Fresh Spirit Award for Chicago's Leading Women Religious Leaders, the 2005 NBC5 Chicago Jefferson Award and the 2005 Mitsubishi Motors Unsung Heroine Award. She sits on the African-American Advisory Board of Lisa Madigan, attorney general for the State of Illinois, the Local Government Advisory Board for Daniel M. Hynes, comptroller for the State of Illinois and the Women's Board of the Goodman Theater.

Harris holds a bachelor's degree from DePaul University, three master's degrees from Columbia University, Governors State University and Loyola University, and a doctorate in ministry from the International Bible Institute and Seminary.

Dr. Mildred C. Harris
President &
Chief Executive Officer
God First Ministries

Rev. Dr. Marshall Hatch Sr.

Pastor
New Mount Pilgrim Missionary
Baptist Church

The Reverend Dr. Marshall Hatch Sr. is pastor of New Mount Pilgrim Missionary Baptist Church in Chicago's West Garfield community. In 1998 he participated in highly coveted fellowships at Harvard Divinity School, and in 2000 he was an adjunct professor of McCormick Theological Seminary. Hatch was awarded the Weston Howland Grant for Civic Leadership from Tufts University in 2006.

His civic involvement includes serving as a moderator for the Friendship Baptist Direct Association, national director of religious affairs for the RainbowPUSH Coalition and a board member for the Academy of Communication and Technology Charter School and Christ the King Jesuit College Prep High School.

Hatch earned doctorate and master's degrees in ministry and theological studies from McCormick Theological Seminary, a master's degree in government from Georgetown University and a bachelor's degree in political science from Western Illinois University in Macomb.

A native of the West Side, he is married to Priscilla and they are the parents of four children.

Rev. Dr. L. Bernard Jakes

Senior Pastor
West Point Missionary
Baptist Church

The Reverend Dr. L. Bernard Jakes serves as the senior pastor of West Point Missionary Baptist Church in Chicago, Illinois. In this office, his successes include West Point Village, luxury townhomes in the community; an additional worship service; the organization of a Christian education department; and a food pantry ministry that serves more than 150 families weekly. He also spearheaded and completed a $500,000 renovation project and developed the West Point Community Development Corporation.

Jakes is a board member at Vision House, an HIV/AIDS assisted-living facility, and he works with the Center for New Horizons Youth Outreach. Additionally, he serves as co-chaplain at Elmhurst College in Elmhurst, Illinois, and is a life member of Alpha Phi Alpha Fraternity, Inc. and the Scottish Rites Masons.

He earned a Bachelor of Arts degree from Elmhurst College, a Master of Arts degree from Garrett-Evangelical Theological Seminary and a Doctor of Ministry degree from United Theological Seminary in Dayton, Ohio.

Jakes is the husband of Carole D. Jakes and the proud father of two children, Miss Erika and Master Brandon.

Charles Jenkins

Pastor
Fellowship Missionary
Baptist Church

Pastor Charles Jenkins has firmly established himself as one of the most dynamic forces in the African-American community. As a community leader, counselor and preacher, 31-year-old Jenkins is respected and revered for his innovative thinking, age-old wisdom, contemporary leadership and business savvy. As pastor of the historic Fellowship Missionary Baptist Church (FMBC), he has more than doubled revenues, implemented cutting-edge programs, increased real estate holdings and created an empowering environment for youth, while impacting nations for God. As a result of his unwavering commitment to adding value to others, more than 5,500 new parishioners have united with FMBC in merely six years.

A graduate of Moody Bible Institute, Jenkins earned a Bachelor of Science degree in Christian education. He is currently completing a master's degree at Trinity Evangelical Divinity School.

A man of balance, he is married to Tara Rawls-Jenkins and has two young daughters, Princess and Paris.

Jenkins is a man that brings people together to ensure mobility and momentum for individuals, communities and organizations. He is considered a yardstick for his generation.

The Reverend Dr. Carl E. King Sr. is the pastor and founder of Christ Community Church – COGIC in South Holland, Illinois, founded in 1987. Additionally, he is a chaplain for the South Holland Fire and Police departments and president of the South Holland Ministerial Alliance.

King serves as district superintendent for the William Roberts Memorial District of First Jurisdiction Illinois and chairman of the national executive board for the Pastors and Elders Council of Church of God in Christ. King was appointed by Bishop Ocie Booker as the chairman of the Pastors and Elders for First Jurisdiction of Illinois. He also serves on the board for High School District 205 and Wheaton College's board of visitors.

A graduate of Governors State University, Trinity Evangelical Divinity School and McCormick Theological Seminary, King is an affiliate faculty for Indiana Wesleyan University in Merrillville, Indiana, where he teaches in the associate, bachelor's and master's programs.

King is married to Marilynn Ruth King and is the father of Carl II, Anna and Marjalene Kelly. He has one son-in-law, Stephen Kelly, and a grandson, Stephen M. Kelly.

Rev. Dr. Carl E. King Sr.
Pastor & Founder
Christ Community
Church – COGIC

Pastor Sheraine Lathon is senior pastor and administrator of Liberty Temple Full Gospel Church. Her fiery and cutting-edge message of godly order and holiness has caused thousands to turn their hearts toward God.

With 23 years of dedicated service, especially in church administration and finance, Lathon has progressed at Liberty Temple from member, to evangelist, to elder, to pastor, teacher and prophet.

Lathon established an annual health fair for Chicago communities, offering free mammograms and screenings. She sponsors shelters throughout the city and feeds 1,500 disadvantaged families biannually. She also helps her overseer in the planting and nourishing of ministries across the nation.

Lathon is an associate professor at Logos Ministerial Training Institute and Friends International University. Her areas of expertise are church history, homiletics and hermeneutics. She holds a bachelor's and a master's degree in church administration, and a doctorate degree in divinity. Her name appears in many Who's Who publications.

Lathon honors her husband, Willie, and her sons, Eric and Chris, for their prayers and encouragement in allowing her to pursue God's plan for her life.

Sheraine Lathon
Senior Pastor &
Administrator
Liberty Temple Full
Gospel Church

John Andrew McBride is pastor of Ebenezer Missionary Baptist Church (EMBC). As pastor of EMBC, he has seen it mature from 65 members in 1996 to 250 members as of 2007. McBride is a pastor, preacher and teacher for this 21st century.

McBride is the former president of North Shore Baptist Ministers' Alliance. He was also Youth Division instructor for the National Baptist Convention USA, Inc., and was featured in *The Heritage Registry of Who's Who*™ 2006-2007 edition.

McBride attended the College of Lake and McKinley Theological Seminary. Additionally, he was city chaplain of North Chicago.

A native of Chicago, Illinois, John is the husband of Kendell R. McBride, formerly Kendell R. Coleman, and the proud father of four sons, Durrell, Jonathan, Joel and Elijah, and one daughter, Jazmine.

John Andrew McBride
Pastor
Ebenezer Missionary
Baptist Church

CHICAGO'S SPIRITUAL LEADERS

Dr. Arnella Elizabeth Pierce

Founder & Pastor
Revelation International
Outreach Ministry

D r. Arnella Elizabeth Pierce, founder of Revelation International Outreach Ministry, has been the pastor of this nondenominational ministry for 16 years. Through Pierce's pastoral leadership, teaching and vision of an "alternative village," holistic programs have evolved. This includes Blessings to Go, a feed the homeless outreach, and Zoe, a motivational prison lecture program. Through The Bridge Project, Pierce conducts workshops essential for healing the soul and mind. A three-story convent houses the ministry's offices, chapel, sanctuary and health spa.

Pierce has authored several inspirational and healing books, such as *But You Say You Love Me* and *The Pregnant Man*. As a playwright, Pierce also writes and directs plays for "soul revelation," including *Destiny's Decision*.

Pierce received a bachelor's degree in journalism from Columbia College, holds a master's degree in religious education, and received a doctorate in theology. She also established the Revelation Institute in 1998, where she is dean.

Bishop Dr. Claude Porter

Chair & Chief Executive Officer
Proviso-Leyden Council for
Community Action, Incorporated

B ishop Dr. Claude Porter became a community organizer through Uplift Community Service Center, helping to organize the West Suburban Organization for Welfare Rights from 1968 through 1970. In 1968 he also founded the Proviso-Leyden Council for Community Action, Incorporated (P.L.C.C.A., Inc.), a not-for-profit community organization with approximately 30 programs and an operating budget of more than $9 million. The agency provides services to 18 municipalities in the Chicago Metropolitan area. He currently serves as chair and chief executive officer of P.L.C.C.A., Inc.

In 1972 Porter became founder and pastor of Proviso Missionary Baptist Church. He serves on the White House Committee on Violent Crimes, is chair of the International Ministerial Alliance Network, chair of the Proviso Township Ministerial Alliance Network, and a member of the 2005 President's Roundtable and Inner Circle.

Porter was the 2005 recipient of the Businessman of the Year Award presented in Washington, D.C., on behalf of President George Bush, and most recently was the 2007 recipient of the Governor's PATH (People Are Today's Heroes) Award.

Dr. Alan V. Ragland

Senior Pastor
Third Baptist Church of Chicago

D r. Alan V. Ragland is the senior pastor of Third Baptist Church of Chicago. He has been extensively involved in lay and ministerial development within the church, church-based community organizing and transformation in the community at large. In publications, he has contributed to the book *Living in Hell - the Dilemma of African American Survival*, and he wrote the meditation for Psalm 95 in the *African-American Devotional Bible*.

Ragland is a native of Memphis, Tennessee, where he completed undergraduate studies at the University of Memphis. He received a Master of Divinity degree from Colgate Rochester Divinity School and a Doctorate of Ministry degree from McCormick Theological Seminary.

In addition to his congregational ministry, Ragland also serves as president of Heritage Community Development Corporation, a community-based, not-for-profit organization whose primary objective is to enhance the quality of life for families through supportive programming.

Ragland is a nationally recognized theologian, scholar and preacher. He is married to Barbara Ollie Ragland, and they have one daughter, Melanie Loren Ragland.

The Reverend Dr. Albert Sampson will celebrate his 51st anniversary in the ministry, as well as his 32nd pastoral anniversary of Fernwood United Methodist Church.

As presiding elder of the United Methodist Church South End Cooperative Parish, Sampson is leadership director of the United Methodist South End Cooperative E3 (Economics, Education and Evangelism) Initiative. He is also founder and president of the faith-based organized Farmers Agribusiness Resource Management and the Neighborhood Social Entrepreneurs Society.

Sampson was one of only three ministers ordained by Dr. Martin Luther King Jr. at Ebenezer Baptist Church in 1966. Additionally, he was inducted into the Martin Luther King Jr. Board of Preachers of Morehouse College.

A distinguished biblical scholar, Sampson is a theological consultant for *The Original African Heritage Study Bible*. President George W. Bush and Mr. Jim Towey, former director of the White House Office of Faith-Based and Community Initiatives, invited him to participate as a panelist in the 2nd White House National Conference on Faith-Based and Community Initiatives. He presented his position paper, "Paradigm Shift Change for Social Strength 2006 and Beyond!"

Rev. Dr. Albert "Al" Sampson

Pastor
Fernwood United
Methodist Church

District Elder Andrew D. Singleton Jr. is pastor and chief executive officer of Victory Apostolic Church, in Chicago Heights, Illinois. Founded in 1996 with 12 members, Victory has grown to 1,700 members with more than 60 ministries. A $16 million, 2,500-seat sanctuary is under construction in Matteson, Illinois, and is to be completed by fall of 2008.

Singleton was chief finance officer and vice president of finance for several nonprofit organizations. While at the Apostolic Church of God in Chicago, he served as associate pastor, and director of prison ministry and the Ministerial Alliance. He is also a member of the executive board and chairs the budget committee for the Illinois District Council.

Having received his bachelor's degree in accounting from the University of Illinois at Chicago, Singleton is a certified public accountant and certified financial planner. Additionally, he became ordained as an elder in the Pentecostal Assemblies of the World in 1989, and holds a master's degree from McCormick Theological Seminary.

Married for 33 years to his wife, Brenda, they are the proud parents of three children and one granddaughter.

District Elder Andrew D. Singleton Jr.

Pastor & Chief Executive Officer
Victory Apostolic Church

Pastor Bennie Stewart Jr. has dedicated a lifetime of service to the people of God. In 1980 he founded the Sanctuary of Holiness Church of God in Christ. A visionary leader, Stewart takes a holistic approach to ministry. The church provides spiritual, educational, professional and social support to the members and community. As superintendent of the Obe Hendricks Memorial District and administrative assistant to Bishop Robert R. Sanders of Illinois' Third Jurisdiction of the Church of God in Christ, his leadership extends to more than 60 churches.

Stewart was ordained by Bishop Louis Henry Ford, former international presiding bishop of the Church of God in Christ who served the administration until his demise. Over the course of nearly 50 years in ministry, he has inspired, influenced and uplifted hundreds of people.

Stewart and his wife, Viola, celebrated 51 years of marriage this year. They consistently maintain a standard of Christian family values for their children and family.

His motto is: "We go to God on behalf of man and to man on behalf of God."

Bennie Stewart Jr.

Pastor
Sanctuary of Holiness
Church of God in Christ

Rev. Clarence E. Stowers Jr.

Senior Pastor
Mars Hill Baptist Church

The Reverend Clarence E. Stowers Jr. was born on December 2 to Dr. Clarence Stowers Sr. (deceased) and his wife, Margaret, in Evanston, Illinois. He began his spiritual pilgrimage at the historic Mars Hill Baptist Church of Chicago under his father's leadership. In 1991 he accepted his call to preach the gospel, and was licensed and ordained at Mars Hill.

In May of 1999, Stowers succeeded his father as the pastor, and consequently, Mars Hill has experienced phenomenal ministry growth under his visionary pastoral leadership. Since his ministry there, more than 1,500 souls have been saved and united with the church. In 2004 the church was awarded the Church Health Award from Rick Warren and Saddleback Church. Mars Hill is an innovative, multicultural and soon-to-be multisite church. With membership now exceeding 2,200, it is one of the fastest growing churches in the Midwest.

Stowers holds a Doctorate of Ministry degree and three master's degrees in divinity, urban ministry and public administration.

He shares his life and ministry with his wife, Lady Shauntai Stowers, and three children, Myles, Joshua and Lauren.

Rev. Michael G. Sykes

Associate Pastor
Trinity United Church of Christ

The Reverend Michael G. Sykes is associate pastor for visitation ministries at Trinity United Church of Christ, where the Reverend Jeremiah A. Wright Jr. is senior pastor. Sykes also holds the ecclesiastical office of cluster dean for the Chicago Metropolitan Association of the United Church of Christ, and he chairs the education committee of the Urban Clinical Pastoral Education Program.

In addition to his church duties, he serves as pastoral care coordinator at Michael Reese Hospital. In his capacity as head of pastoral care, Sykes is a member of the hospital's institutional review board, which provides oversight for medical research involving human subjects. Moreover, he occupies a seat on the institution's biomedical ethics committee.

Sykes holds a Master of Divinity degree from Chicago Theological Seminary. Before entering seminary, he studied political science at the University of Illinois at Chicago and Bradley University in Peoria. Sykes' employment background also includes experience in the field of corporate marketing, where he held management positions with Citibank, assistant vice president, and Time Warner, marketing manager.

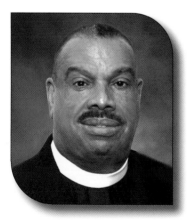

Rev. Dr. Richard L. Tolliver

President &
Chief Executive Officer
St. Edmund's Redevelopment
Corporation

The Reverend Dr. Richard L. Tolliver has been an ordained Episcopal priest since December of 1971, serving churches in New York City, Boston and Washington, D.C. Since June of 1989, he has been the rector of St. Edmund's Episcopal Church in Chicago.

Tolliver also serves as president and chief executive officer of St. Edmund's Redevelopment Corporation, a not-for-profit community development organization that has gained international attention for spearheading the rebuilding of more than 500 units of housing in the church's neighborhood. Previously, he served as associate country director of the United States Peace Corps to Kenya and the country director in the Islamic Republic of Mauritania.

A member of numerous civic, corporate and church-related boards, Tolliver is vice chair of the board of trustees of Chicago State University, a trustee of Seabury Western Theological Seminary in Evanston, Illinois, and a member of the board of directors of Hyde Park Bank of Chicago.

Tolliver holds five university degrees, including a Doctorate of Philosophy degree in political science from Howard University. His work has been widely recognized in numerous books and periodicals.

Bishop Larry D. Trotter was born and raised in Chicago, Illinois, and grew up in one of its most disreputable housing projects. In 1981 he began to pastor The Sweet Holy Spirit Church, which now has a resident membership of more than 8,000 members.

Trotter's unique blend of encouragement and deliverance preaching, in congruence with his perceptible teaching and healing gifts, has afforded him the opportunity to minister in nearly all of the United States and in more than 18 countries worldwide. He has preached to more than 30,000 people in the New Orleans Superdome and to more than two million people in Nigeria. He has also led mission trips to Ethiopia, Finland, Ghana, Zimbabwe, Greece and India.

On December 30, 1993, Trotter was consecrated to the sacred office of bishop, and on June 12, 2004, he was unanimously elected as the presiding prelate of the United Covenant Churches of Christ (UCCC). In this position, he presides over 21 bishops and 250 churches worldwide.

Bishop Larry D. Trotter
Pastor
The Sweet Holy Spirit Church

The Reverend Marvin E. Wiley, a native of Pine Bluff, Arkansas, is the pastor of the Rock of Ages Baptist Church located in Maywood, Illinois. He made history at the Rock of Ages Baptist Church in March of 1991, becoming its second pastor in 40 years.

The church has experienced spiritual, numerical and financial growth under his dynamic leadership. Due to this growth, a new multimillion-dollar worship facility was constructed to the glory of God and service of mankind. Additionally, Wiley helped organize Vision of Restoration, Inc. (VOR), a 501(c)(3) organization. VOR provides educational and economic development, mental/social services, and career development and enhancement for the community.

Under Wiley's innovative leadership, a new Spiritual Growth and Development Center, a four-level, multimillion-dollar facility opened in 2004. The new 40,000-square-foot edifice offers many additional resources for worship, education and business.

Wiley's ability to teach and preach has carried him across the country for leadership, stewardship and evangelistic services.

Rev. Marvin E. Wiley
Pastor
Rock of Ages Baptist Church

The Reverend Reginald Williams Jr. is associate pastor for justice ministries at Trinity United Church of Christ (TUCC). "Rev. Reggie" partners with TUCC justice ministries to advocate for justice on local, national and global levels.

A member of Alpha Phi Alpha Fraternity, Inc., Reginald is a monthly columnist for *Trumpet* newsmagazine, a contributor to the book *Blow the Trumpet in Zion* and a contributor to the Winter 2005 and Summer 2006 editions of the *African American Pulpit*.

Born and raised in Chicago, the son of Dr. Reginald Williams Sr. and the late attorney Marcelle H. Williams, Reginald holds a Bachelor of Science degree from the School of Business and Industry at Florida A&M University. He also earned a juris doctorate from the University of Wisconsin Law School, where he was honored as the State Bar of Wisconsin Public Interest Law Student of the Year, and a Master of Divinity degree from the Samuel DeWitt Proctor School of Theology at Virginia Union University.

Reginald shares his life with Nikita Williams and their daughter, Nia Mar'Celle Williams.

Rev. Reginald Williams Jr.

Associate Pastor
Trinity United Church of Christ

Apostle H. Daniel Wilson

Senior Pastor
Valley Kingdom
Ministries International

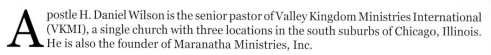

Apostle H. Daniel Wilson is the senior pastor of Valley Kingdom Ministries International (VKMI), a single church with three locations in the south suburbs of Chicago, Illinois. He is also the founder of Maranatha Ministries, Inc.

Additionally, Wilson is the founder and chief executive officer of The Cause Worldwide Outreach, Inc., a faith-based, nonprofit organization established to raise awareness and provide funding to fight the battle against the HIV/AIDS pandemic. He also serves as one of the executive council members for the International Coalition of Apostles (ICA), and as the Illinois state director for Christians United for Israel.

As an end-time apostle with vision, leadership skills and compassion, Wilson is the chief executive officer of Kingdom Entertainment Group, whose mandate is to produce films, docudramas and theatre productions.

Wilson is married to Beverly L. Wilson, who serves with him in ministry as pastor of the women's ministries at VKMI. They have two children and four grandchildren. They also guide more than 150 sons and daughters in ministry, both nationally and internationally.

Dr. Bill Winston

Pastor
Living Word Christian Center

Dr. Bill Winston is a visionary leader whose mission is to restore the self-esteem of individuals and families, and to rebuild communities through entrepreneurship and economic revitalization based on God's word. He shares profound biblical truths through simple, straightforward teaching.

The recipient of an honorary Doctorate of Humane Letters from Friends International Christian University, Winston is the pastor of Living Word Christian Center, a 15,000-member church located in Forest Park, Illinois. The church has a broad range of entities, including a ministry school, a business school, two shopping malls, a Christian academy (grades K-8) and a worldwide television program.

Winston is founder of The Joseph Business School; board chair of Covenant Bank, which is presently in organization; president of New Covenant Community Development Corporation; chief executive officer of Bill Winston Ministries; and founder of Faith Ministries Alliance, an organization of more than 250 churches worldwide. In 2007 he was awarded the U.S. Small Business Administration's Director's Choice Award for his significant impact on entrepreneurship.

Winston is married to Veronica and has three children, Melody, Nicole and David.

Rev. Ramah E. Wright

Associate Pastor,
Adolescents & Women
Trinity United Church of Christ

The Reverend Ramah E. Wright is a graduate of Garrett Evangelical Theological Seminary in Evanston, Illinois, where she received a Master of Divinity degree. Currently, she serves as associate pastor for adolescents (teens) and women at Trinity United Church of Christ (UCC) in Chicago. "Rev. Ramah," as the congregation refers to her, has served as the co-convener of Trinity's annual women's conference, the facilitator of Bible classes for women and teens, and the coordinator of youth revivals, youth retreats and the junior deacon training program.

A native of Chicago, Ramah was the first born to Leonard and Marjorie Bratton. She earned Bachelor of Science and Master of Science degrees in mathematics from Chicago State University, and taught high school mathematics for 19 years.

Ramah is married to the Reverend Dr. Jeremiah A. Wright Jr. They are co-partners in the ministry to more than 8,000 members of Trinity UCC. They are also the proud parents of five children, Janet, Jeri, Nikol, Nathan and Jamila, and the proud grandparents of Jeremiah, Jazmin and Steven Jr.

knowledgeable

qualified

CHICAGO'S

Professionals

PROFESSIONALS

specialist

proficient

guru

diligent

skillful

competent

precise

Sharron Banks

Assistant Vice President
Flowers Communications
Group, Inc.

Sharron Banks is the assistant vice president of Flowers Communications Group, Inc. (FCG), one of the largest African-American-owned public relations firms in the Midwest. Banks joined the agency in 1995 as secretary I, her first job after graduating from college. Over the years, she has held several positions, including account coordinator, senior account coordinator, office administrator and administrative services manager. In her role as account coordinator, she executed and facilitated local and national events for FCG's clients.

Banks is currently responsible for maintaining efficient office operations, including leasing, recruiting, corporate purchasing, administrative and clerical supervision, the company health care program, insurance and benefits package, and personnel orientation and training.

Banks attended historically black Wilberforce University in Ohio, and earned a bachelor's degree in business administration from Robert Morris College. She is currently pursuing a Master of Business Administration degree in human resources from Morris Graduate School.

Robin Y. Boyd

Account Manager
The New York Times

Robin Y. Boyd is an account manager with *The New York Times*, with the responsibility to sell advertising into the newspaper, magazine and Web site. Prior to joining *The Times*, she worked for 13 years at *The Wall Street Journal*, having begun her advertising sales career as a sales intern and progressing to account manager.

A native Chicagoan, Robin attended the University of Illinois at Champaign-Urbana, earning both a Bachelor of Science degree and Master of Science degree in advertising.

Actively involved in the advertising industry and the community, Robin is a board member of the Chicago Magazine Association and chair of the Education Committee of the Soul Children of Chicago, the nationally renowned religious community choir.

She and husband, Phillip, are both members of Salem Baptist Church of Chicago, and are the proud parents of one daughter, Phallon Antoinette.

Melissa Donaldson

Inclusion Practices Manager
CDW Corporation

Melissa Donaldson is the inclusion practices manager for CDW, a Fortune 500 company and a leading provider of technology products and services for business, government and education.

In her current role, Donaldson serves as a strategic partner to all business units to create a diverse workforce, foster an inclusive work environment, and leverage diversity in order to drive CDW's success. Additionally, she is responsible for education and communication initiatives, as well as developing strategic plans for diverse recruiting, and driving diversity and inclusion training. She oversees the development and operation of inclusion councils and affinity groups, and forges partnerships with external networks and organizations.

Donaldson joined CDW in 1999 and played a pivotal role in developing the company's inaugural leadership development program, which earned CDW recognition as one of the Top 50 Training Companies by *Training* magazine.

She holds a bachelor's degree from Wright State University and a master's degree from Central Michigan University. Donaldson is a member of the Chicagoland Chapter of the American Society of Training & Development, the National Association of Female Executives and Jack & Jill of America.

Sylvia Ewing is the cultural intersections producer at Steppenwolf Theatre Company, where she produces multicultural and multigenerational events for Steppenwolf's cultural intersections programming, as well as oversees forthcoming cross-platform programs that enhance Steppenwolf as a destination for cultural and civic dialogue.

Sylvia worked with Chicago Public Radio as a freelance producer of town hall meetings and other Chicago Matters (Edward R. Murrow Award) programming since the early '90s, and was a producer on Eight Forty Eight (Public Radio News Directors, Inc. Award). She is a former producer and correspondent for *Chicago Tonight* and *Art Beat*. As a freelance journalist, she has contributed to *Chicago Parent*, *N'DIGO*, *Chicago Sun-Times*, *NewsHour with Jim Lehrer* and *South Africa Now*, as well as the radio stations WMAQ and WVON. Sylvia is also a part-time professor at Columbia College Chicago. Nominated for three local Emmys, she has received a Peter Lisagor Award and three outstanding awards from the Chicago Association of Black Journalists.

Originally from Erie, Pennsylvania, Sylvia resides in the West Logan Square neighborhood of Chicago with her children, Eve and Matthew.

Sylvia Ewing

Cultural Intersections Producer
Steppenwolf Theatre Company

Derrick T. Gillard is director of customer service and sales for Luxury Motors Bentley Downers Grove. He is responsible for coaching executives on the delivery of complete customer satisfaction. Derrick works with the Customer Service and Sales departments to create harmonious environments for clients and perspective clients. Responsible for the company's relationship with the black consumer market, he builds lasting relationships with valued customers.

Trustworthy and dependable, Derrick has risen quickly through the ranks, working for Luxury Motors Infinity Gold Coast and as a sales associate at Bentley/Lamborghini. In addition to directing customer service, he remains a top sales person. His work includes service and training that influences 11 Luxury Motors dealerships throughout the country. Derrick maintains and serves a national customer base, delivering luxury automobiles to highly satisfied customers.

His first exposure to customer service was with JC Penney, where he was quickly promoted. From there, having heard of Nordstrom's customer service reputation, he rose through the ranks quickly, and was later recruited by Neiman Marcus.

Derrick was born in Flint, Michigan, and attended the University of Michigan.

Derrick T. Gillard

Director of Customer
Service & Sales
Luxury Motors Bentley
Downers Grove

Linda Gorham performs internationally as a storyteller, speaker and workshop presenter. She has been featured on the PBS show *Arts Across Illinois*. WTTW 11 and the Illinois Arts Council produced her story-video, *No Time for a ParTAY*. Her story CD, *Common Sense and Uncommon Fun*, won four national awards. Linda was co-chair of the National Storytelling Conference held in Chicago.

Her dynamic performances inspire her audiences through her use of movement, humor and sometimes zaniness as she creatively tells imaginative, multicultural folktales updated with "attitude." Young listeners tell Linda, "You are better than recess!"

Linda is an accomplished speaker and workshop facilitator for many major national corporations. Her energetic storytelling, together with her 13-year experience as a manager in Prudential Insurance Company's Human Resources and Public Affairs departments, generate powerful and vibrant on-point presentations.

Linda received a Bachelor of Arts degree in mathematics. She is an active member of the National Association of Black Storytellers and the National Storytelling Network.

Linda and her husband, John, live in Aurora, Illinois. They have two wonderful sons, Anwar and Jamal.

Linda Gorham

Professional Storyteller

Kymberly Hunt

Sales Executive
GlaxoSmithKline

K ymberly Hunt is a sales executive for GlaxoSmithKline. In this position, she is responsible for educating and marketing oral health care consumer products to physicians.

Kymberly is also a member of the African American Alliance, whose mission is to create, develop and sustain a work environment that empowers and enables African-American associates to reach their full potential.

She received a Bachelor of Science degree from Lincoln University in Pennsylvania, and a radio, television and film certification from Temple University in Philadelphia.

A native of Pittsburgh, Kymberly resides and works in Chicago. When not working or spending time with her 12-year-old son, Dallas, she takes advantage of the tremendous cultural offerings in the Chicago area including theatre, dance and great restaurants.

Maureen Jenkins

Communications Specialist
The Boeing Company

M aureen Jenkins is a communications specialist for The Boeing Company, where she leads companywide manager-targeted communications and helps coordinate internal international communications. She was previously a "Lifestyles" reporter for the *Chicago Sun-Times* and contributed to the "Food," "Travel" and "Weekend" sections. She joined the *Sun-Times* after spending nearly one year living and working as a freelance writer in Florence, Italy.

Before moving to Italy, Maureen was an award-winning writer for *Boeing Frontiers*, a monthly employee magazine that shares Boeing's global growth strategy with employees and external stakeholders. She has also handled public relations for Sears and Golin/Harris Communications for the national McDonald's account.

Maureen also has worked as a "Features" reporter at the *Rockford Register Star* in Illinois and *The Oregonian* in Portland, Oregon. In 1999 she earned a master's degree in theological studies from Garrett-Evangelical Theological Seminary and covered religion at the *Charlotte Observer* and *Arizona Republic*.

Maureen is a member of the Chicago Council on Global Affairs Young Professionals, the Chicago Sister Cities Milan Committee, Alliance Française de Chicago and Delta Sigma Theta Sorority, Inc.

John H. Nelson

Registered Representative &
Personal Financial Advisor
Ameriprise Financial Services, Inc.

J ohn H. Nelson is a registered representative and personal financial advisor for Ameriprise Financial Services, Inc. He specializes in personal financial planning for investments, retirements and tax management strategies. He is committed to providing sound financial advice to help his clients achieve financial independence.

John is a native of Georgia and earned a Master of Business Administration degree from Atlanta University. He is an avid golfer and is married with two adult children.

Erika D. Patterson serves as the area learning manager of the assurance and advisory business services practice for Ernst & Young's Midwest region. In this capacity, she ensures that more than 1,600 audit professionals in the Illinois, Wisconsin, Indiana, western Michigan, Minnesota, Missouri and Nebraska offices receive appropriate training and have the leading technical development resources needed to provide quality client service. Erika is active in Ernst & Young's diversity and inclusiveness efforts, having led the Chicago African-American affinity group. Additionally, she serves on the Area's People Advisory Council.

Erika was formerly a senior manager in Ernst & Young's audit practice serving clients in the insurance industry. Prior to Ernst & Young, she spent seven years at State Farm Insurance Companies in the internal audit division and in various operations management positions in West Lafayette, Indiana; Dallas, Texas; and Bloomington, Illinois.

Erika earned a bachelor's degree from Butler University in Indianapolis, Indiana. She is a member of Alpha Kappa Alpha Sorority, Inc. and the National Association of Black Accountants, Inc. Her professional designations include a chartered life underwriter and chartered financial consultant.

Erika D. Patterson, CLU, CHFC

Area Learning Manager
Ernst & Young LLP

Jeffery Perry is the transaction integration practice leader with Transaction Advisory Services (TAS) of Ernst & Young LLP in the Americas (U.S., Canada and Latin America). Jeffery advises clients to "bring forward" integration issues early in transactions to mitigate deal risk and to prepare for integration success. He also has extensive experience in divestitures. He has worked with clients in industries including energy, consumer goods, financial services and communications.

At Ernst & Young, Jeffery serves on the TAS Operating and the TAS Inclusiveness Steering committees. He serves on the boards of the Boys and Girls Club of Chicago, Chicago Children's Museum and INROADS, Inc.

Jeffery earned a Bachelor of Science degree in marketing/quantitative methods from Babson College, with high distinction, and a Master of Business Administration from the Harvard Business School. His thought leadership exists in quotes and articles in the *Financial Times*, *BusinessWeek Online*, *Financier Worldwide*, *The Deal*, *Strategy & Leadership*, *Associated Press Watercooler* and *Chicago Tribune*.

He and his wife, Dena Dodd Perry, are the proud parents of two sons and a daughter.

Jeffery S. Perry

Americas Transaction
Integration Practice Leader
Transaction Advisory Services
Ernst & Young LLP

Cappie Pondexter's road to the WNBA has been one of natural progression. Born in California and raised in Chicago, this guard, who stands at 5-foot-9-inches, attended John Marshall High School in Chicago, and was a starter all four years. Cappie became the first player in her state to be named Illinois' Miss Basketball twice (2000, 2001). Also, she was awarded the Illinois Player of the Year (2001).

Cappie attended Rutgers University, broke school records and became the first player in Big East history to be on the All-Big East first team all four years.

In April of 2006, Cappie was drafted in the first round (second overall) by the WNBA Phoenix Mercury. Wearing No. 23 to honor her idol, Michael Jordan, she approaches basketball with a similar voracity. She was named an All-Star (2006, 2007), and was ranked in the top ten for total points in the league.

Cappie has countless achievements and awards with USA Basketball and overseas organizations. She is nowhere near finished adding to the list of her many accomplishments.

Cappie Pondexter

Guard
Chicago Sky

CHICAGO'S PROFESSIONALS

Kimberly Waller

Account Executive
Aon Risk Services, Inc.

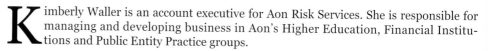

Kimberly Waller is an account executive for Aon Risk Services. She is responsible for managing and developing business in Aon's Higher Education, Financial Institutions and Public Entity Practice groups.

As the national leader of Aon's African-American Networking Group, her focus is building on Aon's commitment to become the destination of choice for the best and the brightest talent. Kimberly, along with other Aon colleagues, has built a practice group which provides unique development opportunities for talented people of color to prepare to assume greater leadership roles within the company.

Keeping in line with her commitment to the community, Kimberly serves as a board member for a number of nonprofit organizations in Chicago, including Family Focus, the National African-American Insurance Association and the Perspectives Charter School.

Kimberly earned a Bachelor of Arts degree in economics from the University of Wisconsin-Madison. She also maintains a professional designation as a chartered property casualty underwriter, and is completing a master's degree in organizational change at Northwestern University.

Kimberly and her husband, Tony Waller, reside in Chicago and have one son, Tony Waller Jr.

Chevon E. Washington

Team Manager
Vitas Healthcare

Chevon E. Washington is a team manager for Vitas Healthcare, where she manages a team of registered nurses, certified nurse assistants, physicians, social workers and chaplains, and coordinates the care of hospice patients and families. She has clinical expertise in hospice, geriatric and oncology nursing, and has worked in the hospital and homecare sectors. Her special certifications include nurse assistant instructor, CPR instructor, and L-NEC trainer for end-of-life care.

Chevon served as a delegate at the U.S.-China Joint Conference on Social Work in Beijing, China. Additionally, she was honored by Vitas Healthcare for outstanding customer service and leadership, and the National Black Nurses Association honored her accomplishments in oncology nursing. She is a member of the Hospice and Palliative Nurses Association.

Chevon earned a Bachelor of Science degree from DePaul University and a Master of Science degree in human service administration from Spertus College. A native Chicagoan, she is the proud mother of one son, Edward (Tracy) and two granddaughters, Yasmine and Shia.

BIOGRAPHICAL INDEX

BIOGRAPHICAL INDEX

ADVERTISER'S INDEX